MILTON'S MESSIAH

Milton's Messiah

*The Son of God in the Works of
John Milton*

RUSSELL M. HILLIER

OXFORD
UNIVERSITY PRESS

OXFORD
UNIVERSITY PRESS

Great Clarendon Street, Oxford OX2 6DP

Oxford University Press is a department of the University of Oxford.
It furthers the University's objective of excellence in research, scholarship,
and education by publishing worldwide in

Oxford New York

Auckland Cape Town Dar es Salaam Hong Kong Karachi
Kuala Lumpur Madrid Melbourne Mexico City Nairobi
New Delhi Shanghai Taipei Toronto

With offices in

Argentina Austria Brazil Chile Czech Republic France Greece
Guatemala Hungary Italy Japan Poland Portugal Singapore
South Korea Switzerland Thailand Turkey Ukraine Vietnam

Oxford is a registered trade mark of Oxford University Press
in the UK and in certain other countries

Published in the United States
by Oxford University Press Inc., New York

British Library Cataloguing in Publication Data
Data available

Library of Congress Cataloging in Publication Data
Data available

Typeset by SPI Publisher Services, Pondicherry, India
Printed in Great Britain
on acid-free paper by
MPG Books Group, Bodmin and King's Lynn

ISBN 978-0-19-959188-6

3 5 7 9 10 8 6 4 2

Dedication

For my wife and parents

... add Love,
By name to come calld Charitie, the soul
Of all the rest

Paradise Lost 12.583–85

Preface

In his *First Prolusion* the young Milton reminded his Cambridge University audience that, 'in every kind of speech, whether demonstrative, or deliberative, or judicial, the exordium should be shaped to win the favour of the Listeners; otherwise the minds of the Listeners could not be moved, nor could the cause succeed as the speaker would wish' (*CE* 12.118). Whether the following study of Milton's Messiah and its re-evaluation of the importance of redemptive theology for Milton's thought will earn the approval of its audience is in the lap of the gods. My study proceeds on the assumption that Milton's poetry serves as the handmaiden to his theology, and not *vice versa*. In his *Commonplace Book* Milton includes Basil the Great's opinion 'that poetry was taught by God to kindle in the minds of men a zeal for virtue', and that verse 'mixed the delight of melody with doctrines so that we might unconsciously receive the benefit of the discourse through the charm and the smoothness of the sounds' (*CPW* 1.382). In *Areopagitica* Milton did not think 'our sage and serious Poet *Spencer*... a better teacher' (*CPW* 2.516) than either Homer or Virgil, but, rather, a greater instructor than Duns Scotus and Thomas Aquinas, the Medieval systematizers and architects of intricate scholastic cathedrals of Christian theology and philosophy. For Milton, the major function of poetry was first and foremost theological and ethical. Moreover, as William Haller illustrates in his lively sketch of the young poet, for Milton 'poetry was a kind of revelation and the poet God's evangel'.[1] Doctrine and dogmatics, terms that have accrued morally dubious connotations of state propaganda, control, and coercion, were once affirmative watchwords for the Puritan way of life. John Diekhoff reminds us:

> we must not forget that to the extent to which one makes allowances for Milton's misfortune in being a Christian in a Christian age and country, one departs from Milton's meaning and falls into the not uncommon error of speculating about what Milton would have thought if he had not thought what he did. The moral principles that we can isolate from Milton's theology were not enough for Milton. They had validity for him only within the framework of his theology. To remove Milton's ethical system from that framework is to separate it from the basis of its validity.[2]

If Diekhoff's recommended approach to interpreting Milton's writings appears outmoded to us, then so, too, are the assumptions on which Milton wrote with both his left and right hands. To divorce Milton the theologian from Milton the man is as grievous an omission as disregarding Harriet Beecher Stowe's vital contribution to the abolitionist movement when reading *Uncle Tom's Cabin*; Upton Sinclair's socialist and humanitarian motives when reading *The Jungle*; or

---

[1] William Haller, *The Rise of Puritanism* (New York, 1938), 310.
[2] John S. Diekhoff, *Milton's 'Paradise Lost': A Commentary on the Argument* (London, 1958), 12.

Dickens's boyhood experience of social hypocrisy and injustice and the tyranny of corporate industry when reading *David Copperfield*.

This book complements such studies as Dennis Burden's *The Logical Epic* (1967), Dennis Danielson's *Milton's Good God* (1982), and Benjamin Myers's *Milton's Theology of Freedom* (2006), which adopt a sympathetic and constructive approach to clarifying Milton's poetic intentions. Their methodology engages with Milton's theological context and understands the theodicy of *Paradise Lost*, as far as one may, on Milton's terms. In later chapters, and particularly in my fifth and sixth chapters, I advance a hermeneutic that rehabilitates and reorients Fishian literary analysis. While, like Professor Fish, I privilege the reader's response, an unavoidable emphasis with a poet whose works concern choice and free will, I argue that Milton's fit readers may be assured by grace as much as they are surprised by sin. Moreover, I contend that unfamiliarity with Reformation and pre-Reformation theological discourse and increased distance from the underlying soteriological meanings of ordinary English words have alienated twenty-first century readers from recognition of how the central theme of salvation is communicated within Milton's epic. My position is therefore opposed to and corrective of the sly brilliance of William Empson, who, in *Milton's God* (1961), famously imputed improbity to Milton's characterization of the divine. Indeed, the title of this study is meant as an implicit rejoinder to Empson's view. I hope to question the readings of that sect of scholars who continue to make Satan the hero of Milton's epic and those of a deconstructionist stripe who might argue that Milton's reader reaches an epistemological, quasi-Satanic impasse where all meaningful readerly access to his poetry is denied. My first two chapters challenge some current trends in Milton studies that interpret the Son as an Arian, Socinian, or 'subordinationist' figure and make a further case for the Son's centrality within Milton's theology and poetry. From Chapter 2 to Chapter 6 I offer an approximately linear reading of *Paradise Lost*. I seek to engage with Milton's view of the atonement and elicit the operation of a crucial redemptive discourse in the epic by drawing upon the influence of classical literature and language and Patristic, Medieval, Reformation, and post-Reformation theology in shaping Milton's major poem. In Chapter 7 I provide a close reading of *Paradise Regain'd* and, building upon Barbara Lewalski's seminal work, I strive to illuminate some of the myriad ways in which Milton makes the poem as much a sophisticated Passion poem as a poem about the wilderness temptations. Throughout the study I draw, *ad fontes*, upon the Latin manuscript *De Doctrina Christiana*, a document that is a persistent and disputed focus of scholarly enquiry. I aim to show how recourse to the original Latin of this theological treatise proves invaluable for a full appreciation of how Milton works.

Russell M. Hillier

Providence, Rhode Island, 2009

Acknowledgements

No work can be conceived and written by the power of one. This book is a revised and expanded version of my doctoral dissertation, completed for Cambridge University, England, in 2008. Valentine Cunningham revealed to me the worth of investigating the confluence of literature and theology. Maxine Hancock shepherded me from delight in Bunyan to fascination for Milton, preventing my thoughts from, like those of the hopeless Belial, fruitlessly wandering through eternity. Without the encouragement and mentoring of two gentle scholars at Cambridge University, Charles Moseley and Douglas Hedley, this book would never have seen the light of day. I am indebted to Jacqueline Baker, Ariane Petit, Kathleen Kerr, and Sara Barnes, my editors at Oxford University Press, for trusting in the manuscript's merits and guiding this work to press, and to Elizabeth Teague for proofreading. I am grateful to my four anonymous readers for their sagacity and advice, and for their tolerance of what was originally an unwieldy manuscript. I would like to thank Andrew McNeillie for his support of the manuscript during its early stages at Oxford University Press. I am also grateful to those who generously gave their time and consideration to sections of this work: to the late and great Albert Labriola, Edward Jones, Dennis Danielson, Edward Donald Kennedy, Andrew Hass, Stephen Honeygosky, David Gay, Derek Wood, Roger Pooley, John Batchelor, William Horbury, Raphael Lyne, Edwin Block, Robert L. Patten, Logan D. Browning, Allyna Ward, and the anonymous reviewers of my various published articles on Milton whose names I am unfortunately unable to record here. These commentators not only helped to give force, clarity, and cogency to my argument, but also taught me that all worthwhile scholarship is collaborative in nature and requires patience in the crafting, 'be it less or more, or soon or slow'.

Some of this material has previously been published elsewhere. A portion of Chapter 3 was published as 'Two Patristic Sources for John Milton's Description of the Sun (*Paradise Lost* 3.591–95)', *Notes and Queries*, 53 (2006), 185–87, and a modified segment of Chapter 7 was published as 'The Wreath, the Rock, and the Winepress: Passion Iconography in Milton's *Paradise Regain'd*', *Literature and Theology*, 22 (2008), 387–405. Both pieces are reprinted with permission from Oxford University Press. A section of Chapter 4 appeared as 'Spatial Allegory and Creation Old and New in Milton's Hexaemeral Narrative' and is reproduced with permission from *SEL Studies in English Literature 1500–1900* 49, 1 (Winter 2009), 121–43. Chapter 5 appeared as 'The Good Communicated: Milton's Drama of the Fall and the Law of Charity', *Modern Language Review*, 103 (2008), 1–21, and is reprinted with permission from the MHRA. Another segment of Chapter 7 was published as 'Milton's *Paradise Regain'd* and Herbert's "Love (3)"', *The Explicator*, 66 (2007), 4–9, and is reprinted with permission from the Taylor & Francis Group and Heldref Publications (www.heldref.org). An earlier draft of Chapter 3 was awarded Cambridge University's Norrisian Prize for

2007. The granting of permissions to use the foregoing material as part of the present study is gratefully acknowledged.

I have delivered various papers deriving from this material at a D-Society Seminar at Cambridge University in November of 2007; the 2008 NeMLA Conference panel, 'John Milton at 400,' in Buffalo, New York; the Ninth International Milton Symposium in London in the Summer of 2008; and the Milton Society of America's 'John Milton at 400' panel, held at the 2008 MLA Convention in San Francisco.

My greatest debt is to my family for their steadfast support and unflagging belief that my dissertation and, eventually, this book would come to fruition. My mother and father would bear my sometime doubts and fears and were able to transform what could seem the most unpromising of showers into rainbows. As the dedication makes plain, it is foremost to my wife Alyssa that my thanks are due. In her tolerance of our pilgrim existence as we passed, for scholarly purposes, between the Old World and the New, she lived out Eve's selfless vow of constancy that:

> In mee is no delay; with thee to goe,
> Is to stay here; without thee here to stay,
> Is to go hence unwilling

Contents

Notes on Texts and Abbreviations

The following editions have been used for citation from the works of John Milton: *The Poetical Works of John Milton*, ed. Helen Darbishire (London, 1958); *The Complete Prose Works of John Milton*, gen. ed. Don M. Wolfe *et al.*, 8 vols (New Haven, 1953–82), cited throughout as *CPW*; *The Works of John Milton*, gen. ed. Frank A. Patterson *et al.* (New York, 1931–38), 18 vols, cited throughout as *CE*. *The Oxford English Dictionary*, ed. J. A. Simpson and E. S. C. Weiner, 20 vols (2nd edn, Oxford, 1989), is cited throughout as *OED*. Where texts are originally in Latin, Greek, Hebrew, French, or Italian, I have attempted a literal translation. All English translations from the Latin of Milton's *De Doctrina Christiana* are my own. My translations from the New Testament derive from *The New Greek–English Interlinear New Testament*, ed. J. D. Douglas, trans. Robert K. Brown and Philip W. Comfort (Wheaton, 1990). Unless otherwise indicated, all references to Milton's poetry are to *Paradise Lost*. In the text and in the notes the following abbreviations are employed: *PR*, *Paradise Regain'd*; *SA*, *Samson Agonistes*; *AV*, *The King James Authorized Version*.

Introduction

> The king-becoming graces,
> As justice, verity, temp'rance, stableness,
> Bounty, perseverance, mercy, lowliness,
> Devotion, patience, courage, fortitude
>
> William Shakespeare, *Macbeth*, IV.iii.91–94

In an intellectual climate where, four centuries after Milton's birth, Miltonists are writing articles and books that defend why Milton matters, it may seem quixotic to be offering a study that is arguing, some might say even more narrowly, for why Milton's distinctive theology matters.[1] Why, in short, should a twenty-first century reader care? Allow me briefly to reason the need. A number of landmark studies in Milton criticism have contended that Milton's God is emphatically *not* good. William Empson is only the most conspicuous among this school, not least for his chilling comparison of Milton's God with an officer at Belsen. In more recent times Michael Bryson has steered a middle course between 'Satanist' and 'Neo-Christian' critics. Bryson provides an almost Gnostic interpretation of Milton's idea of Godhead, where a tyrannous Father, who is representative of Milton's condemnation of kingship, is a foil to the virtues of Milton's Son.[2] In his *Theological Milton* Michael Lieb consciously takes his lead from Empson. Although Lieb fully acknowledges the significance of divine love and compassion for Milton's poetry, his study draws upon the theology of Rudolf Otto to explore 'the subterranean aspects of deity, aspects that suggest the "dark side" of God'.[3] Otto's negative theology makes the case for the hiddenness of a God who is 'Other', not in a Barthian sense, but whose Otherness conceals a *mysterium tremendum*, a dreadful and awesome aspect. Lieb in part bases his interpretation upon a passage in *De Doctrina Christiana* where Milton rejects anthropopathy on the grounds that the ascription of divine feelings to God in Scripture functions as much more than a rhetorical trope.[4] According to Milton's literalist interpretation, when Scripture asserts that

---

[1] Stanley Fish, 'Why Milton Matters; Or, Against Historicism'; Barbara K. Lewalski, 'Why Milton Matters'; Joseph Wittreich, 'Why Milton Matters', *Milton Studies*, 44 (2005), 1–39.
[2] See Michael Bryson, *The Tyranny of Heaven: Milton's Rejection of God as King* (Newark, 2004).
[3] Michael Lieb, *Theological Milton: Deity, Discourse and Heresy in the Miltonic Canon* (Pittsburgh, 2006), 7 and 128.
[4] Ibid. 127–62.

God pities, loves, and laments, we should believe that He does indeed pity, love, and lament. Milton's theology accordingly admits a passible God. Lieb argues that one inevitable consequence of this reasoning is that Milton accepts a God who hates with a perfect hatred and thunders with a perfect wrath. Milton is 'an epic poet for whom the face of divine love finds its counterpart in the face of divine hatred, that is, hate divinized'.[5] The ramifications of what Lieb terms Milton's *theopathy* are considerable. A theopathetic worldview accounts as much for a theology of dread as for one of grace and charity.

The purpose of this study is to restore the balance by returning Milton's reader to that other face of Holy Scripture, that is, to the more affirming side of Milton's poetic theology and his theological poetry. Where Lieb locates in divine passibility the potential for God's hatred and vengeance, there is equally the potential for His love and forgiveness; and where Lieb detects in the idea of a *deus absconditus* a hidden God who embodies living dread, Milton's God is correspondingly a deity who reveals a side of Himself that understands how to compassionate and to love. This face of God is called *chesed* or 'loving-kindness' in biblical Hebrew. The clement aspect to Milton's conception of divinity is manifest in the Son and, admittedly, Lieb grants that Milton's Son is 'the embodiment of the passible in its sublimest form'.[6] More than the dreadful and tremendous, it is this aspect of Milton's positive theology that should recall to Milton's reader all that is worthiest about his poetry. The relevance and importance of this 'Messianic' reading of Milton's major and minor epics will hopefully become apparent in the following pages. Comprehending Milton's Son as an avatar of divine compassion illuminates the nature of Milton's God in ways far removed from Empson's Stalinist deity. Milton's redemptive theology, with its tenets of charity, sacrifice, altruism, and forgiveness, should remind us of all that is most dear in being human and of the essential values with which our humanity, at its best, can invest us. Bryson has maintained the despotic form that the kingship of Milton's God takes. However, in the Son's assumption of his regal sceptre as Messiah, a name that is, among other things, the Hebrew title for King, the reader encounters a digest of the 'king-becoming graces' Shakespeare's Malcolm celebrates in the epigraph to my pre-amble. At a time when Western civilization is perhaps more conscious than ever before of the need for accountable governments, conscientious institutions, and the importance of selfless and magnanimous leadership, Milton's Messiah offers a paradigm, not only of how a demagogue might be the responsible saviour of a people, but also of how individuals might discover a path by which to live as virtuous citizens. Finally, it is the argument of this book that the possible God Lieb construes as a deity who hates and envies is perhaps especially remembered in Milton's poetry both as a God who sacrifices His only Son by sparing him from His side and as a God-man who, as Messiah, willingly accepts the preciousness of that sacrifice. If this study succeeds, then it will make readers attentive to Milton's epic imperative that, in the words of Milton's God, 'Mercy first and last shall brightest

---

[5] Ibid. 167.   [6] Ibid. 160.

shine' (3.134). More than hatred or vengeance or judgement, Milton's God intends, as perhaps Milton himself did, that mercy, a word etymologically consonant with grace, should have the last word.

Milton's lasting appeal is partly owing to his position in intellectual history, bridging the gap between an age of faith and an age of reason; and yet the supremacy of the Enlightenment, of which our epoch is an outgrowth, can diminish our appreciation for, and can even create a bias that reads against, Milton's theological convictions. George Sensabaugh has traced the influence of the moderate Enlightenment upon the critical reception of Milton's poetry so that 'An amiable God, an ethical Christ, and man possessed of infinite possibilities for advancement seemed more acceptable than an angry God, a sacrificial Christ, and man beset with original sin. The old piety had given way to the new moralism.'[7] This 'new moralism' discloses itself as soon as readers 'Socinianize', 'Arianize', or 'humanize' Milton's Son. Once interpreters of Milton's major poetry are prepared to erase the singular or mysterious that Milton so deliberately incorporates into his portrait of the Son, and, in its place, stress his creatureliness, exemplarity, imitability, and, consequently, his ordinariness, the elision of the centrality of redemption from Milton's poetics becomes imaginable.

Sharon Achinstein has suggested that we should replace the portrait of a rationalist Milton with a figure whose thought is moulded by his faith: 'Milton's Christianity has been understood as a rational Christianity, and his theology tending towards Arminian; yet Milton is just as committed to a dependency upon that which is beyond human capacity, upon the affective experience of the regenerative power of divine grace'.[8] Milton's high estimation of an individual believer's explicit faith, of theological doctrines independently and rigorously conceived, is manifest throughout his prose works. Milton's prescript in *Of Education* (1644) that his virtual Academy of young scholars, having received a rudimentary training in ethics, 'will be requir'd a speciall reinforcement of constant and sound endoctrinating to set them right and firm, instructing them more amply in the knowledge of vertue and the hatred of vice' (*CPW* 2.396), may sound authoritarian to modern ears. Yet when Milton imagines within his educational curriculum 'what Religious, what glorious and magnificent use might be made of Poetry both in divine and humane things' (*CPW* 2.405–06), his pedagogical programme, if impracticable, is no hollow rhapsody, but instead would edify youth through poetry that serves to explicate Christian faith. Likewise, in *The Reason of Church Government* (1642) Milton forecasts his epic composition and professes to act in a capacity 'over and above of being a Christian' (*CPW* 1.812) in framing a poem 'doctrinal and exemplary to a Nation' (*CPW* 1.815). Milton affirms a poetic priesthood where a poet's talents 'are of power beside the office of a pulpit' (*CPW* 1.815–16). As Jameela Lares has argued, Milton tended 'to think of poetry in terms of the pulpit'.[9] Concerning the true purpose of epic, Milton

[7] George F. Sensabaugh, *Milton in Early America* (Princeton, 1964), 219.
[8] Sharon Achinstein, *Literature and Dissent in Milton's England* (Cambridge, 2003), 145.
[9] Jameela Lares, *Milton and the Preaching Arts* (Cambridge, 2001), 47.

agreed with the Italian Renaissance poet Torquato Tasso, whose *Gerusalemme Liberata* (1585) Milton esteemed as a model of the epic genre (see *CPW* 1.813–14). In his *Discourses on the Heroic Poem* (1594) Tasso allowed, 'The poet, although he is a maker of images, is more strongly like the dialectician or the theologian [*al dialettico e al teologo*] than the sophist.'[10] Given such a poetic creed, it is difficult not to see Milton's poetry serving as the handmaiden to his theology. Where, then, might we expect to find a reliable account of Milton's theology?

I should here clarify my position on the status of the theological treatise, once readily attributed to John Milton, and commonly known to scholars as *De Doctrina Christiana*. This study will assume the influence of the syntagma *De Doctrina Christiana* upon Milton's poetry. In light of the controversy surrounding the authorship of *De Doctrina Christiana*, Stanley Fish reminds us that the treatise's textual history can be securely traced to Milton's desk, before the opportunistic Daniel Skinner obtained the document.[11] The significant recent investigation conducted by Gordon Campbell, Thomas Corns, John Hale, and Fiona Tweedie has helped to confirm this view. Their research meticulously details the provenance and history of the manuscript from Bunhill Fields to Kew and concludes, '*De Doctrina Christiana* rightfully belongs in the Milton canon'.[12] John Shawcross has made a convincing case for the manuscript's evolution from a 'Theological Index' into a neo-scholastic treatise. Milton's *Commonplace Book* has eleven references, all written in Milton's hand, attesting the existence of such a 'Theological Index' up to 1647 and Shawcross concludes that the 'Index' was constructed in parallel with the *Commonplace Book* and then worked up into a tractate from the late 1640s to the 1650s.[13] If we deny Milton's authorship of the treatise, then how do we account for Milton's retention of the manuscript right up until his death, a document the dedicatory epistle cherishes as that 'than which I have nothing better or more precious' (*CE* 14.8–9)? Kenneth Borris has advocated that, since Milton 'had some substantial and continuing interest in [*De Doctrina Christiana*'s] contents . . . it thus remains a potentially significant Miltonic source, influence, and intertext', and is as close an approximation to Milton's personal theology as a Milton scholar could hope to possess.[14] How else can we explain the various testimonies of his biographer John Aubrey ('*Idea Theologiae* in MS'), his erstwhile amanuensis and friend Cyriack Skinner ('the framing a *Body of Divinity* out of the Bible'), his nephew Edward Phillips ('a Tractate'; 'A perfect System of Divinity'), and the deist John Toland ('a *System of Divinity*') that such a document, of Milton's conception, was in existence and, according to Cyriack Skinner, had been 'finish'd after the Restoration'?[15]

---

[10] Torquato Tasso, *Discorsi Dell' Arte Poetica e Del Poema Eroico*, ed. Luigi Poma (Bari, 1964), 91.

[11] Stanley Eugene Fish, *How Milton Works* (Cambridge, Mass., 2001), 18–19.

[12] Gordon Campbell, Thomas N. Corns, John K. Hale, and Fiona J. Tweedie, *Milton and the Manuscript of 'De Doctrina Christiana'* (Oxford, 2007), 161.

[13] John T. Shawcross, *Rethinking Milton Studies: Time Present and Time Past* (Newark, 2005), ch. 6 (pp. 103–21). For Milton's eleven references to the 'Theological Index', see 200 (fn. 19).

[14] Kenneth Borris, *Allegory and Epic in English Renaissance Literature: Heroic Form in Sidney, Spenser, and Milton* (Cambridge, 2000), 222–23.

[15] Helen Darbishire, ed., *The Early Lives of Milton* (London, 1932), 9, 29, 61, and 192.

If we grant Miltonic authorship to *De Doctrina Christiana* but dismiss the document out of hand, *non vultus, non color*, as unfinalized and untrustworthy, or as a 'palimpsest' or 'ur-text' subjected to an ongoing process of refinement, we ignore both the systematic structure and overall consistency that an applied study of the Latin manuscript yields.[16] We would have to overlook the well-disposed regularity that one Miltonist has commended in 'so plain and logically argued a text' and the analytic rigour that Maurice Kelley found in its design.[17] How, again, do we explain away the numerous correspondences between the treatise and the rest of the Miltonic corpus? For example, there is, as Barbara Lewalski has argued, the resemblance between Milton's two divorce tracts, the second edition of *The Doctrine and Discipline of Divorce* (1644) and *Tetrachordon* (1645), and the digression on marriage in the treatise's tenth chapter. All three texts, in citing Judges 19:2, interpret the word 'fornication' in the same ingenious manner to mean, in addition to adultery, a stubborn disobedience and rebelliousness towards one's spouse (*CPW* 2.334–37, 670–74; *CE* 15.170–79).[18] *Tetrachordon* calls fornication 'any notable disobedience' or 'alienation of mind' (*CPW* 2.672) and *De Doctrina Christiana* correspondingly terms fornication a spouse's 'enmity, perfidy, and disobedience from a manifest alienation of mind [*animi ... alienatione*], rather than of body' (*CE* 15.178).[19]

Maurice Kelley and William Hunter postulated that the difference between the treatise and the epic is a difference in presentation, one that is modal rather than substantial.[20] Balachandra Rajan modifies this approach by forwarding the hypothesis that these two artefacts are 'constitutive of each other'.[21] Given that the treatise is a developed and cogent exposition of Christian doctrine, a biblical exegesis professedly laying forth *aeternae salutis Viam*, 'the Way of eternal salvation' (*CE* 14.4), and *Paradise Lost* is a poetic theodicy justifying God's ways, equivalence between the two works is evident. Therefore my study will proceed from the tenable premise that *De Doctrina Christiana* remains a significant resource and intertext, and that the manuscript's essential integrity provides a reliable means of obtaining an interpretive purchase upon what Milton's poetry has to teach us.

Even if the working manuscript does consist of a developed series of exegetical sayings compiled from other theological treatises, those excerpts were selected and combined at Milton's own choosing and, through a process of 'Miltonic

---

[16] See Campbell, Corns, Hale, Tweedie, 66–68. Lieb writes of the textual and semantic instability of the manuscript: see *Theological Milton*, 15–50.

[17] Mindele Anne Treip, *Allegorical Poetics and the Epic: The Renaissance Tradition to 'Paradise Lost'* (Lexington, 1994), 183; Maurice Kelley, *This Great Argument: A Study of Milton's 'De Doctrina Christiana' as a Gloss upon 'Paradise Lost'* (Princeton, 1941).

[18] Barbara K. Lewalski, 'Milton and *De Doctrina Christiana*: Evidences of Authorship', *Milton Studies*, 36 (1998), 203–28.

[19] In *Uxor Ebraica* (1646) John Selden argued that the Hebrew word for 'fornication' enjoyed such a great semantic range, as *De Doctrina Christiana* avows (*CE* 15.170). See Jason P. Rosenblatt, *Renaissance England's Chief Rabbi: John Selden* (Oxford, 2006), 3.

[20] Hunter has since reneged on this position. See his *Visitation Unimplor'd: Milton and the Authorship of 'De Doctrina Christiana'* (Pittsburgh, 1998).

[21] Balachandra Rajan, 'Milton Encompassed', *Milton Quarterly*, 32 (1988), 89.

appropriation and transformation', merit scrutiny as texts capable of providing guidance towards an understanding of the nature of Milton's explicit faith.[22] An estimation of the document's status as a mosaic of doctrines collated, analysed, and assimilated by one mind, Milton's mind, agrees with everything we know about Milton's Independent theological position and his 'heretical' principle that the faithful individual is both a lifelong seeker of 'the general confirmation of unimplicit truth' (*CPW* 8.438) and a resourceful and self-determining chooser within those domains where spiritual value and doctrinal truth may be found (see *CPW* 2.527, 543, 549; 7.252; 8.419–21). *De Doctrina Christiana* makes a noteworthy assertion when it defines heresy as any belief contrary to gospel teaching: 'In the age of the Apostles, since the gospel books were not yet in existence, that alone was heresy, as often as the word "heresy" was represented as an offence, that opposed the Apostles' doctrine, which was handed down with a living voice... Since that time when the gospel books were written down, with equal reason I reply that nothing except that which opposes those gospels can justly be named a heresy' (*CE* 14.12, 14). Milton's conception of orthodoxy, then, is centrally concerned with a faithful interpretation of Jesus's ministry, death, and resurrection as set forth in the gospel narratives, those chronicles Milton's archangel Michael reveres as 'those writt'n Records pure' (12.513).

The life of Milton's model Christian, as presented in *Areopagitica* (1644), consists of a conscientious interpretive quest for the hewed pieces of 'virgin Truth', disfigured from the age in which 'her divine Master [Jesus] ascended, and his Apostles after him were laid asleep', a formidable task that Milton famously likened to the mythical Isis's assiduous shoring together, 'limb by limb' (*CPW* 2.549), of her beloved Osiris's mangled parts. In the previous year Milton had adopted the same conceit to describe the diligent interpreter's judicious sifting of Christ's utterances from the gospel records: Jesus, 'like a maister, scattering the heavnly grain of his doctrin like pearle heer and there, which requires a skilfull and laborious gatherer; who must compare the words he finds, with other precepts, with the end of every ordinance, and with the general *analogy* of Evangelick doctrine: otherwise many particular sayings would be but strange repugnant riddles' (*CPW* 2.338). The cost of rejecting *De Doctrina Christiana*'s body of doctrines as an aid to comprehending the major poetry, in accordance with Milton's theological priorities, is too great. Unassisted by the treatise, Milton's epic poem inevitably becomes a wax nose whereby *Hic liber est in quo quaerit sua dogmata quisque* – 'Here is a book in which each person seeks his own teachings'. Rather than condemning *Paradise Lost*, in Walter Raleigh's damning phrase, as 'a monument to dead ideas', the poem manifests 'a panorama of doctrine in action'.[23] By reading *De Doctrina Christiana* alongside the major poetry, 'the cool element of prose' illuminating a masterpiece 'of... Empyreall conceit' (*CPW* 1.808), the poem's centre of gravity, its theology, can hold. In short, *De Doctrina Christiana*, the primary witness to

[22] Gordon Campbell, Thomas N. Corns, John K. Hale, David I. Holmes, and Fiona J. Tweedie, 'The Provenance of *De Doctrina Christiana*', *Milton Quarterly*, 31 (1997), 110.
[23] Sensabaugh, 222–23.

Milton's biblical hermeneutics, gives as accurate a guide to the contours of his explicit theology as a reader could hope to find.

My primary intention is to undertake further examination into what Milton's major poetry, especially *Paradise Lost* and *Paradise Regain'd*, and the treatise *De Doctrina Christiana* tell us about the Christology and soteriology of the incarnate and preincarnate Son of God. There have been two notable studies of Milton's God, a study dedicated to Milton's Satan, at least two monographs dedicated to the subject of Milton's angels, one devoted to Milton's Adam and Eve, and another to Milton's Eve.[24] While no previous scholarly engagement with Milton's poetics or theology worth its salt can afford to overlook the Son's role in the Miltonic canon, a book-length exploration of Milton's treatment of the identity and office of the Son of God is warranted within the annals of Milton scholarship. The recent reappraisal of *De Doctrina Christiana* within the Miltonic canon has given Renaissance scholars cause to reconsider the importance of Christology and soteriology for that document and debate is as vigorous as ever concerning the nomination of an orthodox, heterodox, or heretical Milton.

A synopsis of the book's scope may be helpful for its readers. I begin my study by examining Milton's theological and poetic treatment of the Son and the work of salvation. The first chapter challenges the prevailing attitude in contemporary Milton studies that Milton adheres to Arian, Socinian, or psilanthropic tenets. In *De Doctrina Christiana*, and again in Milton's poetry, human restoration is predicated upon divine grace and the doctrine of the redemption is scarcely a 'thing indifferent'. Chapter 2 reconsiders *Paradise Lost*'s exordium and analyses afresh, in fideistic rather than in purely rationalistic terms, its bipartite great argument, the narrator's famous promise to assert eternal providence and justify God's ways to men.

The third chapter offers a new reading of Satan's voyage across Books Three and Four of *Paradise Lost*. I interpret the poem's cosmos as operating according to a sacramental–allegorical poetic that provides a copious manifestation of the Son's mediatorial work of salvation as God-man. In Chapter 4 I develop William Hunter's thesis that the War in Heaven operates as a *temporal* redemption allegory by suggesting further ways in which Raphael's martial narrative displays the saving work of the Son. The chapter goes on to argue that Raphael's hexaemeral narrative in Book Seven serves as a *spatial* redemption allegory, a companion piece to the martial epyllion in Book Six. In Chapter 5 I offer a suggested cause for Milton's representation of the Fall in Book Nine of *Paradise Lost* as Eve and Adam's transgression of the law of charity, violating the love of God, self, and neighbour. Milton's drama of the Fall, while detailing this violation, also anticipates and

---

[24] See, *seriatim*: William Empson, *Milton's God* (Cambridge, 1981); Dennis Danielson, *Milton's Good God: A Study in Literary Theodicy* (Cambridge, 1982); Neil Forsyth, *The Satanic Epic* (Princeton, 2003); Robert Hunter West, *Milton and the Angels* (Atlanta, 1955); Feisal G. Mohamed, *In the Anteroom of Divinity: The Reformation of the Angels from Colet to Milton* (Toronto, 2008); George Musacchio, *Milton's Adam and Eve: Fallible Perfection* (New York, 1991); Diane Kelsey McColley, *Milton's Eve* (Urbana, 1983).

announces the good communicated, namely the restoration of humanity through the Son.

In Chapter 6, my final chapter concerning *Paradise Lost*, I demonstrate how, in addition to surprising Milton's readers by sin, the affective stylistics of Fishian literary analysis can be applied to Milton's treatment of the aftermath of the Fall to assure the poem's readers of the provision of grace. Irony serves an ethical function in Milton's poetics so that, when Milton applies the ironic mode to the fallen world of Book Ten, the action of what I term 'redeeming irony' can bring Adam, Eve, and the reader back from a state of divine curse to divine grace. In Chapter 7 I turn to the soteriological concerns of *Paradise Regain'd* and show how, in myriad ways, the narrative insists upon the importance of redemption. Learned prolepses of the atonement irradiate the poetic narrative. Satan's temptations of Jesus in *Paradise Regain'd* form a fitting culmination to Milton's thought concerning theodicy, redemptive theology, and 'the pattern of a Christian *Heroe*'.

1

The Nature of Milton's Son and his Justification of Men's Ways to God: Things Indifferent?

Thou therefore that sit'st in light & glory unapprochable, *Parent* of *Angels* and *Men*! next thee I implore Omnipotent King, Redeemer of that lost remnant whose nature thou didst assume, ineffable and everlasting *Love*!

Milton, *Of Reformation*

As for those wingy Mysteries in Divinity, and airy subtleties in Religion, which have unhing'd the brains of better heads, they never stretched the *Pia Mater* of mine; methinks there be not impossibilities enough in Religion for an active faith; the deepest Mysteries ours contains have not only been illustrated, but maintained by Syllogism, and the rule of Reason: I love to lose my self in a mystery, to pursue my Reason to an *O altitudo*!

Thomas Browne[1]

Nos itaque in sacris rationi renuntiemus. (Let us therefore renounce reason in sacred matters.)

Milton, *De Doctrina Christiana*

In view of the importance that Milton attaches to comprehending the gospel portrayal of Jesus, the recent emphasis upon Milton's purportedly Arian Christology is infelicitous and misleading. Owing to recent research by Michael Bauman and John Rumrich and, before them, by C. S. Lewis and Maurice Kelley, the epithet 'Arian' has almost become a *datum* in Milton studies for denoting Milton's Son.[2] The term has been challenged by Miltonists, most notably by C. A. Patrides, William B. Hunter, and J. H. Adamson.[3] As early as 1966 Barbara Lewalski was

---

[1] Thomas Browne, *Religio Medici*, ed. W. Murison (Cambridge, 1922), 11.

[2] See Michael Bauman, *Milton's Arianism* (Frankfurt, 1987), 2; John P. Rumrich, 'Milton's Arianism: Why It Matters', in *Milton and Heresy*, ed. Stephen B. Dobranski and John P. Rumrich (Cambridge, 1998), 75–92. See also Gregory Chaplin, 'Beyond Sacrifice: Milton and the Atonement', *PMLA*, 125 (2010), 354–69.

[3] See William B. Hunter, Jr, J. H. Adamson, and C. A. Patrides, eds, *Bright Essence: Studies in Milton's Theology* (Salt Lake City, 1971).

examining Milton's departure from Arius and, in a recent forum concerning the provenance of *De Doctrina Christiana*, she questioned the appropriateness of Arian and Socinian terms, arguing that the treatise diverges from Arian and Socinian models 'in affirming that the Son shares in the Father's substance', if not in the Father's essence.[4] Perhaps the most rewarding contemporary scholarship, welcome for its intervention in scholarly debates about the propriety of applying certain labels to describe Milton's theology, is that of Michael Lieb, who has presented a detailed argument calling into question the scholarly precision of the nomination of either Milton's Socinianism or his Arianism.[5]

Scholars have used the denomination 'Arian' too vaguely and indiscriminately. If we are using the term in its *historical* sense to refer to the archetypal heresy condemned at the fourth-century Council of Nicaea, then revisionist studies advise caution. Maurice Wiles has demonstrated how 'Arianism', as it was defined in AD 325, was 'to a significant degree a creation of Athanasius, designed to further his campaign on behalf of that particular form of Christian self-definition'.[6] The Athanasian agenda to consolidate Jesus's identification as the incarnate Deity, very God and very man, strove to undermine this alternative form of Christology: that the Son had a beginning; was not eternal, but perpetual; was a made thing and the first-born of Creation; was mutable and subordinate to his Father; and, stemming from his creatureliness, was the upshot of divine whimsy rather than the perfect manifestation of God's infinite mercy and love. An Athanasian Christology, enshrined within the Nicene Creed, was 'established, often by unscrupulous means, over against an alternative form of faith that was consistently parodied and misrepresented'.[7]

Michael Bauman's *Milton's Arianism*, advocating this line of enquiry, assumes Miltonic authorship of *De Doctrina Christiana* and determines that 'if what was condemned at the council of Nicaea was Arianism, then John Milton was an Arian'.[8] It is difficult to accept Bauman's assertion because contemporary Church historians and systematic theologians are restricted in their access to documents that can with any confidence define precisely what historical Arianism stood for. As Lieb has shown, posterity did not do much for Arius: 'Arianism as the Other was construed as the spawn of that heresiarch Arius, who was demonized as a Judas-like Antichrist who died with his bowels falling out of his body'.[9] Arius's writings are, at best, of a limited, questionable authority and, at worst, were absorbed into and rendered unreliable by Athanasian polemic that targeted the dogmas Arius held. History has bequeathed to us moderns only three complete texts, allegedly written by Arius, along with sundry extracts derived from Arius's *Thalia*. Rowan Williams alerts us to the scarcity and instability of these surviving Arian texts and cautions that they are 'very far from presenting to us the systematic thought of Arius as he

    [4] Barbara K. Lewalski, *Milton's Brief Epic: The Genre, Meaning, and Art of 'Paradise Regained'* (Providence, 1966), 133–63; Lewalski, John T. Shawcross, and William B. Hunter, Jr, 'Forum: Milton's *Christian Doctrine*', *Studies in English Literature, 1500–1900*, 32 (1992), 151.
    [5] Lieb, *Theological Milton*, 213–78.
    [6] Maurice Wiles, *Archetypal Heresy: Arianism Through the Centuries* (Oxford, 1996), 182.
    [7] Wiles, 183.   [8] Bauman, 2.   [9] Lieb, *Theological Milton*, 265.

himself saw it. In other words, we can never be sure that the theological *priorities* ascribed to Arius by his opponents were his own, even if his *statements* are transmitted correctly.'[10] Arius's own words were stitched together within the anathemas that the Catholic and Apostolic Church drew up to refute Arius's views. These are partial, rhetorical documents of an untrustworthy provenance. The anathemata forming the appendix to the original Nicene Creed, ostensibly direct citations of Arius's doctrines, were grist to the mill of Constantinian, state-driven Christianity. Any kind of absolute claim that Milton's Son is patterned after some paradigm of historical Arianism is therefore fragile and patchy for, as Lieb argues, 'The problematic nature of the Arian label is made evident not only by the polemic that defines it but by the inaccessibility of Arius's own writings.'[11] Such doctrines are 'tainted by the polemic through which they are articulated'.[12]

When Maurice Kelley named *De Doctrina Christiana* 'an Arian document', a decision that helped to revive the imputation of Milton's Arianism, he consciously took certain semantic liberties. Kelley identified Milton's Arianism, adding the caveat, tucked away into a footnote: 'For a variety in diction, I shall frequently employ "Arian" and "Arianism"... as synonyms of "antitrinitarian" and "antitrinitarianism", recognizing as always that Arius and Milton did not hold identical beliefs.'[13] The outcome of using these terms so freely was to equate the broad concept of antitrinitarianism, *ipso facto*, with Arianism.[14] Kelley's Arianism amounts to little more than the subordinationism that Eusebius of Caesarea held, and that was certainly not considered an unheretical and unheterodox position until the vexed politics of the Council of Nicaea outlawed it under the nomenclature of 'Arianism' in AD 325.[15] Larry Isitt follows Kelley in trying to resolve the problem of associating Arianism with Milton's Son by distinguishing the 'two referents' of Arianism, the 'historical' and the 'technical': 'Milton is not an historical Arian, that is, he is not in all points in correspondence with the teachings of the man whose name is affixed to the heresy called Arianism. But he does correspond to the heart of what Arius taught and what was specifically condemned by the bishops meeting at Nicea: Milton denies the perfect equality of Father and Son.'[16] If Milton's Son does not perfectly correspond with a historical Arian Christology, then how far can Isitt extend his claim that Milton was committed as poet and theologian to 'the heart of what Arius taught'? Milton scholarship would benefit from that hobgoblin consistency when using these unstable terms. Arianism cannot serve as a catchall denotation of the inequality between the Father and the Son. In over two millennia of Christian doctrinal history there have been any number of heresies professing to subordinationist, antitrinitarian, and tritheistic

---

[10] Rowan Williams, *Arius: Heresy and Tradition* (London, 2001), 95.
[11] Lieb, *Theological Milton*, 263.
[12] Ibid. 264.
[13] Kelley, 119 (fn. 86).
[14] Kelley, 122; Bauman, 2.
[15] Shawcross, *Rethinking*, 106.
[16] Larry R. Isitt, *All the Names in Heaven: A Reference Guide to Milton's Supernatural Names and Epic Similes* (London, 2002), 192.

tendencies. Such heresies are not automatically Arian, whatever that labile designation might mean.

As J. J. M. Tobin and Michael Lieb have illustrated, Milton's prose gives little indication of an Arian viewpoint.[17] The paucity of evidence within Milton's corpus for explicit Arianism casts doubt upon the soundness of any 'historical' or 'technical' postulate. Tobin details Milton's unflagging disdain for Arius and Arianism:

> Milton makes fifteen explicit references to Arian, Arianism, Arians, and Arius in his prose works, and none in his poetry. Arius himself receives only a single reference, negative in tone, and that in the private *Commonplace Book* under the rubric of the dangerous quality, 'Curiosity' [*CPW* 1.380]. All other references to the associates of Arius and contemporary adherents of Arianism are without exception disapproving in tone. The Arians of the early Church are disorderers or transposers of Biblical texts [*CPW* 6.256], dividers of Christendom [*CPW* 5.115], no true friends of Christ and infectors of the people [*CPW* 1.685; 3.507].[18]

Tobin's example from *De Doctrina Christiana* records Theodore Beza's hypothesis that select passages from the Book of Revelation were inauthentic and had been confused and transposed 'by some Arian [*ab Arriano quopiam*]' (*CE* 14.292–93). The Latin phrase, in its third person address and dismissive use of an indefinite pronoun, distances the convictions of the treatise's author from the Arian persuasion.

The Dutch publisher Daniel Elsevier sent the manuscript of *De Doctrina Christiana* for review to Philippus van Limborch, Professor at Amsterdam's Remonstrant College. Limborch defended his advising against the treatise's publication in an epistle written to the German traveller Zacharias Conrad von Uffenbach: 'because you find that there is, through and through, the severest Arianism within it'.[19] What might the denomination 'Arian' have meant for Limborch, let alone for Arius and Milton? Thomas Hobbes encapsulates what Arianism meant to him: 'the Heresie of *Arrius*, which was denying the Divinity of Christ'.[20] John Shawcross has demonstrated how, throughout the early modern period, the 'term was misused to mean any variation upon or dissection of the concept of the Trinity as "one God in three persons"'.[21] In the seventeenth century 'Arian' was an obfuscating label that clouded more than it clarified, a bugaboo for the early modern thought police. To be slandered as an Arian was comparable to being branded a 'Pinko' in the West during the Cold War. How the mighty could fall once they were stigmatized with this charge! During the Arian Controversy William Whiston was removed from Cambridge University's Lucasian chair in 1710 for maintaining, 'the Arian doctrines are those delivered by our Saviour and his Apostles and all the first Christians

---

[17] See J. J. M. Tobin, 'A Note on Luther, Arius and *Paradise Lost*, X, 504ff', *Milton Quarterly*, 11 (1977), 38–43; in *Theological Milton*, 269–71, Lieb adds *CPW* 1.533–34, 545, 555–60, 613–14, 685, 839; 3.507–8; and see James H. Sims, '*Paradise Lost*: "Arian Document" or Christian Poem?', *Études Anglaises*, 20 (1967), 337–47.

[18] Tobin, 'Note', 39.

[19] 'weil der Arrianismus durch und durch auf das heftigste darinnen zu finden gewesen': Campbell, Corns, Hale, Tweedie, *Manuscript*, 7.

[20] Thomas Hobbes, *Behemoth* (London, 1679), 9.

[21] Shawcross, *Rethinking*, 103.

till philosophy from the ancient heretics, particularly from Tertullian, prevailed at Rome'.[22] Shawcross's verdict should make us question how appropriate so hazy a term as 'Arianism' is today in Milton studies.[23] Yet the Arian denomination has been re-appropriated within the field. Although the label lacks the whiff of scandal that clung to it during the early modern period and although its menacing power for tarring reputations and spreading rumours of heresy has faded, the imputation of Arianism to Milton's Son shares the same unhappy tendency of foreclosing discussion about pivotal Miltonic doctrines, heterodox or orthodox. Above all, the term obscures rather than illuminates the Son's person and function as Saviour in Milton's works.

Repeated assertions of Milton's Arian Christology bring us no closer to grasping the mode Milton's soteriology takes and the role the Son assumes in accomplishing human salvation. Theologians possess fragmentary evidence from antiquity on which to establish a solid basis for Arian soteriology. Robert Gregg and Dennis Groh's work on Arianism is a seminal, if not formative, influence for Michael Bauman's thesis that Milton was an Arian. Bauman's study focuses mainly upon *De Doctrina Christiana*'s fifth and longest chapter, which is devoted to Christology. His study grapples less directly with the mechanism of salvation and his exploration of soteriology is less developed.[24] Like Kelley, Bauman concedes in a footnote the unsoundness of making scholarly assertions regarding Arian soteriology. Bauman confesses that 'this facet of Arian thought' is indebted to 'the recent joint work of Gregg and Groh, *Early Arianism*, upon which I rely heavily for my summary'.[25] Gregg and Groh's rationalistic, soteriological model, which is supposedly Arian, is based upon principles of human self-reliance and improvability, if not perfectibility:

> Elected and adopted as Son, this creature who advanced by moral excellence to God exemplified that walking 'in holiness and righteousness' which brings blessing upon all children of God who would do likewise . . . The central point in the Arian system is that Christ gains and holds his sonship in the same way as other creatures – thus it is asserted that what is predicated of the redeemer can and must be predicated of the redeemed.[26]

In defining Milton's soteriology Bauman supports Gregg and Groh's 'central point of the Arian system': 'Arianism . . . posited a salvation that relied not on the Savior's identification with God but rather with man. If we, like the Savior, conform ourselves to the express will of God, we will, also like the Savior, be amply exalted.'[27] This model of salvation demands from the capable individual 'soteriological adoption', 'moral exertion', and 'moral participation'.[28] The stress upon personal autonomy and initiative in achieving individual salvation reduces the Son's saving work on Earth to that of 'a teacher, and a revealer'.[29] Gregg and Groh maintain that there is no Arian means of grace by 'forensic application, as the Protestant reformers, for example, would later maintain'.[30] Gregg and Groh tender

---

[22] Wiles, 95; see 93–110.   [23] Shawcross, *Rethinking*, 103.
[24] Bauman, 44–46.   [25] Ibid. 66.
[26] Robert C. Gregg and Dennis E. Groh, *Early Arianism – A View of Salvation* (London, 1981), 65 and 67.
[27] Gregg and Groh, 44–45.   [28] Ibid. 45.   [29] Ibid. 46.   [30] Ibid. 45.

this information with certitude, despite the partial Nicene veil through which so much of the piecemeal material by or about Arius is available, and despite the paucity of textual evidence on Arian soteriology. More surprising is the fact that Miltonists continue to promote an exemplarist view of Miltonic salvation when there exists a sizeable body of evidence for a forensic idea of salvation in Milton's works. Michael Bryson, for example, finds that Milton's incarnate Son 'is not so much a savior as an exemplar – he "saves" by showing the way, by providing a roadmap for mankind to follow'.[31] The exemplarist soteriology Gregg, Groh, and Bauman propound appears distinctly more Socinian than Arian, a heresy that, unlike Arianism, has a fully coherent and uncorrupted set of doctrines preserved and articulated within *The Racovian Catechism*.

The identification of Milton's position on the Son with Socinianism is also an inexact fit. Strictly speaking, Socinianism denies the Son's preincarnate existence and his hypostatic union of human and divine natures, testifies to the Son's existence as a real man, advances an adoptionist Christology, and dismisses the doctrines of penal satisfaction and original sin.[32] Each of these fundamental Socinian tenets conflicts with *De Doctrina Christiana* and *Paradise Lost's* representation of the Son, where the Son not only preexists Creation and subsequently assumes his *theanthropic* nature at the Incarnation, but also satisfies for humanity and atones for the effects of original sin occasioned at the Fall. John Rogers and Martin Dzelzainis have suggested that Milton's licensing of *The Racovian Catechism*, the official Socinian manifesto drawn up by Fausto Sozzini's disciples among the Polish Brethren, indicates that Milton had a personal investment in its doctrines.[33] And yet, if we are to take as read the Dutch statesman Liewe van Aitzema's eyewitness report of Milton's interview before the Parliamentary investigating committee, Milton, when asked whether he had approved the publication of this contentious Socinian document, 'said Yes, and that he had published a tract on that subject, that men should refrain from forbidding books; that in approving of that book he had done no more than what his opinion was'.[34] Milton's invocation of his 'tract', which doubtless refers to *Areopagitica* (1644), reveals more about his adherence to his principles, published eight years earlier, concerning the exclusion of the censor and the granting of a free press, than his private theological commitments. Milton's toleration of the publication of uncensored material ultimately neither rendered the book immune from confiscation nor made its author invulnerable to prosecution. *Areopagitica* championed the removal of State censorship so that error might be scanned and presumably condemned – 'the fire and the executioner will be the timeliest and the most effectuall remedy' (*CPW* 2.569) – and so that the truth might be confirmed and applauded. Milton's intention to

---

[31]   Bryson, *Tyranny*, 157.

[32]   For a pithy sketch of Socinianism, see Lieb, *Theological Milton*, 219–21.

[33]   See John Rogers, 'Delivering Redemption in *Samson Agonistes*', in *Altering Eyes: New Perspectives on 'Samson Agonistes'*, ed. Mark R. Kelley and Joseph Wittreich (Newark, 2002), 72–97; Martin Dzelzainis, 'Milton and Antitrinitarianism', in *Milton and Toleration*, ed. Sharon Achinstein and Elizabeth Sauer (Oxford, 2007), 171–85.

[34]   J. Milton French, *Life Records of John Milton*, 5 vols (New Brunswick, 1949–58), 3.206.

promulgate *The Racovian Catechism* among an ideal readership neither cloistered nor fugitive in their virtue need not signify that Milton endorsed Socinianism, but rather that he was acting in a manner consistent with his own limited tolerationist views on the right to a free press.

To return to the idea of an Arian soteriology, Rowan Williams, with reference to Gregg and Groh, cautions those who would mount a purely exemplarist model for Arius's understanding of salvation: that the Son offered humanity the possibility for subjective atonement, a moral paradigm that humans could imitate to earn personal salvation. Williams warns that the 'total lack of allusion to any sort of adoption in Arius' own undoubted works ... must make it doubtful whether the theme was central to his concerns, as has so often been maintained'; and that, 'despite the persuasive arguments of Gregg and Groh, we have to be cautious in ascribing to Arius the exemplarist doctrine of salvation that might be implied in such a scheme, and to be mindful of the fact that Arius himself is *not* speaking of Christ as a human being rewarded for his probity'.[35] Arius 'became the centre of a controversy because of his fusion of ... conservative themes with a very un-conservative ontology'.[36] Arius is likely to have approved of a more orthodox soteriology than some Miltonists have allowed for.

On several occasions *De Doctrina Christiana* and *Paradise Lost* explicitly refute an exemplarist model of salvation. The treatise claims scriptural warrant for its rejection of an adoptionist model: 'those who argue that Christ did not seek death in our place for the sake of redemption, but only for our good, and as though as an example [*velut exempli*], vainly try to elude the evidence of [scriptural] passages' (*CE* 15.318). *De Doctrina Christiana* substitutes for exemplarism an exclusive claim for the universal effects of Christ's redemption: 'Without Christ, who was foreknown, there was no reconciliation for God with humans who were going to fall; no grace was decreed' (*CE* 14.104). God 'foreknew or approved of nobody, except in Christ; no one was a believer, except in Christ' (*CE* 14.122); 'it is credible that the Son is most powerfully called only-begotten because he is the one mediator between God and humanity' (*CE* 14.190). Once informed about the incarnate Son's salvific role, Milton's Adam proclaims that he has been 'Taught this by his example whom I now / Acknowledge my Redeemer ever blest' (12.572–73), but Adam carefully distinguishes the Son's extraordinary office as redeemer even while he proclaims Jesus as his standard of moral excellence. During the Heavenly Council the angelic host proclaims the Son's offer of redemptive love, which no angel is capable of making, as 'unexampl'd love, / Love no where to be found less then Divine!' (3.410–11). God stresses that humanity, unredeemed, 'Attone-ment for himself or offering meet, / Indebted and undon, hath none to bring' (3.234–35). Before the Son volunteers his 'dearest mediation', the epic narrator entertains the awful possibility that 'without redemption all mankind / Must have been lost' (3.222–23). God exclaims that the Son 'onely canst redeeme' (3.281) and is 'the onely peace / Found out for mankind under wrauth, O thou / My sole

---

[35] Williams, *Arius*, 105 and 113.   [36] Ibid. 232.

complacence!' (3.274–76). An exemplarist soteriology is insufficient to explain the exclusiveness of the Son's saving work for Milton's theology.

Milton's reader needs to appreciate the relative weighting in the treatise of the heterodox Milton against the orthodox Milton. To do this, we must be careful to distinguish within *De Doctrina Christiana* the heterodoxies of divine passibility, Christology, mortalism, creation *ex Deo*, and polygamy from the treatise's core of resolutely orthodox elements. One of the strengths of Corns, Campbell, Hale, and Tweedie's monograph on the manuscript of *De Doctrina Christiana* is the cold eye their study casts upon the treatise's contents. In their estimation, despite Milton's adoption of minority positions concerning creation *ex Deo*, mortalism, and the like, the treatise, as an exposition of post-Reformation systematic theology, 'is for the most part unexceptionable'.[37] Overall, 'Milton, like his fellow systematizers, overwhelmingly agrees with received opinion but occasionally champions a minority or personal opinion'.[38] Their study concludes that 'for the most part [Milton's] opinions are part of the theological mainstream. This combination of local heterodoxy and general compliance with mainstream Protestantism can be paralleled among other exponents of systematic theology.'[39] The syntagma's 'general compliance with mainstream Protestantism' is especially pertinent concerning its soteriology.

An understanding of Milton's heterodox Christology should not distract us from the compelling orthodoxy of his soteriology. Scrutinizing the Son's person without appreciating the mode of his accompanying work of salvation, the teaching on what the Son *is* without regard for what he *does*, tells us almost nothing about his exceptionality. To point an analogy, gazing intently at a photograph of Sir Winston Churchill will ultimately render up little information about his vital contribution to the war effort. C. A. Patrides eloquently summarizes the Son's celebrity in *Paradise Lost*:

> The role of protagonist, once assigned to him, is maintained in all subsequent events. As Creator he erects the universal edifice (VII.210 ff.); as Saviour he volunteers to redeem man long before the Fall (III.236 ff.); as Judge he passes sentence on Adam and Eve (X.97 ff.); through his Prevenient Grace he is instrumental in their regeneration (XI.2 ff.); as the incarnate Christ he consummates the salvation for which he had earlier offered himself (III.236 ff., XII.360 ff.); through his Comforter he supports his faithful followers (XII.485 ff.); and as the Supreme Judge he is to return in order to terminate the history of the world.[40]

Critics such as Gordon Campbell detect a reverence for the Son in Milton's verse, but find a corresponding admiration absent from the syntagma: 'In *De Doctrina* Milton argues relentlessly for the secondary status of the Son. The polemic reduces the Son's status by stripping him of the attributes of God. In *Paradise Lost*, this

---

[37] Campbell, Corns, Hale, Tweedie, *Manuscript*, 92.
[38] Ibid. 160.
[39] Ibid. 161.
[40] C. A. Patrides, *Milton and the Christian Tradition* (Oxford, 1966), 261.

attempt to reduce is simply not present. Instead, Milton's attitude is worshipful.'[41] Despite Campbell's claim, the Son's relentless reduction is difficult to locate in the treatise. As the first-born and apogee of God's Creation, the Son is the only entity who can approach and gaze upon the Father; instrumental agent and conserver of Creation; the perfect exponent of God's revealed will; redeemer, restorer, mediator, and perpetual intercessor; archetypal prophet, priest, and king; and fearsome eschatological judge.

The attributes *De Doctrina Christiana* attaches to the Son's person excel the psilanthropic criteria of a merely exemplary human being. The Son's name is above every name (*CE* 14.304–07; Phil. 2:9) and is revelatory of his special relationship with the Father. The Son enjoys 'omnipresence [*omnipraesentia*]' (*CE* 14.314–15); 'omniscience [*omniscientia*]' (*CE* 14.316–17); 'authority [*auctoritas*]' over Heaven and Earth (*CE* 14.318–19); 'omnipotence [*omnipotentia*]' (*CE* 14.318–19); the power to create all things at the Old Creation and to convert fallen creatures at the New Creation (*CE* 14.322–23); the capacity to remit sins, 'even as a man [*Remissionem peccatorum: etiam homo*]' (*CE* 14.324–25) (a phrase logically implying that, in his original, preincarnate state, the Son is superhuman and partakes of divinity); the 'Conservation [*Conservatio*]' of Creation through his redemption (*CE* 14.324–25); 'renovation [*renovatio*]', renewal or remoulding the old Adam into a new, spotless Adam (*CE* 14.326–27); and the conferring of gifts, including 'the mediatorial work, or rather the Passion itself [*Ipsum opus mediatorium vel potius passionis*]' (*CE* 14.328–29); the miraculous potential to resurrect the dead 'to life [*Resuscitationem ad vitam*]' (*CE* 14.330–31), as Jesus did with Lazarus and will do again at the *eschaton*, 'Arriving in judgement [*Adventum in iudicium*]' (*CE* 14.330–31); and, finally, his reception of divine honour and glory (*CE* 14. 330–31, 336–37).

Scripture, *De Doctrina Christiana*, and the God of *Paradise Lost* expound that at time's end Christ will deliver up his restored kingdom because God ultimately is, was, and 'shall be All in All' (see 1 Cor. 15:24–28; *CE* 15.300–03; 16.366–67; *PL* 3.341). Rumrich, commenting upon this monistic theme, maintains that, 'The Son's material being may originally be more refined and exalted than that of other creatures, but eventually parakeets and pachyderms would also qualify as participants in the Godhead.'[42] Rumrich's equation of the Son's status with 'parakeets and pachyderms' would benefit from a consideration of the Son's saving role for the interim in which Milton's reader exists, that interval in salvation-history between genesis and *maranatha*.[43] In the cosmic narrative of Milton's poem the Son comprises the *sine qua non* of human salvation, the Saviour of lapsed Creation, and the tireless sustainer of Creation's welfare. The fit reader's appreciation of Christic heroism increases awareness that the poem's prelapsarian and postlapsarian human characters are always already uplifted by the possibility of redemption.

---

[41] Gordon Campbell, 'The Son of God in *De Doctrina Christiana* and *Paradise Lost*', *Modern Language Review*, 75 (1980), 513–14.

[42] Rumrich, 'Milton's Arianism', 83.

[43] Rumrich, *Milton Unbound: Controversy and Reinterpretation* (Cambridge, 1996), 43.

A temporal continuum of no small importance is presumed. The Son's credentials, 'all in all', boast an impressive résumé for an exceptional figure that exceeds the Arian classification, such as it is: 'a limited, localized, mutable being, not eternal but derived in time from an eternal, substantially omnipresent Father'.[44] Byron, Shelley, and Keats were unable to transcend Milton's vision of Hell for the solace of the Heavenly Council. In a similar way, it is salutary to read beyond *De Doctrina Christiana*'s Christological fifth chapter to its intricate exposition of the covenant of grace. In the enumeration of the Son's cardinal roles, which correspond with the epic's description of his salvific agency, where is the treatise not reverent, if not, to quote Campbell, downright 'worshipful' where the Son is concerned?

As a formal systematic theology, *De Doctrina Christiana* is at bottom an expositional narrative. The *capita* or doctrinal 'heads' of which a systematic theology consists form the building blocks for our modern novels, since from these heads derives the concept of dividing the narrative into corresponding 'chapters'. Across the syntagma the tale of a given systematic theology is told. Typically, the narrative provided by a systematic theology commences with an understanding of God, the Prime Mover, from whom all things proceed. The plot then gives an account of divine providence, the creation of humanity, and the crisis of the human Fall that cries out for resolution. Next, the story normally presents a compensatory hope in the shape of a hero (Christ), indicates his Christology or heroic nature, and explores his soteriology, the manner in which he overcomes the labours set before him to redeem a troubled world. The diegesis ordinarily closes in a grand restorative climax with eschatology, an apocalyptic dénouement dealing with Last Things. *De Doctrina Christiana* abides by this structural pattern. The treatise, like any systematic theology, must give an account of the Son's significance in his nature and saving work. A cursory glance at *De Doctrina Christiana*'s 'Table of Contents' indicates that a major portion of the manuscript – chapters 14 to 28 of Part One – is committed to an exposition of the covenant of grace, the Son's exquisite person, and his mission to save humankind.

The Christology outlined in *De Doctrina Christiana* requires re-evaluation. Williams has reconstructed 'Arius' concern to remove all trace of emanationism and materialism from the relation of Father to Son' and Arius's lukewarm reception of a cosmos 'of "Middle Platonism"; ascent to the first principle by a graded sequence of images, knowledge of God through the created works which show his wisdom and through the primary *eikon*, the Son'.[45] In Williams's view Arian ontology is far removed from the graduated, monist materialism set down in the treatise's seventh chapter on Creation, where 'all things were from God [*fuisse omnia ex Deo*]' (*CE* 15.20), and Raphael's emanationist model of the Cosmic Tree, a cosmos where 'one Almightie is, from whom / All things proceed', that originary 'one first matter all' (5.469–505). The treatise's Christological fifth head demonstrates, if not the Son's coessentiality with the Father, then a consubstantiality that sublimates him above Creation. As the first-born of Creation, the head of the

[44] Rumrich, 'Arianism', 81.   [45] Williams, *Arius*, 9 and 230.

angelic orders, and the medium for heavenly and mundane Creation, the Son is specially created, that is, begotten, produced, or generated, so that, if he does not proceed from God's essence (a logical impossibility, according to the treatise), then he partakes of the Father's immediate substance. As Lewalski and Lieb note, Arianism, in its differentiation of the Father's *ousia* or 'essence' from the *ousia* of the Son, has no precedent for Milton's distinction between the consubstantiality and the non-coessentiality of the Father and the Son. Milton's distinction 'is quite beside the point in Arian thought'.[46]

The fifth chapter's first teaching concerns the Son's 'GENERATION, whereby God begot His only Son from His decree. Whence He is primarily called Father' (*CE* 14.178). God's 'begetting [*genuisse*]' of the Son is 'in a literal, single sense [*uno proprio*]' (*CE* 14.180). The divine begetting of the Son is more rarefied and privileged than the creation of humans of terrestrial mould:

> *Nam Adami ex pulvere facti opifex erat Deus, potius quam Pater: Filii autem ex substantia eius producti proprius erat Pater.*
>
> (For God was the craftsman rather than the Father of Adam, who was made from dust; but He was, properly speaking, the Father of the Son who was produced from His own substance.)   (*CE* 14.186)

Paradise Lost often recurs to Adam's original, crude formation 'of the dust of the ground' from the second Creation account of Genesis 2:7 (see *PL* 7.524–26). The Son, a more refined entity than humans, has the Father's substance imparted directly to him at his generation and, through consubstantiality, 'in him all his Father shon / Substantially exprest' (3.139–40). The Son is the medium through whom all Creation witnesses to God's divine virtues *substantially* reflected (3.63–64, 385–86; 6.680, 719–21; 7.194–96; 10.63–67; *PR* 1.91–93). In *De Doctrina Christiana*'s discussion of the Incarnation the pious tentativeness with which the treatise explores the God-man's ontology dramatizes a struggle between the author's heart and his head, between faith and reason. In his *Artis Logicae* (1672) Milton expresses exasperation at the apparently chopped logic of the Incarnation and eventually skirts the issue: 'Once pettifogging distinctions have been devised, disputing that *Christ's human nature is at the same time an infinite body* [*humanam naturam Christi adeoque corpus infinitum esse*], [Theologians] commit an equal contradiction. But, omitting the paradoxes of Theologians, let us return to the precepts of Logic' (*CE* 2.314–17). Milton's theological treatise cannot sidestep this contradiction, but it nevertheless admits and defers to the impenetrability of the Incarnation, a mystery greater to its author than the Trinity:

> But this Incarnation of Christ by which he, since he was God, assumed human nature and was made flesh and, as a result, did not leave off being numerically one, this Incarnation Theologians deem to be far and away the greatest mystery of our religion, after that mystery of three persons in one essence of God. Indeed, concerning the

---

[46] Lewalski, 'Forum', 151; Lieb, *Theological Milton*, 276–77.

mystery of that triad, no word whatsoever exists in sacred scripture: while this Incarnation is very often termed a *mystery*. (*CE* 15.262)

As the curtain lowers upon Dante's *Divine Comedy*, the pilgrim wonders at the revelation of the Incarnation at the heart of the Celestial Rose. As he gazes, he struggles to comprehend this paradox, just as a geometrician might strive to square the circle (*Par.* 33.133–38). Milton's dilemma within the treatise is an analogous war waged between head and heart to be reconciled with the Incarnation and its redemptive purpose. The struggle is evident in that substantial section of the treatise concerning the Son's saving work and especially in the fourteenth head entitled, 'ON HUMANITY'S RESTORATION AND CHRIST AS REDEEMER'. John Carey has remarked that 'Milton's rational distrust of mystery is clear on every page of *Christian Doctrine*'.[47] However, the manuscript illustrates that, at certain junctures where Milton accepts divine mystery, such cool rationalization allows for divine dispensation. The treatise concedes that Christ's 'NATURE is twofold; divine and human' (*CE* 15.258), yet that 'the fullness of the Godhead that dwells in him bodily', a concept inspired by Colossians 2:9, signifies, 'in every way, the virtue of the Father' and 'the fullness of the promises dwelling in, not hypostatically united with, Christ the man'. The treatise interprets the expression 'bodily' as 'really [*revera*]' (*CE* 15.260). The reader turns the page to find the author inveighing against the vain disputations and subtleties that Christ was *merum hominem* or 'mere man' (*CE* 15.262), an assertion that reflects Satan's frustrated predicament in *Paradise Regain'd*, blind to Jesus's divinity and insisting that the Son is tested 'To th' utmost of meer man both wise and good, / Not more' (*PR* 4.535–36). *De Doctrina Christiana* resists such Satanic reductionism by arguing that the Son is *apud Deum Deus* or 'God with God' and, in its next paragraph, ratiocination again yields to the grand mystery of the Incarnation. Not two pages later, after conceding that 'we should allow the mysteries to remain inviolate and we should be fearful of investigating beyond that which is right' (*CE* 15.264), Milton resumes the enquiry with fresh vigour. The assertion is made that 'from two natures one person comes into being . . . a Hypostatic union' (*CE* 15.266), and that 'there has been the union of two natures in Christ, the mutual hypostatic union of two essences' (*CE* 15.268). After this rally the thesis is once more concessive. While 'the mode is unknown and it is certainly best that it is unknown, that which God wishes to be unknown' (*CE* 15.270), the aim of the Incarnation, the salvation of humanity, is no enigma, but a fundamental article of faith:

> How much more satisfactory, therefore, is it for us to know this only, that the Son of God, our Mediator, was made flesh, that he both is called and is God and human, whom, for this reason, the Greeks most aptly name by the single word θεάνθρωπος ['God-man']. But, in what way [this happens], since God does not show that, we should desist from argumentation and instead be wisely ignorant [*sapienter potius nescire*]. (*CE* 15.272)

---

[47] John Carey, *Milton* (London, 1976), 97.

In the Son's supernatural capacity as God-man the Reformed dogma of the *communicatio idiomatum* or *proprietatum*, the 'communication of properties' between the divine and human natures pertains, where an attribute belonging to one of Christ's natures is transferable to or communicable with the other (*CE* 15.278). The ability to mediate is the exception to this rule and applies to Christ's total person, so that both natures intercede for humankind, 'Not insofar as he was a man, but insofar as he was *theanthropos*' (*CE* 15.278). The consequence is that, as Christ's divine nature was enfleshed and humiliated, so human nature was exalted and purified in God's eyes by the *theanthropos*'s death and resurrection. God is reconciled to humanity, just as the two natures of the *theanthropic* person are reconciled by death and rebirth. Milton's hesitations and vacillations, his checks and balances concerning Christ's person, achieve equilibrium in an affirmation that the Son is divine and human. Underlying this central affirmation concerning the Incarnation is Milton's implied acquiescence to the irrationalism that divinity is passible. The doctrine of theopaschitism or patripassianism maintains that, in some substantial sense, the Father did indeed suffer with humanity through the Son's death. But, then, the treatise does concede, 'let us renounce reason in sacred matters; what divine scripture teaches, that solely let us follow' (*CE* 14.196).

Rumrich has remarked upon the inconsistency of any critical attempt to negotiate an Arian interpretation of the Son, once the treatise's assertion of Christ's divine humanity is granted: 'Milton acknowledges in *Christian Doctrine* that the mystery he refuses to allow in his Arian construction of the deity – the mystery of distinct persons equally participating in a single essence – occurs at the Incarnation . . . He recognizes the inconsistency, but absolves himself by observing that, unlike the mystery of the Trinity, the Incarnation rests on an explicit scriptural foundation. He therefore rejects the judgment of reason.'[48] While Rumrich is surely right to point out that the treatise accepts that Christ's twofold, hypostatic nature baffles any logical solution, Milton is only being 'blithely paradoxical' if, from the outset, one imagines that *De Doctrina Christiana* is construing its Christology in Arian terms.[49] If, however, one sets aside the imputation of Arianism and appreciates Milton's bid to exegete his Christology as an enterprise that is *sui generis*, then Rumrich's valuable insight regarding the treatise's recognition of the mysterious nature of the Incarnation, like the treatise's decidedly non-Arian consubstantiality of the Father and the Son, ceases to be problematic.

T. S. Eliot found Milton's epic oxymora to be a contributory factor to modern poetry's dissociation of sensibility and its poverty of objective correlatives. I would argue that Milton's oxymora supply Christological hints for readers who, like *De Doctrina Christiana*'s author, are willing to renounce reason and accept the Incarnation's mystery. 'Mystic oxymorons' permeate Milton's cosmos.[50] Hell's 'darkness visible' (1.63), 'fiery Deluge' (1.68), 'wide womb of uncreated night' (2.150),

---

[48] John P. Rumrich, 'Milton's *Theanthropos*: The Body of Christ in *Paradise Regained*', *Milton Studies*, 42 (2002), 54.

[49] Ibid. 57.

[50] Leland Ryken, *The Apocalyptic Vision in 'Paradise Lost'* (Ithaca, 1970), 88–94.

and 'Black fire' (2.67); the 'Eternal Anarchie' (2.896) of 'hot, cold, moist, and dry' (2.898) in Chaos; Heaven's 'living Saphire' (2.1049) and 'bright Sea [that] flowd / Of Jasper, or of liquid Pearle' (3.518–19); the stars set like 'living Saphirs' (4.605) in Creation's firmament; and the fruits of 'vegetable Gold' (4.220) clustering down from Milton's Tree of Life. These oxymora train the reader's imagination to grasp the paradox, Milton's ultimate oxymoron, embodied in the incarnate Son's person. The living contradictions inflecting Milton's epic universe imply a Christology where the Son is 'Both God and Man, Son both of God and Man' (3.316). The epic narrator yearns for a glimpse of a 'human face divine' (3.44) and *De Doctrina Christiana* supplies the Origenic oxymoron *theanthropos* to describe Jesus's hypostatic union. This nature is 'twofold [*duplex*]', the 'mutual hypostatic union of two essences' (*CE* 15.268), representing one who 'both is called and is God and human, whom, for this reason, the Greeks most aptly name by the single word θεάνθρωπος' (*CE* 15.272). The contradictions of Milton's infernal, chaotic, celestial, and paradisiacal images anticipate God's crowning paradox of the Incarnation.

I observed above that Milton's God is primarily comprehended as Father relationally, through His paternal association with His Son. The Son's mediation is predicated upon his affiliation with his Father. It is from God's original, preincarnate act of begetting the Son 'in a literal, single sense' that God is considered as Father, and it is through His propinquity to his first-born, only-begotten Son that humans are regarded at their creation and, again, through redemption, as children of God by the soteriological doctrine of adoption. Through the Son's sacrifice 'GOD ADOPTS HIS CHILDREN TO HIMSELF WHO ARE JUSTIFIED THROUGH FAITH' (*CE* 16.50). Humans are God's children 'insofar as we are created by Him' (*CE* 16.50). 'By adoption, we are also constituted *heirs* in Christ' (*CE* 16.54) because we are 'justified by his grace' (Tit. 3:7). Humanity is favoured anew 'with a new generation and, as it were, with the new nature and glory of a child'; we are even elevated to a status where, like the Son, we are 'first-born [*primogeniti*]' (*CE* 16.54). An accompanying proof text sources the restoration of God's prodigal sons and daughters in the Son's resurrection: 'They are equal to the angels, and are children of God, who are children of the resurrection' (Luke 20:36). In *Paradise Lost* the Son exercises his privileges of primogeniture on behalf of a fallen world and ventures his worthiness as an atoning sacrifice for 'Man / Thy creature late so lov'd, thy youngest Son' (3.150–51). The Father is willing to 'spare Thee [the Son] from my bosom and right hand, to save, / By loosing thee a while, the whole Race lost' (3.278–80), so that humans, adopted by the Father through the Son, are once more invited to become God's children.

The Son's intimacy and oneness with his Father secures human salvation and forms the basis for reconciliation between God and humanity. Apropos of this, *De Doctrina Christiana* styles the gospels 'the *ministry* and the *word of reconciliation*, 2 Cor. 5:18–19' (*CE* 16.114). The treatise maintains that Christ 'alone can teach, and does teach' (*CE* 14.210), the many ways that the Son and the Father are one. 'First, because they speak as one, they act as one' (*CE* 14.210). Second, they share 'a most intimate communion' where the Son 'declares that he and the Father are one in the same way as we are one with him: that is, not in essence, but in love, communion, agreement, charity, spirit, and finally glory' (*CE* 14.212). The incarnate Son 'was God only in nearness and love, not in essence' (*CE* 14.254). Enjoying this propinquity, the Son, as God-man, is simultaneously different from and identical to God and humanity so that he can mediate from both sides. Thus Marshall Grossman describes how Milton's Son 'returns man to the center of divine concern and converts difference into identity'.[51] Milton's theology insists upon this puzzling and mystifying paradox. The riddle of reconciliation is that God, 'To whatever God we are reconciled, if he is one God, will not be that God through whom we are reconciled, since he is another God; for, if he is the same God, he must be a mediator between himself and us, he will reconcile us to himself through himself; which is an extremely knotty issue' (*CE* 14.206). Despite this tangled reasoning, *De Doctrina Christiana* affirms the Son's mediatorial office as the eternal reconciliation between God and humanity: 'HE WILLINGLY PERFORMED, AND EVEN NOW PERFORMS, ALL THOSE THINGS BY WHICH PEACE AND ETERNAL SALVATION WITH GOD IS ACQUIRED FOR THE HUMAN RACE' (*CE* 15.284). Under the rubric of 'PEACE WITH GOD' is a string of proof texts focusing on Christ's agency in bringing humanity into a state of reconciliation with the Father; these texts include Romans 5:10, where, through the Son's death, humanity is reconciled to God, and 2 Corinthians 5:18–19, where God 'reconciled us to Himself through Jesus Christ; God was in Christ, reconciling the world to himself' (*CE* 15.286).

Milton's diffuse epic reminds the reader of the hypostatic union that makes this reconciliation feasible. God prophesies that His resurrected Son will exalt humanity by being 'Both God and Man, Son both of God and Man' (3.316), and Michael attests that, in the incarnate Son, 'God with Man unites' (12.382) and 'therefore joines the Son / Manhood to God-head' (12.388–89). The Son knows that 'peace assur'd, / And reconcilement' (3.263–64) will issue from redemption, and he expresses his mediation in the Johannine discourse of reconciliation and interpenetration between the Father and the Son. He also vouchsafes a restored humanity, a sublime at-one-ment, 'when in the end / Thou shalt be All in All, and I in thee / For ever, and in mee all whom thou lov'st' (6.731–33). In his sacerdotal and intercessory role (11.19, 21, 25) Milton's Son petitions God in distinctly Johannine terms that humankind may 'live / Before thee reconcil'd' (11.38–39) so that 'with mee / All my redeemd may dwell in joy and bliss, / Made one with mee as I with thee am one' (11.42–44).

The treatise lists 'Conservation' among the Son's divine attributes. A supporting text is Hebrews 1:3, where the Son 'upholds all things by the word of his power', an action the treatise denotes by the Latin *sustinens* or 'sustaining', and which conveys the Son's caretaking of Creation (*CE* 14.324). The Son of *Paradise Lost* sustains Creation: in Book Three he offers himself to appease his Father, even before humankind has fallen; as Book Ten opens, he clothes and imputes righteousness to the newly fallen Adam and Eve; and, as Book Eleven commences, he hastens to intercede for them within God's heavenly inner sanctum. Michael's prophecy

[51] Marshall Grossman, *'Authors to Themselves': Milton and the Revelation of History* (Cambridge. 1987), 64.

expounds the Son's redemptive role in history and his function at the *eschaton* to judge 'Bad men and Angels' (3.331). As the Father predicts, the Son will revive a New Heaven and Earth, 'purg'd and refin'd' (12.546–51) as in an alchemical process, or flourishing phoenix-like 'from her ashes' (3.333–38), distilled out of the sublunary cosmos's wasted corruptions.

To appreciate the magnitude of Milton's redemptive theology readers must recognize Milton's stress upon human helplessness before sin. Milton's writings are not of a Pelagian complexion and so reject an attainable human perfectibility unaided by grace. At times Milton borders upon espousing the Calvinist doctrine of total depravity. The orthodox 'Anglican' George Herbert figured fallen humanity as 'a brittle crazie glasse' ('The Windows', 2), 'a weak disabled thing' ('The Crosse', 17), and 'A sick toss'd vessel, dashing on each thing' ('Miserie', 76).[52] In Milton's works sin is represented as enervating and pestilential. In *Areopagitica* sin is endemic, ungovernable, and ineradicable by human effort alone: 'a huge heap increasing under the very act of diminishing, though some part of it may for a time be withdrawn from some persons, it cannot from all . . . and when this is done, yet the sin remains entire. Though ye take from a covetous man all his treasure, he has yet one jewell left, ye cannot bereave him of his covetousnesse' (*CPW* 2.527). Milton mistrusts the cultural optimism and social progressivism of Thomas More's *Utopia* (1515), Francis Bacon's *The New Atlantis* (1627), and James Harrington's *The Commonwealth of Oceana* (1656). He laments the gap between spirit and flesh that divides our erected wits from our infected wills.[53] He discredits the utopian literature of a Baconian or Harringtonian stripe and perhaps, by extension, expansionist ambitions in a brave New World, admonishing, 'To sequester out of the world into *Atlantick* and *Eutopian* polities, which never can be drawn into use, will not mend our condition' (*CPW* 2.526). In *Tetrachordon* sin is uncontrollable and immense: 'Besides it is an absurdity to say that law can measure sin, or moderate sin; sin is not a predicament to be measur'd and modify'd, but is alwaies an excess. The least sinne that is, exceeds the measure of the largest law that can bee good; and is as boundlesse as that vacuity beyond the world' (*CPW* 2.657). *De Doctrina Christiana* pictures sin as cumulatively festering and pullulating: 'sin is its own punishment, it is a spiritual death to life, especially since sins are heaped up on sins' (*CE* 15.206, 208).

In *Paradise Regain'd* the Father announces the Son's destined victory over a 'mass of sinful flesh':

> To conquer Sin and Death the two grand foes,
> By Humiliation and strong Sufferance:
> His weakness shall orecome Satanic strength
> And all the World, and mass of sinful flesh
> (*PR* 1.159–62)

---

[52] George Herbert, *The Works of George Herbert*, ed. F. E. Hutchinson (Oxford, 1941), 67, 165, and 102.

[53] See Philip Sidney, *Sir Philip Sidney*, ed. Katherine Duncan-Jones (Oxford, 1989), 217.

The Son stands poised to perform an objective atonement that is worlds apart from the exemplarist, subjective atonement of the Socinian and semi-Pelagian positions. The 'mass of sinful flesh' is an Augustinian expression deriving from the *massa* (Vulgate Rom. 9:21) or common 'lump' of sinful humanity, out of which proceed vessels of mercy (the elect) as well as vessels of wrath (the reprobate). Augustine imagines human peccability arising 'out of Adam [as] a mass of sins and impieties [*ex Adam massa peccatorum et impiorum*]' or 'a mass of perdition [*massa perditionis*]' that requires the second Adam to vanquish it.[54] John Donne preached a homily on the '*Massa damnata* [in which] the whole lump of mankind is under the condemnation of *Adams* sinne'.[55] Milton uses the figure in his *Apology against a Pamphlet* (1642) to relate how the notion that a wise man might be 'exempted out of the corrupt masse of Adam, borne without sinne originall, and living without actuall, is impossible' (*CPW* 1.909). *De Doctrina Christiana* makes the same distinction between 'ORIGINAL . . . sin [ORIGINALE . . . *peccatum*]', the 'evil concupiscence [*concupiscentia mala*]', an innate 'propensity or tinderbox to sin [*habitum . . . sive fomitem . . . peccati*]' of which Adam and Eve were guilty and which they transmitted to their posterity, and 'actual sin [*actuale peccatum*]', the sinner's 'wicked action itself, or the malefaction [*ipsa mala actio, seu malefactum ipsum*]', which may be committed 'by deeds, words, and thoughts, and even by the very omission of good actions' (*CE* 15.192–201). *Paradise Lost* differentiates these two species of sin. The 'mortal Sin / Original' (9.1003–04) arises from Adam's eating the Forbidden Fruit; the indomitable figure of Sin, unleashed from Hell to plague Creation, is described as '*Sin* there in power before, / Once actual, now in body, and to dwell / Habitual habitant' (10.586–88). God's prediction in *Paradise Regain'd* that the Son will overcome this universally benighted 'mass of sinful flesh', whether original or actual, far exceeds the diminished capacities of *l'homme moyen sensuel*.

De Doctrina Christiana's hamartiology provides two further categories for sin: 'SIN, which is either COMMON TO ALL HUMANS or PERSONAL TO EACH INDIVIDUAL' (*CE* 15.180). The sin common to all, actual sin, is tantamount to Augustinian original sin: 'THE SIN COMMON TO ALL IS THAT WHICH, ONCE THEY HAD SQUANDERED THEIR OBEDIENCE AND TASTED THE FRUIT OF THE FORBIDDEN TREE, OUR FIRST PARENTS AND, IN THEM, ALL THEIR POSTERITY, COMMITTED' (*CE* 15.180). A supporting text for this tenet is 1 Corinthians 15:22, '*in Adam all are dead*. Therefore, assuredly, they sinned in Adam' (*CE* 15.182). The treatise justifies this 'perpetual method of divine justice' that, when 'one has violated a sacred thing (in this case, it was the sacred tree), not he alone, but all his progeny, become condemned and a sin-offering' (*CE* 15.184). Penitents must confess their own and their fathers' sins; a family may have to expiate the crime committed by its head; subjects may have to requite their king's transgression; and a nation may have

---

[54] Augustine glosses Romans 9:21 in *Concerning Diverse Questions to Simplicianus* (AD 397), Book 1, section 19, in *Opera Omnia*, vol. 6 (Paris, 1837), column 176; *Contra Duas Epistolas Pelagianorum* (AD 420), Book 2, section 15, *Opera Omnia*, vol. 10 (Paris, 1838), column 837.

[55] John Donne, *The Sermons of John Donne*, vol. 3, ed. George R. Potter and Evelyn M. Simpson (Berkeley, 1953–62), 109.

to recompense for the sins of a single citizen (*CE* 15.188, 190). By the same 'method of divine justice' one perfect individual may atone for all.

In the second category, 'SIN PROPER TO THE INDIVIDUAL' is 'QUITE APART FROM THAT SIN COMMON TO ALL' (*CE* 15.192). *De Doctrina Christiana* jettisons as a misprision Augustine's conception of 'original sin', formulated during Augustine's controversy with Pelagius. The sin of concupiscence did not originate in Adam at the Fall nor was it an infection transmitted within his seed. Sin instead continued to contaminate Adam and Eve throughout their lives: original sin 'is too narrow a term, . . . because that evil of concupiscence, that law of evil, was inborn, not only in us, but inhabited in Adam after the Fall, so that it could not possibly be called Original' (*CE* 15.194). Such sin was rather sin common to all. Augustinian concupiscence is too restricted a definition for common sin, which is so pervasive that it permeates our words, deeds, and even our omission from action (*CE* 15.198, 200).

Neither is there any ambiguity in *Paradise Lost* about humanity's innate depravity. The havoc Sin and Death spread across the cosmos in Book Ten's middle panel, a wave of destruction stemming from Adam and Eve's transgression, conveys the ubiquity and contagion of festering sin. Milton's Sin scoffs, with no small irony for the reader anticipating the redemption, that 'Death from Sin no power can separate' (10.251). The Father's challenge to the Son to redeem humanity reveals Adam's hopeless predicament for, without redemption, he 'with his whole posteritie must die: / Die hee or Justice must' (3.209–10). Adam's long lament conveys Milton's traducianism and his understanding of sin's magnitude. Adam agonizes, 'All that I eate or drink, or shall beget, / Is propagated curse' (10.728–29), and asks, 'what dies but what had life / And sin?' (10.790–91). He continues:

> Ah, why should all mankind
> For one mans fault thus guiltless be condemnd,
> If guiltless? But from mee what can proceed,
> But all corrupt, both Mind and Will deprav'd,
> Not to do onely, but to will the same
> With me? how can they then acquitted stand
> In sight of God?
>
> (10.822–28)

The Son's saving work satisfies Adam's question. Likewise, the Son's renovation of Adam's sinful progeny affords the background to the exordium to *Paradise Lost*, of 'Mans First Disobedience' and the 'one greater Man' who will 'Restore us' (1.1–5). The 'breach / Disloyal' (9.6–7) Adam makes is bridged by the perfect man's obedience. A Pauline verse resonates within this passage: 'For as in Adam all die, even so in Christ shall all be made alive' (1 Cor. 15:22; see Rom. 5:15).

Campbell, Corns, Hale, and Tweedie determine that *De Doctrina Christiana*'s redemptive theology 'is uncontentious' and assert, 'Milton's thinking on many doctrines developed throughout his life, but he always resolutely defended the forensic theory of the atonement'.[56] Milton's theory of the atonement holds that an

---

objective atonement successfully counteracts sin's devastating effects. God's gracious incursion into human affairs becomes necessary because humankind is incapable of saving itself. For this reason a forensic model of salvation constructed along principally orthodox Pauline, Anselmian, and Lutheran lines characterizes Milton's epic, where the Son justifies and satisfies for the human catastrophe of the Fall and reverses humanity's enslavement to Satan, Sin, and Death. One of the most fundamental articles of faith the epic and the treatise propound rests upon belief in the Son's saving action, a deed accomplished within and for all time.

A consideration of the correlations between John Owen's defence of the objective atonement and Milton's definition of salvation in the poetry and the treatise will help clarify Milton's advocacy of an orthodox forensic soteriology. Owen, who in 1655 acted as Vice Chancellor to Oxford University, was commissioned by the Council of State to answer the burgeoning of heretical Socinian, psilanthropic, and subordinationist tendencies. Owen responded with *Vindiciae Evangelicae*, a two-pronged confutation of *The Racovian Catechism* and John Biddle's *Two-fold Catechism*. Owen's rebuttal is a meticulously argued 700-page broadside against the Socinian–Biddelian position. Nearly 200 pages of the polemic are dedicated to corroborating from scripture the Son's objective atonement and efficacious satisfaction. Owen deduces the necessity of the Incarnation in order to render satisfaction for sin.[57] In the chapter 'The Principall Considerations of the Death of Christ' Owen divides the doctrine of satisfaction into three key elements: '1. As a PRICE [or "Ransome"]. 2. As a SACRIFICE. 3. As a PENALTY'.[58] Owen's critique furnishes a template for analysing Milton's soteriology. If the atonement theories of ransom, sacrifice, and penalty are pertinent to Milton's soteriological paradigm, then the cost of discounting the objective atonement from Milton's poetry is substantial.

First, regarding a price or ransom, *De Doctrina Christiana* defines redemption as 'THAT WHEREBY CHRIST, . . . AFTER HE THOROUGHLY PAID, VOLUNTARILY, AT THE PRICE OF HIS OWN BLOOD, REDEEMED ALL BELIEVERS' (*CE* 15.252; see 254, 256). The treatise gleans the idea of a price from 1 Corinthians 6:20 and 7:23; Galatians 3:13; Matthew 20:28; and 1 Timothy 2:6 (*CE* 15.318). The epic implements the language of redemption and the metaphors of debt and restitution. Fallen humanity stands 'Indebted' (3.235) to God and 'to [God] ow / All his deliv'rance' (3.181–82). Sin exacts a 'deadly forfeiture' (3.221) so that the Son must requite the heavy reckoning and, in the mercantile terms of standing surety for another's debt, the Son appeals to his Father to 'Account mee Man' (3.238). As one person covers the debt of another, the Son 'quitted all to save / A World from utter loss' (3.307–08) with the effect that "that debt [is] paid"' (3.246). The metaphor of the cross as ransom, intrinsic to any orthodox appreciation of redemption, pervades the poem. Owen advises, 'The *propriety* of paying a Ransome to any, where it lyes in undergoing the penalty that was due to the *Ransomed*. Consists in the *voluntary* Consent of him to whom the Ransome is paid, and him that *pays* it, unto this *Commutation*.'[59] Thus the New Testament term for ransom, λύτρος (Matt. 20:28;

[57] John Owen, *Vindiciae Evangelicae* (Oxford, 1655), 455–635.
[58] Ibid. 463–64. [59] Ibid. 605.

1 Tim. 2:6), could be defined as 'the price of humanity's redemption'. Fallen humanity has its 'ransom set' (3.221), which the Son, voluntarily made captive to Death, shall free, 'ransomd with his own dear life' (3.297). After the Fall God identifies the Son as 'Both Ransom and Redeemer voluntarie' (10.61) and Jesus's resurrection morning heralds '[Adam's] ransom paid, which Man from death redeems' (12.424).

Milton's treatise maintains Owen's second redemptive category of sacrifice in its explanation of the Son's sacerdotal role: 'THE PRIESTLY OFFICE is that whereby CHRIST OFFERED HIMSELF ONCE TO GOD THE FATHER AS A VICTIM FOR SINNERS, HE ALWAYS HAS INTERCEDED FOR US, AND EVEN NOW HE INTERCEDES' (CE 15.290). The treatise supplies proof texts for the Son as sacrifice, propitiation, and victim (1 John 2:2; Isa. 53:10; Matt. 20:28; Heb. 9:12 and 10:10; Rom. 3:25). The Son sacrifices himself in his twofold nature: 'And, being *theanthropos*, he duly offered himself as God-man' (CE 15.292). Consequently, 'no one would deny that Christ was doubtless a sacrifice in both his divine and human nature' (CE 15.308). The efficacy of his sacrifice extends to those who have no knowledge of him: 'If [Christ] had not been given to the world, God would have called no one at all; . . . how much more perfect is Christ's sacrifice, even for those who have never even heard of Christ's name?' (CE 15.348); 'it should not seem wondrous that many of the Judeans, moreover, many people of other races who were before and even after Christ, to whom Christ was not revealed, and who believed or who still believe in God alone, are saved; yet saved in Christ; because he was given from the beginning of the world and was sacrificed' (CE 15.402, 404). The treatise's sacramentalism holds that lacking a sacrificial understanding of redemption divests the rites of Passover and Communion of their inner meaning. The treatise interprets the Passover typologically so that 'the significance of the Passover was Christ sacrificed' (CE 16.168). Likewise, the bread and wine at the Last Supper teach 'the doctrine of Christ made man, so that he might pour forth his blood for us; a doctrine which, whoever takes it with true faith, no less surely will they live for eternity, just as those among us who eat and drink sustain this mortal life daily, nay, rather more surely than that' (CE 16.194). Milton's narrator styles the Son's redemption 'as a sacrifice / Glad to be offerd, he attends the will / Of his great Father' (3.269–71). The Son's intercession in Book Eleven is an archetypal enactment of ancient Israel's annual atonement sacrifice at *Yom Kippur* where the Son, as God's high 'Priest' (11.25), is granted access before the 'Mercie-seat' (2), the 'Gold'n Altar' (18), and his 'Fathers Throne' (20) within God's empyreal Holy of Holies. Here the Son offers himself as humanity's 'propitiation' (11.34), just as Michael compares the old covenant's 'shadowie expiations weak' (12.291) with the Son's 'bloud more precious' (12.293), shed for the striking of a new covenant.

The poem also reflects Owen's redemptive metaphor of penal substitution. Michael foretells that the Son's obedience to death is 'impos'd / On penaltie of death, and suffering death, / The penaltie to thy [Adam and his progeny's] transgression due' (12.397–99). Closely related to penal substitution is *satisfaction* – that the incarnate Son's death was an act of mercy for humanity that slaked God's wrath and fulfilled the divine justice. A standard ethical objection to satisfaction occurs in *The Racovian Catechism*:

> They say, there is in God by nature justice and mercy . . . that Christ should endure death in our stead, and thus satisfy God's justice in his human nature, by which God had been offended, and at the same time there is a place for God's mercy in condoning sins . . . however that justice and mercy which our adversaries want, we deny is in God's nature . . . in no way was there need for that method, by which he would satisfy mercy and justice, and by which as though he would, between these two poles, conciliate a certain temperament within God . . . For what is the justice, and similarly what is the mercy, that punishes the innocent, and pardons the guilty?[60]

Miltonists have re-echoed this accusation of inhumanity in the picture of an absolutist God who permits the suffering of a non-divine Son, perhaps most notably in the Stalinist, totalitarian deity William Empson imported into *Paradise Lost*.[61] Adopting this view impairs the theodicy of the poetry and the treatise, which allows for the Son's divinity. Thomas Altizer has urged the reclamation of Milton's suffering God:

> even if Christ's nature is both divine and human, Christ totally died upon the cross, and not only both his soul and body died, but his divine nature succumbed to death as well as his human nature. At no point was Milton more revolutionary theologically, a theological revolution inseparable from the epic revolution of *Paradise Lost*, as for the first time in both theological thinking and poetic language itself death is known not only as an ultimate but as a divine event, and an event that is the sole source of redemption. Certainly Luther was reborn in Milton.[62]

An interpretation of Milton's incarnate Son that esteems him as a creature human and divine, at whose Passion, *De Doctrina Christiana* recounts, the Father both sanctioned the piercing and was Himself pierced, permits an unparalleled intimacy between the Father and the Son: 'they transfixed him who poured out the spirit of grace [Rev. 1:10]. But it was the Father who poured out the spirit of grace through His Son . . . Therefore the Father is He whom they pierced in the Son' (*CE* 14.298–99). This matchless oneness, even amid suffering, sets the supernatural phenomenon of the cross outside humanity's moral and epistemological frame of reference. Desmond Hamlet asserts, 'One fundamental reason for our failure to appreciate Milton's fusion of dogma and drama in *Paradise Lost* and for our insistence on the "inexplicability of God's justice" in the poem is the evidently desperately felt need to fit God's ways into our own concepts of justice.'[63] So Hugh MacCallum observes, 'The necessary sacrifice of the Son draws attention to something in the Father which is difficult to assess in terms of man's principles and rules, and the conflict of justice and mercy cannot easily be placed within a

---

[60] *The Racovian Catechisme* (Amsterdam, 1652), 272–74.
[61] 'The picture of God in the poem . . . is strikingly like Uncle Joe Stalin': Empson, *Milton's God*, 146.
[62] Thomas J. J. Altizer, *The Contemporary Jesus* (Albany, 1997), 118.
[63] Desmond M. Hamlet, 'Recalcitrance, Damnation, and the Justice of God in *Paradise Lost*', *Milton Studies*, 8 (1976), 271.

framework of purely human values.'[64] John Owen likewise admonished tendencies to probe too deeply into God's plan of redemption: 'There must some differences be allowed between *spirituall, eternall*, and *civill, corporeall, temporall* deliverances, which yet doth not make Spirituall Redemption to be improper wherein it agrees not thereunto; The one is *Spirituall*, the other *Temporall*, so that in every circumstance it is not expected that they should agree.'[65]

Milton explicitly represents the Son's saving work as a mending of the schism between divine justice and mercy within the Godhead. Even before the Father decrees that sinful Adam requires redeeming, He avouches grace for humankind and promises that 'in Mercy and Justice both, / Through Heav'n and Earth, so shall my glorie excell, / But Mercy first and last shall brightest shine' (3.132–34). Mercy is a fundamental attribute of God and the Son is its avatar and agent. Accordingly, the narrator describes how 'in [the Son's] face, / Divine compassion visibly appeerd' (3.140–41). In an arresting trope Milton's angels celebrate the atonement as a reconciliation of discordant elements within God: the Son 'to appease thy wrauth, and end the strife / Of Mercy and Justice in [the Father's] face discernd . . . Second to [the Father], [the Son] offerd himself to die / For Mans offence' (3.406–07, 409–10). *De Doctrina Christiana* similarly formulates that the incarnate Son endured the full onslaught of divine justice. The Son's 'HUMILIATING STATE is where CHRIST THE GOD-MAN, IN HIS LIFE, AS IN HIS DEATH, SUBJECTED HIMSELF VOLUNTARILY TO THE DIVINE JUSTICE TO ENDURE ALL OF THOSE THINGS BY WHICH OUR REDEMPTION MUST BE CARRIED OUT' (*CE* 15.302). After the Fall the Father sends the Son as 'Mercie collegue with Justice', that is, 'sending [the Son] / [as] Mans Friend, his Mediator, his design'd / Both Ransom and Redeemer voluntarie' (10.59–61). The Son backs God's plan by promising that he 'shall temper so / Justice with Mercie, as may illustrat most / Them fully satisfi'd, and thee appease' (10.77–79).

After almost thirteen years Milton broke his political silence in a prose tract that made plain his espousal of the doctrine of satisfaction. Milton's tolerationist and latitudinarian purpose in *Of True Religion, Haeresie, Schism, Toleration* (1673) was, in the spirit of the Test Act, to weld the various sects of Protestant Christianity into a united front against the potential Papal threat from the continent and Stuart sovereignty. Milton's last gambit to preserve the Commonwealth and godly reformation lends further insight into Milton's theology as he itemizes the mistaken, eccentric, and correct points of doctrine in each Protestant sect's working out of an explicit faith. Milton maintains that sects of all stripes hold in common 'all things absolutely necessary to salvation' (*CPW* 8.424). He faults the Lutheran doctrine of 'Consubstantiation' and finds that the 'Calvinist is taxt with Predestination' (*CPW* 8.424), doctrinal stances that *De Doctrina Christiana* likewise discard.[66] Milton

---

[64] Hugh MacCallum, '"Most perfect Hero": The Role of the Son in Milton's Theodicy', in *'Paradise Lost': A Tercentenary Tribute*, ed. Balachandra Rajan (Toronto, 1969), 100.

[65] Owen, *Vindiciae*, 599.

[66] The treatise lumps Lutheran consubstantiation with Roman Catholic transubstantiation as 'anthropophagy' (*CE* 16.198). It approves predestination of all creatures to election, but

highlights, but does not flatly refute, the Anabaptist belief in infant baptism and the Arminian 'setting up of free will against free grace' (*CPW* 8.425).[67] Among the Arians and Socinians Milton's pamphlet detects two fundamental heterodoxies, antitrinitarianism and disputing the Son's satisfaction:

> The Arian and Socinian are charg'd to dispute against the Trinity: they affirm to believe the Father, Son, and Holy Ghost, according to Scripture, and the Apostolic Creed; as for terms of Trinity, Triunity, Coessentiality, Tripersonality, and the like, they reject them as Scholastic Notions, not to be found in Scripture, which by a general Protestant Maxim is plain and perspicuous abundantly to explain its own meaning in the properest words, belonging to so high a Matter and so necessary to be known; a mystery indeed in their Sophistic Subtilties, but in Scripture a plain Doctrin. Their other Opinions are of less Moment. They dispute the satisfaction of Christ, or rather the word *Satisfaction*, as not Scriptural: but they acknowledge him both God and their Saviour. (*CPW* 8.424–25)

Much ink has been spilt attempting to thread Milton's labyrinthine first assertion concerning the Trinity, unfortunately at the cost of neglecting his second assertion. According to Milton, the second error peculiar to Arians and Socinians lies in their rejection of the doctrine of satisfaction, which holds that the Son was crucified to satisfy God's anger against a disobedient humanity. This distinction, though apparently 'of less moment', is one of only two points of deviant dogma Milton singles out as characteristic of Arian and Socinian belief, inherent in their reading of scripture, and worthy of comment. Milton applies the adversative particle 'but' to defend the Arian and Socinian position – his primary goal *is* to consolidate the Protestant sects – and he permits them a place in God's fold because 'they acknowledge him both God and their Saviour'. The identification of Christ not only as Saviour but also as God would square with Milton's granting of divinity to the Son's person in his poetry and theology. Furthermore, if Milton is of an Arian or Socinian stripe, then why does he so deliberately differ from them by openly affirming the doctrine of satisfaction in his verse?

Milton's early poetry is positive concerning satisfaction. In *On the Death of a fair Infant dying of a Cough* the poem's speaker imagines the departed Christ-like child in Heaven, 'slak[ing] his wrath whom sin hath made our foe' (66); and in *Upon the Circumcision* Christ's first wounding merges into his self-emptying on the cross when he 'that great Cov'nant which we still transgress / Intirely satisfi'd' (21–22). Milton stands by the doctrine of satisfaction in his mature epic, when God predicts of fallen humankind, 'Die hee or Justice must; unless for him / Som other able, and as willing, pay / The rigid satisfaction, death for death' (3.210–12). The Son meets God's terms by offering his 'life for life' (3.236) and he asks, 'on mee [the Son] let thine [the Father's] anger fall' (3.237). God's jubilant response – and His initial reaction *is* jubilant, since His address to the Son begins with an honorific title and is

---

discountenances Calvinism's predestination to reprobation, since God's 'destruction of unbelievers [is] a thing inherently graceless and odious' (*CE* 14.98).

[67] *De Doctrina Christiana*, however, does jettison infant baptism (see *CE* 16.170).

vigorously punctuated by an exclamation mark – honours the Son who, 'as is most just, / Shall satisfie for Man' (3.294–95). As 'the only peace / Found out for mankind under wrauth' (3.274–75), the Son aims 'to appease [God's] wrauth' (3.406). Immediately after the Fall the Son intercedes before God's throne and vouchsafes, yet once more, 'I shall temper so / Justice with Mercie, as may illustrat most / Them fully satisfi'd, and thee appease' (10.77–79). After judging and blessing Adam and Eve, the Son returns to the Father's 'blissful bosom', for whom he has 'appeas'd / All' (10.226–27). Finally, Michael reveals how on the cross humankind's sins will be 'with [Jesus] there crucifi'd . . . In this his satisfaction' (12.417, 419). Milton's extensive use of the doctrine of satisfaction, together with his testimony of Arian indifference to satisfaction in *Of True Religion*, confirms that there is no perfect marriage between Miltonic and Socinian–Arian opinion concerning the Son's person and salvific method.[68]

Miltonic anthropology paints a picture of humanity beset on all sides by sin and death and possessing insufficient intrinsic merit to save itself. *De Doctrina Christiana* attributes an efficacious merit to the Son's person that neutralizes sin's corrosive effects. Because of his intrinsic worth, the Son can satisfy for fallen humanity: 'CHRIST, AFTER HE HAD TRIUMPHED OVER DEATH AND LAID ASIDE THE FORM OF SERVANT, WAS WOKEN BY GOD THE FATHER TO IMMORTAL AND SUPREME GLORY FOR OUR BENEFIT, PARTLY BY HIS OWN MERIT, AND PARTLY BY GOD'S LARGESSE, AND HE WAS RESURRECTED AND ASCENDED AND SITS AT GOD'S RIGHT HAND' (*CE* 15.308). *Paradise Lost* is decisive on this point. The Son's willingness to die for humanity reveals to the Father that he is not merely extrinsically privileged, but intrinsically worthy, and 'hast been found / By Merit more then Birthright Son of God' (3.308–09). God invites the Son, as the founder, preserver, and protector of Creation, to 'assume / Thy Merits' (3.318–19). During the War in Heaven, the Father reminds Abdiel that the Messiah 'by right of merit reigns' (6.43) and He later dispatches the Son in His triumphal chariot as one 'worthiest to be Heir / Of all things' (6.707–08). In a forensic turn of phrase God foretells how the Son's righteousness and 'merit / Imputed shall absolve them who renounce / Thir own both righteous and unrighteous deeds' (3.290–92) and Michael voices God's will that the Son's 'obedience / Imputed becomes theirs [sinners'] by Faith, his merits / To save them, not thir own, though legal works' (12.408–10). In *Paradise Regain'd* God confirms Jesus's worthiness to atone, as being 'by merit calld my Son, / To earn Salvation for the Sons of men' (*PR* 1.166–67).

The Son's merit renders fallen humanity acceptable in God's eyes. With the exception of their saving faith sinners achieve little by their own best lights. *De Doctrina Christiana* promotes Christ's unique immaculacy because 'in no other way are we said not to sin, except that, in Christ, our sins are not imputed to us' (*CE* 16.30). The Son is singular: 'Christ alone was free from contagion, although,

---

[68] The *Racovian Catechism*'s denial of various doctrines does not square with Miltonic Christianity, particularly in its rejection of 'original sin, . . . vicarious satisfaction, and justification by faith alone': Owen Chadwick, *The Penguin History of the Church: Volume Three: The Reformation* (London, 1990), 202.

indeed, he came from Adam's line; but he arose from supernatural generation: Heb 7.26. *holy, without spot*' (*CE* 15.196). The Son of *Paradise Lost* foresees that after the crucifixion his 'unspotted Soule' will not be 'For ever with corruption there to dwell' (3.248–49). In *Paradise Regain'd* the Father describes Jesus as 'This perfet man' (1.166) and the narrator calls him 'sinless' (4.425). The Son's impeccability and meritorious perfection entitle him to redeem peccable humanity. According to the treatise, human fellowship with the Father through the Son arises from 'participation in all the gifts and merits of Christ' (*CE* 16.58). The Son recognizes that the power issuing from his intrinsic merit can perfect sinners when he intercedes as high priest, sacrificial offering, and Paraclete or 'Advocate' for Adam and Eve. He supplicates the Father to bless their penitential prayers:

> Unskilful with what words to pray, let mee
> Interpret for him, mee his Advocate
> And propitiation, all his works on mee
> Good or not good ingraft, my Merit those
> Shall perfet, and for these my Death shall pay.
> (11.32–36)

An early entry in Milton's *Commonplace Book* declares humanity's inability to satisfy because of its estrangement from God. In the 'Ethical Index' the category headed 'Moral Evil' cites Lactantius's teaching on human merit, to which Milton appends his opinion. While Milton approves the virtue of unaided human effort to achieve good works when exercised by evil, he issues a caveat: 'even though these things do not satisfy [*quamvis et haec non satisfaciunt*]' (*CE* 18.128).[69] *De Doctrina Christiana* displays Milton's mature appreciation of this idea, since, alongside justification, the syntagma makes satisfaction the cornerstone of its soteriology. The treatise asserts that the *telos* of mediation was the satisfaction of divine justice and the conformation of the faithful to Christ's image: 'SATISFACTION is where CHRIST THE GOD-MAN, BY FULFILLING THE LAW AND PAYING THE JUST PRICE, FULLY SATISFIED DIVINE JUSTICE FOR ALL' (*CE* 15.314). Universal satisfaction provides the primary means of grace in God's providential plan: 'it necessarily follows that there was satisfaction by Christ for all, sufficiently and efficaciously enough that it meets God's plan and will, since, without that most complete satisfaction, not the least amount of grace can be imparted in any way' (*CE* 15.320, 322). Without satisfaction humanity would have been lost: 'But the gracious call could not have been deemed worthy of anyone, had not Christ's satisfaction interposed, not only sufficient in itself, but also for all, to the extent that it was planted in God's efficacious will' (*CE* 15.324); 'satisfaction is the effect and end of [Christ's] entire administration . . . the effect of this satisfaction is equal to the reconciliation of God the Father with humanity' (*CE* 15.330, 332). Neither human merit nor human endeavour in imitating Christ is sufficient without the human acceptance of grace

---

[69] Ruth Mohl notes, 'This is apparently Milton's own comment. It is not from Lactantius' (*CPW* 1.363 [fn. 4]). The expression appears in neither *Divine Institutes* 5.7 nor Lactantius's treatise *De Ira Dei*, texts Milton cites under this heading.

springing from Christ's satisfaction: 'the restoration of humanity, if we heed Christ's satisfaction and our conformation with him when he was emptied [upon the cross], proceeds from merit . . . Nor should we be afraid lest we are thereby led into a doctrine of our merits. For that conformation of ours [in imitating Christ] adds not a jot to Christ's most complete satisfaction, no more than our works add to our faith . . . the restoration of humanity is solely a matter of grace' (*CE* 15.336, 338; see 16.44).

The treatise exegetes from scripture an objective atonement: 'The external cause of regeneration or sanctification is Christ's death and resurrection' (*CE* 15.376). Neither works nor faith alone can emulate the efficacy of redemption, 'except insofar as they are propped up by God's mercy and Christ's righteousness, and these two things alone sustain them' (*CE* 16.42). The treatise instructs that a sacrament's underlying identity is bound up with Christ's satisfaction because a sacrament is that which, 'through a visible sign, divinely instituted, God sets His seal on believers for His saving grace or Christ's satisfaction' (*CE* 16.164). The Son enjoys an incomparable status as redeemer: 'Scripture nowhere teaches that to approach God, to take away sin, to fulfil the Law, to sustain and conquer God's wrath, Satan's power, and temporal and eternal death, and to recuperate the good things lost to us, can be done by no one except by God, but by him to whom God has given the power to do these things; that is, given by God to His beloved Son in whom He has testified He is well pleased' (*CE* 15.274). According to the treatise's economy of salvation, without satisfaction there is no hope of reconciliation between God and humanity; without the incarnate and redeeming Son there is no prospect of salvation.

Let us now take stock of these findings. If readers are fair-minded in their interpretation of Milton's treatise and his epic, they discover that both documents advocate a high Christology that expounds, if not the Son's strictly Athanasian identity as very God, then his distinctively divine and consecrated nature, set apart from humanity. Both texts work out a complex soteriology. The 'Preface' to the treatise declares its goal is to distinguish between 'what in sacred matters must be believed, and what must be held as only an opinion' (*CE* 14.8). Milton's *Areopagitica* underlines the importance of an individual's ability to discern what constitutes 'all that rank of things indifferent, wherein Truth may be on this side, or on the other, without being unlike her self' (*CPW* 2.565). *Paradise Lost* illustrates *adiaphora*, 'that rank of things indifferent', by frequently supplying readers with a variety of choices on which to fix their opinions.[70] Thus the narrator exculpates the 'Gardning Tools' with which Eve tends her Edenic orchard from the corruptions of fallen technology by offering a series of alternative possible aetiologies. The tools were manufactured 'as Art less rude, / Guiltless of fire had formd, or Angels brought' (9.391–92). Likewise, Satan is able to ventriloquize through the serpent

---

[70] James Sims distinguishes matters of opinion, knowledge, and faith, and offers a fruitful discussion of Milton's things indifferent. See Sims, 'The Miltonic Narrator and Scriptural Tradition: An Afterword', in *Milton and Scriptural Tradition: The Bible into Poetry*, ed. James H. Sims and Leland Ryken (Columbia, 1984), 192–205.

either 'with Serpent Tongue / Organic, or impulse of vocal Air' (9.529–30); and the Son clothes the nakedness of the fallen couple 'with Skins of Beasts, or slain, / Or as the Snake with youthful Coate repaid' (10.217–18). These are speculative flights of exegetical fancy, Christian *midrashim*, not articles of faith upon which one would firmly stake one's salvation. The divine colloquies conducted between the Father and the Son, however, concern matters not indifferent: saving doctrines that require belief. These epic scenes present plain expositions of an objective atonement couched in forensic soteriological discourse that demand from the reader, in no uncertain terms, faith in the exceptional efficacy of the Son's redemption.

Two very different figures living in Milton's age suggest how far Milton's theology abides by orthodox Christian canons. In his quest for a godly reformation, Oliver Cromwell, in whose government Milton served as Secretary for Foreign Tongues, defined the strictest limits of belief and 'peculiar interest' for his idealized, united Protestant front. For Cromwell, as for Milton, the atonement lay at the heart of the matter:

> For . . . undoubtedly this is the peculiar interest all this while contended for. [That] men that believe in Jesus Christ . . . men that believe the remission of sins through the blood of Christ and free justification by the blood of Christ, and live upon the grace of God, that those men that are certain they are so, are members of Jesus Christ and are to him as the apple of his eye.[71]

Elsewhere, in banishing John Biddle, the father of Biddelianism and Unitarianism, to the Scilly Isles, Cromwell cautioned, 'liberty of conscience . . . should never . . . be stretched so far as to countenance those who denied the divinity of our Saviour'.[72] For Milton, too, the Son's divine nature was imperative to the efficacy of his atonement.

The outcast John Biddle deplored various tenets that were, by his account, unscriptural, and yet which somehow passed muster among the supposedly orthodox Protestants of his day:

> Examine therefore the expressions . . . of an Incarnation, of a Hypostatical Union, of a Communication of Properties . . . of Christs making Satisfaction to God for our sins, both past, present, and to come, of Christs fulfilling the Law for us, of Christs merits, or his meritorious obedience both active and passive . . . of Christs enduring the wrath of God . . . of apprehending and applying Christs righteousness to our selves by faith, of Christs being our Surety, of Christs paying our debts, . . . of Christs dying to appease the wrath of God, and reconcile him to us.[73]

Milton's treatise and his epic legitimate all of these soteriological doctrines, doctrines that were, for Biddle, without scriptural precedent. Milton's justification of these dogmas indicates the extent to which his conception of salvation holds to a Christian orthodoxy that does not strictly abide by a principle of *sola scriptura* or, as *De Doctrina Christiana*'s 'Preface' maintains, '*solo Dei verbo*' (*CE* 14.6). Benjamin

---

[71] Barry Coward, *Oliver Cromwell* (London, 1991), 111–12.
[72] Ibid. 122.
[73] John Biddle, *A Twofold Catechism* (London, 1654), preface.

Myers has recently argued that to advocate for an orthodox or a heterodox Milton is to oversimplify and that the 'treatise itself cannot accurately be said to belong to any specific theological tradition, but it draws eclectically on various concepts and traditions, and presses towards its own unique theological position'.[74] Perhaps an anonymous early reviewer of *De Doctrina Christiana*, commenting shortly after the manuscript's publication in 1825, affords a concise and equitable judgement upon Milton's theological system as an argument as orthodox in its major doctrines as it is heterodox in its minor ones:

> The system of theology which is here presented to us, has been characterized as a combination of arianism, anabaptism, latitudinarianism, quakerism, and (in reference to the Author's opinions on polygamy) 'mohammedism.' No existing sect can lay claim to the honour or the shame of having engendered the theological monster, upon which is entailed the fate of all hybrids; it will perpetuate no new variety. No future Miltonists will arise to form an article in the catalogue of sects and opinions. As a theologist, not less than as a poet, its Author must stand alone. The Baptists disown him; the Socinians can have no fellowship with him; he soars above the Arians; he would not be admitted among the gentle followers of Penn. Too heterodox for the orthodox, he is by far too orthodox for the sceptical and misbelieving school. In short, he must be admitted to rank within the pale of the true Church, from the impossibility of classing him with any other than devout and faithful men. But within that divine enclosure, he dwells apart, an intellectual hermit, a sect consisting of the individual, a genus with one species, in society with himself. Yet, though thus isolated as regards his opinions, he is no sectarian in spirit, but most truly Catholic; and of his very aberrations from sound doctrine, it may truly be said,
>
> > 'But yet the light that led astray,
> > Was light from heaven!'[75]

---

[74] Benjamin Myers, *Milton's Theology of Freedom* (Berlin, 2006), 52.
[75] Anon., 'Milton on *Christian Doctrine*', *The Eclectic Review*, 25 (1826), 4–5.

2

Milton's Great Argument

... to sing the victorious agonies of Martyrs and Saints...

Milton, *The Reason of Church-Government*

The *Paradise Lost* is an Epic, or a Narrative Poem, he that looks for an Hero in it, searches for that which *Milton* never intended; but if he will needs fix the Name of an Hero upon any Person in it, 'tis certainly the *Messiah* who is the Hero, both in the Principal Action, and in the chief Episodes.

Joseph Addison[1]

Milton's early poetry, and in particular those occasional poems concerned with the life of the incarnate Son, openly explores the atonement. *The Nativity Ode* (1629) looks forward to a time when the infant Christ, a vision of rosy innocence, will atone for humanity:

> The Babe lies yet in smiling Infancy,
> That on the bitter cross
> Must redeem our loss;
> So both himself and us to glorifie
>
> (151–54)

In *Upon the Circumcision* (c. 1633) Milton apprehends in the first shedding of the Christ-child's blood and his 'wounding smart' (25) a premonition of the 'Huge pangs and strong' (27) experienced on the cross. The poem foresees Christ's many heroic accomplishments upon Golgotha: the act of kenosis whereby he empties his glory even to nakedness (20), his complete satisfaction for humanity (21–22) in shouldering the wrath of divine justice (23–24), and the sealing of his obedience through death and resurrection (25). In the unfinished *The Passion* (1630) Milton depicts the poet striving to convey the ineffable event of a suffering deity. Milton's appended prose statement of failure that, finding himself to be '*above the yeers he had, when he wrote it, and nothing satisfi'd with what was begun, left it unfinisht*', can read as an admission that Milton felt, at that stage of his life, unequal to the task of rendering the Passion in compelling and imaginative verse, rather than, as the statement is too frequently interpreted, as a repudiation of the ode's subject matter.

---

[1] Richard Steele and Joseph Addison, *Selections from 'The Tatler' and 'The Spectator'*, ed. Angus Ross (London, 1988), 426.

According to this reading, the young Milton is consciously being critical of the medium rather than the message of his Passion ode. He finds fault with the restrictions of his poetic vision, the confinement of his 'roving vers' (22), and the binding of his muse and Christ's 'Godlike acts' (24) to a limited 'Horizon' (23). Milton's decision to place *The Passion*, along with *The Nativity Ode*, in a prominent position within his two editions of minor poems of 1645 and 1673 indicates that the ode marked a defining point in his poetic growth. When the mature poet embarked upon his major epic poem, he would successfully reapply himself to the same foundational Passion event with a reinvigorated vision.

In my second chapter I wish to analyse the soteriological implications of Milton's 'great Argument', famously declared in *Paradise Lost*'s exordium, to 'assert Eternal Providence, / And justifie the wayes of God to men' (1.24–26). Richard Strier has argued, upon the premise that *De Doctrina Christiana* is 'essentially a rationalistic project', that, 'While it is true that the desire to "assert Eternal Providence" is not necessarily rationalistic[,] the intention to "justify the ways of God to men" is indeed a rationalistic project.'[2] Strier obtains this reading by halving the epic argument, a method that weakens the force of what I believe are two complementary statements. These statements comprise two sides of a single coin, the 'assertion' and the 'justification' making a joint appeal to faith and proclaiming soteriological purpose. For Strier, the 'goal' of Milton's poetic theodicy 'is rational explanation; "justification" is used in its normal, rationalistic sense rather than in its specialized Reformation one'.[3] This conclusion obviates the poem's emphasis on fideist over rationalist theodicy and downplays the inestimable role that the doctrine of justification by faith has had in Reformation thought, in *De Doctrina Christiana*'s high soteriology, and in *Paradise Lost*, the great epic of Protestant Christianity. For, as Sharon Achinstein acknowledges, Milton 'emerges as a Christian fideist who is attempting to brace against the modernity spoken by scepticism and rationalism'.[4] To consider the highly nuanced vocabulary of the epic argument's two clauses requires interpretive tact and an openness to the theological discourse proper to seventeenth-century Protestantism. To achieve this end, the reader must be willing to take Milton's faith seriously.

JUSTIFYING THE WAYS OF GOD TO MEN

I begin with a consideration of the concept of justification, a key term within Reformed dogmatics. The early commentator Thomas Newton, Bishop of Bristol, in discussing Milton's great argument, granted that '*the ways of God to Men* are justified in the many argumentative discourses throughout the poem, and

---

[2] Richard Strier, 'Milton's Fetters, or Why Eden is Better Than Heaven', *Milton Studies*, 38 (2000), 169–70.

[3] Ibid. 170.

[4] Sharon Achinstein, 'Toleration in Milton's Epics: A Chimera?', in *Milton and Toleration*, 225.

particularly in the conferences between God the Father and the Son'.[5] The poetry of the orthodox Protestant George Herbert may help to dispel the mistaken idea that the justification of God's ways to humanity is incompatible with, or bizarrely inverts, mainline Protestant theology and theodicy. In 'Justice (1)' Herbert's speaker, confounded by the mystery of God's willingness to participate in human suffering, marvels, 'I cannot skill of these thy wayes' (1). After recalling his own missteps and backslidings, Herbert's speaker acknowledges that his redeemer has justified God's ways to him, a wretched sinner, and confesses, in a parallel clause, 'I cannot skill of these my wayes' (12).[6] The dilemma lying at the heart of Herbert's poem in the discrepancy between God's ways and the ways of sinful humanity contains its own solution. The remedy becomes apparent when one views the lyric's two halves as twin cotyledons of a single seed. When the speaker accepts that in the Incarnation and redemption God assumes and cancels out the sinful human burden of 'these my wayes', only then is the speaker empowered to 'skill' of these God's ways in Christ. For Milton, as for Herbert, the human initiative to scan and justify God's ways through Jesus's life, death, and resurrection is the criterion of a resourceful, Miltonic Christian with an explicit faith.

The classic Pauline text for the doctrine of *iustificatio impii*, the justification of sinners by faith in the atonement, is Romans 3. The doctrine expresses the apposite idea of God the Father being justified in the Son's propitiation:

> For there is no distinction, for all have sinned and come short of the glory of God, being justified by His grace as a gift, through the redemption that is in Christ Jesus, whom God put forward as a propitiation by his blood, effective through faith. [God did this] to display His righteousness because, in God's forbearance, He had passed over sins committed previously, and to display at the present time that He himself is just and that He justifies the one who has faith in Jesus.   (Rom. 3.22–26)

During the Heavenly Council of *Paradise Lost* the Son explicitly states that the Father must find grace for humankind and justify Himself in the eyes of humanity through the Son's redemption, else 'So should thy goodness and thy greatness both / Be questiond and blaspheamed without defence' (3.165–66). In *De Doctrina Christiana*'s exposition of the Son's Incarnation and mediation the phrasing of Milton's 'great Argument' is evoked – God's justification of His ways to humanity through His reconciling Redeemer:

> For the great mystery of godliness is not Christ, but God the Father in Christ, as is plain, Colossians 2:2: 'for the knowledge of the mystery of God and the Father and Christ.' 2 Corinthians 5:18–19: 'all these things are from God, who reconciled us to Himself through Jesus Christ: namely because God was in Christ, reconciling the world to Himself, not by imputing their offences to them.' Why, therefore, through all the offices of reconciliation enumerated in this passage of Timothy, should God the Father not have been in the Son? 'God was made conspicuous in the flesh,' namely in the Son, His own image, otherwise He is invisible. Christ did not come to

---

[5] Thomas Newton, ed., *Paradise Lost*, vol. 1 (London, 1749), 10.
[6] Herbert, 95–96.

make himself, but his Father, conspicuous, John 14:8–9. 'He was justified in the spirit,' for who was justified, if not the Father [*quis enim iustificetur potius quam pater*]? . . . namely He who was in the Son, once reconciliation had been made, returned with His Son into glory, or received Himself into greatest glory, which He had brought back in the Son.   (*CE* 14.264, 266)

The archangel Michael repeats this salvific principle that humanity 'may finde / Justification towards God' (12.295–96) through Jesus's 'bloud more precious' (12.293). The treatise's assertion that the Father *is justified* in the Son's saving work, both by Christ's reconciliation between God and humanity upon Earth, and by his resurrection, glorification, and restoration to his Father's right hand, is equivalent to the heroic action recorded in *Paradise Lost*'s exordium. From Adam's Fall, 'one greater Man' will 'Restore us, and regain the blissful Seat' (1.4–5). Accordingly, the second Adam will justify God's ways to men.

God's redemption of humanity and, in the treatise's radical idiom, *God the Father's redemption and justification of Himself* through the God-man's sacrifice distinguish the ways of Milton's God from the 'undecent things of the gods' (*CPW* 1.891). Milton argues in his *Apology for Smectymnuus* (1642) that licentious Homeric epic epitomizes these 'undecent things': unflattering depictions of fallible deities that ruin the sacred truths in classical epic, fable, and romance. Examples from classical epic are plentiful: Hera, whose incestuous marriage to her sibling Zeus is afflicted with so stale and flaccid a sex life that she must not only bribe Sleep into using his soporific powers, but must also trick Aphrodite into procuring an aphrodisiac, an enchanted girdle, to seduce and disarm Zeus and distract the Thunderer from the Trojan War (*Il.* 14.153–360); or, again, the bard Demodocus's scandalous song about the adulterous fumblings of Aphrodite and Ares who, thanks to the crippled cuckold-deity Hephaestus's artifice, are discovered *in flagrante delicto* and openly disgraced before a jeering, ogling Pantheon (*Od.* 8.266–369). The compromised anthropomorphic gods of antiquity stray far from the earnest theodical intentions of *Paradise Lost*. In *Paradise Regain'd* Jesus does not gild the lily, but excoriates the gross indecorousness of ancient epic. The epic grand style is lubriciously 'thick laid / As varnish on a Harlots cheek' (*PR* 4.343–44) to conceal the indignities lurking beneath. Jesus lambastes ancient poets who 'loudest sing / The vices of thir Deities, and thir own / In Fable, Hymn, or Song, so personating / Thir Gods ridiculous, and themselves past shame' (*PR* 4.339–44).

For Milton, Christian salvation soars above these superlunary bedroom farces. Michael measures the superiority of the new covenant's tender mercies of justification and saving grace against the rigidity of the old covenant's Law:

> And therefore was Law giv'n them [the Hebrews] to evince
> Thir natural pravitie, by stirring up
> Sin against Law to fight; that when they see
> Law can discover sin, but not remove,
> Save by those shadowie expiations weak,
> The bloud of Bulls and Goats, they may conclude
> Some bloud more precious must be paid for Man,

> Just for unjust, that in such righteousness
> To them by Faith imputed, they may finde
> Justification towards God, and peace
> Of Conscience, which the Law by Ceremonies
> Cannot appease, nor Man the moral part
> Perform, and not performing cannot live.
>
> (12.287–99)[7]

As Desmond Hamlet has demonstrated, the archangel's brief but dense explication of the cross is readily construable as a transparent rendering of the Lutheran doctrine of justification.[8] *De Doctrina Christiana* interprets the Mosaic Law as a device for discovering, but not remedying, the crisis of human sin. Michael styles sin 'natural pravitie' and the treatise likewise uses the Latin noun 'PRAVITAS'. Yahweh delivers the Law so that the Israelites, 'RECOGNIZING THEREFROM THE DEPRAVITY OF THE HUMAN RACE, AND ACCORDINGLY THEIR OWN, WOULD TAKE REFUGE TOGETHER IN THE RIGHTEOUSNESS OF THE PROMISED CHRIST' (*CE* 16.102). The teaching that one 'more precious' sacrifice, Christ crucified, can accomplish what the blood of bulls and goats tenuously and distantly foreshadows draws upon Hebrews 9:11–15 and 1 Peter 1:18–19 that 'under the Law, though obscurely, both the existence of a redeemer and the necessity of redemption are perceptible' (*CE* 16.98).[9] Michael's idea of the just dying for the unjust, which draws from 1 Peter 3:18, where 'Christ one time suffered for sins, a righteous man for the sake of the unrighteous [δίκαιος ὑπὲρ ἀδίκων]', reiterates God's providential plan for a redeemer, one 'just th' unjust to save' (3.215), but also affirms the victim's exceptionality and immaculacy. Milton's Son is above heroic because he transcends the darkened faculties of a peccable humankind that 'Attonement for himself or offering meet, / Indebted and undon, hath none to bring' (3.234–35). Unsupported by Jesus's saving work, humanity would be incapable of appeasing God (3.210–12) and expunging its corruptions (3.290) or 'the moral part / Perform', because 'To expiate his Treason hath naught left' (3.207). Humanity's 'natural pravitie' attests the extent to which the Son is the hero of a poem in which, 'without redemption all mankind / Must have bin lost' (3.222–23). The 'peace / Of Conscience' gained by the believer's assurance of 'Justification towards God' bears out the Son's function as 'the onely peace' (3.274). According to *De Doctrina Christiana*, such peace is the badge of a justified sinner who has attained 'the peace of God, which

---

[7] The greatest concentration of biblical allusions in Milton's epic tends to occur in passages concerning the redemption (12.285–306; 10.182–92), as though Milton were enunciating the mystery of the Incarnation and redemption with scriptural testimony. In the narrator's gloss on the *protevangelium* the following texts are discernible: *seriatim*, Gal. 3:19; Rom. 3:20, 7:7–8; Heb. 9:13–14, 10:4–5; Rom. 4:22–24, 5:1, 7:18–19, 10:1; Gal. 3:11–12, 23, 4:7; and Rom. 8:15.

[8] Desmond M. Hamlet, *One Greater Man: Justice and Damnation in 'Paradise Lost'* (Lewisburg, 1976), 163–67.

[9] *De Doctrina Christiana* teaches that there was 'a manifestation of the covenant of grace' under Moses, 'as if it were a shadow [*veluti umbra*]', both in the Hebrews' liberation or redemption from Egypt and in the image of the brazen serpent, but also in the Law's 'sacrifices and priests', which were 'symbols of expiation and redemption' (*CE* 16.102).

passeth all understanding' (*AV* Phil. 4:7), where, 'From a sense of justification springs, finally, peace [*pax*] and true tranquillity of mind [*vera tranquillitas animi*]' (*CE* 16.48).

In the previous chapter I observed that in *De Doctrina Christiana* human works finally fail to satisfy and faith is grounded upon the unique Son's inimitable satisfaction. On two occasions the treatise eschews the imputation of merit to humanity and, instead, ascribes accredited merit to Christ's justification of humanity and his satisfaction of divine justice upon the cross. In its bipartite plan of redemption, comprehending, first, Christ's satisfaction and, second, the believer's conformation to Christ's image, the treatise passes over 'a doctrine of our merits', since our conformation to Christ's example 'in no way whatever adds to Christ's most complete satisfaction [*nihilo plus accedit ad satisfactionem Christi plenissimam*]' (*CE* 15.336). Merits are instead vicariously imputed to undeserving humans through Christ's intrinsic worthiness.

Milton's Sonnet Fourteen (1646) meditates upon the same tension between the efficacy of faith and good works. The sonnet is an epitaph to the memory of Catharine Thomason, who was Milton's 'Christian friend' and the spouse of George Thomason, collector of the extensive 'Thomason Civil War Tracts'. The sonnet's second quatrain imagines the deceased Catharine's virtues attending her saintly soul as she ascends to her appointed mansion in Heaven:

> Thy Works and Alms and all thy good Endeavour
> Staid not behind, nor in the grave were trod;
> But as Faith pointed with her golden rod,
> Follow'd thee up to joy and bliss for ever.
>
> (5–8)

Milton, for the purposes of his poetic conceit, dispenses with any suggestion of mortalism, the tenet that the body and soul of the departed slumber until their rebirth on Resurrection Day. He instead envisions the revival of justified souls at the resurrection of the saints. The allegorical figure of Faith is determinative for Catharine Thomason's ascent and, like the treatise, Faith's offshoots of 'Works and Alms', though external signs of faith, are ornamental to the intrinsic value of faith. E. A. J. Honigmann comments that 'the staff of office of Athene in Homer, *Od.* xvi.172, is transferred to Faith', but an equally convincing source for the sonnet's 'golden rod' is Hermes's rod in his divine office as *psychopomp* or conductor of souls to the underworld.[10] Hermes traditionally held the caduceus, a winged golden wand entwined with two serpents, with which he escorted departed souls into Hades. Milton adverts to this emblem in his pastoral elegy *Epitaphium Damonis* (1639), where he prophesies that Damon, Milton's pseudonym for Charles Diodati, will be included among the saints when Hermes, 'he who divides souls with his golden wand [*virga . . . aurea*], would lead you in a procession worthy of you, and would ward far off the entire idle herd of silent dead' (23–25). Milton probably borrowed this conceit of a figure shepherding souls with his golden rod from the final book of Homer's *Odyssey*, which opens with Hermes guiding the spirits of the

---

[10] E. A. J. Honigmann, *Milton's Sonnets* (London, 1966), 136.

slain suitors: 'And Cyllenian Hermes summoned forth the suitors' souls. And he held in his hands a beautiful golden rod, with which he touches the eyes of whosoever he wills with magic; but others, who are asleep, he awakens. With this rod he led and goaded them, and they, squealing, followed him' (*Od.* 24.1–10). Where Hermes ushers his retinue into the murky underworld, the Christ-like figure of Faith in Milton's sonnet shepherds his saints 'up' (8, 11) in a glorious ascent. Homer's souls squeal like pigs being dragged off to the abattoir, whereas Milton's serene saints waft gracefully heavenward. The sonnet's transposing of Hermes's pastoral role to the allegorical figure of Faith bespeaks the Protestant ethic of 'faith alone' and stresses its primary importance for a Puritan over the outward show of 'Works and Alms'. Faith becomes Catharine Thomason's inward passport, guaranteeing her saintly soul safe passage. The sonnet's stress on saving faith is borne out in *De Doctrina Christiana*, which devotes an entire chapter to the subject. Saving faith is contingent upon our efforts to 'BELIEVE ALL THOSE THINGS WHICH GOD PROMISED US IN CHRIST; ESPECIALLY THE GRACE OF ETERNAL LIFE' (*CE* 15.392). In the same way Milton's major epic spells out the fideistic condition of salvation through justification by faith in Christ's atonement. Michael similarly makes faith, and especially the faith of those 'who rightly trust / In this [the Son's] satisfaction' (12.418–19), the foundation for eternal felicity. Christ's death is 'Proclaiming Life to all who shall believe / In his Redemption' (12.407–08). The condition for salvation, as stated in the poem – faith in Jesus's redemption, satisfaction of divine wrath, and cancellation of the debt of human sin – is a wholly orthodox Protestant formulation of those things requisite to salvation.

De Doctrina Christiana's exposition of human salvation privileges the doctrine of justification. Justification is related to 'external growth [*externa auctio*]' and abides by a Lutheran or, properly speaking, a Pauline view of salvation where, in accordance with a sinner's lack of merit, righteousness is found, not *intra nos*, but *extra nos*, in the crucified and risen Christ. Righteousness is imputed to humanity from the fruits of Christ's redemption:

IUSTIFICATIO EST SENTENTIA DEI GRATUITA QUA REGENERATI, CHRISTOQUE INSITI PROPTER EIUS PLENISSIMAM SATISFACTIONEM PECCATIS ET MORTE ABSOLVUNTUR, ET IUSTI CORAM DEO NON EX OPERIBUS LEGIS SED PER FIDEM REPUTANTUR.

(JUSTIFICATION IS THE GRATUITOUS SENTENCE OF GOD WHERE THOSE WHO ARE REGENERATED AND ENGRAFTED IN CHRIST ARE ABSOLVED FROM SINS AND FROM DEATH BECAUSE OF HIS MOST COMPLETE SATISFACTION AND ARE REPUTED RIGHTEOUS IN THE SIGHT OF GOD, NOT FROM WORKS OF THE LAW, BUT THROUGH FAITH.) (*CE* 16.24)

Milton's is a classic, 'Christ-centred' Lutheran and Calvinist formulation, stated in forensic terms, of Pauline 'justification by faith', a dogma firmly entrenched in the fiduciary principle that all 'are justified freely by His grace through the redemption that came through Jesus Christ' (Rom. 3:24) and that justification is 'reckoned to those who believe in Him who raised Jesus Christ from the dead' (Rom. 4:25). Campbell, Corns, Hale, and Tweedie adroitly summarize the treatise's position on this doctrine: 'In *De Doctrina*, Milton appears to take the standard line that justification is by faith alone . . . but he adds that a saving faith cannot be devoid of works.'[11] The chapter 'ON ENGRAFTING IN CHRIST AND ITS EFFECTS' describes the imputation of righteousness in Christ to all believers: 'By this method those who act strenuously in that struggle and continuously and assiduously strive to attain perfection in Christ, though they are really imperfect, yet by imputation and divine mercy they are often called *perfected* and *blameless* and *not sinning* in the scriptures; because sin, though it clings to them, does not reign over them' (*CE* 16.22). Yet once more:

> Therefore, our justification is plainly gratuitous for us; but it is not gratuitous for Christ. For, after the debt was thoroughly discharged, and he imputed to himself our sins, he voluntarily washed them away and expiated them. Paying nothing, we accept his righteousness, which is imputed to us only by believing in his gift. Subsequently, the Father, appeased, pronounces all believers 'Just,' and there could not be any other clearer or more equitable method of satisfaction.   (*CE* 16.26, 28)

Michael repeats this doctrine, prophesying that 'such righteousness [is] / To them by Faith imputed' (12.294–95). The same concept of washing away Adam's primordial sin through justification by faith in Christ's satisfaction (Rom. 5:18–6:13) prevails in the invocation to *Paradise Regain'd* where Eden, 'By one mans disobedience lost', is regained by Jesus's victorious obedience, 'By one mans firm obedience fully tri'd . . . And *Eden* rais'd in the wast Wilderness' (*PR* 1.2, 4, 7).

Augustine understood that justification entailed humanity being *intrinsically* rendered righteous. The Protestant tradition construed a distinctive process whereby humanity was *extrinsically* reckoned, rendered, and imputed righteous, in the words of *De Doctrina Christiana*, CORAM DEO or 'IN GOD'S SIGHT,' by virtue of Christ's intrinsic worth as a sacrifice glad to be offered. Faith is requisite to God's gift of grace, but that grace is imparted on the basis of Christ's saving work, because humanity is enthralled to sin and incapable of self-liberation. Humanity's reception into grace is effected in spite of its inherent sinfulness and on the condition of possessing saving faith so that the whole human being is, in the Lutheran axiom, *simul iustus et peccator*, 'simultaneously righteous and a sinner'. Humanity is righteous in God's eyes, but sinful without the benefit of Christ's righteousness. Luther regards justified humanity as simultaneously inwardly depraved and speciously purified by Christ's alien righteousness. The treatise endorses this position: 'Just as our sins are imputed to Christ, so the righteousness or merits of Christ are imputed to us through faith' (*CE* 16.26). Michael's vision of the Consummation and of the saints being invited into God's presence appropriately describes the 'New Heav'ns, new Earth', predicated upon the Son's justification of humanity and therefore 'Founded in Righteousness and Peace and Love' (12.549–50). It is noteworthy that the New Testament term δικαιοσύνη can be translated 'righteousness' as well as 'justification'.

---

[11] Campbell, Corns, Hale, and Tweedie, *Manuscript*, 111.

Common biblical symbols that were drawn from scripture or early modern typology to convey this process of justification include metaphors of covering. Jesus imagines himself in relation to Israel as a mother hen sheltering her chicks under her wings (Matt. 23:37; Luke 13:34) and Luther's *gnadenstuhle* or Tyndale's 'Mercy-seat' covers the Ark of the Covenant. In each case divine mercy supersedes divine wrath (Exod. 25; Heb. 9). The treatise figures justified sinners as being protected by a garment of grace: 'hence we are said to be *clothed* [*induti*]' (*CE* 16.28). Once fallen, Milton's Adam and Eve cover their genitals with fig leaves 'broad as *Amazonian* Targe' (9.1111) that fail to cloak their sin, providing 'vain covering if to hide / Thir guilt and dreaded Shame' (9.1113–14). Adam yearns to hide his shame from God's sight 'in some glade / Obscur'd, where highest Woods impenetrable / To Starr or Sun-light, spread thir umbrage broad' (9.1085–87). He beseeches, 'Cover me ye Pines, / Ye Cedars, with innumerable boughs / Hide me' (9.1088–90). In Book Ten Adam, 'hid in gloomiest shade' (10.716), attempts to conceal his fallen self from himself, Eve, and God deep within a wild wood. Through a deft stroke of dramatic irony Milton's reader knows what the fallen pair does not. Even as the Son judges the guilty couple, he covers Adam and Eve's outer and inner culpability from God's sight:

> then pittying how they stood
> Before him naked to the aire, that now
> Must suffer change, [the Son] disdaind not to begin
> Thenceforth the forme of servant to assume,
> As when he washd his servants feet, so now
> As Father of his Familie he clad
> Thir nakedness with Skins of Beasts, or slain,
> Or as the Snake with youthful Coate repaid;
> And thought not much to cloathe his Enemies:
> Nor hee thir outward onely with the Skins
> Of Beasts, but inward nakedness, much more
> Opprobrious, with his Robe of righteousness,
> Arraying coverd from his Fathers sight.
>
> (10.211–23)

In Genesis 3 God walks in the garden, searches for Adam and Eve, and judges them. Milton's innovation is not only to identify the Son with this divine figure, but also to trump God's harsh sentence, Eve's pains in childbearing, and the sweat of the toiling Adam's brow, with the Son's gracious words and deeds. Before the Son's epiphany Adam and Eve are walled into a maze of sin and error. They adopt a language of justification that is faulty and parodic. Eve scoffs at Adam, 'Imput'st thou that to my default' (9.1145) and, because neither possesses the intrinsic merit to make themselves righteous or to impute righteousness to themselves or each other, they can only exchange 'mutual accusation . . . but neither self-condemning' (9.1187). The arrival of Milton's Son reverses the situation by providing mercy amid justice and hope amid despair.

Michael Lieb and Dennis Danielson have analysed how the Son's actions of divestiture and investiture enact the kenotic Christology of Philippians 2:7.[12] The narrator's comment that the Son 'disdaind not to begin / Thenceforth the forme of servant to assume' apprises the reader that the work of salvation has already begun. The atonement is historically manifested at the cross where Jesus 'emptied himself, taking the form of a servant, being in the likeness of humans; and, according to this scheme, being found as a human, he humbled himself, becoming obedient until death, and that the death of the cross' (Phil. 2:7–8). As Michael Lieb notes, 'the Son's clothing of man prefigures what will be the effect of his future self-humiliation. He will voluntarily take upon himself the corruption of man so that man may be purified, and given the possibility of regeneration.'[13] Milton extensively amplifies the half-verse at Genesis 3:21b where 'the Lord God made coats of skins, and clothed them' (*AV*). By identifying the God of Genesis 3 with the Son, Milton juxtaposes the Son, the second Adam, with the first, fallen Adam and, in the Son's generosity towards Adam and Eve, he anticipates Christ's future, vicarious sacrifice. The Son shields Adam and Eve's 'outward' nakedness from the harsh weather with 'the Skins / Of Beasts'; he also covers their 'inward nakedness' with a 'Robe of righteousness' and imputes to them his princely righteousness. Milton's poetic recension makes one further allusion to a future Christic service. The narrator posits equivalence between the Son's clothing of Adam and Eve and Jesus's washing of his disciples' feet on Maundy night, when he officiated as servant-king on the eve of his Passion (John 13). Milton's fusion of these two biblical events concentrates upon two symbolic actions, the covering of Adam and Eve's corrupted souls and the cleansing of the apostles' soiled feet. The Son's two rituals prefigure Christ's heroism in his vicarious atonement before a lapsed, ignorant, and unsuspecting world. Milton's verbatim inclusion of the Lutheran formula *coram Deo*, 'from his Fathers sight' (10.223), and the detail of the Son's 'Robe of righteousness' support the association of the Son's action with justification, the fallen couple standing before God as simultaneously righteous and sinful. Poignantly, the Son 'thought not much to cloathe his Enemies', a detail that anticipates the redemption. During his ministry Jesus teaches humans to love their enemies (Matt. 5:43–44) and realizes this teaching when, from the cross, he petitions his Father to pardon his persecutors and 'forgive them, for they do not know what they do' (Luke 23:34).

So far I have attempted to delineate the epic's commitment to justification by faith, that doctrine which is arguably the cornerstone of orthodox Protestant belief. With great sophistication Milton melds this tenet within his poetics and accommodates aspects of this doctrine to key dramatic moments. The claim of the epic's great argument to justify the ways of God to men should not be divorced from an

---

[12] Michael Lieb, *The Sinews of Ulysses: Form and Convention in Milton's Works* (Pittsburgh, 1989), 38–52 (ch. 4); Dennis Danielson, 'Milton, Bunyan, and the Clothing of Truth and Righteousness', in *Heirs of Fame: Milton and Writers of the English Renaissance*, ed. Margo Swiss and David A. Kent (Lewisburg, 1995), 247–69.

[13] Lieb, *Sinews*, 51.

appreciation of the far from negligible status of justification by faith in the Son's atonement within the poem's action.

ASSERTING ETERNAL PROVIDENCE

The proem to *Paradise Lost* projects the full scope of God's providence throughout human history. In any epic proem the poet is at his most self-conscious, declaring his allegiance to and divergence from his predecessors, and recuperating and revitalizing established epic conventions. The invocation inevitably exerts significant interpretive pressure upon its readers. Readers must be prepared to compare and contrast new epic poems with their antecedent models and be attentive to innovations within the genre when succeeding epic poets recast the form. The exordium of classical epic has a regular taxonomy and displays a three-part structure. First, there is a declaration of subject matter, which is customarily followed by, second, the epic-narrator's formal invocation to the Muse or, at least, a declared intention to sing. Attendant upon the invocation is the exordium's third segment, a relative clause introduced by a relative pronoun (ἥ, ὅς, or *qui*) expounding the epic subject matter. In the literary–critical digression to his *Second Defence* (1654) Milton remarks upon this structural principle of ancient epic:

> In the same manner as that poet who is called an Epic poet, if he is even the slightest bit learned and doesn't swerve from the rules, regarding the Hero whom he declares to sing about in verse, he undertakes to sing about, not the hero's entire life, but normally a single action in his life [*unam fere vitae actionem*] and passes over the rest – consider Achilles at Troy, or Ulysses's return, or Aeneas's arrival in Italy, all of which are embellished in verse. (*CE* 8.252)

Thus the *Iliad* sings 'of the accursed wrath of Achilles, son of Peleus, / Which brought countless ills upon the Achaeans' (*Il.* 1.1–2); the *Odyssey* 'of that many-sided man who / Roamed far and wide' (*Od.* 1.1–2); and the *Aeneid* of the refugee Aeneas, 'Of arms and the man I sing, of he who first left the shores of Troy' (*Aen.* 1.1).[14] Given these entrenched generic expectations, Milton's professed subject, the single historic action in the life of his epic hero, is instead divided into the catastrophic fall and compensatory rise of two heroes. The first Adam initiates humanity's decline and fall, while the second Adam accomplishes its restoration:

> Of Mans First Disobedience, and the Fruit
> Of that Forbidd'n Tree, whose mortal tast
> Brought Death into the World, and all our woe,
> With loss of *Eden*, till one greater Man

[14] References to Homer's and Virgil's poetry derive from Homer, *Opera*, ed. David B. Monro and Thomas W. Allen, 5 vols (Oxford, 1966–69); Virgil, *Eclogues; Georgics; Aeneid I–VI*, trans. H. Rushton Fairclough, ed. G. P. Goold (London, 1999); and *Aeneid VII–XII*, trans. H. Rushton Fairclough, ed. G. P. Goold (London, 2000).

> Restore us, and regain the blissful Seat,
> Sing Heav'nly Muse
>
> (1.1–6)

Paradise Lost concerns itself with Adam's tumble from an immaculate Edenic state and his expulsion into a dark world and wide. What else, other than humanity's falling off from a paradisiacal state, should one expect from a poem named *Paradise Lost*? But Milton's declared subject matter is more extensive and far more ambitious than a history of the Fall, which is only the first element in the exordium's bipartite summary of epic content. The proposed subject is inclusive of the restoration of humanity by 'one greater Man' in his life's ministry, his redeeming work on the cross, and his regaining of his heavenly seat at God's right hand. The poem's opening lines, then, encompass a chronicle of universal history extending from the first Adam's Fall to the second Adam's redemption, that is, his suffering, death, resurrection, and ascension, and, implicitly, his glorified session, interceding for humanity until the *eschaton*. Across the initial five lines Milton has already imparted the cosmic panorama of his epic from Genesis to Revelation or, as John Lightfoot roundly spanned Christian history, 'from *in the beginning*, to *come Lord Jesus*'.[15] Milton professes that the parameters of his epic song are the reaches of Holy Scripture: the loss of the human Fall cross-thwarted and reclaimed by the Son.

The exordium resumes by re-invoking and re-engaging with this providential pattern. A series of allusions charts the continuum of biblical history from the primeval history of Genesis to the gospels:

> Sing Heav'nly Muse, that on the secret top
> Of *Oreb*, or of *Sinai*, didst inspire
> That Shepherd, who first taught the chosen Seed,
> In the Beginning how the Heav'ns and Earth
> Rose out of *Chaos*: Or if *Sion* Hill
> Delight thee more, and *Siloa's* Brook that flowd
> Fast by the Oracle of God; I thence
> Invoke thy aid to my adventrous Song
>
> (1.6–13)

After the narrator has invoked the heavenly Muse, he delineates the Muse's inspiring activity within scripture in a tricolon crescendo of periphrases traversing biblical history. In the first segment the 'Shepherd' is Moses. Mount Horeb is the geographical site where Yahweh, through the Angel of the Lord in the Burning Bush, surprises the fugitive Moses while he tends his father-in-law Jethro's flocks (Exod. 3 and 4). During this epiphany Yahweh commissions Moses to deliver His people, the 'chosen Seed', out of Egypt and lead them into the Promised Land. Mount Sinai, the next sacred site, constitutes the locus for Yahweh's delivery of the Law to the Hebrews from the cloud-enshrouded mountain's 'secret top', which is, etymologically speaking, the holy mount's 'secluded' or 'sacred' summit (Exod. 19–32). '*Sion* Hill' or Zion is the eminence upon which the fortress or citadel

---

[15] John Lightfoot, *Erubhin* (London, 1629), 115.

named the City of David stood. The citadel of Zion later became a metonym for the Temple of Jerusalem. '*Sion* Hill' thus refers to the age of King David and Israel's succeeding kings. In the context of the Muse's inspirational activity Zion is a metonym for the genre of the biblical Psalms or, as Jesus calls them in *Paradise Regain'd*, '*Sions* songs, to all true tasts excelling' (*PR* 4.347). Although the nomination of the third element of the crescendo has been vigorously contested among Miltonists, the evidence for '*Siloa's* Brook' indicates 'the water of Siloam [τὴν κολυμβήθραν τοῦ Σιλωάμ]' (John 9:7).[16] In his commentary on John's gospel John Calvin identifies Siloam with 'a fountain, which was near the Temple', just as Milton locates his Siloa 'Fast by the Oracle of God', the sanctuary housed within the resplendent Herodian Temple (*OED*).[17] Siloa's brook marks the body of water within which, in the Johannine gospel, Christ bids the blind man wash the mud from his eyes so that he might miraculously see his Messiah, the Light of the World. Calvin draws upon the evangelist's etymology for Siloa as 'one sent', a prophetic name that 'daily reminded the Jews of the Christ who was to come'.[18] In the exordium Siloa's brook, which springs close by Mount Zion, represents the imparting of Messianic illumination, much as Aganippe on Mount Helicon inspired the poets of classical antiquity.

In literal–historical terms the invocation's tripartite, periphrastic crescendo moves chronologically and typologically through the three most prominent figures of Jewish–Christian history: first, Moses, Israel's deliverer, whose name, some believed, was rooted etymologically in the title of Messiah; next, King David, a Messiah or 'Anointed' King, the true founder of Israel's monarchic dynasty and propagator of the Messianic line stemming from his father Jesse (Isa. 11:1); and, finally, Jesus the Messiah, the supreme Christian archetype, who was prophesied to be the deliverer of nations and the fulfilment of Old Testament types. This invocatory crescendo simultaneously generates a scriptural–generic catena proceeding through the main biblical sites for the reception of divine revelation. The epiphanic origins of the three great collections of biblical texts are invoked: the Mosaic Torah, the Davidic Psalms, and the gospels. The Hebrew word *Torah* only

---

[16] Gerald Snare, 'Milton's "Siloa's Brook" Again', *Milton Quarterly*, 4 (1970), 55–57. The identity of Siloa's brook has been extensively debated: see Paul Lauter, 'Milton's "Siloa's Brook"', *Notes and Queries*, 5 (1958), 204–05; Anthony Low, 'Siloa's Brook: *Paradise Lost*, I, 11', *Milton Quarterly*, 6 (1972), 3–5; Leo Miller, ' "Siloa's Brook" in *Paradise Lost*: Another View', *Milton Quarterly*, 6 (1972), 5–7. Miller offers other possible biblical references to Siloa's brook in 'the water of the Shiloach' of Isaiah 8:6 (*AV* 'Shiloah') and 'the Shelach' of Nehemiah 3:15 (*AV* 'Siloah') (6). Miller argues that Nehemiah and John's gospel refer to the same geographical pool or fountain. As the evangelist explains, the verbal root of the Hebrew word *Siloa(m)* means 'having been sent [Ἀπεσταλμένος]'. In Hebrew *Shiloah* translates as 'a sending of water' and Nehemiah's word *Shelah* is a 'sending'. Both geographical names probably derive from the 'sending forth' of waters from the earth into a pool, brook, or fountain. The evangelist may be playing here upon the fancy that the title of Messiah and *missus*, the Latin participle for 'sent', were linked.

[17] John Calvin, *Calvin's Commentaries: The Gospel according to St. John*, trans. T. H. L. Parker, ed. David W. Torrance and Thomas F. Torrance (Edinburgh, 1959), 242.

[18] Ibid. 242. Other possible biblical sources for Siloa do not match: the reparations made to the wall of Siloah's pool by the Remnant (Neh. 3:15); the gentle waters of Shiloah that, in Isaian prophecy, contrast with the raging river of the Assyrian King (Isa. 8:6); and Siloam Tower's catastrophic fall (Luke 13:4).

secondarily means 'Law': its primary meaning is 'Teaching' or 'Instruction'. The exordium plays upon this etymology when it narrates that Moses 'taught' Torah to the 'chosen Seed', Israel's wilderness generation. Milton's exordium confirms this association by remembering the opening words of Torah. The Yahwistic account of Creation with which the Book of Genesis begins is introduced by the Hebrew phrase *Bereshit*, just as the epic exordium reads 'In the Beginning' (1.9). The ancient Jewish tradition attributed the authorship of Torah to Moses and named the separate books of Torah after the initial Hebrew words to each book, so that the Book of Genesis, for example, is designated 'In the Beginning'.[19] Over a mere eight lines the exordium recapitulates two major series of Messianic characters and biblical genres, the first sequence consisting of Moses–David–Jesus and the second of Torah–the Psalms–the gospels. These two providential series reach fruition in the new covenant in Christ, but *Paradise Lost* itself serves as a kind of second scripture, the poetic efflorescence of these mutual catenae of allusions. The gospel passage narrating the healing of the blind man beside Siloam's waters broadens out into Milton's stated epic subject. Milton's resumptive clause, 'I thence / Invoke thy aid to my adventrous Song', enlists the Muse's aid 'thence', a word that signifies either temporally 'from that point in time' or locally 'from that place'. Thus the adverb could indicate a site that is geographical, historical, or even textual. The word 'thence' gathers up all of the prior instances and provenances of biblical inspiration that occurred before *Paradise Lost* makes its own claim to divinely sanctioned revelation. The origin of divine revelation is affiliated with the source of Mosaic and Psalmic inspiration, which is located spatially upon Mount Sinai and Mount Zion and textually in Torah and the Davidic Psalms. The preeminent source of inspiration, though, is ultimately linked with Jesus's imparting of clarified sight to the blind man beside Siloam's pool. The blind man's predicament as a creature burdened by affliction who is nonetheless granted the sight of his Messiah reflects the condition of the blind poet and the reader, whose inspired perceptions will, in the process of composing and experiencing the poem, be irradiated by a vision of God's Son and his redemptive significance.

It is well established that the Johannine gospel and the Johannine epistles are remarkable for their literal and figurative use of images of light and darkness. John Painter has found that the evangelist's treatment of Jesus's healing of the blind man inculcates a message of '*universal significance*' 'as a parable or narrative symbol on the theme of "spiritual perception"' and plays upon the double sense of Christ's imparting of physical sight and the inner vision that faith brings.[20] The gospel identifies the blind man by the generic noun ἄνθρωπος or 'humankind' and not by the specific τις ἄνθρωπος or 'a certain individual'. The omission of a definite or indefinite article and the choice of the Greek word ἄνθρωπος to denote the species

---

[19] The Hebrew title for Exodus is *Shemoth*, 'And these are the names'; for Leviticus, *Vayikra* or 'And he called'; and, for Numbers, *Bamibdar* or 'In the wilderness'.

[20] John Painter, *The Quest for the Messiah: The History, Literature, and Theology of the Johannine Community* (Edinburgh, 1991), 274; see 274–85. I am indebted to Painter's interpretation of this pericope for my interpretation of Milton's first epic invocation.

of 'humankind' rather than the individuated ἀνήρ or 'human' establish the blind man as an everyman figure. The blind man's broadening vision converges with that of the reader of the miracle story. The actual miracle takes up a scant three verses, while the ensuing narrative explores the human response to the miracle in the interrogations of the healed man conducted by his neighbours, the Pharisees, and sceptics. These interrogations strive to determine what actually happened at Siloa's brook. Jesus's imparting of sight to the blind man catalyses the narrative proper and provides the basis for the narrative's more momentous consideration of the sighted man's growth in spiritual perception. The Johannine metaphor of vision encapsulates the eye of faith as much as bodily sight. At first the sighted man calls Jesus merely 'The man named Jesus' (9:11); next, officially, a 'Prophet' (9:17); next, 'Christ' or 'Messiah' (9:22); then, honorifically, one from God like Moses (9:28–33); and finally, mysteriously, 'the Son of Man' and 'Lord', a fit object of worship (9:35–38). Milton's allusion to John 9 in the epic exordium aligns Jesus's investing of the blind man with physical sight and the blind man's crystallizing perception of his Messiah with Milton's epic narrator and reader, who must treat the poem's underlying meaning as a Messianic revelation of salvation by 'one greater Man' (1.4). Across the exordium all of Christian providence is here. The narrator asserts divine dispensation from Adam's disobedience in Eden to Jesus's obedience on the cross. He next reasserts God's dispensation in an intertextual series that spans Moses to King David to Jesus; Genesis to the Psalms to the gospel of John; and the hexaemeron to a vision of the incarnate Word. In each case the culmination of the series is the 'one greater Man' of the gospels, who gifts humanity with an intimate revelation of God's ways.

De Doctrina Christiana supplies a comprehensive definition of God's providential care that thematically duplicates the exordium's patterning from the Fall to redemption and from the first to the second Adam: 'God's PROVIDENCE, regarding humanity's Fall, is first discerned in his sin and the wretchedness that followed from it, then in his restoration' (*CE* 15.179).[21] Divine providence anticipates the human tragedy of cancerous sin and forestalls it with the panacea of grace. Throughout the poem God's providence, expressed by the machinery of salvation available through the Son, is always going ahead before human error and reconciling human ways to God by prevenient grace.[22] One of the epic's strongest examples of prevenient grace occurs soon after the human Fall. The Father instructs the Son to dispense a tempered divine judgement to humanity's first parents that will render 'Mercie colleague with Justice' (10.59). The Son enters Eden and pronounces the riddling *protevangelium* of Genesis 3:15. This oracle portends that the seed of woman shall bruise the serpent's head and that the serpent shall bruise the seed of woman's heel. Joseph Duncan has chronicled how Genesis 3:15 was first interpreted as a

[21] 'PROVIDENTIA *Dei lapsum hominis respiciens cum in peccato eius et miseria inde consecuta cernitur, tum in eius restitutione.*'

[22] Elsewhere I illustrate how Milton's Nineteenth Sonnet on his blindness is a miniature theodicy that dramatizes the action of prevenient grace: see 'The Patience to Prevent that Murmur: the Theodicy of John Milton's Nineteenth Sonnet', *Renascence*, 59 (2007), 247–73.

Messianic prophecy by the Church Fathers Justin Martyr and Irenaeus; later, all three magisterial Reformers, Luther, Melanchthon, and Calvin, endorsed this Patristic reading.[23] Milton relies upon this hermeneutic tradition when the Son meets Adam and Eve in a spirit of justice and mercy as 'mild Judge and Intercessor both / To sentence Man' (10.96–97), words that convey the tact and sensitivity of his reproof, but also the salvific message that their future redeemer brings. The epic narrator supplies an interpretive gloss to the Son's delivery of the *protevangelium* that expounds the importance of this riddle for *Paradise Lost*'s theodicy. The *protevangelium* is 'then verifi'd' at the Son's Passion:

> So spake this Oracle, then verifi'd
> When *Jesus* son of *Mary* second *Eve*,
> Saw Satan fall like Lightning down from Heav'n,
> Prince of the Aire; then rising from his Grave
> Spoild Principalities and Powers, triumphd
> In op'n shew, and with ascension bright
> Captivity led captive through the Aire,
> The Realme it self of *Satan* long usurpt,
> Whom he shall tread at last under our feet;
> Eevn hee who now foretold his fatal bruise
>   (10.182–91)

Thomas Newton is rare among Milton's commentators for having pieced together this jigsaw of primarily Pauline allusions that decrypts God's secret method of human salvation. The Son will regain lost Paradise by undergoing the Incarnation, crucifixion, and resurrection (Luke 10:18; Eph. 2:2; Col. 2:15) and then by experiencing the ascension (Ps. 68:18; Eph. 4:8; Rom. 16:20).[24]

Unlike Milton's privileged reader, Adam and Eve do not benefit from an amplified explication of the proto-gospel until Michael's revelation in the epic's closing two books. Michael is insistent about the momentousness of Christ's extraordinary victory on the cross in which he overcomes Satan and defeats Sin and Death. The archangel also alerts Adam to the spiritual destitution that would have resulted had the Son not made saving grace available from this superhuman, 'God-like act':

>   this God-like act
> Annulls thy doom, the death thou shouldst have dy'd,
> In sin for ever lost from life; this act
> Shall bruise the head of *Satan*, crush his strength
> Defeating Sin and Death, his two maine armes,
> And fix farr deeper in his head thir stings
> Then temporal death shall bruise the Victors heel
>   (12.427–33)

[23] Joseph E. Duncan, *Milton's Earthly Paradise: A Historical Study of Eden* (Minneapolis, 1972), 129–32.
[24] Newton, *Paradise*, vol. 2, 225, commenting on 10.184.

From Books Ten to Twelve Milton sustains the narrative suspense after the Fall's catastrophe by gradually unveiling, through revelatory glimpses of reconciliation and grace, the soteriology underlying the Son's oracle. Existing studies have already explored the unfurling of the *protevangelium* across the last three books; to reiterate their efforts would be superfluous.[25] That said, insufficient attention has been given to the ways in which the narrator grants the reader access to heavenly realms and to the providential purpose of the *Deus* or, rather, the *Christus ex machina* who actively intercedes for humanity and propitiates his Father off-stage of Milton's fallen domestic drama in Eden. The fruits of grace outpouring from the Son's saving work are always already taking effect in Milton's Eden after the Fall occurs and nature feels the wound, and even before Adam and Eve repent of their transgressions. The Son's bestowal of the merciful *protevangelistic* covenant, even as he dispenses judgement, is one example of this interlacing of justice and mercy. *De Doctrina Christiana's* glosses of the nature of God's commissioning of the *protevangelium* squares with the demeanour of Milton's Son in his role as clement judge:

> For, even before man had, not without malignity [*non nisi maligne*], confessed his sin to God, God, in pronouncing punishment on the serpent, promised one whom He would raise up from the seed of woman, one who would bruise the serpent's head, Genesis 3:15; [He did this] before He had passed judgement on man. And so He preceded the condemnation of humanity with His gratuitous redemption [*condemnationem hominis gratuita redemptione praevertit*].   (*CE* 15.252)

In identical fashion Milton's Adam and Eve approach their 'gracious Judge', one who speaks 'without revile' (10.118), while nursing a brood of negative emotions, with 'Love . . . not in thir looks, either to God / Or to each other, but apparent guilt', 'shame', 'perturbation', 'despaire', 'Anger', 'obstinacie', 'hate, and guile' (10.111–14). Despite their ingratitude, the Son still administers the *protevangelistic* cure for their lapsed condition.

Divine compassion, then, waits patiently in the wings, even before faulty humanity seeks grace. This soteriological aspect of the postlapsarian portion of Milton's epic may be somewhat obscure to modern readers who are estranged from, and perhaps out of sympathy with, the speech community of the Christian tradition. Our contemporaries are understandably alienated from the discourse of redemption and the metaphoric language of exchange, debt, and surety with which Milton's diffuse and brief epics explain the mystery of salvation. The average modern reader is probably desensitized to, and at a disadvantage in recognizing, the extensive lexicon of nowadays mostly neutralized redemptive terminology at play in the early modern English vernacular, a terminology to which Renaissance readers were necessarily acculturated. As this study aims to show, these terms continually inflect the semantics of Milton's verse, animating the poetry with soteriological wordplay: terms such as 'absolute', 'absolve', 'prevent', 'sufficient', 'safe', 'gift',

---

[25] See, for example, Georgia B. Christopher, *Milton and the Science of the Saints* (Princeton, 1982), 175–98; and Russell M. Hillier, '"So Shall the World Goe on": A Providentialist Reading of Books Eleven and Twelve of *Paradise Lost*', forthcoming in *English Studies* (2011).

'thanks', 'mercy', 'satisfaction', 'exempt', 'exact', 'account', 'well-pleased', 'stand', 'withstand', 'patience', 'propitious', 'cover', 'recover', 'restore', 'reconcile', 'interpose', 'companion', 'assure', 'surety', 'complacence', 'consummate', 'answer', 'answerable', 'partake', 'impart', 'union', 'communion', 'communicate', 'amend', 'recompense', 'pass', 'compass', 'easy', 'bent', 'burden', and 'exonerate'. The list goes on. *De Doctrina Christiana* privileges this redemptive discourse, because 'the restoration of humanity, if we consider Christ's satisfaction and our shaping ourselves to him when he emptied himself, is a matter of merit: in which manner those passages should be understood which indicate a system of recompense and paying a reward' (*CE* 15.336). Readers of *Paradise Lost* should be equally receptive to this redemptive system of recompense and reward if they are fully to comprehend the epic's assertion of eternal providence.

To conclude, whether or not the exordium's assertion of eternal providence can be construed as an amplification or a re-emphasis of Milton's justification of God's ways to men, both of the clauses comprising Milton's 'great Argument' (1.24) serve the poem's didactic goal of championing the machinery of salvation. As I hope to show, the great argument to Milton's *Paradise Lost* is a stirring reminder of the Christian example of humiliation before exaltation, descent before ascension, and kenosis as requisite to theosis, all of which the poem enacts and memorializes in its justification by faith in God's ways through His redeemer.

3

'Matter new to gaze': Satan's Blindness and the Manifestation of Milton's Sacramental Universe

[T]o the characters participating in an allegory, nothing is allegorical. They live in a world compact of wonders, beauties, and terrors, which are mostly quite unintelligible to them. Secondly and contrarily, our own experience while we read an allegory is double. It is divided between sharing the experiences of the characters in the story and looking at their life from somewhere outside it, seeing all the time meanings that are opaque from within.

C. S. Lewis[1]

A frequently discussed interpretive crux in *Paradise Lost* occurs after the Heavenly Council, when the epic narrator appears to add his voice to the angelic polyphony celebrating the Son's offer to redeem. The angels sing:

> O unexampl'd love,
> Love no where to be found less then Divine!
> Hail Son of God, Saviour of Men, thy Name
> Shall be the copious matter of my Song
> Henceforth, and never shall my Harp thy praise
> Forget, nor from thy Fathers praise disjoine.
>
> (3.410–15)

Interpreted along slightly different lines, this promise could be being independently couched within a solo performance given by each member of the angelic choir. Angelic curiosity concerning the redemption is supported by scripture (1 Pet. 1:10–12) and also by the archangel Raphael's willingness to 'inquire / Gladly into the wayes of God with Man' (8.225–26). *De Doctrina Christiana* concurs that God's angels 'desire to contemplate the mystery of our salvation because of love, not need' (*CE* 15.98–101). Indeed, the 'High matter' (5.563) of Raphael's twofold narrative fulfils the angels' vow of making the Son the 'copious matter' of angelic lays, both in his capacity as *Messias victor*, overthrowing Satan during the War in Heaven, and as God's creative Logos, founding and ordering Creation. In the epic's final two books the *protevangelium* permeates the temporal continuum of Michael's narrative, more 'High matter' that

[1] C. S. Lewis, *Spenser's Images of Life*, ed. Alastair Fowler (Cambridge, 1967), 29.

charts the gradual historical inbreaking of the archetypal one just man and the flowering of salvation history in Adam's 'Redeemer ever blest' (12.573). The owner of the possessive pronoun in the phrase 'my Song' remains ambiguous and, in all probability, deliberately so. Nevertheless, in a recurrent *topos* in Milton's early occasional pieces the poetic persona adds his voice to a company of angels (see *The Nativity Ode* 22–28; *The Passion* 1–4). If William Hunter and Stevie Davies are correct to identify the Son as the focus of Book Three's invocation, the Father's 'Bright effluence' (3.6) and the 'ofspring of Heav'n first-born' (3.1), then this choral statement re-emphasizes the Son's importance in inspiring a book that commences with the Christocentric Heavenly Council.[2] Above all, the choral statement makes a bold programmatic claim for the epic's total content by asserting that the Son, as 'Saviour of Men', comprises the poem's 'copious matter'.

Milton's debt to rhetoric in the phrase 'copious matter' is suggested by his adoption of technical, oratorical language. *Copia* or 'copiousness' was first defined by Quintilian and was then exhaustively treated by Desiderius Erasmus in his rhetorical guide *De duplici copia verborum ac rerum* (1512). The term *copia* ordinarily describes a richness and versatility of expression and the demonstration of variety and invention. In treating any given subject, a skilled rhetorician draws upon '*copia rerum ac verborum*', 'an abundance of subject matter and words'.[3] Quintilian writes that an orator's resources 'consist of a copious supply of words and subject matter. But the subject matter is peculiar to its specific case or common to a few cases, whereas words should be prepared for each and every case.'[4] Milton heeds Quintilian's formula in his *First Defense* (1651) when he begins his polemic by avouching that he would not be as 'profuse of words, empty of matter [*profusus verborum, vacuus rerum*]' (*CE* 7.3) in vindicating the English people as his opponent Salmasius had been in championing the English monarch. Milton's appropriation of Quintilian's terminology would appear to attest that *Paradise Lost*'s single predominant *res* or 'subject' is God's saving Son. The poem adorns its Christological matter with diverse registers and discourses across a spectrum of verbal tropes, schemes, styles, and genres. In conveying the Son's significance the epic displays a panorama of rhetorical invention 'more literal or more ornate or more powerful or richer sounding'.[5] If the epic is to function as a 'copious' representation of the Son, a work manifesting the nature and salvific office of the 'Saviour of Men' in literal, figurative, and mysterious ways, then its strategies must approach the allegorical mode.[6]

---

[2] See William B. Hunter, Jr, 'Milton's Muse', in *Bright Essence*, 149–56; and Stevie Davies and William B. Hunter, Jr., 'Milton's Urania: "The Meaning, Not the Name I Call"', *Studies in English Literature, 1500–1900*, 28 (1988), 95–111. William Kerrigan has persuasively challenged Hunter and Davies's identification of the Son with the 'holy Light' of the second invocation in *The Sacred Complex: On the Psychogenesis of 'Paradise Lost'* (Cambridge, Mass., 1983), 143–57.

[3] Quintilian, *Institutio Oratoria*, vol. 4, trans. H. E. Butler (London, 1953), *Inst.* 10.1.5–6: '*Eae constant copia rerum ac verborum.*'

[4] Ibid.: '*Sed res propriae sunt cuiusque causae aut paucis communes, verba in universas paranda.*'

[5] Ibid. *Inst.* 10.1.6: '*magis propria aut magis ornata aut plus efficientia aut melius sonantia*'.

[6] A further figuration of Christ's saving office is the angels' symbolic action of casting down and taking up their amaranthine crowns. For the soteriological overtures to these angelic curtseys see my note, 'To Say it with Flowers: Milton's "Immortal Amarant" Reconsidered (*Paradise Lost* 3.349–61)', *Notes and Queries*, 54 (2007), 404–08.

I

Recent critical appraisals of *Paradise Lost* have acceded that the epic abides by allegorical tenets.[7] Norman Council has proposed that Milton favoured 'an epistemology that was able to discard the distinction between literal and figurative meaning in scriptural statements and in interpretation of them by redefining all the accumulated meanings as literal when properly understood by the individual believer'.[8] Arising from the twofold sense of scripture laid out in *De Doctrina Christiana*, which privileges the internal, unwritten rule of the Spirit within the believer over the external rule of the biblical text, the final authority for scriptural meaning is displaced from the God-breathed text onto the reader. The Rabbinic interpretation of Torah according to *peshat* or the 'literal' interpretation was originally indistinguishable from *derash*, the more liberal, allegorical reading. The verbal root *pashat* translates as 'to stretch out' and implies a more generous way of interpreting scripture that is inclusive of figurative readings. Likewise, Miltonic literalism can become surprisingly mobile and elastic, demonstrating complex figurative meanings, obliquely expressed, that are variously metaphoric, metonymic, allegorical, and anagogical.

In order to appreciate how Milton's theology informs his poetic allegoresis, we must first consider three doctrines: the Incarnation, Creation, and sacramentalism. *De Doctrina Christiana*'s account of the Incarnation maintains that the Son preexisted his incarnate self as the 'firstborn of every created thing' and that, 'through him, all things both on Earth and in Heaven were made, even the very angels' (*CE* 15.262). Although the treatise avoids anatomizing the precise mode of the Incarnation, preferring ignorance and an acceptance of the doctrine as 'by far the greatest mystery of our religion' (*CE* 15.262; see 270–73, 278), nonetheless the syntagma makes a number of bold dogmatic assertions. The Son assumes a twofold nature that is divine and human (*CE* 15.258). While the 'respective properties of each may remain distinct among themselves' (*CE* 15.270), a single person is formed from the 'mutual hypostatic union of two natures, that is, of two essences, substances, and, inevitably, persons' (*CE* 15.270), a state the treatise designates by the Patristic term *theanthropos* (*CE* 15.272) or 'God-man'. The Son is not a mediator for humankind as he is human, but as *theanthropos* (*CE* 15.278; 15.272), so that redemption is achievable only in his *theanthropic* state. 'Indeed, the *theanthropos* offered himself as *theanthropos*' (*CE* 15.292), and 'CHRIST, AS THEANTHROPOS, OFFERED HIMSELF VOLUNTARILY TO DIVINE JUSTICE IN LIFE AS

---

[7] See, for example, Kenneth J. Knoespel, 'The Limits of Allegory: Textual Expansion of Narcissus in *Paradise Lost*', *Milton Studies*, 22 (1986), 79–99; Stephen M. Fallon, 'Milton's Sin and Death: The Ontology of Allegory in *Paradise Lost*', *English Literary Renaissance*, 17 (1987), 329–50; Kenneth Borris, 'Allegory in *Paradise Lost*: Satan's Cosmic Journey', *Milton Studies*, 26 (1990), 101–33; Borris, 'Union of Mind or in Both One Soul: Allegories of Adam and Eve in *Paradise Lost*', *Milton Studies*, 31 (1995), 45–72; Borris, *Allegory and Epic*, 183–252; Treip, *Allegorical Poetics*; Norman Council, '"Answering His Great Idea": The Fiction of *Paradise Lost*', *Milton Studies*, 32 (1996), 45–62; Catherine Gimelli Martin, *The Ruins of Allegory: 'Paradise Lost' and the Metamorphoses of Epic Convention* (Durham, 1998).

[8] Council, '"Answering"', 47.

WELL AS IN DEATH' (*CE* 15.302). As Hugh MacCallum has argued, Milton's sacrificial God-man resembles an orthodox soteriology, because 'Only a Son who is divine but not God, and whose humanity takes existential and individual form, can act as mediator.'[9] The efficacy of the Son's mediation applies not only to the historical time within which he redeems humanity, but his redeeming influence extends 'virtually from the beginning of the world' (*CE* 15.294).

In all that the incarnate Son experiences, in his birth, ministry, humiliation, and exaltation, he performs his mediatorial office from within his divine humanity. 'Indeed, that Christ was human demonstrates that he had a body' (*CE* 15.276), but he was hypostatically God-man. One mark of the treatise's heterodoxy, yet a doctrine consistent with its mortalism, expounds that, when Jesus died, 'his soul died with his body on the same day' (*CE* 15.306). Because Jesus's humiliation pertains to both natures, 'each of Christ's natures must have suffered with patience to some degree' (*CE* 15.302–05) so that 'the whole sacrifice, therefore the whole Christ, that whole sacrificial lamb, should be immolated' (*CE* 15.308). Both natures enjoy the Son's exaltation, as both natures once endured humiliation: 'Christ's exaltation is according to both his natures, just as his self-emptying was. His divine nature [was exalted] by his restoration and manifestation, his human nature by an accession' of glory (*CE* 15.314). It is vital to the treatise's eschatology that the Son's humanity enjoys resurrection and exaltation along with his divinity because otherwise, at Christ's Second Coming and the resurrection of the dead, 'If it is not so, we will not be conformed to Christ; who himself entered into glory with the identical body, the identical body and blood, with which he had died and with which he rose again' (*CE* 16.352).

As Kenneth Borris observes, the treatise's conceptions are reflected in the physics and the metaphysics of the Incarnation and redemption discussed in the Heavenly debate in Book Three.[10] The Son accepts that he will be 'Made flesh . . . of Virgin seed' (3.284), yet his divinity is distinguished from his humanity, since 'Nor shalt thou by descending to assume / Mans Nature, less'n or degrade thine owne' (3.303–04). Thus Michael describes the Incarnation as a hypostatic union, 'So God with Man unites' (12.382). In line with the treatise's heterodox death of Christ's soul and body, the Son acquiesces to immolation on the cross of 'All that of me can die' (3.246). The Father foresees that both humiliated natures will be exalted to God's throne:

---

[9] Hugh MacCallum, *Milton and the Sons of God: The Divine Image in Milton's Epic Poetry* (Toronto, 1986), 225.

[10] Borris has defended the importance of the treatise's formulation of the Incarnation for *Paradise Lost*. See his 'Milton's Heterodoxy of the Incarnation and Subjectivity in *De Doctrina Christiana* and *Paradise Lost*', in *Living Texts: Interpreting Milton*, ed. Kristin A. Pruitt and Charles W. Durham (London, 2000), 264–82. Other critical discussions of the Incarnation include: Lewalski, *Milton's Brief Epic*, 133–63; MacCallum, *Milton and the Sons of God*, 210–25; Marshall Grossman, '"In Pensive trance, and anguish, and ecstatic fit": Milton on the Passion', in *A Fine Tuning: Studies of the Religious Poetry of Herbert and Milton*, ed. Mary A. Maleski (Binghamton, 1989), 205–20.

> Therefore thy Humiliation shall exalt
> With thee thy Manhood also to this Throne;
> Here shalt thou sit incarnate, here shalt Reigne
> Both God and Man, Son both of God and Man,
> Anointed universal King
>
> (3.313–17)

According to *De Doctrina Christiana,* by lowering himself and then returning to the Godhead as *theanthropos,* Christ satisfies for humankind and enables every believer's future exaltation. Christ's humiliation and exaltation recover the vast ontological distance between lapsed humanity and the God humans have fallen away from. Christ's achievements establish the groundwork for the treatise's machinery of salvation. This machinery, the beneficial effects of the Incarnation and redemption, comprises the core of the treatise's First Part: renovation and supernatural regeneration, repentance and saving faith, justification and implanting in Christ's body, adoption as God's children, union and communion with the Father in Christ, and, finally, incomplete glorification in this life and complete glorification at the *eschaton.* The external motive force for this soteriological process is the God-man's ministry and death, but the instrumental and contributory cause is the believer's faith. Humans, if they so choose, can be made new creatures, liberated from sin and restored to God's image by faith in Christ's salvific humiliation and exaltation.

De Doctrina Christiana insists that God has planned this state of grace, a preconceived purpose in Christ, and made it virtually and efficaciously available to humankind since the world's foundation (*CE* 14.90, 100; 15.402, 404). *De Doctrina Christiana* affirms that, before Christ, such grace was available to 'the illustrious men . . . Abel, Enoch, Noah etc.' (*CE* 15.404) catalogued in the cloud of witnesses of Hebrews 11, the same just men who culminate typologically in Christ in Michael's patterned history (11.429–60, 664–82, 700–11, 712–901). This condition stands because the Son mediates as intercessory priest and a sacrifice glad to be offered for all time (*CE* 15.284, 290, 300, 302). Granted that salvation has already been and still is being accomplished, the responsibility now rests upon each individual to recognize the opportunity the Son makes possible. Part of this recognition requires the kind of acknowledgement Adam makes of his redeemer and the Paradise within. *De Doctrina Christiana*'s sacramental theology encourages an allegorical mode of interpretation *and perception.* This allegorical mode permits a willing participant to perceive how the spatial phenomena decorating Milton's poetic cosmos may be otherwise than those phenomena appear to be.[11]

De Doctrina Christiana's sacramentalism maintains that it is incumbent upon the participant to accept the sacraments as a seal upon 'saving grace or Christ's satisfaction through a visible sign' (*CE* 16.164). The baptismal waters or the

---

[11] Elsewhere I argue how Milton adopts astrology to clarify his theodicy and champion a strong Christology. See my '"Betwixt Astrea and the Scorpion Signe": The Conjunction of Astrology and Apocalyptic in Milton's Psychostasis', *The Cambridge Quarterly,* 37 (2008), 305–23.

elements of bread and wine in Holy Communion signify symbolically and figuratively and there is one common analogy between all sacraments, despite their
different modes of signification (*CE* 16.176, 178). That analogy is the seal of
grace provided by the Son's atonement. Thus baptism signifies 'COALITION [literal-
ly, "TAKING ROOT"] WITH CHRIST THROUGH HIS DEATH, BURIAL, AND RESURREC-
TION' (*CE* 16.168), 'a seal of grace now exhibited, remission of sins, sanctification,
and a sign of our death and resurrection with Christ' (*CE* 16.178). Baptism
represents, 'figuratively, Christ's painful life, death, and burial' (*CE* 16.184; see
16.190). In a Zwinglian sense Communion is a *commemoration* of the Last Supper,
an event figuring Christ's death and its benefits. The idea that the bread and wine
materially metamorphose into Christ's flesh and blood is a nonsense: 'Certainly
consubstantiation and especially that transubstantiation and Papist *anthropophagy*
[Greek "cannibalism"] are not only contrary to all reason, sense, and human
custom, but also to sacred doctrine, to the nature and fruit of a sacrament' (*CE*
16.198). A communicant's worthiness to partake is premised upon 'faith alone',
not upon 'teeth as they chew flesh' (*CE* 16.194). The interpretive burden of
recognizing the baptismal waters and the bread and wine as 'signs and seals' of
grace rests upon the faithful perception of the communicant. Therefore infants are
precluded from baptism because they are spiritually immature and unteachable.
They lack the faith and understanding to undertake an obligation and cannot
answer for themselves (*CE* 16.170ff.). According to John Ulreich's reconstruction
of Milton's theory of 'sacramental participation', 'Our communion with Christ in
the sacraments depends upon the activity of this spiritual and rational faculty, upon
the operation of mind and will. It is in this sense . . . that it is appropriate to speak
of Milton's participating in the sacrament by a conscious act of imagination.'[12]
De Doctrina Christiana appropriates the language of poetics to describe the communicant's imaginative perception of the meaning underlying the sacramental
elements of water, bread, and wine. The treatise understands sacramental participation as an imaginative act occurring in the participant's mind. A sacrament is a
trope or figure of speech that illustrates or signifies, not what it is in itself, but the
higher redemptive reality it illustrates or signifies (*CE* 16.198). Sacrament and
allegory resemble one another. Both the sacramental and allegorical modes figure
forth 'something other' than is initially apparent. Interpreters of sacramental and
allegorical discourse need to adjust their perceptions in order to admit the 'something other' that is being conveyed.

   There is much in the sacramental hermeneutic outlined above that is characteristic of Reformed theology. Above all, there is the idea that the natural order,
Creation's sights and sounds, must be reinterpreted in light of biblical revelation.
Robert Entzminger re-evaluates what Milton's monist ontology *ex Deo*, rather than
ex nihilo, guarantees for divine revelation in the poetry: 'God's creation of the

---

[12] John C. Ulreich, Jr, 'Milton on the Eucharist: Some Second Thoughts about Sacramentalism', in
Milton and the Middle Ages, ed. John Mulryan (Lewisburg, 1982), 48; and Ulreich, 'Making the Word
Flesh: Incarnation as Accommodation', in *Reassembling Truth: Twenty-First-Century Milton*, ed.
Charles W. Durham and Kristin A. Pruitt (Selinsgrove, 2003), 129–44.

universe out of himself rather than *ex nihilo*, the accounts of angelic as well as Edenic lovemaking and digestion, and Raphael's promise that sustained obedience may lead to progressive refinement all point to matter as the medium for the revelation of spirit [see 5.496–505 and 7.154–61].'[13] Milton peppers his prose with references to a revealed theology of God's image in the Incarnation. Milton's educational goal, for instance, is 'to repair the ruins of our first parents by regaining to know God aright, and out of that knowledge to love him, to imitate him, to be like him', and to arrive at 'a knowledge of God and things invisible, as by orderly conning over the visible and inferior creature' (*CPW* 2.366–69). Milton here recommends that, by acquainting ourselves with our divine likeness, we might approach God through the renewed image of the Son. The famous Christological frame of reference from *Areopagitica*'s parable of picking up the pieces of Virgin Truth in a fallen world recalls that, originally, 'Truth indeed came once into the world with her divine Master, and was a perfect shape most glorious to look on: but when he ascended', Truth was 'scatter'd . . . to the four winds . . . till her Masters second coming' (*CPW* 2.549). Similarly, the Incarnation subtends *De Doctrina Christiana*'s theory of accommodation, which teaches that our best conception of God arises from the fact that 'He Himself has stooped to meet us at our level, lest we are carried away beyond human comprehension and beyond what is written' in scripture (*CE* 14.32). Scripture most perfectly imagines such divinely conceived *anthropopathy* that God might suffer as a human suffers, in Christ's advent. *Paradise Lost* reflects the Son's importance as God's medium for humanity, 'the image of the invisible God' (Col. 1:15). He is the 'radiant image' (3.63) of God's glory and 'in him all his Father shon / Substantially exprest' (3.139–40). The Son crowns Creation's vertical architecture as 'of all Creation first' (3.383), 'Second to [God]' (3.409), and 'great Vice-gerent' (5.609), next in eminence. He is appointed 'Head' (5.606) of angels and humans and 'Second Omnipotence' (6.684), answerable only to his Father. Kenneth Borris discerns in the Son's person and mediation an overarching structural principle for the epic: 'The Son is the medium of creation in *Paradise Lost*, so that, even when not formally incorporated in him as head, the constituents of Milton's universe are at least expressions of him as Word.'[14] Because the cosmos articulated within Milton's poem and treatise expresses an animist and monist materialism, a Creation manifested *ex Deo* and suffused with the physical and spiritual, the poetry lends itself to an allegorical–sacramental form where the Son irradiates Creation as its creative Logos and divine–human intercessor.

II

The figure of the Cosmic Plant with which Raphael expounds God's cosmos to Adam and Eve is construable as an allegoresis of the Son entrenched within the sacramental context of a meal spread for Raphael. Anthony Low has demonstrated

---

[13] Robert L. Entzminger, *Divine Word: Milton and the Redemption of Language* (Pittsburgh, 1985), 49.
[14] Borris, *Allegory*, 196–97.

how this paradisiacal meal approximates to Communion and he contrasts it with the Catholic Mass.[15] When this simple repast begins, a prandial rite pregnant with visible signs of grace, the epic narrator puns upon angelic digestion as a process of transubstantiating food (5.438). Raphael's capacity 'with keen dispatch / Of real hunger, and concoctive heate / To transubstantiate' (5.436–38) is more than a crude anti-Catholic jibe. Raphael's reference to angelic sustenance proceeds via the biblical discussion of the manna that the Exodus generation was supported by in the wilderness as 'angels' bread' (Coverdale translation, Ps. 78:26), the 'bread of heaven' (Coverdale, Ps. 105:40), and, in the Wisdom of Solomon, as 'angels' food' (*AV* Wisd. 16:20), to the idea of Christ as the living bread of heaven (John 6). This sequence of images formed the biblical substructure of Medieval teaching on Eucharistic transubstantiation. The sacramental directions inscribed within Raphael's discourse prepare Milton's fit reader to come to the table as a willing participant. The figure Raphael selects for the emanationist model of Creation's 'one first matter all' that from body up to spirit works is that of a Cosmic Plant or Vine: 'So from the root / Springs lighter the green stalk, from thence the leaves / More aerie, last the bright consummat floure / Spirits odorous breathes' (5.479–82). As if it were a palimpsest, the New Creation renewed in the Son allegorically overlays unfallen Creation. With a similar metaphor Satan's plot aims 'to confound the race / Of mankind in one root' (2.382–83). As early as *The Tenure of Kings and Magistrates* (1649) Milton traces the fractured 'image and resemblance of God himself . . . from the root of *Adams* transgression' (*CPW* 3.198–99). The epic's newly fallen Adam plays upon the Latinate meaning of 'propagation' from *propago*, a 'slip' or 'shoot', when he laments that his progeny will be a 'propagated curse' (10.729) and questions 'what can proceed / But all corrupt?' (10.824–25). In Michael's vision-narrative the World Deluge typologically foreshadows a new root growing in Christ after human corruption stems from Adam's root or room. As Albert Labriola has shown, the biblical Noah, destined 'to raise another World' (11.877), was long established as a prefiguration of Christ, standing 'Betwixt the World destroyd and World restor'd' (12.3), from whom 'Man as from a second stock [will] proceed' (12.7), 'This second sours of Men' (12.13).[16] Michael is careful to insert the comparative particle 'as', since Noah does not renew humanity through his bloodline as Christ is destined to do. Instead, more human corruption ensues from Nimrod's tyranny.

   De Doctrina Christiana's doctrine of 'INSITION' or 'IMPLANTING IN CHRIST' is a consequence of regeneration, 'where God the Father plants the faithful in Christ, that is, renders them participants in Christ, and, moreover, as sufficient to grow together [*coalescant* – "take root"] in one body with Christ' (*CE* 16.1). Two outcomes of implanting are 'NEW LIFE' and 'GROWTH' or 'Spiritual increase' (*CE* 16.2, 4, 16). Proof texts for implanting in Christ include, revealingly for Raphael's choice of figure, Christ's Johannine statement that 'I am the vine' (John 15:1–17), where Jesus imagines himself as a revitalizing plant in whom his followers will be

---

[15] Anthony Low, 'Angels and Food in *Paradise Lost*', *Milton Studies*, 1 (1969), 135–45.
[16] See Albert C. Labriola, 'The Medieval View of Christian History in *Paradise Lost*', in *Milton and the Middle Ages*, ed. John Mulryan (Lewisburg, 1982), 115–32.

engrafted and prosper. But the treatise's base scriptural text for exegeting the doctrine of insition is Romans 6:5: 'For if we have been planted together in the likeness of [Christ's] death, we shall be also in the likeness of his resurrection' (*AV*; see *CE* 16.4). The Vulgate's Latin verb for 'planted together' is *complantati*. The Father accordingly foretells the identical benefits of 'new life' and 'growth' for fallen humanity, implanted by the Son's restorative work:

> be thou in *Adams* room
> The Head of all mankind, though *Adams* Son.
> As in [Adam] perish all men, so in [the Son]
> As from a second root shall be restor'd,
> As many as are restor'd, without thee none.
>
>   .   .   .   .   .
>
> And live in thee transplanted, and from thee
> Receive new life.
>   (3.285–89, 293–94)

Raphael admonishes Adam that carnal love, 'the sense of touch whereby mankind / Is propagated' (8.579–80), is subordinate to spiritual love. Adam falls partially because, transported by fleshly, propagating touch, he decks Eve with excessive superlatives and thinks her 'so absolute... / And in her self compleat' (8.547–48). Proportionately, fallen Adam rises by spiritual propagation, effected through the Son's love for humankind. When the Son intercedes for fallen humanity, he supplies the treatise's image of implanting or engrafting when he asks that, by his 'propitiation, all [humanity's] works on mee / Good or not good [will] ingraft, my Merit those / Shall perfet, and for these my Death shall pay' (11.34–36), and that 'All my redeemd [will be] Made one with mee as I with [God the Father] am one' (11.43–44).

Milton's Son, whom the Father honours as 'perfet Man' of 'consummat vertue' (*PR* 1.165–66), constitutes the entire radical structure, from the root to the bright consummate flower, in whom Creation participates and is sustained.[17] As, at the angelic level, the Son is head and, under him, all are embodied in one, throughout Creation the Son stands nearest to God, receiving divine gifts and benefits, bestowing them through his person, and distributing divine grace throughout Creation. Jonathan Goldberg suggests that the 'bright consummat floure' forming the apex to Raphael's Cosmic Plant may hint at the *virga Jesse* of Isaiah 11:1.[18] But the image may equally allude to Balaam's oracle at Numbers 24:17, a text the early

---

[17] William Madsen asserts, 'In this definitive vision of the Incarnation Christ is not merely the moral exemplar so many critics have seen in *Paradise Regained*, He is the Head of mankind in Adam's room; He is the second root; He is the new Garden in which man will live transplanted. His descent into the flesh is the true pattern of the humiliation that exalts. [These patterns] are possible because Christ is the symbolizing center of the poem': William Madsen, *From Shadowy Types to Truth: Studies in Milton's Symbolism* (New Haven, 1968), 121–22. Stephen Fallon finds that 'the plant begins as a metaphor for the steps of the hierarchy of matter only to become a synecdoche for the process by which creatures ascend the hierarchy': Stephen M. Fallon, *Milton among the Philosophers: Poetry and Materialism in Seventeenth-Century England* (Ithaca, 1991), 105.

[18] The Lady Chapel of St Laurence's Church, Ludlow, boasts an intricate fourteenth-century Jesse window. Milton would have had the opportunity to appreciate this device in 1634 when he presented *A Maske* at Ludlow Castle.

Christians interpreted as an *ex eventu* Messianic prophecy. Goldberg importantly adds: 'In Raphael's image of history as a tree Christ is implicit as the root and the flower, as the creative principle and the re-creative force.'[19] In Christian *testimonia* Balaam's prophecy of the star (Num. 24:17) and the Isaian oracle of the ancestral branch rooted in the stem of Jesse (Isa. 11:1) were interfused to make a composite Messianic statement, conspicuous in a kerygmatic text traditionally associated with the Heavenly Son: 'I am the root and offspring of David, the bright morning star' (Rev. 22:16). Milton's 'bright consummat floure' resembles the 'God-like fruition' (3.307) the Father dubs His redeeming Son. Justin Martyr (*c.* AD 100–165), whom Milton often cites, melds Balaam's star oracle with the stem of Jesse in his *First Apology* to read, 'A star shall rise out of Jacob, and a flower shall spring from the root of Jesse.'[20] The Incarnational tree of Being described by the seventeenth-century Platonist Peter Sterry evokes Milton's image of the New Creation nested within the Old Creation and recalls the biblical image of Christ as the invigorating vine: 'The Word made Flesh, is the *whole Tree* of Being Uncreated and Created, the *Root*, the *Body* with all the branches putting forth themselves into one little top-branch now withering, that through its death they may renew all unto a fresh and flourishing spring.'[21]

III

Raphael's Christological figuration of the 'one first matter all' is not an isolated example of Milton challenging the reader to adopt an allegorical–sacramental view of his poetic universe. Subsequent to the epic's angelic–narratorial–Miltonic claim that the Son will be the copious matter of their song, there is the 'matter new to gaze' (3.613) of Creation, freshly conceived out of Chaos's 'Matter unformd and void' (7.233). It is reasonable to ask why Milton elected to foreground Satan's voyage through the cosmos with the Father and Son's elaborate disquisition upon the theology of Incarnation and redemption. One plausible explanation is that the celestial scenes that follow body forth a copious manifestation, a divine patefaction, of the Son's *theanthropic* mediation – 'to recapitulate all things in Christ, things in Heaven and things on Earth' (Eph. 1:10).

That Milton's Christocentric universe, charged with the Son's grandeur, has largely escaped critical notice may be due to the fact that the cosmic panorama is filtered through Satan's soured and limited perspective. In the direct narrative of Satan's expedition the reader's scope is curbed to seeing 'as farr as Angels kenn' (1.59). From Satan's departure from Hell's brink in Book Two to his voyeuristic gaze in Book Four the reader shares Satan's sensations when his ear is 'peald / With

[19] Jonathan Goldberg, '*Virga Iesse*: Analogy, Typology, and Anagogy in Milton's Simile', *Milton Studies*, 5 (1973), 185.

[20] Justin Martyr, *Writings of Saint Justin Martyr*, trans. Thomas B. Falls (Washington, DC, 1948), 68–70.

[21] Peter Sterry, *A Discourse of the Freedom of the Will* (London, 1675), 232.

noises loud' (2.920–21) at Chaos's hubbub, his eye struck by the 'sudden view' (2.890; 3.542) of the Deep and the concentric world, and his sense of smell arrested by Eden's 'odorous sweets' (4.166). Indistinct forms take shape for the reader as and when they are adapted to Satan's vision so that, from the perspective of Chaos, 'Farr off th' Empyreal Heav'n' appears 'undetermind square or round' (2.1047–48), and the world's outermost orb 'a Globe farr off / It seemd, now seems a boundless Continent / Dark, waste, and wild' (3.422–24). The wealth of verbs connoting sight and vision that describe Satan's beholding, viewing, looking, surveying, gazing, seeing, observing, discerning, descrying, spying, marking, and perusing is unprecedented in the poem. The reader is drawn entirely into a Satanic worldview that, like his flight, is unremittingly 'oblique' (3.564). The vision Creation's unfallen creatures enjoy is usually accompanied by an instinct for worship. Uriel assumes that Satan sees eye to eye with him ('I saw', 3.708; 'as thou seest,' 3.719) in wishing to visit God's works, 'to glorifie / The great Work-Maister' (3.695–96). Adam and Eve's unpremeditated vespers, delivered 'under op'n Skie' (4.721; see 4.720–35), and their matins, prompted in 'op'n sight / Of day-spring' (5.138–39; see 5.136–208), correspond formally with the Creation Psalms 8 and 19 and witness God's goodness in Creation. Adam combines seeing and praising when he reasons that 'Millions of spiritual Creatures...with ceaseless praise his works behold / Both day and night' (4.677–80). But because Satan a Hell within him brings as he surveys a world he hopes to waste and colonize (see 4.18–26, 75–78, 838–40), his aggravated voyage initially grants the reader an occluded perspective of a creature blinded and sunk within his own fallenness.[22] Consider the infinite distance between Satan's abomination and Adam and Eve's adoration of their sun-fashioning God (4.32–39; 5.171–74; 8.273–82).

James Dougal Fleming has argued that Satan is gripped by 'an inexcusable determination not to see what he in fact sees'.[23] Like the discussion of inhabitants within Dante's *Inferno*, Satanic *agitprop* evades all mention of the Son. William Hunter identifies Monarchianism as chief among Satan's heresies. Monarchianism stresses God's unity and insists upon a 'denial of the independent existence of the Son or of the divinity of Christ'.[24] Of course, Satan gives 'envie against the Son of God' (5.662) as the suggested cause for committing angelic sedition. In his quarrel with Abdiel, arguably the Rubicon moment of Satan's apostasy, the fiend recoils from granting the Son any special distinction, 'by whom / As by his Word the mighty Father made / All things' (5.835–37), to the point of absurdly denying the historical fact of this 'strange point and new' (5.855) when he insists that the angels were 'self-begot, self-rais'd / By our own quick'ning power' (5.860–61). Uriel's rhapsody on God's Creation, which was brought about 'at his Word', that is,

[22] Merritt Y. Hughes interprets Milton's Hell as a locality in the fastness of Chaos and the psychological state of Satan and his devils. See Hughes, '"Myself Am Hell"', *Modern Philology*, 54 (1956), 80–94.
[23] James Dougal Fleming, *Milton's Secrecy and Philosophical Hermeneutics* (Aldershot, 2008), 28.
[24] William B. Hunter, Jr., 'The Heresies of Satan', in *Th' Upright Heart and Pure: Essays on John Milton Commemorating the Tercentenary of the Publication of Paradise Lost*, ed. Amadeus P. Fiore (Pittsburgh, 1967), 29.

through the agency of God's Son, revives the issues of Satan's argument with Abdiel over the Son's primacy. Uriel's implicit praise of the Son as God's creating Word provides as good an explanation as any for Satan's splenetic descent to Earth, 'inflam'd with rage' (4.9), and moves Satan to rant against the Son-sun. In Hell the devils alter the facts and rewrite history to forget God's Messiah and his victory during the War in Heaven. The Son's Heaven-quaking triumph, guiding the divine chariot's 'rapid Wheeles / That shake Heav'ns basis' (6.711–12), becomes a heavenly disturbance that the rebel angels, in their delirium, attribute to the havoc they have themselves wrought 'In dubious Battel' (1.104). The Christless propaganda of diabolic rhetoric variously expunges the Son's role as 'Sole Victor from th' expulsion of his Foes' (6.880). First, Satan focuses on the Father's person as Heaven's 'Conquerour' (1.143) and 'Sole reigning' (1.124). Second, the devils blank the Son's name with an indefinite title like 'fierce Foe' (2.78) or 'Almighty Foe' (2.769), or they reduce his initiative to instrumental means by metonymy or synecdoche, calling him 'the Thunderers aime' (2.28), an 'Almighty Engin' (2.65), or 'Heav'ns afflicting Thunder' (2.166). Finally, they disperse the Son's being amid myriad persons so that his preeminence becomes diffused through phrases like 'Ministers of vengeance' (1.170) or 'swift persuers' (1.326).[25] Yet, although the narrator teaches that Satan avoids the subject of Deity – 'God and his Son except, / Created thing naught valu'd he nor shunnd' (2.678–79) – the narrative reminds us, often most unexpectedly, of the Son's providential role in defeating the fiend. In Book Two, for instance, when Satan and Death are about to lock horns, the narrator uses a circumlocution to evoke the Son's consummate victory at the Last Judgement, since 'never but once more was either like / To meet so great a foe' (2.721–22; and see 10.629–37 and 12.537–51). Given that the demonic party line wholly elides the Son's past accomplishments in reordering Heaven and successfully evicting the devils, it is unsurprising that Satan convinces himself to disregard Christic evidences during his voyage.

Cary Nelson describes Satan's 'incoiling psychic landscape' and deems that 'the anguished space of fallen perception is the limited measure of Satan's alienation', an alienation that makes 'dramatic conflict between satanic and innocent spaces'.[26] Satan's admiring encounters with cosmic wonders are coloured and finally warped by the destructive emotions of rancour, spite, pride, jealousy, and rage. As Gilbraith Miller Crump explains, Milton's blistering pun during the War in Heaven, where Satan's 'Eye so superficially surveyes' (6.476) Heaven's bounties, signifies that, 'In seeing beyond Heaven, Satan has discovered Hell; in place of Heaven's "ambient light," he would substitute "infernal flame".'[27] Crump's observation glosses over an essential aspect of Satanic psychology. Although Satan's fascination is hobbled by his envy, scorn, and disdain, his worldview is a distortion, not a negation, of a true perspective. His festering envy of the Son and his 'jealous leer maligne' (4.503),

---

[25] James A. Freeman makes a similar case in *Milton and the Martial Muse: 'Paradise Lost' and European Traditions of War* (Princeton, 1980), 141–42.

[26] Cary Nelson, *The Incarnate Word: Literature as Verbal Space* (Urbana, 1973), 81.

[27] Gilbraith Miller Crump, *The Mystical Design of 'Paradise Lost'* (Lewisburg, 1975), 104.

intemperately cocked at Creation, true to its Latin etymology of *in-vidia* or slanted vision, is a 'seeing awry', an obscuring of what was once clear and lucid.[28] *De Doctrina Christiana* teaches that the effects of sin and the Fall are a privation. '[A]n obliquity or anomaly [*obliquitas sive anomalia*] from a lawful rule is properly evil' (*CE* 15.198), rather like the 'oblique way' (3.564) Satan describes in his flight or the shiftiness with which Satan, disguised within the serpent, pursues his 'tract oblique' (9.510) and, 'side-long' (9.512), sidles up to Eve. Milton's simile of the scout admiring an exotic city is an imprecise fit with Satan's cankered view of Creation. Although, for the scout, 'Such wonder seis'd', for Satan, 'much more envy seis'd' (3.552–53). Once the reader recognizes that the passageway Satan peers into is a conduit for grace into a grateful world, Satan's submerged awareness of all he has lost explains his envious seizure. His five soliloquies are catalysed by what Satan terms 'the hateful siege / Of contraries' (9.121–22), his estimation of the ontological distance between his vitiated self and Creation's beauty. Two soliloquies are prompted by visions that remind Satan of God's glory expressed through His Son: the orb of the Son–sun shining 'like the God / Of this new World' (4.33–34) and Adam and Eve, expressing 'Divine resemblance' (4.364).[29]

Two strategies are open to Milton's reader to negotiate the spaces through which Satan flies, over a stretch of text in which Satan's perspective virtually monopolizes our gaze. The first strategy is to attend to the outer frame controlled by the narrator, who corrects Satan's crooked observations with more 'objective' comments, similes, and interjections. The second strategy is to adopt a sacramental attitude by accepting the Son as Word, creatively disposing Milton's imaginative world, while Satan has made it his rule to reject God's providence. Yet, even in Milton's embroiled Chaos, through which Satan scrabbles towards Heaven's Gate, Chaos is defined, when Satan and Sin first set eyes upon it, by the absent presence of the Logos's becalming and ordering hand. Chaos's domain is a 'dark / Illimitable Ocean without bound, / Without dimension, where length, bredth, and highth, / And time and place are lost' (2.891–94). The narrator's description of Chaos alludes to the Pauline passage on the Son's loving *pleroma* or 'plenitude', maintaining the cosmos as the head governs the body, as the foundation supports the building or, in Raphael's allegory, as the root sustains a tree or plant.[30] In all three extended metaphors Christ fits and coalesces his members, even while those members make for the growth and edification of themselves in love:

> For Christ may make his home in your hearts through faith, you who are rooted and founded in love, so that you may be exceptionally strong to grasp intellectually,

---

[28] The young Milton described 'Envy's twisted glance with its goatish, sideways look [*Invidiaeque acies transverso tortilis hirquo*]' (*Ad Patrem* 106). The Latin *hircus* can refer to squinting from the corner of one's eye.

[29] *Seriatim*: On Satan's beholding the sun, 'O thou that with surpassing Glory crownd' (4.32–113); gazing at Adam and Eve, 'O Hell! what doe mine eyes with grief behold' (4.358–92), and 'Sight hateful, sight tormenting!' (4.505–35); sighting Paradise, 'O Earth, how like to Heav'n' (9.99–178); and ogling at Eve, 'Thoughts, whither have ye led me' (9.473–93).

[30] For Milton, these two terms are interchangeable. Milton's narrator calls the Tree of Life 'that life-giving Plant' (4.199).

together with the saints, what is the breadth and length and height and depth [of Christ's love] and to know Christ's love, which surpasses knowledge, so that you may be filled with all of God's fullness.   (Eph. 3:17–18)

The infinite dimensions of the Son's love are absent from this chaotic scene of uncreation. Here, in this thankless place, 'length, bredth, and highth . . . are lost'. Two lines earlier, the narrator refers to the Pauline epistle's description of depth in 'the hoarie Deep' (2.891). Milton's Chaos embodies real bathos, the ontological nadir next to the splendours of Creation. The chaotic dregs churning at the bottom of the cosmos are chronically unordered, untouched, and unrefined by the Son's harmonizing hand. What signifies to Satan only a turbulent crossing actually constitutes a maelstrom signally unhallowed by the Son's composing and compassionate touch.

In *Areopagitica* Milton clusters the traditional images of Christ's mystical body to defend the stability of an infinitely varied Church, should there be a reformation of Reformation itself. Milton adopts the Pauline metaphors of Christ's body both as a building and as a plant. As a building or temple, Christ's body demonstrates 'perfection', a 'goodly and gracefull symmetry that commends the whole pile and structure' (*CPW* 2.555–56). To the image of the Christic plant Milton adds Satan's ridicule of the project: 'The adversarie again applauds, and waits the hour. when they have brancht themselves out, saith he, small anough into parties and partitions, then will be our time. Fool! [Satan] sees not the firm root out of which we all grow, through into branches' (*CPW* 2.555–56). Milton rebuts by asserting Satan's blindness before the cornerstone, foundation, or 'firm root' of the Son. Milton's illustration indicates how, as early as 1644, he was confidently developing his sacramental hermeneutic. For, as with the allegorical portents of Satan's journey, the reader must actively participate in Milton's allegories to supply the Son's identity upon which Milton's ideal Church body is established.[31]

IV

Book Three's prose 'Argument' furnishes an itinerary of key sites visited throughout Satan's cosmic flight: '*The Limbo of Vanity*', '*the Gate of Heaven, describ'd ascending by stairs*', and '*the Orb of the Sun*'. The first of these spaces, Milton's 'Paradise of Fools' (3.496), is a frequent point of embarrassment for critics. Dr Johnson savaged it. Addison deplored it. Richard Bentley believed it was a rude, unMiltonic interpolation perpetrated by an obtrusive editor. Merritt Hughes salvaged Milton's Fools' Paradise from its demeaned status as 'an outcropping of religious bigotry blocking the channel of epic narrative', and Roy Flannagan conceded, 'It is obviously satire, it is propaganda, and it is out of place – except that it is in a satiric setting.'[32] In addition to complementing Satan's crazed flight, Milton's Limbo has its own theology. Described

---

[31] For Satan's flight as an extended allegory, see Borris, 'Cosmic Journey', 101–33.

[32] Merritt Y. Hughes, 'Milton's Limbo of Vanity', in *Th' Upright Heart*, 9; Roy Flannagan, 'Reflections on Milton and Ariosto', *Early Modern Literary Studies*, 2.3 (1996), 4.15 (published online 16 Dec. 1996) <http://purl.oclc.org/emls/02–3/flanmilt.html> accessed 21 Nov. 2009.

as 'a *Limbo*' (3.440–97), its name plays upon the Latinate meaning of *Limbus* as a 'Borderland', an outpost of Chaos situated at the edge of the world's outermost orb and not, as Catholic tradition holds, along Hell's rim. Milton owes much to Ariosto's account of the English paladin Astolfo's quest to the Moon of Lost Things, in which John the Divine accompanies the knight to retrieve Orlando's wits. Milton's relocation of Ariosto's 'Paradise of Fools' from the 'argent Fields' of 'the neighbouring Moon' (3.459–60) testifies to Milton's acknowledged literary debt, as does Milton's adoption of Ariosto's leitmotif of lunar vacuity and vanity. Milton's anti-Catholic congeries of 'Reliques, Beads, / Indulgences, Dispenses, Pardons, Bulls, / The sport of Winds' (3.491–93) complements Ariosto's own anti-clerical cluttering of his moonscape.[33] But, much more than the lunatic fringe of Ariosto's satirical allegory, although Milton's Limbo resembles a cipher – there are 'None yet' (3.444) and the region remains 'now unpeopl'd, and untrod' (3.497) – still, *Paradise Lost*'s 'windie Sea of Land' (3.440) represents a circumscribed zone in Milton's cosmography, akin to the antechamber of Dante's *Inferno* with which, quite aptly, Milton's *Commonplace Book* compares Ariosto's Moon (*CPW* 1.418).[34]

Amid these abortive future enterprises the narrator offers one single spatio-temporal constant, namely the creating Word's present absence within this Limbo. The Son's present absence reverses the rhetorical effect and reinforces the same providential point as the absent presence of Christ in Chaos. I am referring to the vignette of pilgrims 'that strayd so farr to seek / In *Golgotha* him dead, who lives in Heav'n' (3.476–77).[35] The figures thronging this vacuity have spent their lives groping vainly for a guarantee of their own immortality, for 'fond hopes of Glorie or lasting fame' (3.449). The narrator lists the tyrant Nimrod and the builders of Babel, who strove to construct for themselves a reputation; the frenzied acquisitioning of expiatory indulgences and pardons; the habiting of dying sinners who hope to steal their way into Heaven; the Greek philosophers Empedocles, who sought apotheosis by hurling himself into Etna's crater, and Cleombrotus, who, intoxicated by Plato's treatise *On the Soul*, drowned himself in the hope of laying eyes on the Elysian fields. The hubbub of their futile activity, all the more a blustery nullity because their persons do not yet exist to inhabit the actual time of

[33] Milton singles out from the dust-heap on Ariosto's moon the Donation of Constantine to Sylvester and a meagre mess of porridge that symbolizes the sum of an average human life's parsimonious alms-giving (*CPW* 1.418, 559–60). Ariosto's other objects of oblivion include dominion, reputation, and wealth, but also innumerable prayers and vows, lovers' sighs and tears, time squandered in gambling, chronic indolence, fruitless plans, flatteries, patronizing verses, ponderous and violated treaties, and frivolous trysts. See Ludovico Ariosto, *Orlando Furioso*, trans. Guido Waldman (Oxford, 1974), 419; Canto 34.68–92.

[34] Irene Samuel compares Milton's Limbo with Renaissance commentary surrounding the third canto of Dante's *Inferno* in *Dante and Milton: The Commedia and 'Paradise Lost'* (Ithaca, 1966), 85–93.

[35] Could there be an implied debunking here of Tasso's *Gerusalemme Liberata*? Tasso's epic celebrates Godfrey's liberation of Christ's Sepulchre in Jerusalem and the carving of an open passage for pilgrims, a chivalric deed and an epic subject that Milton, judging by his treatment of the pilgrim fools of Limbo, would have found at the very least inconsequential, if not unheroic. Tasso's exordium promises, 'I sing the reverent armies, and that Chief / who set the great tomb of our Savior free' (canto 1.1.1–2): *Jerusalem Delivered; Gerusalemme Liberata*, ed. and trans. Anthony M. Esolen (Baltimore, 2000), 17.

Satan's flight, acts as a foil to the reality of the Son's exalted presence at God's right hand.

When Milton's reader encounters this region, the Heavenly Council has just elucidated that the Son altruistically assumes mortality to secure immortality for others. The effect of the clause 'lives in Heav'n' (3.477), made vivid by its historic present tense 'lives', is to telescope the distance between the present timeframe of the journeying Satan, the commentating narrator, and Milton's attentive reader. In the poem's time, the Son now 'lives in Heav'n', for the reader has just encountered him at the Heavenly Council, offering to sacrifice himself. In the reader's time, any time after the epic's original publication of 1667, the Son, his redeeming work accomplished, now 'lives in Heav'n' to intercede for others, as Milton has Christ do in his sacerdotal role after their Fall (11.1–71). In the poem and in the sacramental reader's formulation of history, the Son's session 'at Gods right hand, exalted high / Above all names in Heav'n' (12.457–58) is the only enduring reality and the single solidity in a space destined for 'this Worlds dissolution' (3.459). For Satan, the Fools' Paradise is neither an evanescent Limbo nor a parodic contrast to the Son's securing of an everlasting habitation for humankind. Instead, all Satan can experience are the scatological 'Aereal vapours' (3.445) blown 'ore the backside of the World farr off' (3.494). Disconsolate and gracelorn, Satan bears an incoiling and desolate psyche as, in Milton's pleonasm, he 'Walkd up and down alone bent on his prey, / Alone' (3.441–42).

V

The spectacle of the cosmic Ladder, a scalar 'Structure high' (3.503) providing a vertical passage from the lip of Heaven's Gate to 'the blissful seat of Paradise' (3.527), does not function as a simile, but demarcates the passage of grace from Heaven to Earth. There is a misprision in Christopher Ricks's determination that the Ladder operates as a disjunctive simile contrasting Satan as 'the arch-enemy of God' with Jacob as God's 'chosen hand', a simile that 'forces' the reader 'to choose between damaging irrelevance, or likeness turning grimly into disparity'.[36] The reader is told that 'The Stairs were such as whereon' (3.510) Jacob beheld the travelling angels 'And waking cri'd, This is the Gate of Heav'n' (3.515), a claim denominating a specific structure in its replication of Jacob's deictic biblical exclamation: 'How dreadful is this place! this *is* none other than the house of God, and this *is* the gate of heaven' (*AV* Gen. 28:17). Alastair Fowler comments that Milton is comparing Satan's impious indifference with Jacob's pious awe before the same phenomenon (Fowler's note on 3.510–15). Satan has little reverence for either Heaven's frontispiece or its Ladder. Inaugurated as the primal fool in Milton's Fools' Paradise, Satan does reach 'the lower stair', whereas future fools will be blown transverse when 'at foot / Of Heav'ns ascent they lift thir Feet'

---

[36] Christopher Ricks, *Milton's Grand Style* (Oxford, 1963), 128.

(3.485–86). Satan's access to the structure is denied and the Ladder's extension 'aggravate[s] / His sad exclusion from the dores of Bliss' (3.524–25). Satan's relation to the stairs is ruthlessly utilitarian and pragmatic. He literally turns his back on the celestial marvel, here reduced to the status of a ledge affording Satan a prospect of the new world he is bent on destroying. The 'wonder' (3.542, 552) Satan feels at this 'goodly prospect' (3.548) is shortly marred by 'envy' (3.553). Satan misses the fact that the Ladder affords a channel for God's grace, a means for God's angelic emissaries to aid His creatures (3.526–39), and, in postlapsarian times, for the Son to descend as *theanthropos* and ascend in triumph after his resurrection.

There is more to this almost emblematic scene than Satan's reprobation. C. A. Patrides and George Whiting have rehabilitated the many typological expositions of Jacob's Ladder as symbolizing the traffic of prayers, the way of salvation, the *scala mundi*, Christ's descent from the cross, the soul's climb to perfection, and the Messianic genealogy.[37] One particular interpretation, the Ladder as a fore-shadowing of Christ's mediation, predominates, since it enjoys biblical warrant. Milton's earliest commentators, such as Patrick Hume, were aware that 'Christ indeed may well be represented by this Heavenly Ladder, for by him not only the angels, but all the Saints and faithful Servants of God, (who in Heaven shall be like the Angels, *Matth.* 22. Vers. 30) *do ascend and descend*, that is, have free access to God, and the Throne of Grace, and attain by his Merits Everlasting Happiness.'[38] Hume omits the more obvious gospel intertext John 1:51, which repro-duces the biblical formula that Jacob saw 'Angels of God ascending and descending on [the Ladder]' (Gen. 28:12). Milton interpolates this Johannine phrase to read, 'whereon *Jacob* saw / Angels ascending and descending' (3.510–11). The Johannine gospel has Christ modify the Hebrew expression to incorporate himself as the mystical scalar body upon which God's creatures are transported: 'Truly, truly, I tell you, you will see Heaven opened and the angels of God ascending and descending on the Son of Man.'[39] The gospel's supplementation of 'on the Son of Man' for the Hebrew text's stark preposition *bo* or 'upon it' illustrates how the incarnate Son is the cosmic principle stretching from Heaven's giddy heights to the Earth's utter depths. Griffith Williams, William Guild, and Samuel Mather supply compendia of typological expositions of the Ladder as shadowing forth the Son's incarnate role.[40] However, Milton's Ladder does

[37] See C. A. Patrides, 'Renaissance Interpretations of Jacob's Ladder', *Theologische Zeitschrift*, 18 (1962), 411–18; George Wesley Whiting, *Milton and This Pendant World* (Austin, 1958), 59–87.

[38] Patrick Hume, ed., *The Poetical Works of Mr. John Milton* (London, 1695), on 3.516.

[39] In biblical Hebrew, *'we-hineh malachey elohim olim we-yoredim bo'*; literally, 'and behold! Angels of God ascending and descending on it'; and, in Greek, 'τοὺς ἀγγέλους τοῦ θεοῦ ἀναβαίνοντας καὶ καταβαίνοντας ἐπὶ τὸν υἱὸν τοῦ ἀνθρώπου'.

[40] Williams expounds, 'the *Tree* of *Life*, the *Arke* of *Noah*, the *Ladder* of *Iacob*, the *Mercy Seat*, the *Brazen Serpent*, and all such mysticall *Types*, and typicall *Figures* that we reade of in the Old *Testament*; what were they else but *Christ*?': Williams, *Seven Goulden Candlesticks* (London, 1624), 258. Samuel Mather interprets the Ladder as respecting '*Christ* as the means of Intercourse between God and Man[,] some dark Shadow of the *Person, Natures and Office of Christ*'. For Mather, 'There is no ascending to Heaven, but by the Spiritual Ladder Jesus Christ, no Salvation but by Christ . . . it is through Christ

more than prefigure the Son's mediation. The structure actively substantiates that intercession, since the Heavenly Council scene and *De Doctrina Christiana* establish the efficacy of the Son's sacrifice for humanity before the Fall (and, in the treatise, from before the world's foundation).

This tradition of interpreting the Ladder is ecumenical. On the basis of Jesus's personal testimony that the Ladder embodies his mediatorial office, Augustine avers:

> Christ is the ladder reaching from earth to heaven, or from the carnal to the spiritual... There is thus both an ascent and a descent upon the Son of man. For the Son of man is above as our head, being Himself the Saviour; and He is below in His body, the Church. He is the ladder, for He says, 'I am the way.' We ascend to Him to see Him in heavenly places; we descend to Him for the nourishment of His weak members. And the ascent and descent are by Him as well as to Him.[41]

For Augustine, Jacob's anointing of the stone he uses for a pillow somehow anticipates Jesus as Messiah or 'Anointed One' and, closer to Milton's epoch, the Christian Hebraist John Reuchlin (1455–1522) came to espouse this view.[42] Martin Luther endorsed Nicholas of Lyra's account that the Ladder's rungs refer to each of the Hebrew Patriarchs in the Matthean genealogy of Christ (Matt. 1:1–17), and that the angels scaling it 'refer to the revelation of the incarnation of Christ – the revelation which took place through the fathers, the prophets, and the apostles'.[43] Luther concludes that 'by means of this new picture' Jacob's epiphany enabled Abraham and Isaac to 'teach and transmit [this picture] to their descendants... and expect a Savior from their own flesh'.[44] Luther interprets, concerning the ascent and descent, 'it is this very mystery that in one and the same Person there is true GOD and man' and that 'GOD, who created all things and is above all things, is the highest and the lowest'.[45]

The Lutheran understanding of the Ladder was admired in early modern England. In a delightful exegesis of the significance of Jesus's skill as a carpenter, one of John Donne's Lenten sermons teaches, 'That that Jesus, whom they knew to be that Carpenters Son, and knew his work, must be believ'd to have set up a frame, that reached to heaven, out of which no man could, and in which any man might be saved'.[46] Again, in a homily on Jacob's vision, Donne glosses, 'God hath let fall a

that God enters into Covenant, and renews his Covenant with us': Mather, *The Figures or Types of the Old Testament* (2nd edn, London, 1705), 131–32. William Guild unfolds, '*So Christ, albeit he was humbled in shape of sinfull flesh, touching the earth as it were, yet hee was the most High God, reaching so to heauen, and reconciling, as the two natures in himselfe by personall Vnion: so God and us together by his death and mediation*, Rom 5.10'; further, 'At the foote of this Ladder, *Iacob* did repose and sleepe. *Shadowing the rest and peace of conscience, which the godly haue vnder the shadow of Christs intercession*': Guild, *Moses Unuailed* (London, 1626), 33–34, 35.

[41] Augustine, *The Writings against the Manichaeans and against the Donatists*, ed. Philip Schaff (Peabody, 2004), 192.

[42] John Reuchlin, *De Rudimentis Hebraicis* (Pforzheim, 1506), 297.

[43] Martin Luther, *Lectures on Genesis: Chapters 26–30*, ed. Jaroslav Pelikan (Saint Louis, 1968), 216.

[44] Ibid. 217.

[45] Ibid. 218–19.

[46] Donne, *Sermons*, vol. 3, 220.

ladder, a bridge between heaven, and earth, that Christ, whose divinity departed not from heaven, came downe to us into this world.'[47] Lucy Hutchinson's early Restoration poem *Order and Disorder* celebrates the Ladder in limping couplets as 'the Christian's only way, / The blessed Messiah, Heaven's gate . . . The mediator between Earth and Heaven' (19.162–63, 165):

> His merit and his intercession are alone
> The stairs by which from God's eternal throne
> His sacred ministers bring to mankind
> The sweet refreshments they from his grace find.
> (19.171–74)[48]

That the Ladder, 'Ascending by degrees magnificent' (3.502), 'That scal'd by steps of Gold to Heaven Gate' (3.541), belongs to a larger imagistic network across Milton's epic becomes clear when the terms 'degree', 'degradation', 'grade', and 'scale' are understood as wordplay upon the metaphor of the cosmos embodied in Christ as a 'Ladder' (Latin *scala*) divided into 'steps' or 'degrees' (Latin *gradus*).[49] Thus Raphael describes the cosmic order as a 'gradual scale sublim'd' (5.483), imbricated into a series of 'degree[s]' (5.490). Abdiel admonishes Satan that God's Son as Word created all things 'in thir bright degrees' (5.838). Adam speculates that humans may be promoted upon 'the scale of Nature set' (5.509) so that 'By steps we may ascend to God' (5.512). Raphael later confirms that 'Love . . . is the scale / By which to heav'nly Love thou maist ascend' (8.589, 591–92) and Adam reaffirms the doctrine that 'Love thou saist / Leads up to Heav'n, is both the way and guide' (8.612–13). The magnitude of that scale may be measured by the Son's love for Creation. Contrastingly, Satan simply does not make the grade and the degradation of 'The Fiend' (3.524) upon the stairway, as no friend to human or angel, is realized by the position of that 'Spirit maligne' (3.553) 'on the lower stair' (3.540). Conversely, God reassures the Son that he will stoop 'de-graded' several rungs on Creation's Ladder in order to save humankind:

> Nor shalt thou by descending to assume
> Mans Nature, less'n or degrade thine owne.
> Because thou hast, though Thron'd in highest bliss
> Equal to God, and equally enjoying
> God-like fruition, quitted all to save
> A World from utter loss
>
> (3.303–08)

The stairs outline a redemptive pattern where the Son participates in Creation at every level of a *scala humilitatis* so that 'Christ, reducing himself through his humiliation, passes us on the way and, through lowering himself, insures our safe

---

[47] Donne, *Sermons*, vol. 2, 226.
[48] Lucy Hutchinson, *Order and Disorder*, ed. David Norbrook (Oxford, 2001), 244.
[49] *De Doctrina* uses analogous language to describe matter admitting graded ontological 'steps [*gradus*]' (*CE* 15.20).

arrival at our unmerited destination'.[50] Don Cameron Allen has noted that the world that, from the perspective of Chaos, initially seems to be 'link't' (2.1005) or 'hanging in a gold'n Chain' (2.1051) eventually resolves itself, at Satan's closer inspection, from a suspended golden chain into the Heavenly Ladder itself.[51] The golden chain derives from Homer's *Iliad*, where Zeus's rage at his gods and goddesses' meddling in the Trojan War inflames him to dare them to a superhuman contest. The Thunderer is singly pitted against his pantheon from either end of a golden chain strung between Olympus and Heaven (*Il.* 8.19–22). Milton's celestial Ladder is a clarification of what initially appears to be a golden chain. The Son's mediatorial way, represented by the Ladder, constitutes Milton's literary and metaphysical refinement of the frolics of Homer's deities, who sport with Troy's fate in a gigantic tug-of-war.

The epic narrator further encourages a sacramental reading of the stairway when he hints, 'Each Stair mysteriously was meant' (3.516). *De Doctrina Christiana* defines the Incarnation as 'the greatest mystery [*mysterium*]' (*CE* 15.262), which accords with the Pauline tendency to reserve the word 'mystery' for the Incarnation.[52] In Milton's epic the six uses of the word 'mystery' and its cognates are traceable across one perspicacious axis of meaning, namely the generative powers of Adam and Eve that come to redemptive fruition in the Messianic line. Eden's 'mysterious parts' (4.312) denote the happy couple's organs of increase; the narrator's epithalamium praises 'the Rites / Mysterious of connubial Love' (4.742–43) and 'wedded Love, mysterious Law, true sourse / Of human ofspring' (4.750–51); and Adam pays 'mysterious reverence' to 'the genial Bed' (8.598–99). Milton's epithet 'mysterious' commonly betokens the means of grace occulted within sexual union and the Messianic genealogy culminating in '*Marie*, second *Eve*' (5.387) and Jesus 'Our second *Adam*' (11.383). The poem's final occasion for the word 'mysterious' is fittingly at the revelation of the *protevangelium*, prophesying Incarnation and redemption, 'apply'd . . . in mysterious terms' (10.172–73).

Another more ambitious device that may also subtend the Incarnational meaning of the 'mysteriously meant' stairs of Milton's cosmic Ladder is borne out by the rhetorical scheme of the *climax*, which presents a graduated blueprint for the Son's mediation across the Ladder's divisions. The *climax*, which Quintilian Latinized as *gradatio*, is named after its ladder-like arrangement of cross-hatching terms. The scheme links echoing words that mount by degrees in a parallel arrangement resembling the consecutive rungs of a ladder. The term's origin resides in the

---

[50] Stevie Davies, *Images of Kingship in 'Paradise Lost': Milton's Politics and Christian Liberty* (Columbia, 1983), 143.

[51] Allen, 'Two Notes on *Paradise Lost*', *Modern Language Notes*, 68 (1953), 360–61.

[52] The treatise gives a string of Pauline proof texts for the 'mysteriousness' of the Incarnation, including Rom. 16:25; 1 Cor. 2:7; Col. 1:26–7, 2:2–3, 4:1–4; Eph. 1:9–10, 3:4,9; and 1 Tim. 3:9, 16. Milton's early biographer John Toland demonstrates with numerous Patristic sources that the word 'mystery' refers to 'the gracious Manifestation of Christ and his Gospels': Toland, *Christianity not Mysterious* (London, 1702), 95–99 and 114ff. Francis Cheynell, Toland's disputatious answerer, concurs that New Testament instances of the word 'mystery' 'more naturally point at the *Mystery* of our Redemption, in the Incarnation of the Son of God': Cheynell, *The Christian Belief* (London, 1696), 98.

Greek *klimax* [κλῖμαξ], which translates 'ladder', the same word used in the Septuagint to designate Jacob's Ladder.[53] Not 200 lines before Satan settles upon the lower stair, Milton's God offers the Son a comprehensive scheme for human salvation through atonement in just such an elaborate, interlacing *climax*:

> As in [Adam] perish all men, so in [the Son]
> As from a second root shall be restor'd,
> As many as are restor'd, without thee none.
> [Adam's] crime makes guiltie all his Sons, [the Son's] merit
> Imputed shall absolve them who renounce
> Thir own both righteous and unrighteous deeds,
> And live in thee transplanted, and from thee
> Receive new life. So Man, as is most just,
> Shall satisfie for Man, be judg'd and die,
> And dying rise, and rising with him raise
> His Brethren, ransomd with his own dear life.
> So Heav'nly love shall outdoo Hellish hate,
> Giving to death, and dying to redeeme,
> So dearly to redeem what Hellish hate
> So easily destroyd, and still destroyes
> In those who, when they may, accept not Grace.
>
>   (3.287–302)

The first series of rungs narrates the soteriological process of Passion and resurrection (judge – die – rise – raise – ransom). At the Ladder's centre 'Heav'nly Love' outfaces 'Hellish hate' across a single line of verse. Across the *climax*'s second round Heaven claims the victory and the redemption's eschatological effect is impressed upon those creatures that accept or spurn God's grace (*die – redeem – destroy*). It behooves the reader to superimpose this *climax* expounding the Son's salvific method upon the physical scale of mysterious meanings sweeping from Heaven's Gate to Earth.

Milton's epic narrator darkly prophesies that the aperture through which the cosmic Ladder passes will diminish after the Fall.[54] Milton's Son, the archangels Raphael, Gabriel, and Michael, and lesser angels travel down this Ladder to bring counsel and succour to Adam and Eve. The scalar portal will increasingly constrict throughout human history, during the ages of Abraham, Moses, and Joshua, to the size of the Promised Land, and then, as the chosen people break faith with God, will shrink further to the proportions of the Jerusalemic Temple (3.526–39). The Heavenly Ladder, with its diachronously straitening Gate and narrowing Way, has, as its infernal counterpart, a widening gate with a broadening way in Sin and Death's construction of a facile highway for the damned. The staggeringly broad

---

[53] Other synonyms for this scheme, such as *anabasis* and *ascensus*, have soteriological nuances in Christian theology, reinforcing the idea that the Son's mediation between God and humanity works by processes of humiliation and exaltation.

[54] Harry F. Robins, 'Satan's Journey: Direction in *Paradise Lost*', *Journal of English and Germanic Philology*, 60 (1961), 699–711.

dimensions of Hell's Gate, from which the causeway proceeds, is the keynote
sounded when Sin opens wide Hell's doors:

> the Gates wide op'n stood
> That with extended wings a Bannerd Host
> Under spred Ensigns marching might pass through
> With Horse and Chariots rankt in loose array;
> So wide they stood
>
> (2.884–88)

Sin and Death's overpass contends with the Heavenly Ladder for the purchase of
human souls, since the 'ridge of pendent Rock' (10.313) gains ingress into God's
Creation, 'to the self same place where [Satan] / First lighted from his Wing, and
landed safe / From out of *Chaos* to the outside bare / Of this round World'
(10.315–18). Book Ten's iteration of this phrase from Book Three, when Satan
plants his 'willing feet / On the bare outside of this World' (3.73–74), emphasizes
the scope of Satan's gaze at this point, the Ladder of Heaven sweeping through 'the
op'ning' (3.538) in the world's shell. The aperture in the world's rind is a junction
for Heaven's stair and Hell's mole. The gospel source is Jesus's teaching on the
rough, hard way to earn God's grace: 'Enter ye in at the strait gate: for wide *is* the
gate, and broad *is* the way, that leadeth to destruction, and many there be which go
in thereat: Because strait *is* the gate, and narrow *is* the way, which leadeth unto life;
and few there be that find it' (*AV* Matt. 7:13–14). A broad, smooth, and high way
has pejorative connotations in Milton's early poetry, and Milton's 'Bridge of
wondrous length' (2.1028), interrupting Chaos and spanning Earth and Hell,
conforms to this 'broad and beat'n way' (2.1026) and supplies 'Spirits perverse /
With easie intercourse' (2.1030–31).[55] The infernal bridge offers 'a passage broad, /
Smooth, easie, inoffensive down to Hell' (10.304–05), and Satan gloats that 'By
Sin and Death a broad way now is pav'd' (10.473). Now that Sin and Death's crude
construction obtrudes upon this opening, a 'new wondrous Pontifice' (10.348) has
been founded 'by wondrous Art / Pontifical' (10.312–13). This pontifical pun,
aside from its low anti-Papist barb, makes the Hellish causeway a mock of the
Ladder that bodies forth the archetypal bridge-builder, *Christus mediator*. *De
Doctrina Christiana* styles one of the Son of God's mediatorial functions, along
with his priestly role and resurrection, that of the reconciliatory *pontifex* or 'bridge-
builder' (Latin *pons* + *facere*), a word John Carey imprecisely translates as 'priesthood' (*CPW* 6.208; *CE* 14.184). The poem's cosmos presents Milton's reader with
two antithetical forms of mediation – devilish vagabonds preying over the black
bridge between Hell and Earth and the Son's gentle condescension upon the
Golden Ladder reaching from the shining Heavens to this dim spot.

---

[55] In Sonnet Nine (*c.* 1643) Milton praises his 'Lady' (1) for having 'shun'd the broad way and the
green' (2), the enticing 'paths of all that forget God' (Job 8:12–13). In *Ad Patrem* (*c.* 1632) Milton
thanks his father for permitting him to serve 'the slender muses' and forgo that worldly path 'on which
the road stretches out broadly [*Qua via lata patet*], where the ground is more inclined to one's
advantage, and the certain, golden hope of producing ready cash shines forth' (67–70).

VI

During his voyage Satan is repeatedly drawn to 'the sacred influence / Of light' (2.1034–35), the 'glimmering dawn' (2.1037), and 'a gleame / Of dawning light' (3.499–500), until the light's source manifests itself once Satan enters the world's shell and sees 'The gold'n Sun in splendor likest Heaven [that] / Allur'd his eye' (3.572–73). Despite Satan's attraction to this solar, 'all-chearing Lamp' (3.581) that draws the surrounding stars into its presence, Satan meets the heavenly body 'Undazl'd' (3.614) and treats it with loathing and contempt in his Niphates speech. For Philip Gallagher, this scene, in which Satan assumes a cherub's guise to exploit Uriel's knowledge of Eden's whereabouts, exculpates Eve from her deception: 'Since his "goodness thinks no ill / Where no ill seems" (688–89), the angel bright cannot even suspect Satan, much less penetrate his disguise'; 'the beguiling of Uriel is *the* paradigm of sinless deception'.[56] A further aspect to Uriel's deception suggests itself. As Gabriel notes, Uriel's 'perfet sight' (4.577) in the sun's vantage makes him 'The sharpest sighted Spirit of all in Heav'n' (3.691), and yet the sun 'sharp'n'd [Satan's] visual ray / To objects distant farr' (3.620–21), presumably refining his vision from its former state. The narrator emphasizes Satan's 'visual ray' and dwells upon the ideal physical conditions for visibility while Satan stands in the sun. Satan's eye commands 'farr and wide' and is impeded by 'no obstacle' or 'shade' (3.614–15). The noonday sun stands at its meridian over the equator (compare 10.672) and 'the Aire, / [is] No where so cleer' (3.619–20). These ideal climatic factors imply that Satan lacks something perceptually. The narrator's sermonological excursus upon the angelic and human inability to discern hypocrisy applies to Satan as well as to Uriel (3.681–91). When Satan perches upon Heaven's lowest stair and the aperture's rim, he uses each prospect as a vantage point and overlooks its intrinsic significance. Similarly, the sun, like Uriel, serves as a beacon in Satan's voyage towards Eden, his destination. The angelologist Henry Lawrence reasoned that fallen angels never see God as upright angels do, but rather that 'what they see, they see but by halfe lights'.[57] Milton's narrator protests too much about Satan's vision, clarified by the sun, so that the reader understandably forgets that Satan's spiritual perception is confined 'within kenn' (3.622). A double meaning may apply to the invisibility of the sun's virtuous effects that 'to each inward part / With gentle penetration, though unseen, / Shoots invisible vertue eev'n to the Deep' (3.584–86). Once spread into distant and inward parts, the sun's rays may escape the eye of the beholder and therefore be 'unseen' and 'invisible', but, equally, Satan is undazzled by the sun's glories, with his attention bent upon corrupting Eden.

Kenneth Borris details the ramifications of Satan's aberrant behaviour after he arrives at this splendid location:

---

[56] Philip J. Gallagher, *Milton, the Bible, and Misogyny*, ed. Eugene R. Cunnar and Gail L. Mortimer (Columbia, 1990), 54–55.

[57] Henry Lawrence, *An History of Angells, Being A Theologicall TREATISE of our Communion and Warre with them* (London, 1649), 29 and 61.

The solar setting, a marvelous realm of especial perceptual clarity (III, 694–707), implicitly rebukes the satanic enterprise. The sun had long commonly symbolized enlightenment, and also Christ or Christian truth, essential for Miltonic wisdom. Here Satan's epistemological perversity stands most brightly revealed because he undertakes his demonic 're-connaissance' of the poem's cosmos only for destructive vengeance against its proper ultimate object for created intellect, God.[58]

The Renaissance conjunction of the homonym Son–sun is a commonplace. Peter Sterry paeans 'the Lord Jesus in his spiritual Glories' as 'the *Original* form of the Sun, the *Suns Sun*'.[59] This conceit activates strong Christological resonances throughout *Paradise Lost* and especially when Satan lands upon the sun. On the first day of Milton's hexaemeron the Son, acting as God's agent of Creation, draws from the Deep 'Ethereal Light', that 'quintessence pure' (7.244) or rarefied fifth element, and next lodges it 'in a cloudie Tabernacle' (7.248). On the fourth day the Son retrieves 'the greater part' of this luminous deposit, 'Transplanted from her cloudie Shrine' (7.359–60), so that the porous mould of the Sun's orb might 'drink the liquid Light' (7.362). The marvellous image of entabernacled light derives from Psalm 19, a Creation Psalm where, 'In [the Heavens] hath [God] set a tabernacle for the sun' (*AV* Ps. 19:4), but the image carries over into Johannine Christology too. The Johannine gospel's induction, from its opening words 'In the beginning', is deliberately structured after the Creation narrative in Genesis 1. The induction celebrates the Son as the preexistent Word who was with God in the beginning and through whom all things were created (John 1:1–2). The Son is figured as 'the light of humanity', a light shining in darkness that darkness did not grasp, and 'a true light which enlightens every human' and 'was coming into the world' (John 1:4–5). This allusion to the Incarnation is sustained in a refigured image of the Son, when 'the Word became flesh and was entabernacled' (John 1:14). The etymology of the Greek ἐσκήνωσεν or 'entabernacled' stems from the idea of being placed in a tent or tabernacle, much as the sun's source in Milton's hexaemeron and Psalm 19 is entabernacled light, and much as the Johannine Son, the Light of the World, is entabernacled or enfleshed. Accordingly, in *Paradise Regain'd* Jesus is 'enshrin'd / In fleshly Tabernacle, and human form' (*PR* 4.598–99). In the poem's first chronological association with Creational light or sunshine Milton assembles powerful Christological metaphors.

When Satan alights on the sun's surface, the narrator stresses his estrangement from its beauty by comparing Satan's reaction to the spot on which he lands and the place which an 'Astronomer in the Suns lucent Orbe / Through his glaz'd Optic Tube yet never saw' (3.589–90). As in the comparison between Satan's vision of Creation and the scout's admiration for the golden city, the phenomenon Satan could enjoy, had he the eyes to see, excels in wondrousness what the human astronomer strains to sight through his telescope. Furthermore, the astronomer is more distant from the sun than Satan and his vision is mediated through a fragile,

---

[58] Borris, 'Journey', 118.
[59] Sterry, *Discourse*, 39.

inaccurate instrument, a telescope with a 'glaz'd' or blurred lens. Even so, the astronomer's contemplation of the sun, despite his imperfect gaze, surpasses Satan's, even though Satan's privileged vision is one that the astronomer 'never saw'. The narrator's subsequent four analogies arise from a comparison between the sun's status, 'beyond expression bright, / Compar'd with aught on Earth, Mettal or Stone' (3.591–92). Satan has never travelled to Earth before; he is visiting Eden for the first time. Consequently, he is ill equipped to make such comparisons, so that the focalizer for these four analogies remains the astronomer. This perspectival shift thus matches the astronomer's thought-world and experiential frame of reference, the perception of a fallen, imperfect human, with the reader's own perspective. Satan is excluded from such a perspective, since the arch-fiend, self-deceived, meets the marvellous solar 'matter new to gaze . . . Undazl'd' (3.613–14).

Milton's four similes liken the sun's matter to earthly metals (a glowing lump of iron; a gold and silver alloy) and precious stones (the jewels set in Aaron's breastplate; the philosopher's stone). All four analogies are strong Incarnational metaphors, deriving from Patristic thought and Protestant theology and poetics, that aid explanation as to how the Son's divinity mysteriously partakes of humanity and how, as with Milton's sun, in the incarnate Son's person there are 'Not all parts like, but all alike informd / With radiant light' (3.593–94). *Paradise Lost* imagines the Son's substance as visions of light when divine virtue is transferred from the Father to the Son (3.62–64, 138–43, 383–89; 6.680–84, 719–22; 7.194–96; 10.63–67; *PR* 1.91–93). I have shown elsewhere how the two analogies of the 'glowing Iron with fire' (3.594) and the electrum or amalgam that 'part seemd Gold, part Silver cleer' (3.595), succeed as Incarnational metaphors.[60] The glowing iron occurs in Origen's *On First Principles* where Christ's 'soul which, as if it were iron in a fire, is placed always in the word, always in wisdom, always in God, is God in everything it does [and], by being ceaselessly charged with fire, possesses permanence from its unity with the word of God'.[61] According to Origen, at the Incarnation the Son's humanity is suffused with the glory of his divinity, just as Milton's sun appears to be 'all Sun-shine' (3.616). Tertullian used his amalgam conceit to rebut the Monarchian 'heretic' Praxeas, and we noted above how Milton's Satan propounds this Monarchian heresy. Tertullian regards the Son's hypostatic union as both unified and separate in its divine and human natures. He maintains that the image of a substance naturally occurring through the fusion of two metals, when properly applied to the Incarnation, allows for two distinct natures, even while it produces a new and unique third nature in the amalgam:

> Jesus will now be one substance made from two substances, from flesh and spirit, a kind of mixture, as electrum is made from gold and silver, and it grows to be neither gold, that is, spirit, nor silver, that is, flesh, since one metal is changed by another metal, and some third thing is produced . . . And so out of two substances one thing is produced which is neither the one nor the other, but a third something, very different

---

[60] See my note, 'Two Patristic Sources for John Milton's Description of the Sun (*Paradise Lost* 3.591–95)', *Notes and Queries*, 53 (2006), 185–87.

[61] Origen, *Opera Omnia*, vol. 11 (Berlin, 1847), *De Principiis*, Book 2.6.6.

from either... We see a twofold mode of being, not confused but conjoined in one person, Jesus, who is God and a human.[62]

Milton was not alone in adopting Tertullian's electrum image. Brian Walton included John Baptista Villalpandus's commentary *Explanations on Ezekiel* (1596–1604) in his monumental *Biblia Sacra Polyglotta* (1655–1657). As the Council of State's censor, Milton condoned Walton's scholarly efforts by personally petitioning Parliament to grant Walton the right to publish his polyglot Bible.[63] Villalpandus conflates Origen and Tertullian's images in a chapter entitled 'On the Electrum [or Amber] Immersed in Fire'. He writes how, 'The ignited electrum,... because of the mixture of silver with gold, signifies Christ the Lord, in whom there is a divine and human nature.'[64]

The third analogy, 'the Twelve that shon / In *Aarons* Brest-plate' (3.597–98), refers primarily to Exodus 28, where Jehovah mandates to Moses the twelve precious stones encrusting, in four rows of three, the high priest Aaron's breastplate, and the placing of the mantic stones Urim and Thummim 'upon Aaron's heart' (Exod. 28:30). Christian typology had biblical precedent from Hebrews for deeming Jesus an archetypal high priest (Heb. 4:14–5:10) and it correspondingly associated Aaron's breastplate with Jesus's person. Thomas Taylor, a contemporary of Milton's at Christ's College, Cambridge, reflected that, since *Urim* was the Hebrew word for 'Lights', it could signify the Son, who 'is the sun, nay he is lights'; and that *Thummim*, meaning 'Perfections', also designated Jesus, who 'is perfection in all parts'.[65] As the breastplate served as an oracular medium for Israel to communicate with Jehovah, so the Son intercedes between God and God's creatures, 'as to whom all secrets and Mysteries are perfectly knowne... For as the Oracle by Urim was certaine for direction: so Christ is the most perfect rule and direction shadowed by that.'[66] During the War in Heaven the Son enters the fray wearing an oracular breastplate to execute the Father's will, 'in Celestial Panoplie all armd / Of radiant *Urim*' (6.760–61), and, in *Paradise Regain'd*, Satan flatters Jesus about the divine intimacy of his 'Counsel [that] would be as the Oracle / *Urim* and *Thummim*, those oraculous gems / On *Aarons* brest' (*PR* 3.13–15).

Milton's fourth and final analogy is alchemical and compares the sun with the philosopher's stone. Stanton Linden has delineated a tradition that analogized the philosopher's stone with Christ and linked the perceived powers of the stone and the God-man to regenerate, respectively, dull and base metals or sinful human flesh. Linden demonstrates that before John Donne and George Herbert's devotional poetry alchemical discourse had ordinarily served the ends of poetic satire and burlesque, but that the 'Metaphysical' poets harnessed alchemical reference, simile, and allusion to denote the transformative operation of grace upon the human spirit

---

[62] *Adversus Praxean Liber*, ed. and trans. Ernest Evans (London, 1948), 124; section 27.

[63] See Barbara K. Lewalski, *The Life of John Milton* (Oxford, 2003), 288 and 634 [fn.52].

[64] Jerome de Prado and John Baptista Villalpandus, *In Ezechielem Explanationes et Apparatus Urbis, ac Templi Hierosolymitani*, vol. 1 (Rome, 1596–1604), 52: '*Electrum ignitum... propter mistionem argenti cum auro, significat Christum Dominum, in quo est divina et humana natura.*'

[65] Thomas Taylor, *Christ Revealed* (London, 1635), 120.

[66] Ibid., 120–21.

and the Protestant process of conversion within the repentant sinner.[67] In Donne's
'The Father', the first section of his long poem 'The Litanie', the speaker asks to be
restored, that 'From this red earth, O Father, purge away / All vicious tinctures, that
new fashioned / I may rise up from death, before I'm dead' (7–9).[68] In 'Resurrection, Imperfect' Christ, who 'was all gold when he lay downe' in death, 'rose / All
tincture' at his resurrection and, possessing this tincture or quality of transmuting
base matter, he can not only 'dispose / Leaden and iron wills to good, but is / Of
power to make even sinfull flesh like his' (13–16).[69] Herbert's 'Easter' likewise re-
appropriates alchemy to convey the transforming effects of Christ's death and
resurrection upon others who 'likewise / With him mayst rise: / That, as his
death calcined thee to dust, / His life may make thee gold, and much more, just'
(3–6).[70] Robert Herrick wrote a slight, though grave, verse entitled 'Sin' in which
God, the Chemist of chemists, distils good from evil through an alembic:

> There is no evill that we do commit,
> But hath th' extraction of some good from it:
> As when we sin; God, the great *Chymist*, thence
> Drawes out th'*Elixar* of true penitence.
>
>   (1–4)[71]

The most heavily sustained use of alchemical terminology to convey spiritual
regeneration is probably Herbert's 'The Elixir':

> All may of thee partake:
> Nothing can be so mean,
> Which with his tincture (for thy sake)
> Will not grow bright and clean.
>
> A servant with this clause
> Makes drudgerie divine:
> Who sweeps a room, as for thy laws,
> Makes that and th' action fine.
>
> This is the famous stone
> That turneth all to gold:
> For that which God doth touch and own
> Cannot for lesse be told. (13–24)[72]

[67] See Stanton J. Linden, *Darke Hierogliphicks: Alchemy in English Literature From Chaucer to the Restoration* (Lexington, 1996), 34–35, 154–55, 188–92, 214–19. I refer throughout to Linden's selection of alchemical examples from Herbert and Donne's poetry.
[68] John Donne, *The Complete Poetry and Selected Prose of John Donne*, ed. Charles M. Coffin (New York, 2001), 249.
[69] Ibid. 247.
[70] Herbert, 41–42.
[71] Robert Herrick, *Poems*, ed. L. C. Martin (London, 1971), 386.
[72] Herbert, 184–85.

Janis Lull builds upon Richard Strier's appreciation of the importance of justification by faith for Herbert's thought and recognizes that Herbert's parenthetical
phrase '(for thy sake)' encodes Christ's utterance and embodies the 'clause' denoting his vicarious sacrifice, 'the elixir' with which believers' deeds and spiritual states
are made 'divine'.[73] Like that 'famous stone / That turneth all to gold', the Son
makes the meanest person 'bright and clean' in God's sight. Christ's sacrifice
making 'th' action fine' 'is a complex pun reflecting both "the tincture" that
makes base things fine and Christ's sacrifice that "puts fine" to the action (for
debt) brought against humanity by the Old Testament God'.[74]

Milton's philosopher's stone analogy develops this trend in religious verse of
equating the alchemical process with the Christian scheme of regeneration through
the Son. In Raphael's hexaemeron the sun is a 'Fountain' whence the stars 'in thir
gold'n Urns draw Light' and the moon 'guilds his horns' so that, by the sun's
'tincture' (7.364–69), the celestial bodies become burnished gold. In the last and
most extensive of Milton's four analogies the sun is compared with:

> a stone besides
> Imagind rather oft then elsewhere seen,
> That stone, or like to that which here below
> Philosophers in vain so long have sought,
> In vain,
>
> .   .   .   .
>
> Draind through a Limbec to his Native forme.
> What wonder then if fields and regions here
> Breathe forth *Elixir* pure, and Rivers run
> Potable Gold, when with one vertuous touch
> Th' Arch-chimic Sun so farr from us remote
> Produces with Terrestrial Humor mixt
> Here in the dark so many precious things
> Of colour glorious and effect so rare?
>
> (3.598–602, 605–12)

The immediate comparison is between the mythical philosopher's stone that
alchemists imagine exists rather than attest to have actually seen. The futility of
the alchemists' quest, searching 'here below' for a figment, is conveyed by the
repetitio, 'Philosophers in vain so long have sought / In vain'. The philosophers'
hopeless pursuit of the occult stone recalls those pilgrims in Milton's Fools' Paradise
'that strayd so farr to seek / In *Golgotha* him dead, who lives in Heav'n' (3.476–77).
The stone that deserts the philosophers' expectations on Earth may be 'elsewhere
seen' where it has been 'Drained through a Limbec to his Native forme.' In early
modern English the pronoun 'his' was equivalent to the indefinite pronoun 'its',
but the ambiguity suggests the Son who after his crucifixion was, in alchemical

---

[73] Janis Lull, *The Poem in Time: Reading George Herbert's Revisions of The Church* (London, 1990),
94–100; and see Clarence H. Miller, 'Christ as the Philosopher's Stone in George Herbert's "The
Elixir"', *Notes and Queries*, 45 (1998), 39–41.

[74] Ibid. 97.

terms, 'Draind through a Limbec' or resurrected, purified, and restored 'to his Native forme', exalted at God's side. Milton's epithet 'Native' may even retain a Latinate pun upon Christ's Sonship from the Latin word *natus*.

Linden reads Milton's description of lands perfumed with elixir and rivers flowing with drinkable or 'Potable Gold' as indicative of solar sites, but the anaphora of 'here below', 'here', and 'Here in the dark' designates the Earth. In particular, the description designates the Earth as seen from the astronomer's and the reader's own fallen perspectives, darkened by sin.[75] Milton's reader may associate the virtuous action of the sun's influence with the transmuting property of the philosopher's stone and, governing these two ideas, with the regenerative effects of the 'Arch-chimic' Son's intercession for humankind radiating from Heaven. Linden cites two other instances in *Paradise Lost* that may interpret the Son's fulfilment of his duties as a mighty chemist or alchemist. First, Linden notes Raphael's allegorical Plant through which terrestrial creatures, engrafted upon Christ's exalted body, advance to a spiritual state and are 'more refin'd, more spiritous, and pure' (5.475) and 'sublim'd' (5.483). Second, Michael predicts how at the *eschaton* Christ, 'Now amplier known thy Saviour and thy Lord', will chemically distil the old, sinful corruptions and 'dissolve' and 'raise / From the conflagrant mass, purg'd and refin'd', a New Heaven and Earth (12.546–48). As the sun shines upon the Earth, converting 'Terrestrial Humor' into gold 'with one vertuous touch', so the Son, exalted to his 'Native forme', operates with his spiritual alchemy of grace to regenerate the hearts and minds of believers upon Earth, 'Here in the dark'.

'Potable Gold' is the closest transliteration Milton could render for the *aurum potabile* of alchemy. Under Paracelsus alchemy evolved from being a search for the means of transmuting objects into gold into a quest for drinkable gold, a substance believed to be a panacea, offering the remedy for all diseases and housing the properties for creating the elixir of life. Milton's alchemical analogy may further allude to the *Treatise of Aurum Potabile* (1656), an alchemical–theological work attributed to the physician, herbalist, and astrologer Nicholas Culpeper. The treatise schematizes three levels of reality, the 'Elimentary', 'Celestiall', and 'Intellectual, or Aetheriall'.[76] One discipline is regnant over each level: 'Naturall Philosophy' over the Elementary sphere, 'Astrology' over the Sun, and 'Divinity' over the Ethereal. Each level has, at its centre, one presiding entity: 'In the Elementary World there is one Philosophers Stone, the instrument of all Naturall virtues, having the quintessence of the virtues of all Elementary bodies compacted in it selfe'; 'In the Celestiall World there is one Sun, the Author of Generation and preservation in the Elementary World, the giver of light, life, and motion to the Creation.'[77] To grasp the Ethereal level 'in and to the Processe of the Aur[um] Potabile is required a serious Active and Contemplative Spirit'.[78] The treatise's final

---

[75] Linden, *Darke Hierogliphicks*, 252–53.
[76] [Nicholas Culpeper?], *Treatise of Aurum Potabile, Being A Description of The Three-fold World Viz. Elimentary, Celestiall, Intellectual* (London, 1656).
[77] Ibid. 161–62.
[78] Ibid.

chapters enumerate 'What points in Divinity must be practiced such as intend the attainment of *Aurum Potabile*'. These doctrinal heads centre upon 'The restitution of Man, and his being united to the God-head, by the person of Jesus Christ, who took part both of God and man [and] thereby man is brought into an Estate far above the Angels'.[79] Milton's reader needs only to ascend from the simile of the 'Elementary' philosopher's stone and the potable gold to the 'Celestiall' Sun to perceive the solar orb as an analogy for the 'Aetheriall' Godhead and the incarnate Son's radiant person.

According to this hermeneutic, the sun's radiance that 'to each inward part / With gentle penetration, though unseen, / Shoots invisible vertue eev'n to the Deep' (3.584–86) recalls 'the hermetic images of the dove brooding over the primordial waters at Creation' in 'the sun's impregnation of the universe with fructifying virtue'.[80] Linden's insight succeeds because the creating Spirit of *Paradise Lost*'s first invocation penetrates the universe's depths as it 'satst brooding on the vast Abyss / And mad'st it pregnant' (1.21–22). *De Doctrina Christiana* describes the Holy Spirit's *virtus* or 'power' proceeding from the Father through the Son as a divine power capable of suffusing the universe. William Hunter has remarked that the 'Bright effluence of bright essence increate' (3.6) fulfils a Father–Son model. So, too, Milton's depiction of the sun may present the reader with a trinal model for the Father, the Son, and the Spirit's outpouring of grace upon Creation that is similar to Hunter's Patristic metaphors of the fountain and the sun: 'For why should not the Spirit easily fill with its virtue what the sun fills with its light?' (*CE* 14.386).[81] Michael alludes to God's virtuous suffusion of the universe when he comforts a fallen Adam who pines for God's 'Presence Divine' (11.319). Michael teaches that Adam may experience God's grace throughout the cosmos, because God's 'Omnipresence fills / Land, Sea, and Aire, and every kinde that lives, / Fomented by his virtual power and warmd' (11.336–38). God's imparting of grace and humanity's participation in such 'invisible vertue' escape Satan's notice since, as the Elder Brother of *A Maske* says of the wicked:

> He that has light within his own cleer brest
> May sit i'th center, and enjoy bright day,
> But he that hides a dark soul, and foul thoughts
> Benighted walks under the mid-day Sun;
> Himself is his own dungeon.
>
>   (381–85)

To adopt an aphorism, 'Noonday is as midnight to a blind man.'[82]

---

[79] [Nicholas Culpeper?], *Treatise of Aurum Potabile*, 177–78; for the closing chapters, see 179–93. Without an appreciation for these doctrines, the treatise asserts, 'you can never attain the making of *Aurum Potabile*' (169).

[80] Linden, *Darke Hierogliphicks*, 249.

[81] The treatise enlists this comparison between the Spirit and the sun to disprove the Spirit's omnipresence. This rhetorical move in no way detracts from the positive force of the assertion that the Spirit's virtue may fill 'the compass of the Earth with all the firmament, that is, this entire world's frame' (*CE* 14.386).

[82] Samuel Taylor Coleridge, *Aids to Reflection*, ed. John Beer (London, 1993), 361. The aphorism is Archbishop Leighton's.

VII

I wish to conclude by considering Satan's devious use of the Tree of Life. Book Four's 'Argument' stresses the Tree's convenient location for Satan's plotting of his dark designs '*as highest in the Garden to look about him*'. For Satan, the Ladder and the sun are devoid of all Christological and soteriological meaning and serve pragmatic ends as ledges or projections. From these vantage points an undazzled and unimpressed Satan conspires to wreak havoc in Eden. The Tree of Life upon which Satan perches provides a ready nook for a voyeur, whence he might see 'undelighted all delight' (4.286). Satan's ignorance and the reader's need to exercise a sacramental poetics expressive of salvation are again central to an unobscured interpretation of Satan's symbolic situation:

> Thence up he flew, and on the Tree of Life,
> The middle Tree and highest there that grew,
> Sat like a Cormorant; yet not true Life
> Thereby regaind, but sat devising Death
> To them who liv'd; nor on the vertue thought
> Of that life-giving Plant, but onely us'd
> For prospect, what well us'd had bin the pledge
> Of immortalitie. So little knows
> Any, but God alone, to value right
> The good before him, but perverts best things
> To worst abuse, or to thir meanest use.
>
> (4.194–204)

Milton's earliest commentators acknowledged the potent ironies of this frozen, almost iconic moment. Jonathan Richardson expostulated, 'What a Picture is here! *Satan* Boldly Perching on the Tree of Life, He had no Regard to its Dignity, but finding it most Convenient for his Accursed Purpose Us'd it accordingly.'[83] An enquiry into the Tree's 'Dignity', its sacramental value, should make clear the symbolism of this arrested narrative moment.

In Milton's Edenic topography an unnamed 'River large' (4.223) wells up from an anonymous 'fresh Fountain' springing near the Tree of Life that 'with many a rill / Waterd the Garden' (4.229–30). The Fountain sustains all natural life in the paradisiacal enclosure. The poem's imagery intimates that this fluvial landmark is the Water of Life, the scriptural complement to the Tree of Life, since, just as 'blooming Ambrosial Fruit' (4.219) clusters down from the Tree of Life, 'Nectar' purls in the 'crisped Brooks' of the 'Saphire Fount' (4.237–41). Ambrosia and nectar were the food and drink of the classical pantheon, and these elements are concentrated in the Forbidden Tree whose 'sciential sap, deriv'd / From Nectar, drink of Gods' (9.837–38), and whose boughs 'ambrosial smell diffus'd' (9.852).[84] Milton's Eden reflects the New

---

[83] Jonathan Richardson, Jr and Sr, *Explanatory Notes*, 147; commenting upon 4.203.

[84] The epic narrator appears to suggest that the 'the Tree of Life', 'the Fount of Life,' and 'the river of Bliss', like the flower amaranth, were all 'for Mans offence / To Heav'n remov'd' (3.353–59) before the destruction of the Paradisiacal Mount at the Flood (11.829–35), to remain there until the *eschaton*.

Jerusalem destined for the saints in the vision of John of Patmos, where the Water or 'fount' of Life mirrors Milton's Eden by spreading into a river running beside the Tree of Life:

> And [the angel] showed me a river of the Water of Life, bright as crystal, flowing forth out of the throne of God and the lamb. In the middle of [the city's] street and on each side of the river stands the Tree of Life, producing twelve Fruits and yielding its Fruit each month; and the Tree's leaves are for the healing of nations.   (Rev. 22:1–2)

The identification of Milton's anonymous Fountain with the Water of Life appeals because, in Satan's second Edenic intrusion, the common enemy again perverts best things to worst abuse as when he roosted upon the Tree of Life. After Satan again decides against entrance through Eden's gates, from which all pernicious spirits are prohibited access (4.579–81), he contrives to misuse the same 'Fountain by the Tree of Life . . . In with the River sunk' (9.73–74) by exploiting the conduit as an opportune water chute along which he sneaks rather sportively into Eden.

John Steadman has examined the regard that the post-Reformation tradition had for the *arbor vitae* as a sacrament offering eternal life on the condition of obedience. Steadman favours this interpretation because of the Tree's typological importance as a symbol of eternal life, a concept dating from at least the time of Irenaeus.[85] Milton's poem bears out Steadman's reading. The Son intercedes and pleads before the Father that, until the saints' resurrection 'To better life' (11.42), a human being's 'days [might be] / Numberd, though sad, till Death' (11.39–40). God responds by directing Michael to remove Adam and Eve from Eden, partly lest with an unmerited 'bolder hand / [they] Reach also of the Tree of Life, and eat, / And live forever' (11.93–95). God's precaution forestalls humans from taking, eating, and then suffering an interminable and deathless fallen state. God also closes off 'all passage to the Tree of Life' (9.122) lest 'Spirits foule' steal its Living Fruit, 'Man once more to delude' (11.124–25). In *Paradise Regain'd* sacramentalism underlies the climactic celestial banquet, where the victorious Jesus partakes of ambrosial fruits and nectarous refreshment 'fetcht from the Tree of Life, / and from the Fount of Life' (*PR* 4.589–90), as spoils earned from Satan's defeat and his raising of Eden in the waste wilderness (*PR* 1.5–7). In Milton's brief epic the Tree of Life embodies the Christian expectation of everlasting life as an eternal reward for a patient life of Christian virtue, patterned upon Christ's example.

De Doctrina Christiana underlines the Tree of Life's sacramental associations and the Forbidden Tree's importance as a pledge of obedience. The treatise teaches concerning the Forbidden Tree that where 'the Tree of the Knowledge of Good and Evil was not a sacrament . . . because sacraments are for use, not for abstinence [*ad usum, non ad abstinentiam*]', the Forbidden Tree is 'a pledge and memorial [*pignus et monumentum*] of obedience' (*CE* 15.114). *Paradise Lost* buttresses *De Doctrina Christiana*'s position on the Forbidden Tree as, in itself, a 'thing indifferent', but as, symbolically, 'The onely sign' (4.428) and 'Sole pledge' (3.95; 8.325) of human

---

[85] John M. Steadman, 'The Tree of Life as Messianic Symbol', in *Milton's Epic Characters: Image and Idol* (Chapel Hill, 1968), 82–89.

obedience and faith. The poem's Tree of Life, however, is a 'life-giving Plant' and possesses intrinsic 'vertue'. The narrator's emphasis upon Satan's 'abuse' and 'meanest use' of the Tree conforms to *De Doctrina Christiana*'s definition of a sacrament: 'Sacraments are for use, not for abstinence.' Neither, for that matter, are they meant for abuse. Like Milton's epic, *De Doctrina Christiana* is actually more willing to attribute sacramental meaning to the Tree of Life than the treatise's previous translators have allowed for. The Latin prose reads literally, 'I do not know at all whether it should rather be called a sacrament than a symbol, or even the food of eternal life ... Revelation 2:7. *to the victor I will give to eat from the tree of life*' (*CE* 15.114).[86] The difference between Jesus's and Satan's attitudes to the Tree of Life mirrors the degree to which each perceives the Tree to be endowed with sacramental dignity and immortalizing Fruits. Counterbalancing Jesus's merited enjoyment of the Fruit and the Water of Life and his regaining of Paradise, Satan's sedentary squat as a cormorant fruitlessly 'not true Life / Thereby regaind'. It is fitting that Satan's voyage, which requires the reader's attentive participation in Milton's sacramentally illuminated universe, the mediating Ladder and the life-giving sun, should culminate in Satan's obliviousness, even in plain view, to the Tree of Life's virtue as a reified sacrament dispensed from Heaven.

Anne Ferry has diagnosed how Satan's view of 'Physical reality is totally sundered from moral meanings'.[87] In Satan's view the sacred Tree provides only a limited prospect of Eden. The dramatic irony is accentuated by the fact that Satan over-hears Adam discoursing about the Forbidden Tree (4.411–39, 512–27), the means by which Satan will devise humanity's ruination, from a branch on the Tree of Life, a sacramental symbol flourishing with immortal Fruits that promises salvation and the solution to the Fall that Satan is levelling at. The Tree of Life, Satan's final vantage point at his journey's end, is Milton's ultimate sacramental signifier and signified. The Tree is the symbol and presence of the eternal life offered by its immortal Fruits and the eternal reward of the regenerate life after the Son's triumph.

In demonstrating the gap between a Satanic and a sacramental appreciation of Milton's cosmos, this reading endeavours to reinforce John Leonard's claim that Christ, 'of all unnamed names, is the central hidden name in the poem', and Kenneth Borris's thesis that, 'For Milton the Incarnation is the master sign, in effect, which can render all others most fully intelligible for humankind.'[88] Borris asserts that Milton's universe, which, Raphael explains, 'Is as the Book of God before thee set' (8.67), can be read as a Book of Nature or an *explicatio Dei*.

---

[86] '*Arbor vitae haud scio an sacramentum potius, quam symbolum, aut etiam alimentum quoddam dici debeat vitae aeternae.*' Steadman denies Milton's attachment of any sacramental significance to the Tree of Life on the basis of Charles Sumner's rather free translation: 'The tree of life, in my opinion, ought not to be considered so much of a sacrament, as a symbol of eternal life, or rather perhaps the nutriment by which that life is sustained' (*CE* 15.115).

[87] Anne Ferry, *Milton's Epic Voice: The Narrator in 'Paradise Lost'* (Chicago, 1983), 138.

[88] John Leonard, *Naming in Paradise: Milton and the Language of Adam and Eve* (Oxford, 1990), 104; Borris, *Allegory*, 231.

Milton's cosmos equally reads as a Book of Christian Revelation or *explicatio filii Dei*, a principle as inveterate within the Reformed tradition as Calvin's and Hooker's theologies. A sacramental reading of Milton's universe requires a sustained dialectic between natural theology and the revealed theology of regeneration through grace. Without this dialectic, without the knowledge of Christ, and without the providential consolation of the promised seed, the reader can advance epistemologically to the point of the Fall, but no farther.

At least one early illustrator of the epic was aware of Satan's blindness to the Christ-saturated media of Milton's cosmos. John Baptist Medina's illustration to Book Three, included in Jacob Tonson's 1688 ornamental first folio edition of *Paradise Lost*, depicts a scene that has no epic counterpart, but which could arguably stand as Satan's defiance of 'a christocentric kind of structuralist universe'.[89] Medina's drawing depicts Satan gazing heavenward and gesturing ambivalently – he is either protectively shading his eyes with his arm or peevishly shaking his fist – while a glaring shaft of light arcs down from a dazzling angel choir that encompasses the incarnate Son. The angels uphold Christ as he bears his cross. Satan's sightline is paralleled by another sightline that reaches up to the sun, creating two corresponding lines that implicitly associate the exalted Son with the sun. Medina's arrangement of Satan's incensed countenance before the Son–sun might stand for any of the set pieces on Satan's journey during which, from his various prospects, the fiend rages against or is undazzled by 'matter new to gaze' (3.613): the Heavenly Ladder, the edge of the glorious world's aperture, the sun's inexpressible brightness, and the Tree of Life's golden Fruit. In *Paradise Regain'd* Satan shows symptoms of the same defiance when he refuses to conceive of a world apart from the 'Real' (*PR* 4.390), infected soulscape of his own making. For Satan brings about his own blindness by repudiating the very idea of an 'Allegoric' kingdom (*PR* 4.390). Yet, in *Paradise Lost*'s delineation of a sacramental–allegorical universe filled with and substantially expressed by God's love, blazing through His Son, the cosmic *omen est nomen* and the poem's inaugural name is Messiah. In a treatise published one year after Milton's death Peter Sterry pronounced a doctrine harmonious with Milton's sacramental poetic: 'The Lord Jesus now [is] an Universal Person . . . the Original frame of the whole Creation in its utmost Latitude, as the Seed of the whole Creation spread through all the parts of it.'[90]

[89] Borris, *Allegory*, 231.
[90] Sterry, *Discourse*, 232.

4

'On other surety none': Raphael's
Temporal and Spatial Passion Allegories

[*Paradise Lost*] contains the history of a miracle, of Creation and Redemption; it displays the power and the mercy of the Supreme Being.

Samuel Johnson[1]

[S]ince the precipitous fall of man from heaven has left his mind in a vertiginous whirl and since, according to Jeremiah, death has come in through the windows to infect our hearts and bowels with evil [Jer. 9:21], let us call upon Raphael, the heavenly healer, that by moral philosophy and dialectic, as with healing drugs, he may release us.

Giovanni Pico della Mirandola[2]

In a classic essay on Jewish Medieval allegory the respected Hebraist Frank Talmage defined the exoteric or 'outer' meaning and the esoteric or 'inner' meaning of what he termed 'reification allegory'. Talmage held that 'reification allegory is the heir of the Greek allegorizers of Homer, Hesiod, Ovid, and of Philo of Alexandria, an "imposed allegory" in which the surface meaning of a classical or canonical text... is taken to envelop higher esoteric truth, the way the shell envelops the nut'.[3] Raphael's two narratives, which span Books Five to Seven of *Paradise Lost*, treat the Son's anointing, the War in Heaven, and the mundane Creation. Critics have long recognized that these narratives behave allegorically. If Raphael's histories are read exoterically, they constitute God's gracious response to Adam and Eve's morning prayer, 'To give us onely good' (5.206). These histories have a dual purpose, to inform Adam that he has 'Happiness in his power left free to will' (5.235) and to warn him of 'His danger, and from whom, what enemie' (5.239), namely Satan, that 'terrible' (6.910) and 'dire example' (7.42). Once Raphael's narratives are interpreted as allegories, their esoteric meaning functions proleptically to console Milton's readers with the prospect of Adam's future salvation. This salvation is obtainable through the Son's salvific work.

---

[1] Samuel Johnson, *Lives of the English Poets*, vol. 1, ed. George Birkbeck Hill (Oxford, 1905), 174.
[2] Giovanni Pico della Mirandola, *Oration on the Dignity of Man*, trans. A. Robert Caponigri (Washington, DC, 1956), 33.
[3] Frank Ephraim Talmage, 'Apples of Gold: The Inner Meaning of Sacred Texts in Medieval Judaism', in *Apples of Gold in Settings of Silver: Studies in Medieval Jewish Exegesis and Polemics*, ed. Barry Dov Walfish (Toronto, 1999), 109.

PASSION ALLEGORY IN RAPHAEL'S NARRATIVES

Raphael's capacity to convey heavenly matters through narratives accommodated to human language has been the subject of critical commendation and condemnation alike. William Poole finds that, regarding the capability of archangelic utterance, Raphael is unable to relate celestial histories competently so that he 'grows less confident of communicative valence'.[4] It is not so transparent that, as Poole claims, the poem demonstrates a progressive semantic attenuation so that Raphael loses his grip on a mediated narrative that breaks down from simile to metaphor to *aporia*. Admittedly, Raphael does punctuate his histories with admissions that his diegesis amounts formally to a vast similitude or parable (see 5.750–54, 760–63; 6.73–76, 310–15, 573–75), but, over almost 2,000 lines, Milton's divine historian never abandons his narrative nor does he fling up his wings in exasperation. The archangel perseveres in his diplomatic task of conveying his narrative's intelligible truth 'By lik'ning spiritual to corporeal forms' (5.573). More appealing is Mindele Anne Treip's constructive reading of Raphael's commission. Although Treip grants that Raphael's undertaking is, in one sense, an act of heavenly condescension to the more limited faculties of discursive human perception, she discerns, beyond this accommodation, a 'more subtle upward sense, in which the reader makes a conscious effort to recognise . . . that the thing represented both is and is not shown "as [it] really is"', so that the angelic narrative stoops to uplift the human intellect into a greater intimacy with God's ways.[5] As with the telling of a parable or a proverb, a moral fable or a Socratic myth, the recipient of Raphael's narrative, whether Adam, Eve, or Milton's reader, is arrested with a sense of something simultaneously exotic and familiar and leaves the transformative narrative experience in some way edified.

Raphael's concession, 'though what if Earth / Be but the shaddow of Heav'n, and things therein / Each to other like, more then on Earth is thought?' (5.574–76), qualifies the assessment of those critics who find that Raphael's speech act is, at best, a capitulation to frustrated heuristic possibilities. Rather, *Paradise Lost* regularly intimates that the Earth is, to some degree, a resemblance of Heaven, and that even Hell's blasted dungeon somehow constitutes Heaven's warped, infernal counter-type (2.267–73; 4.208; 7.160, 328–31; 9.99–109). Milton had ample biblical and theological precedent for supposing that heavenly matters were assimilable to human epistemology. In the gospels Jesus accommodates heavenly mysteries to the exigencies of mediated narrative, telling his disciples, 'insiders' to Christian truth, that the hermetic meaning of his teachings is all Greek to the uninitiated: 'To you has been given the mystery of God's kingdom, but, to those who are on the outside [ἐκείνοις . . . τοῖς ἔξω], everything comes in parables' (Mark 4:11). Conversely, for the initiated 'on the inside', the Epistle to the Romans holds that, from Creation, 'the unseen things [τὰ . . . ἀόρατα]' (Rom. 1:20) of God are clearly discernible. Pauline rhetoric frequently speaks idiomatically, in accommodated

---

[4] William Poole, *Milton and the Idea of the Fall* (Cambridge, 2005), 177.
[5] Treip, *Allegorical Poetics*, 193.

terms, of communicating heavenly truth 'humanwardly [ἀνθρώπινον], because of the weakness of your flesh' (Rom. 6:19) and revelation unveiled 'according to humanity [κατὰ ἄνθρωπον]' (Rom. 3:5) or 'according to the flesh [κατὰ σάρκα]' (1 Cor. 10:2). Hebrews is possibly the Pauline text to set forth most explicitly an analogical cosmography likening heavenly to earthly horizons with technical terms such as 'character' (1:3), 'image' (10:1), 'comparison' (9:9; 11:19), 'example' (8:5; 9:23), 'Shadow' (10:1), 'antitypes' (9:24), and reflections 'of things in heaven' (8:5). First Corinthians goes further, arguing that it is possible to speak, 'not in didactic words of human wisdom, but in didactic words of the spirit, syncretizing spiritual things with spiritual things' (2:13).

Raphael's lecture on adjusting invisible to visible matters may have been influenced by a celebrated passage concerning analogical cosmography in Origen's *Homilies on the Song of Songs*. Origen draws upon the Pauline doctrine of analogy outlined in Romans 1:20 and 2 Corinthians 4:18 and argues for a metaphysics capable of legitimating universal analogy and correlation:

> The Apostle Paul teaches us that the invisible things of God are understood from the visible things, and that those things which are not seen are contemplated from those things which, in their similitude and relation, are seen; showing by this that this visible world may instruct us about the invisible realm and that this earthly situation may contain certain patterns of celestial things; so that we can rise up from things below to things above, and from these things which we see on the Earth, we can sense and comprehend those things which are had in Heaven. By the certain likeness between these things, the Creator gave to His creatures on Earth an imitation so that, in this fashion, their differences might be able to be inferred and sensed.[6]

Poole's gloss that Raphael's 'final question, "who...can relate"...expects the answer, "no-one"', is not strictly borne out by the epic narrative, because the archangel's discourse concedes to no such interpretive cul-de-sac.[7] Despite Raphael's admission, at least in theory, to a degree of ineffability regarding the heavenly events he is attempting to communicate to the happy couple (see, for instance, 8.172–73), in practice Milton's ethereal storyteller scarcely falters. Raphael's full statement, which regrettably Poole's quotation brackets out, reads, 'for who, though with the tongue / Of Angels, can relate' (6.297–98). Raphael's concessive clause alludes to Paul's renowned exposition of agapic love, the same love that impels and validates Raphael's narration: 'If I speak with the tongues of humans and angels, but I have not love, I am become as a sounding brass or a clanging cymbal' (1 Cor. 13:1). Once more Raphael reminds his audience of this Pauline conceit in the preface to his hexaemeral narrative: 'though to recount Almightie works / What words or tongue of Seraph can suffice, / Or heart of man suffice to comprehend?' (7.112–14). Raphael's pre-echo of Paul's rhapsody on the imperfection of all communication that is divorced from love's catalyst, whether that love is human, angelic, or divine,

[6] Origen, *Patrologiae Cursus Completus, Serie Graeca*, ed. J. P. Migne, vol. 13 (Paris, 1862), 172–73: *Homiliae in Canticum canticorum*, Book 3.81, commenting on Song of Songs 2:9.
[7] Poole, *Idea*, 177.

illustrates that Raphael's narrative is motivated by an avowed love of God and a charitable concern for human welfare. The agapic love of God and humanity that inspires Raphael to forewarn unfallen humankind through narrative is founded upon the same self-giving love with which Milton's Son redeems humanity. The inexpressible love enacted through the Son's atonement constitutes the 'esoteric' meaning and allegorical substance of Raphael's narratives. This deeper meaning is reflected in Raphael's loving initiative to instruct Adam through narrative. Redeeming love, God's surety for human salvation, defines the 'incomparable way' (1 Cor. 12:31) that fires Raphael's allegorical narratives. Raphael's knowledge of this redeeming love that, earlier in the epic chronology and during the Heavenly Council, God promises in his Son and divulges to His angels, arguably actuates the archangel to relate his two histories. As *De Doctrina Christiana* teaches, citing 1 Peter 1:12, the angels 'very gladly inquire into the mystery of human salvation [*in mysterium humanae salutis libentissime inquirunt*]' (*CE* 15.98).

Book Five's 'Argument' explains that the main aim of Raphael's mission to Eden is '*to render Man inexcusable*'. A. D. Nuttall and William Poole link this apparently merciless phrase to the inexorable rigidity of high Calvinist doctrine and they object to the expression as 'a strongly Calvinist statement [that] does not inspire hope'.[8] In fact, the phrase 'to render Man inexcusable' pre-dates Calvin's *Institutes* and is biblical in origin. According to Pauline natural theology, those who behold the handiwork of God's Creation and deny His sustaining hand 'are without excuse [ἀναπολογήτους]' (Rom. 1:20). The Johannine Jesus prophesies that humans who reject the redemption no longer have 'an excuse' (John 15:22) or, literally, lack 'a cloak around their sin'. Christ's cloak image, enveloping and concealing human sin, recalls the 'Robe of righteousness' (10.22) with which the Son arrays fallen Adam and Eve and covers their sins from God's sight. *De Doctrina Christiana*'s chapter 'ON RENOVATION' details the benefits of Christ's redemption that are bestowed upon humanity. Milton's definition of vocation includes a similar expression: 'VOCATION is that natural method of renovation where GOD THE FATHER, OUT OF HIS PRECONCEIVED PURPOSE IN CHRIST, INVITES FALLEN HUMANS TO A RECOGNITION OF HOW TO SATISFY AND WORSHIP DIVINITY AND, OUT OF GRATUITOUS KINDNESS, INVITES BELIEVERS TO SALVATION SO THAT THOSE WHO DO NOT BELIEVE ARE DEPRIVED OF ALL EXCUSE [*NON CREDENTES AD TOLLENDAM OMNEM EORUM EXCUSATIONEM*]' (*CE* 15.344). The treatise marshals two familiar proof texts, namely John 15:22 and Romans 1:18–20. For Milton's treatise, 'to be without excuse' means, for those existing after Christ's redemption, to refuse to believe in both a Creator and an atonement that, fulfilled through '[GOD'S] PRECONCEIVED PURPOSE IN CHRIST', invites fallen humanity to trust to their salvation. The chapter

---

[8] Ibid. 176; A. D. Nuttall, *The Alternative Trinity: Gnostic Heresy in Marlowe, Milton, and Blake* (Oxford, 1998), 96–97. Nuttall cites *Institutes* 2.2.22, 'The purpose of natural law, therefore, is to render man inexcusable [*ut reddatur homo inexcusabilis*]'. Calvin refers to Romans 1:20, a common biblical proof text for substantiating the doctrines of natural theology and natural law. See Calvin, *Institutes of the Christian Religion*, ed. John T. McNeill and Ford Lewis Battles, vol. 1 (Philadelphia, 1960), 282.

argues that even those who preexisted Christ, indeed all humanity, are called to participate in the sufficient grace deriving from the redemption, 'even for those who have never heard Christ's name [*pro iis etiam qui nomen Christi nunquam audiverunt*]' (*CE* 15.348). Adam and Eve would presumably belong among this number.

Inexcusability has a twofold function across Raphael's narratives. These narratives are explicitly communicated to an Edenic audience, Adam and Eve, 'who have never heard the name of Christ', and are implicitly imparted to a virtual, intended audience, Milton's readership, who are privileged by knowledge of Christ's work in the interval of salvation history between the cross and the *eschaton*. The direct recipients of Raphael's discourse are the prelapsarian couple, whom the narratives overtly advise to resist Satan and remain sufficient to stand, but the indirect audience, though postlapsarian, is distinguished from the happy couple by the consolation of redemption. Raphael teaches a cautionary lesson about Satan's fall to forestall Adam's lapse, but the archangel's words also convey to the fit, fallen audience an allegorical redemption song and the solution to Adam's Fall. Without the Son, Milton's poem argues, postlapsarian humanity would be 'without excuse'. Raphael's martial and Creation narratives demand the application of two different but associated hermeneutics. The first hermeneutic, available at the literal, 'exoteric' narrative level, warns original, immaculate Creation against succumbing to the possibility of the Fall, while the second hermeneutic, accessible at the allegorical, 'esoteric' narrative level, consoles vitiated Creation with the promise of a New Creation regenerated in Christ.[9]

Milton motions towards the esoteric, redemptive subtext to Raphael's histories of Heavenly War and mundane Creation when he gives Raphael a didactic preamble to his total narrative. Raphael forewarns Adam and Eve that humanity will be safe, 'if ye be found obedient' (5.501; see 5.513–14):

> My self and all th' Angelic Host that stand
> In sight of God enthron'd, our happie state
> Hold, as you yours, while our obedience holds;
> On other surety none; freely we serve,
> Because we freely love, as in our will
> To love or not; in this we stand or fall
>   (5.535–40)

During the War in Heaven, Milton's reader and Adam learn that Satan and his seditious angels fell 'without redemption' (5.615). Earlier, during the Heavenly Council, the narrator has already revealed that, without the Son's sacrifice, like the fallen angels, 'now without redemption all mankind / Must have bin lost' (3.222–23). Raphael's admonition deliberately leaves the godsend of human redemption open for Adam. Yet Raphael's words intimate a cardinal difference between the angelic and human states in the availability of redemption and salvation for each creaturely order

---

[9] Book Eight's colloquy between Adam and the shape Divine employs a similar hermeneutic. See my article, 'Milton's "Genial Angel": The Identity and Salvific Office of the Son in Adam's Narrative of Creation and Recreation', *Studies in Philology*, 107 (2010), 366–400.

after their lapse. At the Heavenly Council God explains that angels and humans can elect either to stand or fall, but that He has installed a safety mechanism that favours the exclusive possibility of human salvation, a mechanism that, if humanity so chose, could recover the faithful from a potential Fall (3.129–34). Interpreted on another level, Raphael's terse phrase 'On other surety none' alludes to the redemptive failsafe that would follow should Adam and Eve choose to fall. A 'surety', deriving from the Latin *securitas*, is a 'security', an assurance that guarantees *se-curus* or 'freedom from care'. Paul uses the word 'surety' to describe Christ's atoning sacrifice, that 'By so much was Jesus made a surety of a better testament' (*AV* Heb. 7:22). Lancelot Andrewes expounded this text in his Good Friday sermon of 1604. Andrewes extrapolates from the legal–commercial principle of a surety to Christ's vicarious atonement:

> Pity it is to see a man pay that he never tooke; but if he will become a Surety, if he will take on him the person of the Debtor, so he must. Pity to see a sillie poor Lambe lie bleeding to death; but if it must be a Sacrifice, (such is the nature of a sacrifice) so it must. And so Christ, though without sinne in himselfe, yet as a Suretie, as a Sacrifice, may justly suffer for others, if he will take upon him their persons; and so, God may justly give way to his wrath against him.[10]

In a chapter of *The Ark of the Covenant Opened* entitled 'Christ the Surety of the Covenant' the radical Covenanter Patrick Gillespie specified:

> The general *adequate* condition of the Covenant of Suretiship can be no narrower than Christ's whole undertaking... for carrying on, and perfecting the work of Redemption from beginning to end... the *formal* condition of the Covenant of Suretiship... was his whole obedience active and passive, even unto death, *Phil. 2.8 ... even the death of the cross.*[11]

Milton's Son offers to stand surety for humanity and the fruits of the 'Attonement' (3.234) will be 'peace assur'd, / And reconcilement' (3.263–64). Raphael uses the loaded phrase 'On other surety none' to evoke the gift of redemption, which has been denied to the angels, but vouchsafed to the human race through the Son. Fallen Adam and Eve come to a postlapsarian understanding of salvation through Christ, who acts as humanity's 'surety' or guarantor of grace. Raphael's allegorical narratives sustain an 'esoteric' interpretation that upholds an atoning subtext to the archangel's caveat to Adam and Eve that, as with the lapsed rebel angels, a Fall may leave humanity without surety.

Below I first wish to develop William Hunter's insight that Raphael's account of the three-day War in Heaven works as a *temporal* Passion allegory. Second, I aim to show how Raphael's hexaemeral narrative functions complementarily as a *spatial* Passion allegory. The martial epyllion and the hexaemeron have a joint purpose in

---

[10] Lancelot Andrewes, *The Sermons of Lancelot Andrewes*, ed. Marianne Dorman, vol. 2 (Edinburgh, 1993), 158. The New England Puritan John Norton comments, 'the man Christ Jesus... satisfied Justice as [the elect's] Surety, and so fulfilled both Law and Gospel': Norton, *A Discussion of that Great Point in Divinity, the Suffering of Christ* (London, 1653), 7.

[11] Patrick Gillespie, *The Ark of the Covenant Opened* (London, 1677), 91, 92–93; see also 368–444.

that both narratives cooperate allegorically. Both histories intimate, to use Talmage's terms, an encrypted, 'esoteric' level of meaning beyond the literal, 'exoteric' meaning. The allegorical reading reveals how, despite the potentiality of Adam's Fall, the Son's redemption can justify God's ways to men. Equipped with this esoteric sense, Milton's fit readers may discover themselves 'on the inside' as well as 'on the outside' of Raphael's narratives.

RAPHAEL'S TEMPORAL PASSION ALLEGORY: THE SON'S ANOINTING AND THE WAR IN HEAVEN

William Hunter was the first to appreciate that Milton's War in Heaven abides by a structural principle of temporal allegory. His theory that throughout the War Milton 'telescope[s] time' merits further commentary. It is the purpose of this section to fulfil that need.[12] According to Hunter, Milton applies a 'metaphorical interpretation of time' to the Heavenly War's chronology. When interpreted as a temporal allegory, the War, which lasts for four days and three nights, parallels the Paschal *triduum*, the three days of Passion Week that culminate in Jesus's resurrection, namely Good Friday, 'Black' or Easter Saturday, and Easter Sunday.[13] Hunter maintains that Milton's temporal allegory subsists under the sign of Jonah (Jonah 1:17; Matt. 12:38–41; Luke 11:29–30), the timeframe of three days and nights that spans Christ's suffering on the night of his Agony in Gethsemane to his resurrection morning in the garden. Like all effective allegory, Raphael's martial epyllion functions simultaneously in literal and metaphorical senses, literally and actually recounting the War, while also metaphorically and virtually adumbrating the Son's humiliation and resurrection.[14]

Thomas Jackson, an Oxford clergyman and Platonist, had enquired into the propriety of attributing the computation of hours and days to the period before the mundane Creation. Related to this issue, Jackson also disputed the decorum of ascribing space to heavenly matters:

> No event [in Heaven] is observed by sense, but is husked in the circumstance of *place* and *time*, whence it is, that these two accompany many Phantasmes, after they be winnowed from all the rest, into the closet of the understanding. The conceit of mathematicall or metaphysicall space, is so naturally annexed to our imagination of *time* and *place* physicall; that albeit reason, aswell as Scripture demonstrates the world to be, for Physicall magnitude, finite; yet our Phantasies cannot be curbed from

---

[12] William B. Hunter, Jr, 'The War in Heaven: The Exaltation of the Son', in *Bright Essence*, 123. For an in-depth analysis of Book Six, see Stella Purce Revard, *War in Heaven: 'Paradise Lost' and the Tradition of Satan's Rebellion* (Ithaca, 1980).

[13] Ibid. 124.

[14] Spenser's Redcrosse fights a symbolic three-day battle with the Dragon, emerging victorious, like the resurrected Christ, on the third day. See Carol V. Kaske, 'The Dragon's Spark and Sting and the Structure of Red Cross's Dragon-Fight: *The Faerie Queene*, I.xi–xii', in *Essential Articles for the Study of Edmund Spenser*, ed. A. C. Hamilton (Hamden, 1972), 425–46.

running into imaginary locall distance, beyond the utmost surface of this goodly visible worke of God, yea beyond the heaven of heavens... And (which is much to bee admired) some Schoole-braines have beene so puzled in passing this unfoundable gulf, as to suspect that God, which is now in every place of the world created by *Him*, was as truly in these imaginary *distances* of place and time, before the creation was attempted. Thus have they made *place* commensurable to his *immensitie*, and succession, or time coequall to his *eternitie*.[15]

Like Jackson's 'Schoole-braines', Raphael without hesitation imputes the '*distances* of place and time' to the Heaven that existed before the mundane Creation was founded. Both Milton's prose 'Argument' to Book Six and Raphael's martial narrative fastidiously chronicle the three days and nights spanning the War in Heaven. In the 'Argument' Satan and his cohorts retire at the close of the first day '*under Night*', Michael and the angels are repulsed '*in the second dayes Fight*', and the Messiah's decisive victory occurs '*on the third day*'. Raphael meticulously punctuates his narrative with *chronographiae* or temporal signposts as one day's battle passes into the next (see 5.642–45; 685–86; 6.406–07, 524–28, 748–49).[16] Raphael begins his tale with a justification for assigning minutes and hours, daytime and nighttime, to heavenly conditions. The archangel commences with a parenthetical explanation, 'when on a day / (For Time, though in Eternitie, appli'd / To motion, measures all things durable / By present, past, and future)' (5.579–82). Raphael's apologetic parenthesis enlists a scientific proof from Aristotle's *Physics* that time is the measure of motion: 'it is plain that time is a measure of motion according to its beforeness and afterness, and it is continuous (because time is continuous)' (*Phys.* 220a.25–27).[17] *De Doctrina Christiana* twice has recourse to this Aristotelian proof in upholding the existence of heavenly and pre-creational time. In its first reference to Aristotle's *Physics* the treatise argues for the angels' creation and the rebel angels' apostasy at specific, quantifiable moments before God's foundation of the world:

> Certainly nothing compels assent that motion and time [*motum et tempus*] – time, which is a measure of motion, according to the categories of 'before' and 'after' – could not have been before this world was founded, as is popularly believed; since Aristotle taught that motion and time were no less granted in this world, which he decided was eternal. (*CE* 15.34)

The treatise's second Aristotelian reference explains the soul's ontological state as it 'sleeps' between its death and its resurrection at the *eschaton*:

> Because, if there is no time without motion [*tempus nullum sine motu*], what of the story of those who were said to be sleeping at the temple of the Heroes, those who bound together, seamlessly, the moment they went to sleep with the moment they

[15] Thomas Jackson, *A Treatise of the Divine Essence and Attributes* (London, 1628), 42–43.

[16] The others are 5.579, 582, 603, 618, 662, 667, 674–75, 699–700; 6.1–2, 4–15, 87, 170, 246, 423–24, 492, 521, 544, 684–85, 699.

[17] Aristotle, *The Physics*, vol. 1, trans. Philip H. Wicksteed and Francis M. Cornford (London, 1929): "Ὅτι μὲν τοίνυν ὁ χρόνος ἀριθμός ἐστι κινήσεως κατὰ τὸ πρότερον καὶ ὕστερον, καὶ συνεχής (συνεχοῦς γάρ), φανερόν.'

were woken up and were completely oblivious to any intervening time (Arist. *Phys.* 4.11)? (*CE* 15.240)

Michael likewise styles the soul's state between death and resurrection as 'a death like sleep' (12.434). Lest the reader's attention should be diverted from Raphael's symbolic use of time during the War, Milton begins Book Six by introducing God's celestial timepiece with the *locus est* motif of classical poetry:

> There is a Cave
> Within the Mount of God, fast by his Throne,
> Where light and darkness in perpetual round
> Lodge and dislodge by turns, which makes through Heav'n
> Grateful vicissitude, like Day and Night
>
> (6.4–8)

Raphael's allusions to Aristotle's *Physics* and his testimony concerning heavenly time, his invention and inclusion of the celestial timepiece, and his scattering of temporal markers throughout his martial history orient the reader towards the importance of heavenly temporality for understanding Raphael's temporal Passion allegory. One might suppose that critics had cast every conceivable penny at construing God's anointing of the Son, an event that has become something of an interpretive *bête noire* in Milton studies.[18] One detail that is indispensable to understanding how Milton's temporal Passion allegory works is the correlation between Raphael's account of the Son's anointing and the gospel episode that describes the nameless woman's faithful anointing of Jesus. The gospel story occurs upon, or shortly before, Maundy Thursday and so corresponds to Milton's anointing scene, which is placed at the beginning of the four-day narrative, on the equivalent day in the Paschal time-scheme to Maundy Thursday. Jesus's anointing is one of the few pericopes to appear in all four canonical gospels (Mark 14:3–9; Matt. 26:6–13; Luke 7:36–50; John 12:1–8). In Matthew, Mark, and John, the nameless woman's anointing of Jesus occurs at the beginning of the Passion narratives and prior to the Last Supper. The Markan version reads:

And while [Jesus] was in Bethany at the house of Simon the leper, as he was reclining at the table, a woman came with an alabaster jar of ointment, which was expensive, pure nard, and she broke the alabaster jar and poured the contents over his head. Now some persons present were angered and said to one another, 'Why has this ointment been wasted? For this ointment could have been sold for more than three hundred denarii and given to the poor.' And they reproached her. But Jesus said, 'Let her be. Why do you grieve her? She has done a service for me. For you always have the poor with you, and you benefit them whenever you wish, but you do not always have me. She did what she could. She prepared, ahead of time, to anoint my body for burial [προέλαβεν μυρίσαι τὸ σῶμά μου εἰς τὸν ἐνταφιασμόν]. And truly, I say to

---

[18] See, for example: Hugh F. McManus, 'The Pre-existent Humanity of Christ in *Paradise Lost*', *Studies in Philology*, 77 (1980), 271–82; Danielson, *Milton's Good God*, 219–24; Richard S. Ide, 'On the Begetting of the Son in *Paradise Lost*', *Studies in English Literature, 1500–1900*, 24 (1984), 141–55; MacCallum, *Sons of God*, 79–87; Borris, *Allegory*, 192–97.

you, wherever the good news is preached throughout the whole world, what this woman did will be spoken of in remembrance of her.'   (Mark 14:3–9)

The anonymous woman's honorific anointing of Jesus's head functions, however unconsciously on her part, as a prophetic, symbolic action that foretells, in addition to Jesus's excellence, his imminent redemptive death and subsequent entombment.[19] According to the customs of ancient Israel, annealing the head was a significant ritual that distinguished prophets, priests, and kings. Jesus was traditionally thought to have fulfilled these three prophetic, sacerdotal, and regal offices in his person during his earthly ministry.[20] In the Synoptic gospels Jesus's corpse is never actually anointed because God raises him from the dead. Jesus's devout female disciples come to the tomb to anoint his body only to discover that the tomb is empty and Jesus is raised from the dead. In the gospel story the woman's unction of Jesus with oil from an alabaster flask comprises a Markan 'Passion prediction' that foretells Jesus's heroic suffering and anticipates his Messianic victory.[21]

In the Matthean and Markan accounts some disciples object because they misinterpret the woman's anointing as a lavish and irresponsible waste of ointment. They fail to realize that the one the woman honours is the Messiah destined to rule despite and because of his suffering and death. In the Johannine and Lukan versions the unction seems to move Jesus's indignant disciple Judas Iscariot, in the subsequent pericope, to betray his teacher for thirty pieces of silver. In the same way, in Raphael's narrative some of the angels who congregate to witness the Son's anointing, like some of Jesus's disciples in the gospels, are piqued by God's tribute to His Son, so that 'All seemd well pleas'd, all seemd, but were not all' (5.617).[22] Satan, who is as outraged by the Son's elevation as Judas is by the woman's anointing of Jesus, resolves to apostatize. Satan heads north to prepare 'Fit entertainment' (5.690) for the Messiah, just as Judas resolves to betray his anointed master. In three of the gospel accounts the scene immediately following the anointing episode shows the remaining disciples celebrating the Last Supper. Correspondingly, in Raphael's history those angels who do not murmur against and take umbrage at the Son's unction celebrate a celestial Eucharist. As Hunter notes, according to the time-scheme of the Paschal *triduum* the angels' celebration of the Son's anointing corresponds with the Last Supper on Maundy Thursday night.[23] The disciples' partaking of bread and wine is reflected in 'Angels Food, and rubied Nectar' (5.633). In the lines Milton added to the later 1674 edition of *Paradise Lost* the verses of 'They eate, they drink, and in communion sweet / Quaff immortalitie and joy' (5.637–38) consolidate this Eucharistic connection. The

[19] For an invaluable commentary on this passage, to which this reading is indebted, see John R. Donahue and Daniel J. Harrington, eds, *The Gospel of Mark* (Collegeville, 2002), 383–91.
[20] *De Doctrina Christiana* breaks down Jesus's mediatorial office into its threefold function of prophet, priest, and king (*CE* 15.284–303).
[21] Donahue and Harrington, 387: For Jesus's other Markan Passion predictions, see Mark 8:31, 9:31, and 10:33–34.
[22] My observation strengthens the analogy Hunter draws between Satan and Judas here. See Hunter, 'War', 127.
[23] Ibid. 126–27.

inserted lines allude to Jesus's breaking of the shewbread and his injunction to 'take, eat [Λάβετε φάγετε]; this is my body' (Matt. 26:26; see Mark 14:22; 1 Cor. 11:23–24).[24] Moreover, the idiom 'Fruit of delicious Vines' (5.635) is a Semitism describing the provenance of the angels' 'rubied Nectar'. The phrase conjures up the language Jesus uses to describe his blood as wine and evokes his eschatological promise to his apostles that 'I will never again drink of the fruit of this vine [ἐκ τούτου τοῦ γενήματος τῆς ἀμπέλου] until that day when I drink it anew with you in my Father's kingdom' (Matt. 26:29; see Mark 14:25). In the opposing angelic camp, in their night whispering Satan and Beelzebub conspire against the Father and the Son. Their plotting celebrates an anti-Eucharist that divides them from, rather than unites them with, the Son. Satan's address to Beelzebub as 'Companion dear' (5.673) plays upon the etymology of *com-panis* as 'bread-breakers'. His familiar address also suggests an impious solidarity where the bread of sedition is broken to unify the rebel angels into a hostile body composed of a schismatic, Satanic army of 'irregulars'.

As with Judas's betrayal, the grounds for Satan's revolt arise from his gross ignorance regarding the symbolism that lies behind the Father's rite of unction. Satan wilfully disregards the Son's unconditional, self-giving love that is inseparable from and implicit within the honorific meaning of the anointing. The Son's title of 'Messiah' derives from the Hebrew *Masiah* or 'Anointed One' and Satan almost obsessively harps upon the injustice and inequity of God's choice in preferring and anointing the Son. Satan reviles the Son's superior status as '*Messiah* King anointed' (5.664) and 'great *Messiah*' (5.691) and chafes that his own star-bright eminence as God's luminary, at a time when he bore the name Lucifer, has been 'eclipst under the name / Of King anointed' (5.776–77). However, *De Doctrina Christiana* acknowledges that God's begetting or exaltation of the Son, rather than merely signifying distinction, includes the idea of his humiliation and mediation, and specifically 'resurrection from the dead or anointing to the office of mediator [*suscitationem a mortuis aut ad mediatoris munera unctionem*]' (*CE* 14.182). The treatise applies the Latin *unctio* for 'anointing' to describe unction to servant-kingship. John Carey's translation somewhat clouds the connection between the Son's anointing and his redemptive office by translating the Latin term as 'appointment' (*CPW* 6.206). Not unlike *De Doctrina Christiana*, Patrick Gillespie advocated an indivisibility between the Son's anointing to kingship and his mediatorial office as Saviour: 'Christ's qualification for the Office of Mediatorship, is his *Unction;* this was consequent unto his personal union; so that as we called the union of the two natures in Christ's Person, the principal and chief qualification of him for this office.'[25]

In the oft-quoted altercation between Abdiel, the representative of the loyalist angels, and Satan, the spokesperson for the seditious angels, Milton's reader can

---

[24] The obverse of this pious communion is Adam and Eve's eating from the Forbidden Tree, an anti-sacrament that is enacted with the same refrain. Adam has a rapacious urge 'To pluck and eate' (8.309) and, when Eve actually yields, 'she pluckd, she eat' (9.781).

[25] Patrick Gillespie, *The Ark of the Couenant Opened* (1677), 201.

gauge the widely divergent perceptions among God's creatures of what service to the Son entails. The reader is also invited to compare the poem's very different formulations of a self-giving Messiah, who sacrifices and serves, and a haughty despot, who demands and tyrannizes. Milton adopts the bowed knee of loving admiration and, conversely, the bended knee of subjugated service as epic motifs for antithetical attitudes of glad service and demeaning servility in the Messiah's presence. These motifs are touchstones for Abdiel and Satan's personal philosophies. From Satan's perspective, to bend the knee before the Son would signify undignified servility, not fit service, 'Knee-tribute yet unpaid, prostration vile' (5.782). For the fiend, Messiah's rule is a 'Yoke' to which the rebel angels would 'submit your necks, and chuse to bend / The supple knee' (5.785–88). From Hell's floor Satan reminds his troops of the reason for their late ruin from Heaven. The apostate angels refused 'To bow and sue for grace / With suppliant knee, and deifie [God's] power' (1.111–12). David Loewenstein has illustrated the contradictions, ambiguities, inconsistencies, and, above all, the element of 'verbal equivocation' that pervade Satan's political discourse in his diabolic plot to drum up volunteers for his heavenly rebellion.[26] Satan's forked-tongued slipperiness is such that 'at one moment he can use his "potent tongue" (6.135) to speak like a radical or militant Puritan who abhors the constraint of a political yoke and at another to speak like a royalist or a defender of Lords who would justify the ancient authority of magnific titles and powers'.[27] The two-faced hypocrisy of Satan's words that Lowenstein detects is pronounced when, shortly after Satan has lambasted God for exacting knee-tribute, the newly fallen angels, submissively declaring Satan their Lord, 'Towards him they bend / With awful reverence prone; and as a God / Extoll him equal to the highest in Heav'n' (2.477–79). In counterpoint, the grateful angels observe the Son's redemptive offer with approval and deference. Freely and consensually, 'lowly reverent / Towards either Throne they bow, and to the ground / With solemn adoration down they cast / Thir Crowns' (3.349–52). The biblical motif of the bowed knee derives from Isaiah 45:23, 'That unto me every knee shall bow, every tongue shall swear' (*AV*). In the New Testament the Pauline doxology of Philippians 2 re-invokes the Isaian motif. In this biblical passage, because of Jesus's heroic humiliation even to death upon the cross, all creatures deferentially bend their knees and with their tongues confess the Son's majesty:

> [Jesus] emptied himself, taking the form of a servant, being in the likeness of men; and, according to this scheme, being found as a man, he humbled himself, becoming obedient until death, and that the death of the cross. Because of this, God highly exalted him and gave him a name above every name in order that, at the name of Jesus, every knee of creatures in Heaven and on Earth and under the Earth should bend and every tongue confess that Jesus Christ is Lord, to the glory of God the Father.   (Phil. 2:7–11)

---

[26] David Loewenstein, *Representing Revolution in Milton and His Contemporaries: Religion, Politics, and Polemics in Radical Puritanism* (Cambridge, 2001), 204; see 202–41.

[27] Ibid., 217–18.

In Milton's poetics, as in the New Testament, the bowed, in distinction from the bended, knee characterizes the fit response of all celebrants to the Son's restoration of fallen Creation. Milton's God chimes in with the Philippians doxology when He predicts the effects of the Son's crucifixion and exaltation, that, *ex eventu*, 'All knees to thee shall bow, of them that bide / In Heav'n, or Earth, or under Earth in Hell' (3.321–22). God's identification of the doxology's 'creatures … under the Earth' with Hell's inhabitants 'under Earth in Hell' foretells that even the reluctant devils will ultimately bow to humanity's redeemer, the anointed Son.[28] It may be Milton's jest that, when Abdiel subdues Satan in plain view of the heavenly host that is ranged for battle, Satan is chastened in his pride to an identical position of subjugation before God's army and 'ten paces huge / He back recoild; the tenth on bended knee' (6.193–94). Albert Labriola has observed that, in electing not to fall, God's devoted angels have no definite foreknowledge of the redemption. And yet, unlike Satan and his cohorts, Abdiel appreciates that the Son is qualitatively capable of assuming a servant-king's responsibility by 'reducing' himself and altruistically bestowing himself for others, an act that merits the worship of all God's creatures.[29] Thus, in words suggestive of the soteriology of the Philippians doxology, Abdiel defends the 'just Decree of God' and insists that Satan has no right to condemn God's decree:

> That to his onely Son by right endu'd
> With Regal Scepter [so that] every Soule in Heav'n
> Shall bend the knee, and in that honour due
> Confess him rightful King
>
> (5.814–18)

According to the gospel Passion chronologies, immediately after the Last Supper on Maundy Thursday Jesus undertakes his solitary Agony in Gethsemane. As a Passion event of lonely psychic turmoil that occurs prior to the physical agony of the cross, the Agony is rehearsed in Abdiel's isolated outfacing of Satan and the rebel horde. Abdiel's Hebrew 'speaking name' *Ebed-El* or 'Servant of God' recalls the 'Suffering Servant' Songs of Isaiah 52:12–53:12, which the Christian tradition interpreted as Messianic prophecies and which speak of a 'Man of Sorrows' by whose wounds humanity is healed. Alone, Abdiel withstands Satan and the rebel angels. In Gethsemane Jesus's slumbering disciples disappoint and forsake their teacher in his time of need. Abdiel's situation is similar. 'Though single' (5.903), Abdiel remains vigilant, upholding and justifying God while, throughout the same night, the majority of God's angels, blissfully unaware that Satan's rebellion is

---

[28] Michael, too, incorporates the Philippians doxology into his account of the crucifixion and resurrection. Where, in Philippians, because of the cross, 'God highly exalted him and gave him a name above every name' (Phil. 2:9), Michael predicts that after the resurrection the Son will be 'exalted high / Above all names in Heav'n' (12.457–58).

[29] Albert Labriola discerns that a Passion allegory is at work in Raphael's anointing scene and determines that the Son's begetting is a kind of angelic incarnation. To Abdiel's observation that the Son 'the Head / One of our number thus reduc't becomes' (5.842–43) Labriola comments that 'the begetting of the Son represents a humiliation of the deity ("thus reduc't") that serves, in effect, to "exalt" the angelic nature it has chosen to assume': ' "Thy Humiliation Shall Exalt": The Christology of *Paradise Lost*', *Milton Studies*, 15 (1981), 35.

brewing, 'slept / Fannd with coole Winds' (5.654–55). God the Father commends
Abdiel the morning after his ordeal by invoking Abdiel's speaking name as 'Servant
of God' and recapitulating the themes of Christ-like service:

> Servant of God, well done, well hast thou fought
> The better fight, who single hast maintaind
> Against revolted multitudes the Cause
> Of Truth, in word mightier then they in Armes
>   (6.29–32)

'Fighting the good fight' is a Pauline idiom from 1 Timothy 6:12 that translates
literally as a martyr's ordeal, 'agonizing the noble agony of faith [ἀγωνίζου τὸν
καλὸν ἀγῶνα τῆς πίστεως]' by making a 'good confession'. Through his Christ-
like Agony and resistance Abdiel enacts a 'good confession' by defying Satan his
antagonist. Milton's Pauline allusion confirms the connection God draws between
the persecuted Abdiel and the victimized Jesus, since Paul fittingly provides, as the
supreme example of a martyr's 'good confession', Christ's testimony to Pilate only
hours before his death (1 Tim. 6:13).

Appropriately for Raphael's temporal Passion allegory, following Abdiel's Agony
on the 'Maundy Thursday' night Abdiel's Passion experience takes place at midday
on the equivalent day to Good Friday. The crucifixion is the central Good Friday
event and some veiled reference to the Passion on the second day of the Heavenly
War would logically be warranted. I mentioned in Chapter 2 how Michael's
revelation to Adam draws upon the *protevangelium* of Genesis 3:15, an encrypted
Passion prediction. Michael describes the atonement as a bruise inflicted upon the
brow of Satan-the-serpent by Christ-the-Son-of-woman:

> But to the Cross he nailes thy Enemies
>
>   .   .   .   .
>
>   this God-like act
> Annulls thy [Adam's] doom, the death thou shouldst have dy'd,
> In sin for ever lost from life; this act
> Shall bruise the head of *Satan*, crush his strength
> Defeating Sin and Death, his two maine armes
>   (12.415, 427–31)

At noon on 'Good Friday' of the War Abdiel further fulfils his Christ-like name and
office as 'Servant of God' by foreshadowing the Son's redemptive bruising of Satan.
Abdiel publicly flytes Satan before the loyalist and rebel armies; he then brains Satan
with a sword-stroke. Abdiel's blow upon the crest of Satan's head is comparable with the
protevangelistic seed of woman's bruising of the serpent's head: 'So saying, a noble stroke
he lifted high, / Which hung not, but so swift with tempest fell / On the proud Crest of
Satan' (6.189–91). Milton's punning word-choice 'Crest' can equally signify the
decorations upon a warrior's helmet or the markings upon a serpent's head and thereby
strengthens the possible associations of Abdiel's actions with the *protevangelium*.

Abdiel's victory-blow is imbued with soteriological resonances, not least in the
peal of hosannas that his palpable hit upon Satan's crest elicits from the mouths of

God's angels (6.202–05). The Hebrew apostrophe *hosi'a-nna* translates as 'save' or 'deliver us, we pray'. The paronomasia between the words 'hosanna' and 'Joshua', the Hebrew form of the Greek name 'Jesus', a name that means 'Salvation', reinforces the redemptive resonances of Abdiel's bruising stroke. In the Matthean birth narrative an angel instructs Joseph in a dream to call his son by the speaking name of Jesus 'because he will save his people from their sins' (Matt. 1:21). On Palm Sunday, the first day of Holy Week, Jesus's adherents shower their Messiah with hosannas and recite Psalm 118:25–26 as he rides into Jerusalem on a donkey to face his Passion ordeal (Matt. 21:9,15; Mark 11:9,10; John 12:13). The adoration 'hosanna' is almost synonymous with the Hebrew name Joshua, the Grecized form of which is Jesus or 'Salvation'. Milton stresses his awareness of the resonances between these two speaking names in Michael's historical revelation. Michael makes a standard typological play upon the names of Joshua and Jesus, who were both regarded as deliverers of God's people:

> But *Joshua*, whom the Gentiles *Jesus* call,
> His Name and Office bearing, who shall quell
> The adversarie Serpent, and bring back
> Through the Worlds wilderness long wanderd Man
> Safe to eternal Paradise of rest.
>
> (12.310–14)

To summarize, the bruising blow that Abdiel, the eponymous, Christ-like 'Servant of God', deals to Satan's crest, an act that meets with an angelic accolade of salvific hosannas, foreshadows that grave and more lasting bruise that the Son inflicts upon Satan at the Passion. During Milton's Heavenly Council the angels appropriately answer the Son's offer of self-sacrifice with 'loud Hosanna's [that] filld / Th' eternal Regions' (3.348–49). The acclamation 'hosanna' is cryptically suggestive of the Son's future name of Jesus and his role as the means to humanity's 'Salvation'.

Milton orchestrates a structural crescendo of military encounters out of Satan's skirmishes with God's champions. The crescendo guides the reader up God's celestial hierarchy as the Devil opposes, in ascending order of combat, first an angel, then an archangel, and, finally, God's Son. After the angel Abdiel crushes Satan's head, the archangel Michael draws Satan's first blood or, rather, first ichor, after which, climactically, the Messiah routs Satan and his minions in his Father's terrific chariot. In Satan's order of combat Michael, a suitable Christ-figure, is ranked between the plebeian angel Abdiel, the suffering 'Servant of God', and the archetypal Messiah. *De Doctrina Christiana* makes clear the parallel between Michael and the Messiah:

> There seems to be some prince among the good angels, and he is often called Michael [Milton's proof texts are Josh. 6:2; Dan. 10:13, 12:1; Rev. 12:7, 8]. A very great number want Michael to be Christ. But Christ is the sole victor and the absolute treader upon the devil [*Sed Christus victor solus et conculcator diaboli*]. Michael, as leader of the angels, is introduced, as it were, as Antagonist against the prince of the devils; between whom, once their respective forces had been led out in battle formation, they went their separate ways after a fairly equal contest. (*CE* 15.104)

The Latin neologism *conculcator* or 'absolute treader' conveys the Son's total redemptive achievement as he crushes and bruises Satan-the-serpent's head. What is more, Michael's infliction of pain upon Satan during the Heavenly War anticipates the surprised Satan's bafflement and bruising by the Son at the cross. The stress Milton lets fall upon the rebel angels' first experience of pain points not only to future diabolic defeat but also to God's salvific method. The spread of hurt and injury 'through the faint Satanic Host[,] first with fear surpris'd and sense of paine' (6.392–94), predicts the Passion. The Son is also a celestial being but, unlike Satan's troops, he *willingly* debases himself, assumes human flesh, and undergoes humiliation as *theanthropos*, saving humankind as 'Both God and Man, Son both of God and Man' (3.316).

Good Friday yields to 'Black' or Easter Saturday, a day of spiritual darkness in the Christian calendar when Christ's cold body lies entombed. Yet it is also a day pregnant with the promise of resurrection. George Steiner captures this day's spiritual devastation: 'the long day's journey of the Saturday. Between suffering, aloneness, unutterable waste on the one hand and the dream of liberation, of rebirth on the other.'[30] In the War's temporal scheme the equivalent day to Black Saturday is fittingly bleak, desolate, and harrowing. On this day Satan unleashes engines of mass destruction. Satan's offensive results in a futile stalemate between seditious and loyalist angels that seems destined to terminate in catastrophic uncreation as 'horrid confusion heapt / Upon confusion rose' (6.668–69). Thomas Taylor describes the apparent hopelessness of Easter Saturday in terms evocative of the War's second day when, 'as Jonah was in the belly of the fish, three dayes and three nights, so must Christ bee detained in the grave, and lie under buriall three dayes and three nights . . . till the case seemed desperate in both'.[31]

To those cognizant of the sign of Jonah and its portended three days and nights of the Passion, the otherwise desperate events that lead up to Christ's death and burial are not all doom and gloom. The risen Christ and the promise of a New Creation offset these grim events on Easter Sunday. On the War's third day Milton builds the resolution to this crisis of augmenting evil into the fabric of the poem's syntax through the adoption of a device from ancient epic. I will term this grammatical, clausal arrangement *the intervention motif*. The arrangement typically runs, 'And then/now [event *x*] would have occurred, had not [event *y*] occurred.'[32] In classical epic the intervention motif conventionally indicates a dramatic peripety in the action through the initiative of divine or human intercession. The epic poet adopts the intervention motif in order to offer the reader two alternative chains of cause and effect, two potential outcomes, before supplying the actual outcome. The conditional, subordinate clause anterior to the main clause narrates how things might have been, and the intervening main clause overrides this now subordinate, potential circumstance with a description of what has really taken place, normally by outlining the interceding agent and their manner of intervention. Instances of

---

[30] George Steiner, *Real Presences* (Chicago, 1989), 232.
[31] Taylor, *Christ Revealed*, 86.
[32] In ancient Greek the grammatical structure, with occasional variations, runs: καί νύ κεν + optative verb + εἰ μή.

this clausal arrangement abound in ancient epic. In Homer's *Iliad*, for instance, Aeneas would have perished in battle, had not Aphrodite come to his protection (*Il.* 5.311–13); the Trojans would have been defeated by the Achaeans, had not Helenus encouraged Hector and Ares (*Il.* 6.73–76); Hector would have killed Menelaus without Agamemnon's intervention (*Il.* 7.104–08); the Achaeans would have failed in battle, had not Odysseus goaded Diomedes (*Il.* 11.310–12) and Alexander wounded Machaon (*Il.* 11.504–07); Hector would have gained Patrocles's armour, if Iris had not spurred on Achilles (*Il.* 18.165–68); Achilles would have slain Aeneas, if Poseidon had not come to his aid (*Il.* 20.288–91); and Hector might have escaped the jaws of death, had not Apollo bereaved him of his strength (*Il.* 22.202–04). Likewise, in Homer's *Odyssey*, after Odysseus's routing of Penelope's suitors, Athene prevents the slain suitors' vengeful relatives from committing an outrage upon Odysseus and his companions (*Od.* 24.528–30). In Apollonius of Rhodes's *Argonautica* Hera prevents Medea from poisoning herself by impelling the Colchian witch to flee with Jason and the Argonauts (*Arg.* 4.20–23).

Milton employs the epic intervention motif throughout *Paradise Lost* to celebrate how the Son's interposition redeems God's creatures from what would otherwise have been a catastrophe. The motif first occurs in a grim parody of the Son's mediation. Sin intervenes to prevent Satan and his son Death from clashing in arms: 'and now great deeds / Had been achiev'd, whereof all Hell had rung, / Had not the Snakie Sorceress...with hideous outcry rusht between' (2.722–26). Satan reflects upon Sin's intercession in words that pervert the soteriological terms that traditionally describe the Son's accomplishment of prevenient grace and reconciliatory interposition: 'So strange thy outcry, and thy words so strange / Thou interposest, that my sudden hand / Prevented spares' (2.737–39). Sin's intercession prevents Satan and Death's overtures from committing the impious crimes of parricide and filicide. And yet Sin's intervention between her father and son serves as a dreadful foil to the cooperative and harmonious paternal–filial relationship between the Father and the Son dramatized in Book Three. The epic's plainest example of the intervention motif is free from diabolic parody or allusion. During the Heavenly Council the Son makes his offer of prevenient grace, that is, of grace preventing or 'coming before' the human Fall:

> And now without redemption all mankind
> Must have bin lost, ajudg'd to Death and Hell
> By doom severe, had not the Son of God,
> In whom the fulness dwels of love divine,
> His dearest mediation thus renewd.
>
> (3.222–26)

Chiming in with this passage, *De Doctrina Christiana* replicates the syntactical structure of the intervention motif in its chapter 'ON THE ADMINISTRATION OF REDEMPTION': 'But no one could have been thought worthy of a calling by grace, had not Christ's satisfaction been interposed [*nisi interposita Christi satisfactione*]. It was a satisfaction not only sufficient in itself but also efficacious for all people insofar as it was permitted by God's will, if indeed He calls in earnest' (*CE* 15.324).

Raphael weaves the intervention motif into his martial narrative on at least two occasions. In the first instance God limits the effects of Abdiel's *protevangelistic* stroke and checks the loyal angels' battle prowess:

> now storming furie rose,
> And clamour such as heard in Heav'n till now
> Was never
>
> .   .   .   .   .   .
>
> all Heav'n
> Resounded, and had Earth bin then, all Earth
> Had to her Center shook.
>
> .   .   .   .   .   .
>
> Had not th' Eternal King Omnipotent
> From his strong hold of Heav'n high over-rul'd
> And limited thir might
>
> (6.207–09, 217–19, 227–29)

Book Six's prose 'Argument' reveals that God curbs His angels' powers to underscore the Son's decisive conquest of the rebel angels on the third day, *'for whom [God] had reserv'd the glory of that Victory'*. Concordant with the temporal Passion allegory's esoteric meaning, the third day's events are consistent with Easter Sunday, a coup after the protracted emptiness of Black Saturday. On Easter Sunday Christ wins a second victory over Satan and, resurrected from the grave, conquers death. Raphael's second implementation of the intervention motif again confirms God's ultimate purpose through His Son in deciding the War's outcome. At daybreak on the third day of warfare the Son ascends his chariot to thwart Satan and restore the celestial landscape:

> And now all Heav'n
> Had gone to wrack, with ruin overspred,
> Had not th' Almightie Father where he sits
> Shrin'd in his Sanctuarie of Heav'n secure,
> Consulting on the sum of things, foreseen
> This tumult, and permitted all, advis'd:
> That his great purpose he might so fulfill,
> To honour his Anointed Son aveng'd
> Upon his enemies, and to declare
> All power on him transferrd
>
> (6.669–78)

As the Son ascends the chariot of paternal deity, 'the third sacred Morn began to shine / Dawning through Heav'n' (6.748–49). Hunter remarks how Michael's description of the morning of Christ's resurrection to Adam similarly stresses the revitalizing and hopeful dawn of the third day of the Paschal *triduum*: 'ere the third dawning light / Return, the Starres of Morn shall see him rise / Out of his grave, fresh as the dawning light' (12.421–23).[33]

---

[33] Hunter, 'War', 128–29.

Michael Lieb's survey of the more troubling side to Milton's God treats the Son's routing of the rebel angels in the 'Chariot of Paternal Deitie' (6.750) as a primary instance of the *odium Dei* or 'God's hatred'.[34] The Son's testimony to his Father that 'whom thou hat'st, I hate, and can put on / Thy terrors, as I put thy mildness on, / Image of thee in all things' (6.734–36), is realized when, before Satan and his minions hurl themselves headlong from Heaven's verge, the furious Son 'into terrour chang'd / His count'nance too severe to be beheld / And full of wrauth bent on his Enemies' (6.824–26). Yet, as Lieb makes clear, the rebel angels' reaction to the chariot is to be 'hard'nd more by what might most reclame' (6.791), so that the Chariot is a vehicle of reclamation as much as a divine weapon of mass destruction.[35] By Lieb's rationale the '*odium Dei* and the *amor Dei* are complementary aspects of the same idea: they cannot be isolated. The dialectic of Milton's epic is such that the *odium Dei* is always ultimately restorative.'[36] Thus, although the Son acts immediately as 'the emissary of the *odium Dei*', his function as charioteer is equally to regenerate and replenish the vandalized Heavens.[37] In Book Seven, too, the Son rides his 'restorative chariot' to compensate for the loss brought about by hate in heaven with a spectacular act of creativity in which, as demiurge, he founds the world and fills it with teeming life.[38] Therefore, although this portion of the epic is working out a rigorous dialectic between *odium Dei* and *amor Dei*, Lieb concedes that this relationship 'is ultimately consummated in the realization of divine love'.[39]

De Doctrina Christiana defines the soteriological process of restoration, which flourishes in a New Creation, as having two major components, redemption and renovation. The War's third day dramatizes this process. The Son's re-creative advent upon the battle-scarred plains of Heaven evokes the renewal of Creation through the incarnate Son's resurrection. After the Messiah has triumphed over Satan, he passes in his chariot over the ravaged celestial plains, shedding his healing influence:

> At his command th' uprooted Hills retir'd
> Each to his place, they heard his voice and went
> Obsequious, Heav'n his wonted face renewd,
> And with fresh Flourets Hill and Valley smil'd.
> (6.781–84)

Images of recreation, restoration, and renewal spring from the Son's regenerative 'command' and calming 'voice'. These circumstances recur when the Son, acting as God's creative 'Omnific Word' (7.217), shapes the mundane Creation and summons light out of darkness, cosmos out of Chaos, and order from waste. The poem later recollects the smiling hills and valleys of a salvaged post-bellum Heaven in

---

[34] See Lieb, *Theological Milton*, 163–83.
[35] Ibid. 177.
[36] Ibid. 180.
[37] Ibid. 176.
[38] Ibid. 179.
[39] Ibid. 183.

Adam's sudden apprehension of a newly minted world where 'all things smil'd' (8.265).

Satan, the ape of God's Son, feebly mimics the Messiah's gracious ushering in of Heavenly re-creation and Creation's gladness. The fiend briefly renews and re-inspirits his own dejected acolytes, recently fallen from Heaven, in a simile where, over a 'dark'nd lantskip' (2.491):

> If chance the radiant Sun with farewell sweet
> Extend his ev'ning beam, the fields revive,
> The birds thir notes renew, and bleating herds
> Attest thir joy, that hill and valley rings.
>
> (2.492–95)

An earlier simile compares Satan to a false God and likens him to a false sun that has 'yet not lost / All her Original brightness' (1.591–92). In this solar comparison the disgraced Satan is 'Shorn of his Beams' (1.596) and 'In dim Eclips disastrous twilight sheds / On half the Nations' (1.597–98) as a poor restorer and comforter of his minions' hopes. Compared with the rejuvenating and revitalizing power the Son sheds upon Heaven's fields on the War's third day, and contrasted with Christ's future renewal of Creation at his resurrection, the vehicle of Satan's simile as a 'radiant Sun' bestowing an ephemeral and valedictory 'farewell sweet' is elegiac, fragile, and even despondent. Unlike the war-torn heavens and the distempered, fallen Earth, which *are* revisited by the healing sunshine of the Son's curative influence to 'revive' each day and 'renew' their nature, the apostate angels plunge into a physical and psychic state of 'utter darkness' (1.72), 'Ordaind without redemption, without end' (5.615). A third resurrection dawn *will not* shine for the devils and, in Milton's simile, the short-lived effect of Satan's encouragement of his dejected troops amounts to a false cheer that is fleetingly imparted and without salve.

The idea of a sunless or even a 'Son-less' world haunted Milton's imagination long before he constructed his compressed and comfortless 'Inferno' for the first two books of *Paradise Lost*.[40] In his first Prolusion, 'Whether Day or Night is Superior', the young Cambridge scholar's fantasy of a sunless world resembles his epic's graceless Hell or uninhabitable Chaos: 'With the world's eye extinguished all things would decay and utterly pass away. At this calamity humans would certainly not survive long, who would inhabit a world engulfed in gloom, since nothing could supply them with nourishment. What is more, nothing would ultimately prevent all Creation from tumbling into ancient Chaos' (*CE* 12.140–42).[41] By the time Milton wrote *Animadversions* (1641) this nightmarish cataclysm had evolved into the religious conceit of a Son-less or Christ-less world, devoid of all possible intercession, redemption, or restoration. In this anti-prelatical tract Milton reveres

[40] See my note, 'Milton's Dantean Miniatures: Inflections of Dante's *Inferno* and *Purgatorio* within the Cosmos of *Paradise Lost*', *Notes and Queries*, 56 (2009), 215–19.

[41] '*extincto mundi oculo, deflorescerent omnia et penitus emorirentur; nec sane huic cladi diu superessent ipsi homines, qui tenebricosam incolerent terram, cum nihil suppeteret unde victitarent, nihil denique obstaret, quo minus in antiquum Chaos ruerent omnia*'.

and apostrophizes the Christian Saviour: 'let us feare lest the Sunne for ever hide himselfe, and turne his orient steps from our ingratefull Horizon justly condemn'd to be eternally benighted. Which dreadfull judgement O thou the ever-begotten light, and perfect Image of the Father, intercede may never come upon us, as we trust thou hast' (*CPW* 1.705). At the War's climax, though, re-creation *is* a possibility. Raphael's complex temporal Passion allegory prefigures and proclaims a Messianic victory, attainable through patience, across the three days of the Son's anointing, Agony, Passion, and resurrection. Raphael's exoteric, literal narrative of 'hate in Heav'n' (7.54), Satanic rebellion, and angelic expulsion, 'Ordain'd without redemption' (5.615), encases an esoteric, allegorical Passion narrative that proclaims new life through death and human redemption, recovery, and re-creation through the Son's self-sacrifice.

RAPHAEL'S SPATIAL PASSION ALLEGORY: CREATION OLD AND NEW IN RAPHAEL'S HEXAEMERON

We noted above how Aristotle's proof maintained that space, the necessary complement to time, establishes the parameters of creaturely experience and that, according to Raphael's testimony, this spatio-temporal state pertains, in some sense, to Heavenly conditions. If Raphael conveys the esoteric, Passional meaning underlying his martial epyllion through temporal allegory, then the corollary is that the spatial axis provides the coordinates for interpreting the esoteric Passion allegory couched within Book Seven's hexaemeral narrative. Patterns of descent and re-ascent are a cardinal component of the symbolic structure of the process of restoration throughout *Paradise Lost* and the Miltonic corpus generally. These movements of descent and re-ascent chiefly recapitulate the Son's self-bestowing within the turmoil of fallen Creation at the Incarnation, followed by his humiliation and sacrifice within this dark world and wide. A reverse process of exaltation attends this humiliation, which is first accomplished by the incarnate Son's resurrection, and next by his ascension and glorification.

Milton makes plain the salvific significance of this 'V-shaped' activity of humiliation and exaltation in the exordium to *Of Reformation* (1641). Milton describes the *exitus–reditus* formation of the Son's saving work as he initially goes forth from God's Presence to redeem humanity and then returns to his Father's side:

> Amidst those deepe and retired thoughts, which with every man Christianly instructed, ought to be most frequent, of *God*, and of his miraculous *ways*, and *works*, amongst men, and of our *Religion* and *Worship*, to be perform'd to him; after the story of our Saviour *Christ*, suffering to the lowest bent of weaknesse, in the *Flesh*, and presently triumphing to the highest pitch of *glory*, in the *Spirit*, which drew up his body also, till we in both be united to him in the Revelation of his Kingdome: I do not know of any thing more worthy to take up the whole passion of pitty, on the one side, and joy on the other. (*CPW* 1.519)

In his analysis of this passage's grammatical and ideational symmetry, Thomas Kranidas illustrates how Milton expresses the Son's saving, vertical motion in neat, parallel, corresponding clauses. As Christ, the Son declines 'to the lowest bent of weaknesse, in the *Flesh*', and triumphs 'to the highest pitch of *glory*, in the *Spirit*', a theme exciting 'the whole passion of pitty, on the one side, and joy on the other'. Thus, Kranidas remarks, 'God descends in incarnation to save man, suffers, dies and rises again. The Church too descends from Christ, suffers, dies and rises again, and again, and again.'[42] In *De Doctrina Christiana* Christ's mediation is patterned after his exaltation, which is contingent upon his humiliation: 'first his humble state, then his exaltation of the redeemer Christ [*in redemptoris Christi cum humili statu tum exaltatione*]' (*CE* 15.302).

The Son's humiliation involves his inbreaking into a corrupt world as *theanthropos* or 'God-man' and 'VOLUNTARILY SUBMITTING TO ALL THOSE THINGS WHICH SHOULD BE SUBMITTED TO, TO ACCOMPLISH OUR REDEMPTION FULLY' (*CE* 15.302). His humiliation comprises hardships 'IN LIFE...from the very crib...in his circumcision...the flight into Egypt...his manual labour as a carpenter...baptism... temptation...poverty...persecutions, insults, dangers; this, along with the whole of his Passion' (*CE* 15.304); and 'IN DEATH' by his Agony and '*the death of the cross* [Phil. 2:8] with its extreme shame' (*CE* 15.304). The treatise delineates Christ's merited exaltation as an anterior descent and a posterior ascent:

> Exaltation follows a humble state. [*Statum humilem sequitur exaltatio.*]
>
> Where CHRIST, ONCE HE HAD TRIUMPHED OVER DEATH AND PUT ASIDE THE FORM OF SERVANT [*DEPOSITA SERVI FORMA*], WAS AWAKENED BY GOD THE FATHER, INDEED FOR OUR OWN GOOD, TO THE UTMOST STATE OF IMMORTALITY AND GLORY, PARTLY BY HIS MERIT, PARTLY BY THE FATHER'S GENEROSITY, AND ROSE AGAIN, AND ASCENDED, AND SITS AT GOD'S RIGHT HAND.   (*CE* 15.308)

As God informs the Son, 'thy Humiliation shall exalt / With thee thy Manhood also to this Throne' (3.313–14). The treatise divides Christ's exaltation into 'three steps: resurrection, ascension into Heaven, and session at God's right hand... which, by a Hebrew idiom, is equivalent to saying [Christ] was conveyed upwards to power and glory next to that of God' (*CE* 15.312). Michael recapitulates these three steps in his exposition of God's soteriological scheme. The warrior angel reveals that, after the entombed Christ 'soon revives' (12.420) and 'rise[s] / Out of his grave' (4.422–23):

> Nor after resurrection shall he stay
> Longer on Earth
>
> .   .   .   .   .
>
> Then to the Heav'n of Heav'ns he shall ascend
> With victory, triumphing through the aire
> Over his foes and thine
>
> .   .   .   .   .
>
> Then enter into glory, and resume

[42] Thomas Kranidas, *Milton and the Rhetoric of Zeal* (Pittsburgh, 2005), 54.

His Seat at Gods right hand, exalted high
Above all names in Heav'n
(12.436–37, 451–52, 456–58)

This heroic mode of winning ascent from descent, exaltation from humiliation, and resurrection, ascension, and session from Incarnation and crucifixion receives its most compact biblical expression in the Philippians doxology, but it is also clearly articulated in the Apostles' Creed. Of the three major creeds of the Christian Church, the other two being the Niceno-Constantinopolitan and the Athanasian, the English Reformers singled out this creedal formula for inclusion in *The Book of Common Prayer*. The treatise reveres the articles of the Apostles' Creed and at one stage seems to espouse the apocryphal legend, which enjoyed a legitimacy from as early as Ambrose's *Explanatio Symboli*, that each of the twelve apostles commissioned the Creed's Twelve Articles immediately after the Pentecostal gifting of tongues:

> Everywhere the Apostles confirm the same opinion... For here, when the Son shall have fulfilled his mediatorial office and nothing will remain to him, no less will he be restored to his pristine glory as the only-begotten Son, yet he will be subject to his Father. This is the faith of the saints concerning the Son of God, this same is the celebrated confession of that faith, this alone is taught, is accepted by God, and has the promise of eternal salvation... Finally, the Apostles' Creed [*symbolum... apostolicum*] proposes no other more ancient and more widely accepted faith to us in the Church. (*CE* 14.350, 352, 356)

This portion of the treatise endorses the Apostles' Creed with the sanction of numerous gospel and Pauline texts and kerygmatic utterances that the Son's suffering precedes his glorification. The Creed's articles recapitulate Milton's salvific pattern of humiliation and exaltation and of dying to rise again. The first seven Articles run:

> [I believe] in Jesus Christ his only Son, our Lord, who was conceived of the Holy Spirit, born of the virgin Mary, suffered under Pontius Pilate, was crucified, dead, and buried; he descended into the lower depths; on the third day he rose from the dead, ascended into Heaven, sits at the right hand of God the Father Almighty; from there he will come to judge the living and the dead.[43]

The passive and active terms of Passion and resurrection victory, of life, death, rebirth, and restoration, are reflected in the treatise and in Michael's threefold sequence of rest, peace, and session, glorified at God's right hand: *seriatim*, 'conceived', 'born', 'suffered', 'crucified', 'dead', and 'buried', 'descended', 'rose', 'ascended', and 'sits'.

As early as Milton's pastoral elegy *Lycidas* (1637) the Cambridge scholar Edward King, who was drowned in the Irish Sea and whom Milton remembers in his monody as the saintly shepherd Lycidas, will be, at the end of days, in imitation of his Saviour's death and resurrection, 'sunk low, but mounted high, / Through the

---

[43] Translated from H. B. Swete, *The Apostles' Creed: Its Relation to Primitive Christianity* (Cambridge, 1908), 16; see also Adolf Harnack, *The Apostles' Creed*, trans. Stewart Means, ed. Thomas Bailey Saunders (London, 1901).

dear might of him that walk'd the waves' (172–73). In *Paradise Lost* the arc of
downward followed by upward movement figures Satanic lapse and hauteur,
angelic and human Fall and expulsion, and Christic descent and re-ascension.
Jackson I. Cope has charted this aspect of the epic's metaphoric structure, its
vertical imagery of falling to rise and rising to fall, Christic descent into resurrection
and ascension, and Satanic fall and resurgence to hubristic heights.[44] The opening
imperative to Book Seven's invocation, 'Descend from Heav'n', signals the book's
preoccupations with strategies of spatio-spiritual descent and re-ascent. However,
the narrator's request is but one of the epic's myriad, repeated movements from the
plane of Heaven to Earth and back again. Book One's invocation, for example,
sings of humanity's 'fall[ing] off' (1.30) and 'loss' (1.4) until 'one greater Man /
Restore us, and regain the blissful Seat' (1.4–5). God's angelic emissaries Raphael
and Michael recycle this configuration, descending from Heaven to grace Adam
and Eve with revelations of divine providence, just as the incarnate Son descends
into the world to convey his Father's will for humanity.

Straight after the Fall the Son rehearses in cameo the descent and re-ascent he
will undertake at his Incarnation. Forsaking his exalted position of 'high collateral
glorie' (10.86) next to the Father, and then descending as 'both Judge and Saviour
sent' (10.209) to impute internal righteousness to Adam and Eve (10.209–23), the
Son assumes 'the forme of servant' (10.214), an unmistakable allusion to the
Philippians doxology, where Jesus 'emptied himself, taking the form of servant
[μορφὴν δούλου λαβών]' (Phil. 2:7). The Pauline allusion connects the Son's self-
lowering to benefit Adam and Eve in Book Ten with his future Incarnation to
advantage humankind. The Son's symbolic descent–humiliation past, his ascent–
exaltation commences so that 'with swift ascent' (10.224) he returns to God's
'blissful bosom' and 'appeas'd / All...mixing intercession sweet' (10.225–28).
This action prefigures his mediation after redemption when, restored to God's
right hand, he intercedes for humanity as the archetypal High Priest (11.1–72;
Heb. 7:25). In Book Six the Son's restoration of a disrupted Heaven after the havoc
of celestial warfare is bracketed by his session and re-session at God's right hand.
First, the Son 'rose / From the right hand of Glorie where he sate' (6.746–47) to
mount his chariot and, after his triumph, as after his resurrection, God 'into Glorie
him receav'd, / Where now he sits at the right hand of bliss' (6.891–92). Similar
examples of symbolic vertical movement abound across Milton's epic. In each
instance the essential pattern to the restorative process is identical. The Son leaves
his throne beside his Father and descends to allay, repair, or reorder matters,
whether he works to renew the disfigured celestial plains in Book Six; or founds
Creation out of the seething cauldron of Chaos in Book Seven; or sparks the
renovation of a world groaning from the wound caused by the human Fall in Book
Ten. In each case, once the Son has completed his remedial task, he re-ascends and
seats himself at God's side. The paradigmatic model for each of these descents and

---

[44] See Jackson I. Cope, *The Metaphoric Structure of 'Paradise Lost'* (Baltimore, 1962), 50–148; and
Rosalie L. Colie, 'Time and Eternity: Paradox and Structure in *Paradise Lost*,' *Journal of the Warburg
and Courtauld Institutes*, 23 (1960), 127–38.

re-ascents is the incarnate Son's humiliation and exaltation. Nowhere is this paradigm put to greater poetic effect than in Raphael's Creation song.

I observed above that Raphael's hexaemeral narrative complements his martial narrative since it primarily concerns space rather than time, that other indispensable coordinate to human experience. The total scope of Raphael's Creation story is grandly framed by the Son's descent from and his ascension back into collateral glory next to his Father. J. B. Broadbent notes this redeeming pattern: 'The six days are enclosed by the descent and reascension of the Son, counters to Satan's activity.'[45] Despite Jason Rosenblatt's claim that 'Raphael, unlike Luther and Calvin, forbears emphasizing Christ's recreation', the Creation narrative evinces what C. S. Lewis dubs Milton's 'ritual style', a formalized poetic technique that, in this instance, spells out the Son's future humiliation and exaltation.[46] In Book Seven the Son acts out God's providential principle that goodness will prevail, despite the depredations of evil. Raphael prefaces his hexaemeron with the information that:

> [God's] wisdom had ordaind
> Good out of evil to create, in stead
> Of Spirits maligne a better Race to bring
> Into thir vacant room, and thence diffuse
> His good to Worlds and Ages infinite.
>
> (7.187–91)

After the Son has completed the work of Creation, an exuberant angelic chorus celebrates his re-ascent into the Empyrean with a corresponding affirmation that:

> Who seekes
> To less'n thee, against his purpose serves
> To manifest the more thy might: his evil
> Thou usest, and from thence creat'st more good.
>
> (7.613–16)

The hymn's central apothegm that 'to create / Is greater then created to destroy' (7.606–07) reminds us that the mundane Creation compensates for the loss of one third of the angelic company from Heaven. Moreover, the angels' sententia anticipates humanity's recreation by Christ's redemption. Milton's Adam evokes God's providential, restorative principle of wresting good out of evil and remaking the fallen Creation through Christ by praising redemption and recreation in the biblical and Raphaelite language of the Creation story of Genesis 1:[47]

> O goodness infinite, goodness immense!
> That all this good of evil shall produce,
> And evil turn to good; more wonderful

---

[45] J. B. Broadbent, 'Some Graver Subject': An Essay on 'Paradise Lost' (London, 1960), 236.

[46] Jason P. Rosenblatt, Torah and Law in 'Paradise Lost' (Princeton, 1994), 156; C. S. Lewis, A Preface to 'Paradise Lost' (Oxford, 1971), 61.

[47] For analyses of Milton's providential principle of evil's transmutation into good, see G. A. Wilkes, The Thesis of 'Paradise Lost' (London, 1961); and J. R. Watson, 'Divine Providence and the Structure of Paradise Lost', Essays in Criticism, 14 (1964), 148–55.

Then that which by creation first brought forth
Light out of darkness!

(12.469–73)

De Doctrina Christiana reinforces the tenet Adam advances that Christ's fashioning of a New Creation through redemption is 'more wonderful' (12.471) than the original Creation. The treatise teaches that 'HUMANITY'S RESTORATION is where it is freed by God the Father through Jesus Christ from sin and death; it is lifted up to a far superior [*longe praestantiorem*] state of grace and glory than that state from which it fell' (*CE* 15.250). In its chapter 'ON GOD'S PROVIDENCE' *De Doctrina Christiana* parallels Adam's words of jubilation by analogizing the New Creation made possible by redemption, the archetypal working of good from evil, with God's yielding of light from darkness at Creation:

> But wickedness, or the evil of a sin, God, who is the supreme good, cannot effect; rather, out of humanity's wickedness He may create good.
>
> The goal, then, which the one who sins proposes to himself, is nearly always evil and iniquitous, out of which God always elicits something good and just, just as He creates light out of darkness.
>
> It was so in Christ, who was to be crucified... God, *whose hand and counsel had decreed whatever things were to be done* (Acts 4:28), through their cruelty and violence He redeemed the human race.   (*CE* 15.68, 74, 80)

Just as Adam and the treatise recognize a metaphysical correspondence between the Son's wresting of light from darkness on the first day of the hexaemeron and Jesus's wresting of good from evil upon the cross in forging a New Creation, so Raphael inscribes within his exoteric account of the Son's act of Creation the esoteric meaning of Jesus's forthcoming redemption and recreation, in short, his establishment of a renewed world. Milton accomplishes this in his detailing of the Son's descent into the wild abyss of Chaos and his ascent into Heaven from a newborn cosmos, but also in a skein of scripturally allusive details that weave an alternative narrative articulating the promise of the New Creation cradled within the Old.

One biblical allusion comes into play during the Son's descent from the Heaven of Heavens into the realm of Chaos, an action of self-lowering that, at the level of the spatial allegory, corresponds to the Son's future descent into a fallen world at the Incarnation. Raphael tells Adam that the Son's descent is accompanied by God's 'overshadowing Spirit and might' (7.165). The rare biblical epithet 'overshadowing' occurs in the gospels during the Annunciation, when Gabriel heralds the Incarnation to Mary. Gabriel announces that 'The Holy Spirit will come upon you and the power of the Highest will overshadow you [δύναμις ὑψίστου ἐπισκιάσει σοι]. Therefore the one born will be called holy, the Son of God' (Luke 1:35). The Lukan gospel's compound verb *epi-skiasei* or 'it will over-shadow', which Gabriel adopts to describe the Holy Spirit's generative action within Mary's womb, is conveyed by the Latin verbs *inumbrabit* in *De Doctrina Christiana* and *obumbrabit* in the Vulgate. On the three occasions on which *De Doctrina Christiana* interprets Gabriel's use of the word, the treatise identifies the overshadowing entity, first, with 'the Father himself' (*CE* 14.362, 364), second, with 'either God the Father himself or His divine power' (*CE* 14.388), and, third, with 'the Father's virtue and spirit' (*CE* 15.280). In Raphael's narrative God empowers the Son with His 'overshadowing Spirit and might' so that he might descend into Chaos and sculpt Creation out of Chaos's waste and wild. Raphael's biblically allusive words anticipate not only the Son's incarnational descent into the sin-worn chaos of a fallen world, but also the Holy Spirit's advent and the overshadowing of 'the power of the Highest' at Jesus's conception. God's redeeming method accounts for the enwombing of the God-man within Mary and the ushering in of a New Creation in Christ to replace and surpass the corrupted, Old Creation.

Just before the Son embarks upon his divinely commissioned task, Raphael's hexaemeron once again takes up the redemptive subtext to express the Incarnation through biblical allusion. The angels who overture in hymnody the wonders of the Son's six days' work a world also foretell the *Gloria in excelsis Deo* or *Laus angelorum* of the Lukan birth narrative. In Luke's nativity story the angel choir sings of the miraculous Incarnation to the shepherds:

> Δόξα ἐν ὑψίστοις θεῷ
> καὶ ἐπὶ γῆς εἰρήνη ἐν ἀνθρώποις
> εὐδοκίας.
> (Glory in the highest places to God and on Earth peace
> and goodwill towards humanity.)
>
> (Luke 2:14)

Milton inserts this Lukan text within Raphael's hexaemeron when the angels break into songs of praise at witnessing the Son's departure from Heaven to accomplish the work of Creation: 'Glorie they sung to the most High, good will / To future men, and in thir dwellings peace' (7.182–83). Thomas Newton commented here, 'The Angels are very properly made to sing the same divine song to usher in the creation, that they did to usher in the second creation by Jesus Christ, Luke 2:14.'[48] *De Doctrina Christiana* corroborates Newton by including this Lukan text among proof texts illustrating how the unfallen angels 'very gladly inquire into the mystery of human salvation' (*CE* 15.98). In Luke the angels paean God's masterminding of the Incarnation and the Son's subsequent restoration of humanity just as in Raphael's hexaemeron the angels glorify the Son's imminent production of the marvel of Creation. Milton's gospel appropriation preserves the Lukan tricolon of glory, peace, and goodwill, but the poet wittily inserts the qualifying epithet 'future' to accommodate the fact that humanity is, as yet, uncreated, and that Raphael's unfallen audience do not, at this juncture, need to depend upon the Son's recreative powers.

Once the Son reaches Chaos, Milton introduces an evocative, imaginative device by which the Son stretches out 'the gold'n Compasses, prepar'd / In Gods Eternal store' (7.225–26), to pacify and civilize that region of Chaos demarcated for Creation. In an action that develops the spatial Passion allegory, the Son uses the golden compasses to circumscribe Creation's bounds and lay its foundations.

---

[48] Thomas Newton, ed., *Paradise Lost*, vol. 2, 19.

The compasses belong to the rich iconographic tradition of the divine architect, a tradition William Blake powerfully visualized in his etching *The Ancient of Days*. Milton's compasses are of immense esoteric significance for Raphael's re-creational allegory. To a Latinate ear the English word 'compass' lends itself lexically to Milton's fondness for interlingual puns. The paronomasia of the word 'Compass' suggests *com-passion* or *sym-pathy*, the capacity of the God-man for 'suffering with' the tribulations of God's fallen creatures in his life and Passion. The Son's spatial circumscription of Creation with his 'gold'n Compasses' thus adumbrates his compassionate embrace of a fallen, groaning world on the cross, patiently extending his love to the limits of the Old Creation and, through his Passion, founding a New Creation upon redemptive principles. According to the exoteric sense the Son descends into the darkness of Chaos and establishes the boundaries of original Creation within the span of his golden compasses. In the esoteric, allegorical sense Christ descends in the flesh into a world darkened by Satan, Sin, and Death to complete the groundwork for a New Creation by redeeming humanity on the cross within the gracious span of his encompassing arms. My hypothesis is not fanciful. The Latin abstract noun *compassio*, which denotes fellow suffering, has a cognate deponent verb *compatior* that connotes empathy. Both *compassio* and *compatior* are Late Latin words that have their origins in Ecclesiastical Latin and the writings of the Church Fathers Tertullian and Augustine, precisely in the context of the atonement. Let us briefly consider Tertullian and Augustine's innovative soterio-logical treatment of compassion.

Tertullian's *Against Praxeas* contains the first recorded instance of the idea of 'compassibility', that is, of God's capacity for suffering with and for humanity through the Son. Tertullian is discussing patripassianism, the heretical doctrine that the Father participated in the Son's suffering upon the cross:

> And therefore the Father did not suffer with the Son . . . For what is it to have compassion, except to suffer with another? If the Father is impassible, then He is incompassible; or if He is compassible, He is passible . . . For you are afraid to call passible the one you call compassible. But the Father is as incompassible as the Son is impassible, insofar as he is God.[49]

Tertullian's riddling argument dismisses the notion that the Father suffers, but concedes that the Son's divine humanity suffers in the anointed part of his person, that is, insofar as the God-man can assume humanity or fleshliness.

Tertullian explores compassibility further in *On the Resurrection of the Flesh*. He interrogates the Pauline teaching from Romans 8 that Christians should imitate and compassionate with Christ. Tertullian examines Paul's text and concludes that a believer compassionating with Christ through suffering opens up an improving way, an *imitatio Christi* that leads to glorification: 'if, indeed, we suffer with

---

[49] Tertullian, *Adversus Praxean Liber*, 127; section 29: '*ergo nec compassus est pater filio . . . quid est enim compati quam cum alio pati? porro si impassibilis pater utique et incompassibilis; aut si compassibilis utique passibilis. nihil ei vel hoc timore tuo praestas. times dicere passibilem quem dicis compassibilem. tam autem incompassibilis pater est quam impassibilis etiam filius ex ea condicione qua deus est.*'

[*compatimur*] Christ in order that we may also be glorified with him; for I deem that the sufferings of this time are not as worthy as that future glory which will be revealed to us' (Rom. 8:17–18).[50] Tertullian cheers persecuted Christians with the consolation of a glorious future:

> Rather, if we suffer together through the flesh and it is characteristic for us to be ruined by sufferings, to this flesh will be granted that which is promised by suffering together... This is how it will be for those who are glorified together and suffer together. Accordingly, out of those who are colleagued in hardships will also necessarily arise those who will be partnered in rewards.[51]

Tertullian teaches that, as Christ suffered and was glorified for humankind, so should his followers be prepared to suffer, as he did, assured by the knowledge of salvation.

Augustine's *Confessions* develops a singular, though related, idea of compassion to Tertullian's. Augustine's ethical theory of compassion re-forms an Aristotelian poetics of *pathos* into a Christian poetics. He compares compassion with the *misericordia* or 'pity' that Aristotle's *Poetics* taught could be cathartic for an audience beholding a dramatic, mimetic representation of extreme suffering. Augustine redefines Aristotle's understanding of tragic *pathos* as the eliciting of fear or pity from an audience. He finds Aristotle's theory, as it stands, insufficiently compassionate: 'When a person suffers alone, we call it misery [*miseria*]; when a person suffers along with others, we call it pity [*cum aliis compatitur, misericordia*]. But, ultimately, what kind of pity resides in sufferings that are fabricated and dramatized?'[52] Augustine contends that a person truly capable of pity or compassion and genuinely able to empathize with the misfortunes of others would surely wish to abolish all suffering: 'For even if a human who sorrows for a wretched person may be approved of for their charity, someone who is a true brother to pity would prefer that no creature should sorrow.'[53] Accordingly, the Aristotelian account of *pathos* is at worst specious and at best unrepresentative of perfect compassion. Augustine replaces Aristotelian *pathos* with a model of true compassion based upon the example of the Son's vicarious suffering at the crucifixion. Augustine quotes 1 Corinthians 2:16 to this purpose: 'For this love which you, Lord God, have for our souls, and the pity which you feel are far higher and purer, far more incorruptible, than that which we ourselves feel, because you are wounded by no pain. And

---

[50] Tertullian, *De Resurrectione Carnis Liber*, ed. and trans. Ernest Evans (London, 1960), 112; section 40.41–43.

[51] Ibid. 112; section 40.44–46 and 40.53–55: '*porro si per carnem compatimur cuius est proprie passionibus corrumpi, eiusdem erit et quod pro compassione promittitur... ita amborum erit etiam conglorificari sicut et compati: secundum collegia laborum consortia quoque decurrant necesse est praemiorum*'.

[52] Augustine, *St. Augustine's Confessions*, vol. 1, trans. William Watts (London, 1918), 100; Book 3.2: '*quamquam, cum ipse patitur, miseria, cum aliis compatitur, misericordia dici solet. sed qualis tandem misericordia in rebus fictis et scenicis?*'

[53] Ibid. 104; Book 3.2: '*nam etsi adprobatur officio caritatis qui dolet miserum, mallet tamen utique non esse quod doleret, qui germanitus misericors est*'.

who is sufficient for this task?'⁵⁴ Paul's rhetorical question asks the Church at Corinth to supply as its solution the paradigm of a compassionate redeemer.

The Christian concept of atoning compassion, then, was originally a Pauline conceit and later, through the Pauline writings, it became a Patristic ethical category. In the early modern period the theory influences the poetry and sermons of John Donne. God's loving compassion towards humanity becomes reflected, in Donne's penchant for puns, in the compass of Jesus's arms, which are transfixed to the cross to redeem the world in an inclusive, worldwide embrace. In 'Goodfriday, 1613. Riding Westward' the speaker asks, 'Could I behold those hands which span the Poles, / And tune all spheares at once, peirc'd with those holes?' (21–22).⁵⁵ In one homily Doctor Donne scolds reprobates who are 'loth that Christ should spread his armès, or shed his bloud in such a compasse, as might fall upon *all*', and in another sermon Donne envisions the cross as a fence or 'Paile, and [Christ's] *Mercy compasses us about*'.⁵⁶

Paradise Lost inherits this legacy of linking redemptive love, imagined as the Son's compassionating with humanity, with the crucified Son's encompassing, salvific embrace of the world. When the Son makes his redemptive offer at the Heavenly Council, the narrator emphasizes the corresponding 'Divine compassion' (3.141) manifested in the Son's countenance, which is expressive of the Father's will to save. The Father responds by enjoining His angels to praise the Son for his willingness to redeem and to 'Adore him, who to compass all this dies' (3.342). In Raphael's hexaemeron God's words prophesying the redemption are literalized as the Son spreads the golden compasses 'to compass all this' world. In the Son's extending of the golden compasses Milton fashions a vivid emblem of redemptive compassibility, that is, of Christ's *theanthropic* suffering with and for humanity. The spatial reach of the Son's creative embrace as he marks out Creation's circumference with his golden compasses is commensurable with his compassionating embrace in establishing a New Creation by his future atonement. The Son's spatial mapping of the Old Creation with the arms of God's golden compasses foreshadows his future spiritual embrace of the New Creation when Christ crucified, indeed, spreads wide his arms and, to compass all, dies.

Satan, aping God's Son, caricatures the Son's creative and recreative encompassing of the world. Satan's two sorties to uncreate mundane Creation in Books Four and Nine of *Paradise Lost* conflict with the Son's zeal to redeem it in Book Three. In the interval between these two assaults, between Satan's thwarted and then finally successful temptations, the Devil '*compast the Earth*' ('Argument' to Book Nine) like a noisome fly buzzing about some choice delicacy or a bird of prey circling above its quarry. In a sermon entitled *Satans Compassing the Earth* the Puritan divine Henry Smith explicated a passage from Job that describes Satan's action of compassing. In the Geneva Bible translation of 1560 Satan tells God that he comes

⁵⁴ Ibid. 104; Book 3.2.
⁵⁵ John Donne, *The Divine Poems*, ed. Helen Gardner (Oxford, 1969), 31.
⁵⁶ John Donne, *Sermons*, vol. 9, 119 and 410.

'From compassing the earth to and fro, and from walking in it' (Job 1:7).[57] The Geneva Bible's accompanying marginal note characterizes Satan's revolutions about the Earth as predatory actions: 'Herein is described the nature of Satan, which is ever ranging for his pray.'[58] Smith finds in this passage evidence for a Satan who hunts down human game by compassing it. He opens the scriptural text by arguing that Satan's compassing signifies 'the divils pilgrimage' and that 'his name Satan . . . doth tell us why he compasseth. Because it signifies an adversarie, it giveth us to understande that hee compasseth the earth like an adversarie. God doth compas the earth like a wall to defend it: the devill compasseth the earth like an enemie to besiege it.'[59] In Milton's poem Satan's compassing effectively comprises a blockade of the Earth, because he is poised to make his second attempt to claim Eden and, in gaining Eden, Satan thinks that he wins the world. But Satan's compassing also counterfeits the six days during which the Son elaborates Creation by extending and rotating the golden compasses and thereby expresses his divine love and compassion for the world he has delivered. The fiend 'returnd / From compassing the Earth . . . The space of sev'n continu'd Nights he rode / With darkness' (9.58–59, 63–64). On attaining Eden, Satan boasts that he will 'mar[] / What hee *Almightie* stil'd, six Nights and Days / Continu'd making' (9.136–38), namely the Son's 'Six Days work, a World' (7.568). Satan's restless shadowing of his kill for seven days and nights acts as a foil to the Son's six-day-long circumscription and perfection of Creation's splendours, crowned by humanity's stewardship and consecrated on the seventh day with the worshipful recreation of a Sabbath rest.

As well as the opposition between the Son's seven-day labour of love in adorning Creation and Satan's seven-night flight, contriving Creation's destruction, the narrator evokes the Son's atoning antidote to the Fall in another symbolic spatial movement. The poem counterpoints Satan's characteristically destructive descents with the Son's recreative ascents. The narrator describes Satan's voyage to defile Eden in a series of prepositional 'downs', a litany of aggravated declivities. From Hell's gates, 'down he drops / Ten thousand fadom deep, and to this hour / Down had been falling' (2.933–35). From the lower stair of Heaven's Gates Satan 'Looks down' (3.542) upon the world and then 'Down . . . throws / His flight precipitant' (3.562–63). 'Down from th' Ecliptic' (3.740) he lights on Niphates and, like the Dragon of Revelation, 'Came furious down to be reveng'd on men . . . came down' (4.4, 9). On reaching his destination, unrelentingly 'down / The way he went' (4.125–26) and, from Satan's perch on the Tree of Life, 'Down he alights among the sportful Herd' (4.396). Trespassing upon Eden's bounds, Satan degenerates further ontologically. On Earth he degrades himself on Nature's scale by likening himself to or imbruting himself within successive zoomorphic shapes: first, as 'a prowling Wolfe' (4.183); then perched on the Tree of Life 'like a Cormorant'

---

[57] The Geneva translation probably obtained the verb 'compassing' for describing Satan's movement at Job 1:7 from the Vulgate's *circuire*, which means 'to travel around' or 'to encompass'.

[58] The Geneva Bible supplies 1 Peter 5:8 as an accompanying scriptural proof text: 'Be sober and watch: for your aduersarie the deuil as a roaring lyon walketh about, seking whome he may deuoure.'

[59] Henry Smith, *Satans Compassing the Earth* (London, 1592), 9–10.

(4.196), a bird of prey and a Renaissance symbol of greed; next 'A Lion now he stalkes with fierie glare, / Then as a Tiger' (4.402–3); and last, basely 'Squat like a Toad, close at the eare of *Eve*' (4.800).[60] Finally, Satan receives his just deserts in a humiliating theriomorphosis. Having 'Ascended his high Throne' (10.445), he is silenced in midboast and, 'supplanted down he fell / A monstrous Serpent on his Belly prone' (10.513–14). These destructive Satanic downfalls, spatio-ontological markers of his compulsion to sin, are matched by the Son's recreative rises after Creation is completed. The Son's rises anticipate the resurrected Christ's drawing of renewed Creation to himself. The Son and his angelic train re-ascend in an anaphora of Christic 'ups' that counterbalance Satan's diabolic 'downs': 'up returnd [the Son], / Up to the Heav'n of Heav'ns his high abode' (7.552–53), and 'Up he rode' (7.557), 'The glorious Train ascending' (7.574). The 'bright Pomp' of the Son's angelic escort 'ascended jubilant' (7.564). This epithet 'jubilant' signifies the Hebrew year of Jubilee, which commemorates the remission of God's people from slavery and their restitution to a condition of prosperity. The festival was traditionally celebrated every fiftieth year in remembrance of the Exodus and the Hebrews' enfranchisement from Egyptian tyranny (see Lev. 25:8–55). Raphael's jubilant angels proleptically honour God's Son, the re-ascending, creative Word, as the future *Christus liberator*, who ushers in a new Jubilee by emancipating humanity from the bondage of sin and death.

I showed above how Milton incorporates scriptural intertexts within Raphael's hexaemeron to sharpen our perception of the presence of Christic humiliation and Incarnation in the Son's descent into Chaos. Once the Son finishes the work of Creation, biblical allusion associates the Son's ascent with Jesus's future ascension. Mary Ann Radzinowicz has explored how the New Testament's reinterpretation and reformation of the Book of Psalms impinge upon 'the decisive doctrines and decisions of the Christian faith' underpinning Milton's poetry.[61] Above all, Radzinowicz asserts, the Psalms gave Milton 'authority for his understanding of the meaning of the Son's life, the quality of the Son's thought, and the nature of the Son's heroism'.[62] Two prominent Psalms, Psalm 24 and Psalm 68, inform the nature of the Son's ascent in Raphael's hexaemeron. Appropriately, Christians reinterpreted both Psalms as Ascension Psalms and categorized them within that subgenre of Psalms thought to foretell the resurrected Son's '*reascention into Heaven*' ('Argument' to Book Seven). The 'Argument' glosses that '*the Angels celebrate with Hymns the performance*' of the Son's Creation. A familiarity with Milton's angelic hymns in Book Seven reveals their debt to these two Ascension Psalms.

---

[60] For Renaissance instances of the cormorant's proverbial greed, see Shakespeare's 'cormorant devouring Time' (*LLL* I.i.4) and Spenser's 'Cormoyraunts . . . birds of rauenous race' (*FQ* II.xii.8.5): William Shakespeare, *The Riverside Shakespeare*, ed. G. Blakemore Evans and J. J. M. Tobin (2nd edn, Boston, 1997), 213; and Edmund Spenser, *The Faerie Queen*, ed. A. C. Hamilton (2nd edn, Harlow, 2007), 271.

[61] Mary Ann Radzinowicz, *Milton's Epics and the Book of Psalms* (Princeton, 1989), 48.

[62] Ibid.

Once the Son is equipped to sally forth and create the world, Heaven opens 'Her ever during Gates' (7.206) to release 'The King of Glorie, in his powerful Word' (7.208). The honorific title 'King of Glorie' is unique to Psalm 24, where it is mentioned five times (see Ps. 24:7–10). After the Son founds, conglobes, and moulds the world, he is able to ascend victorious. Milton engrafts the refrain to Psalm 24 upon the hymn with which the angels welcome the returning Son: 'Lift up your heads, O ye gates; and be ye lift up, ye everlasting doors; and the King of glory shall come in' (AV Ps. 24:7). Milton's jubilant angels echo this:

> Op'n, ye everlasting Gates, they sung,
> Op'n, ye Heav'ns, your living dores; let in
> The great Creator from his work returnd
> Magnificent, his Six Days work, a World;
> Op'n, and henceforth oft; for God will deigne
> To visit oft the dwellings of just Men
> Delighted
>
> (7.565–71)

Newton's commentary correctly identifies Milton's allusion to Psalm 24 here. Furthermore, Newton remarks how Christians understood this Psalm as a prophecy of Christ's exaltation: 'This hymn was sung when the ark of God was carried up into the sanctuary on mount Sion, and is understood as a prophecy of our Saviour's ascension into Heaven; and therefore is fitly applied by our author to the same divine Person's ascending thither after he had created the world.'[63] Psalm 24 invites this interpretation since it appears to enumerate the Son's eligibility, his worthiness to create, recreate, and be restored to his Father's side: 'Who shall ascend into the hill of the Lord? or who shall stand in his holy place? He that hath clean hands, and a pure heart; who hath not lifted up his soul unto vanity, nor sworn deceitfully. He shall receive the blessing from the Lord, and righteousness from the God of his salvation' (AV Ps. 24:3–5). *Paradise Lost* and *De Doctrina Christiana* declare that the Son's ability to create and restore resides in his intrinsic merit as the one 'worthiest to be Heir / Of all things ... thy deserved right' (6.707–09; and see 3.290–94, 308–09; PR 3.196–97). The treatise analogously asserts that the Son earns exaltation 'BY HIS OWN MERIT [SUO MERITO]' (CE 15.308).

The vast equipage of God that escorts the Son on his descent into Chaos and ascent into Heaven – the 'numberless ... Cherube and Seraph, Potentates and Thrones, / And Vertues, winged Spirits, and Chariots wingd, / From th' Armoury of God' (7.197–200) – is inspired by Zechariah 6:1, which speaks of God's arsenal, stored between 'mountains of brass'. The Son's impressive triumphal procession of heavenly spirits also evokes Psalm 68:

> The chariots of God are twenty thousand, even thousands of angels: the Lord is among them as in Sinai, in the holy place. Thou hast ascended on high, thou hast led captivity captive: thou hast received gifts for men; yea, for the rebellious also, that the Lord God might dwell among them. Blessed be the Lord, who daily loadeth us with

---

[63] Newton, ed., *Paradise Lost*, vol. 2, 56–57.

122 The Son of God in the Works of John Milton

benefits, even the God of our salvation. Selah. He that is our God is the God of salvation; and unto God the Lord belong the issues from death. (*AV*, Ps. 68:17–20)

De Doctrina Christiana teases out Psalm 68's 'enlarged' meaning in light of the fulfilment of the new covenant. The treatise distinguishes not one, but two divine agents in the passage: 'Here . . . mention is made of two figures, *God* and *the Lord*' (*CE* 14.276). Raphael correspondingly argues that God's 'uncircumscrib'd' (7.170) omnipresence allows the Father to join the Son on his creative mission, while He simultaneously remains enthroned in the Empyrean: '[God] also went / Invisible, yet staid (such priviledge / Hath Omnipresence)' (7.588–90; and see 7.192–96, 207–09, 218–20). The preincarnate Son, though, even when he is seated next to God, 'is in a circumscribed place, and is not ubiquitous [*definito in loco est, et non ubique*]' (*CE* 15.314). Milton's presentation of the physics and metaphysics of the Son's ascent into the Heaven of Heavens to rejoin his Father after completing the work of Creation replicates the physics and metaphysics of Christ's ascension after his resurrection, as set forth in *De Doctrina Christiana*. According to the treatise, God the Father, 'who was in the Son, once reconciliation had been made, returned with His Son into glory, or received Himself into the greatest glory, which supreme glory He had obtained in the Son' (*CE* 14.266). At Ephesians 4:9 Paul interprets Psalm 68 in soteriological terms and, consequently, *De Doctrina Christiana* comprehends the Psalm as a prediction of Jesus's post-resurrectional ascension: 'From which [Paul] wanted to show this much, that Christ our Lord, once dead, now received into heaven, gave gifts to men which he had received from his Father' (*CE* 14.276). Ephesians 4, citing and expounding Psalm 68:18, maintains that at the resurrection Jesus led captivity captive and overcame Sin and Death:

> 'Having ascended on high he led captivity captive; he gave gifts to humanity.' What does [Psalm 68] mean by 'he ascended,' unless it means that he previously descended into the lowest parts of the Earth? The one who descended is also the one who ascended far above all the heavens that he might fill all things. (Eph. 4:8–10)

Milton's narrator endorses this Pauline re-rendering of Psalm 68, a translation of old wine into new bottles, by describing the exalted *Christus victor* who 'with ascension bright / Captivity led captive through the Aire' (10.187–88; see 3.254–56). Milton fittingly appropriates the Ascension Psalms 24 and 68 and incorporates them into his angels' celebrations of the Son's ascent. He thus assimilates the resources of ancient psalmody to serve Raphael's spatial Passion allegory. The exoteric Creation narrative of the Son's descent, his composing of Creation, and his ascension to God's right hand tells another esoteric story that articulates the future historical process of human salvation through the incarnate Son's humiliation and glorification.

In concluding his narrative, Raphael informs Adam that in God's eyes the Son's work of Creation was successful in 'Answering his great Idea' (7.557). That the Son 'answers' the divine plan of Creation to his Father's satisfaction speaks to the soteriological preoccupations underpinning Raphael's hexaemeral narrative, since the verb 'answer' originally connoted redeeming, atoning for, and standing surety for another (*OED* def. 1.2, 3, 6–10). One does not have to peel back too many semantic layers to perceive the importance of the atonement for the 'answerable stile' (9.20) of Milton's epic and to discern the Passional subtext to Raphael's complementary narratives. Adam's gracious response to Raphael's gift of narration hints at the *sensus duplex* attaching to Raphael's histories. These narratives work simultaneously as martial and hexaemeral poetic histories and, to borrow William Hunter's phrase, as enormous metaphors or, more exactly, temporal and spatial Passion allegories. Adam, thanking Raphael for his history, 'gratefully repli'd . . . / What thanks sufficient, or what recompence / Equal have I to render thee, Divine / Historian' (8.4–7)? With a dramatic irony so dense it is almost tangible the redemptive economy of Adam's language previews his future fallen state, when humankind will require a surety. The sufficient 'thanks' or grace (Latin *gratia* – 'thanks') afforded by the atonement will 'recompense' and 'render' back to Adam's descendants, burdened by sin's debt, what they have lost. Their redeemer will deliver them as God's 'grateful' subjects, relieved, renewed, and full of grace. Milton's readers can appreciate how these dual Passion allegories function by discerning how the exoteric and esoteric senses work together within Raphael's narratives. Being 'on the inside', as well as 'on the outside', of Raphael's narratives helps readers to recognize the vital message suggested by the sociable archangel that, without the security God guarantees through the Son's redemption, fallen humanity can rely 'On other surety none'.

5

The Good Communicated: Milton's Drama
of the Fall and the Law of Charity

I am long since perswaded, that to say, or doe ought worth memory, and
imitation, no purpose or respect should sooner move us, then simply the love
of God, and of mankinde.

John Milton, *Of Education*

> *Love God, and love your neighbour. Watch and pray.*
> *Do as ye would be done unto.*
> O dark instructions; ev'n as dark as day!
> Who can these Gordian knots undo?

George Herbert, 'Divinitie'[1]

In Book Twelve of *Paradise Lost* Michael explains that upon the cross, 'The Law of
God exact [Christ] shall fulfill / Both by obedience and by love, though love / Alone
fulfill the Law' (12.402–04). *De Doctrina Christiana* makes clear what Milton
means by this point of doctrine. In the treatise's consideration of redemption,
Christ 'fulfilled the law by his most perfect love of God and his neighbour until,
obedient to his Father in all things, he sought death for the sake of his brethren'
(*CE* 15.316). The treatise further subdivides charity towards one's neighbour into
two familiar categories as it 'EMBRACES THE UNIVERSAL DUTY OF LOVE BOTH TOWARDS
ONESELF AND TOWARDS ONE'S NEIGHBOUR' (*CE* 17.196). In *Of Civil Power* (1659)
Milton confirmed the universal applicability of this doctrine of charity: 'our whole
practical dutie in religion is contained in charitie, or the love of God and our
neighbour, no way to be forc'd, yet the fulfilling of the whole law; that is to say, our
whole practise in religion' (*CPW* 7.256). In the Synoptic gospels Christ teaches
that these two loves, the love of God and the love of oneself and of one's neighbour,
comprise the heart of Torah (Matt. 22:34–40; Mark 12:28–34; Luke 10:25–28),
and elsewhere Jesus more radically recommends love of one's enemy (Matt.
5:43–48). *De Doctrina Christiana*, as is standard for Reformed dogma, interprets
the Mosaic Law as a forerunner to the gospels, as a means to, in Michael's words,
discovering but not removing 'natural pravitie' (12.285–306). Only Christ's
redemption can abolish sin so that humanity may thereby 'finde / Justification

---

[1] Herbert, 135.

towards God' (12.295–96). Thus, 'Even under the law, though more obscurely, both a redeemer and the necessity for redemption are perceived . . . Under the gospel, more openly, both a redeemer and the truth of the redemption are perceived' (*CE* 16.98, 100). *De Doctrina Christiana* chronicles the gradual disclosure of the redemption throughout biblical history, first, darkly portended before the giving of the Mosaic Law, then dimly veiled within the Law, and, finally, brightly revealed in Christ. But although 'the whole Mosaic Law is abolished by the gospel' (*CE* 16.140), the heart of the Law still endures:

> It may be evinced, first, from all these Scriptural authorities, next, from the accompanying arguments, that the whole Mosaic Law is abolished by the gospel. And yet, by this abolition of the Law, the Law (that is, the sum of the Law) is not in fact really abrogated, but its goal is attained in that love of God and one's neighbour, which is born out of faith through the Spirit. On this basis Christ truly championed the Law, Matt. 5:17 . . . Therefore the sum of the Law [which], as I said before, [is] certainly the love of God and neighbour, should by no means be considered as abolished. (*CE* 16.140, 142)

Christian tradition interprets the two tablets upon which God inscribed the Ten Commandments as a bodying forth of this principle. One tablet was engraved with those commandments pertaining to the love of God, the first four 'vertical commandments' concerning the relationship between humanity and God; the other tablet was inscribed with those commandments pertaining to the love of neighbour, the remaining six 'horizontal commandments' concerning interhuman relationships. *De Doctrina Christiana*'s advocacy of this concord between the heart of the Mosaic Law and the essence of the gospels is important for understanding the treatise's soteriological method in Christ. *De Doctrina Christiana* cites Jerome Zanchius as an authority on the importance of the fulfilment of the double love for salvation. Milton's *Second Defence* (1654) had esteemed Zanchius among those 'theologians of highest repute' (*CE* 8.66) and that rank of blind worthies, alongside the Hebrew Patriarchs Isaac and Jacob, Timoleon of Corinth, and Appius Claudius. *De Doctrina Christiana* quotes from, and adds to, Zanchius's *Commentary on the Epistle of Saint Paul to the Ephesians* that '*it is not possible for the Scriptures to be properly understood, especially concerning the doctrine of justification and good works*, indeed, I should have said the entire gospel, *unless that article concerning the abrogation of the Law is understood*' (*CE* 16.146), namely the retention of the significance of the double love. Milton's interpolation within Zanchius's statement emphasizes the double love of God (Deut. 6:4, 5) and love of one's neighbour (Lev. 19:18; Matt. 19:19) as the kernel to the Old and New Testaments.

The cross, then, is the meeting-point between God and humanity in which Jesus the God-man reconciles and consummates the double love. The epiphany of Jesus, the perfect man, accomplishes the striking of a new covenant, an internalized law that preserves the sum of the old Mosaic Law. The Pauline writings maintain, 'you show that you are an epistle of Christ, cared for by us, written, not with ink, but with the spirit of the living God; not on stony tablets, but on tablets that are hearts of flesh' (2 Cor. 3:3). Moreover, *De Doctrina Christiana* asserts that the double love pertains to those who existed even before God delivered the Law to Israel. Just as the double love is the epitome of the Mosaic Law and Jesus's gospel teachings, it also constitutes the essential basis for human natural law. Milton scholars are wont to cite *De Doctrina Christiana*'s manifold definition of primal sin as a stew of vice:

> Under this [actual sin] what did humankind not perpetrate? Credulousness of Satan, disbelief in God that humanity would be virtually damned, faithlessness, ingratitude, disobedience, gluttony, he for behaving uxoriously, she for not heeding her husband, both for not heeding their offspring, for not heeding the entire human race, parricide, theft, and plundering another, sacrilege, deceit, conspiring to gain Godhead, and an undeserved striving, pride, presumptuousness. (*CE* 15.180, 182)

The treatise abridges this catena of vices and prefixes one simple compendious phrase indicating that original sin constituted 'a most atrocious transgression of the entire Law [*atrocissimum . . . totius legis transgressionem*]' (*CE* 15.180). *De Doctrina Christiana* first defines the nature or substance of sin as '*anomia*, or the transgression of the law [*legis transgressio*]' (*CE* 15.178); what, in modern parlance, we call anomie or lawlessness. The treatise derives this anomie from 1 John 3:4: 'All who commit sin also commit anomie, and sin is anomie.' The Greek word νομός is the standard New Testament designation for the Mosaic Law, but *De Doctrina Christiana* specifies that 'here, by the name of law, is primarily understood that which is inborn and implanted in the human mind', 'for the Law through Moses was written long after' (*CE* 15.178–80). 'GOD'S LAW is either unwritten or written': the law 'not written is that natural [law] given to the first man [Adam] of which a remnant or a kind of light persists in the hearts of all mortals' (*CE* 16.100). The essence of 'God's will either under the [Mosaic] Law or the gospel' (*CE* 16.100) was originally Edenic natural law. In their prelapsarian state and created in God's image, Adam and Eve possessed an innate and implanted conscience: 'Since humanity was made in God's image, and had the whole law of nature born with them, and had it implanted within them, they were not lacking a precept to hold them to that law' (*CE* 15.114). Formally unlike, but essentially identical to the written precepts of Mosaic Law, this natural law is a universal, inborn, unwritten moral law that resembles Christian liberty under the gospels whereby, 'within the regenerated, the Holy Spirit's work is being renovated daily to its primeval perfection' (*CE* 16.100). Anomie or lawlessness, sin's foundation, is an anomaly or perversion of human natural law. In Eden Adam and Eve could perfectly observe that natural law, the love of God and one another. For postlapsarian humanity existing in primeval history before the divine commission of Torah, that natural law, though obscured by the Fall, was still implanted within humanity. Upon Yahweh's delivery of the Law, the Law evinced humanity's fallen sinfulness, which comprised their repeated transgression of the double love, but humanity alone could neither cancel nor satisfy the penalty for those transgressions. According to Michael's teaching, which alludes to Colossians 2:14, the redeemer's advent fulfils the Law: 'But to the Cross he [Christ] nailes thy Enemies, / The Law that is against thee, and the sins / Of all mankinde, with him there crucifi'd' (12.415–17). The Son reconciles God to humanity by his death, fulfilling the Law and, enshrined within the Law, the double love marred since Adam's loss of that 'primeval perfection'.

Paradise Lost scrupulously records Adam and Eve's falling off from their perfect observance of the double love. When the reader first encounters the immaculate pair, they impeccably observe the inviolable double love, 'Hee for God onely, shee for God in him' (4.299). Adam fears that Satan will maliciously strive to convince them to desecrate this double love somehow: 'Whether his first design be to withdraw / Our fealtie from God [love of God], or to disturb / Conjugal Love [love of one another]' (9.261–63). Once Adam and Eve have fallen, their physical deportment betrays that they have transgressed both elements of the double love because 'Love was not in thir looks, either to God / Or to each other' (10.111–12). Adam's tragically reckless comment following his Fall inadvertently binds together God's single prohibition not to eat the Forbidden Fruit and the ten prohibitions of the Decalogue: 'if such pleasure be / In things to us forbidd'n, it might be wisht, / For this one Tree had bin forbidd'n ten' (9.1024–26). The violation of the single prohibition by Adam and Eve and the transgression of the Ten Commandments by fallen humanity are restituted by Christ's affirmation of the double love upon the cross. This double affirmation is exactly what the Edenic prohibition was established to preserve and what the Decalogue was instituted to protect. Where the Decalogue works prohibitively to prevent or limit transgression, Christ was thought to cancel transgression by his atonement and to become the exemplar of the double love. Adam's words are ironized and hint that both the single and tenfold prohibitions, which implicitly affirm the maintenance of the double love, are collapsible and show the correct way for humans to behave morally towards God, themselves, and one another. Adam and Eve's transgression of God's single Edenic prohibition, the warning not to 'easily transgress the sole Command, / Sole pledge of his obedience' (3.94–95), violates 'This one, this easie charge' (4.421), and 'transgress, and slight that sole command' (7.47) is, at its core, as Milton's drama of the Fall illustrates, a transgression of the double love that constitutes a digest of the Decalogue and an abridgement of gospel teaching.

When in Book Nine Adam and Eve deliberate whether to fall, they travesty and parody the double love that finds its fulfilment in their Saviour. Luther's teaching on the *viva vox Christi* or 'living voice of Christ' maintained that Christ ubiquitously inhabited scripture so that 'Whether *in, with, by, through,* or *under* the verbal sign, Christ was assumed to be present'.[2] In the same way, the redeemer's kenotic, self-emptying attitude is partially or perversely expressed in Milton's drama of the Fall through irony and scriptural allusion. The strong suggestions of the Son's restoration of humanity constitute the mainspring of Milton's poetic across Book Nine. In Milton scholarship motive-hunters have proffered a spectrum of causes for Milton's Fall, from C. S. Lewis's simple disobedience to Edwin Greenlaw's unreason, from James Holly Hanford's lust to Charles Williams's ' "injured merit" ', and from E. M. W. Tillyard's ' "levity and shallowness of mind" ' to J. B. Broadbent's 'alienation'.[3] It is my contention that, more than these motives, the root cause of

[2] Christopher, *Science*, 121.
[3] Lewis, *Preface*, 124–28; Edwin Greenlaw, 'A Better Teacher than Aquinas', *Studies in Philology*, 15 (1917), 196–217; James Holly Hanford, 'The Temptation Motive in Milton', *Studies in Philology*,

Milton's Fall is Adam and Eve's travesty of the double love, reversed and recovered by Christ's life, death, and teaching.

I

Among the possible outlines for tragedies Milton submitted in the Trinity Manuscript, he included, together with two versions on the Fall entitled 'Paradise Lost' and 'Adam unparadiz'd', hypothetical versions on redemption – 'Christ bound', 'Christ Crucifi'd', and 'Christus patiens' (*CPW* 8.554–60). Earlier I examined how the first invocation proclaims the epic subject to be the first Adam's Fall and the second Adam's rise. Book Nine's invocation similarly highlights the redeeming Son, before narrating Adam and Eve's Fall and their fallen education regarding the atonement's meaning. The invocation begins with a fusillade of negations explaining how the narrator is 'Not sedulous by Nature to indite / Warrs' (9.27–28). This formal *recusatio* systematically rejects the stuff of martial epic in a mere six lines (9.13–19). The great heroes jostle together: 'the wrauth / Of stern *Achilles*', Hector, 'Thrice Fugitive about *Troy* Wall', Odysseus, rudely termed 'the *Greek*', Aeneas, periphrastically nominated as '*Cytherea's* Son', and the 'rage / Of *Turnus*'. Milton condenses the divine wrath fuelling the action of the *Odyssey* and the *Aeneid* into the throwaway phrase, '*Neptun's* ire or *Juno's*' (9.18). The gewgaws of Tasso and Ariosto's chivalric blockbusters are as speedily dispatched, their heroes tricked out in 'Bases and tinsel Trappings, gorgious Knights / At Joust and Torneament' (9.36–37), their status fictive and 'fabl'd', their deeds ridiculed as 'long and tedious havoc' (9.30), and their triumphs debunked as 'Battels feignd' (9.31). In their stead the invocation promises an 'argument / Not less but more Heroic' (9.13–14) than such human or divine belligerence, 'hitherto the onely Argument / Heroic deemd' (9.28–29). The heroic mode the narrator intends is nested within barely two verses, 'the better fortitude / Of Patience and Heroic Martyrdom / Unsung' (9.31–33). *De Doctrina Christiana* treats these two virtues of fortitude and patience and associates both ethical qualities with Christ: 'FORTITUDE [*FORTITUDO*] shines out most greatly in repelling or not fearing evils . . . The greatest example of fortitude is our Saviour Jesus Christ in his whole life and death . . . PATIENCE [*PATIENTIA*] consists of strongly enduring evils and injuries' (*CE* 17.246, 248, 252).[4] Milton's Adam, too, links unexampled fortitude with Christ's heroic self-sacrifice, acknowledging that 'suffering for Truths sake / Is fortitude to highest victorie' (12.569–70).

---

15 (1918), 176–94; Milton, *The English Poems of Milton*, ed. Charles Williams (Oxford, 1940), introduction; E. M. W. Tillyard, *Milton: Revised Edition* (New York, 1967), 266; Broadbent, 254.

[4] '*FORTITUDO elucet maxime in malis propulsandis aut non metuendis.* [. . .] *Fortitudinis exemplum maximum est servator noster Iesus Christus tota vita ac morte* [. . .] *PATIENTIA est in malis atque iniuriis perferendis.*' The treatise's proof texts supporting Christ's exemplary fortitude refer to his endurance on the cross: 'Let him take up his cross and follow me' (Matt. 16:24; see Matt. 16:21); 'but if we do not see what we hope for, we eagerly expect [the redemption of our bodies] with patience' (Rom. 8:25); and 'for this reason I assent to infirmities, injuries, hardships, persecutions, and distresses, for Christ's sake' (2 Cor. 12:10).

If the better fortitude of patience and heroic martyrdom in Book Nine's invocation involves the suffering Christ, then the 'answerable stile' (9.20) the narrator seeks to obtain is a poetic mode that will 'answer' or 'redeem' the dismal ensuing narrative of the Fall. This poetic mode will, in effect, transmute into Christian comedy those notes that have, with humanity's falling away from God, been changed to tragic. The primary early modern understanding of 'answerability' – to satisfy, to suffer, to justify, to discharge a debt, to atone (*OED* 2, 3, 5–10) – speaks to the epic's broader imperatives, which explore humanity's atonement prevailing before, during, and after the Fall. To be 'answerable' means to be capable of response, to be magnanimous enough to be responsible, and this Miltonic, heroic state includes Christ's mediation and reconciliation, which is responsive to human suffering. Angus Fletcher thus speaks of the poem's total design as being 'built upon the most massive symmetries and mysteries of narrative structure, all of which turn upon the answering role of Christ the Redeemer'.[5] Milton uses his much-loved paralleling technique, a point–counterpoint of phrases echoing across the epic, to show that the free grace purchased by Christ's sacrifice to cancel out the Fall's effects is the same grace empowering the fallen narrator to sing his epic redemption song. The narrator sings of his Muse and how 'Her nightly visitation' comes 'unimplor'd' (9.22), just as the Son asks his Father whether, through sacrifice, 'shall Grace not find means, that finds her way . . . To visit all [God's] creatures, and to all / Comes unprevented, unimplor'd, unsought' (3.228–31). The verbal resonances between the Son's testimony of 'unimplor'd' grace, bequeathed through atonement, and the heavenly Muse's 'unimplor'd' gracious visitation are luminous and clarifying. Only the suffering Christ's fortitude and patience 'justly gives Heroic name / To Person or to Poem' (9.40–41). Of sufficient grace, the narrator, like all humans, 'hath none to bring' (3.235), except the grace 'sufficient of it self to raise / That name' (9.43–44). Christ is the name being raised or exalted. This is the same 'name' the narrator earlier saluted and raised when, joining his voice to the angelic company, he invoked the 'Son of God, Saviour of Men, thy Name / Shall be the copious matter of my Song / Henceforth' (3.412–14). This is also the name Hebrews 1:4 refers to when it exalts the atoning Christ who, 'having made purification for sins, sat down at the right hand of the majesty on high, and inherited a name, having become so much greater than the angels, so much more excellent than them'. Michael glosses this text when he prophesies Jesus's humiliation and exaltation, when he will be 'exalted high / Above all names in Heav'n' (12.457–58). John Carey complains that Milton's promise to narrate the patient and fortitudinous heroism left unsung 'never materializes'.[6] Carey overlooks the fact that restoration by one greater man, Christ suffering, underwrites the declared subject of the epic exordium, Adam unparadized. The disjunctive prefixes of Book Nine's invocation – 'distrust', 'Disloyal', 'disobedience', and 'distance and distaste' (9.6–9) – though portentous of the Fall, are equally anticipatory of its panacea in the *ordo salutis*, God's atoning answer through the Son.

---

[5] Angus Fletcher, *The Transcendental Masque: An Essay on Milton's Comus* (London, 1971), 249.
[6] Carey, *Milton*, 122.

II

Following Book Nine's invocation, the first character to appear is Satan, who embarks upon his temptation of Eve and purposes, in a ghastly parody of the Incarnation, to possess the serpent. In Satan's former animal disguises he metamorphoses to appear 'like a Cormorant' (4.196) or as 'A Lion now[,] Then as a Tiger' (4.402–03). Satan's union with the serpent, however, marks the first and only time that the accuser substantially combines his angelic nature with an inferior, feral nature. The mere idea of a hypostatic union between his angelic substance and brute matter repulses Satan, 'This essence to incarnate and imbrute' (9.166). The word 'imbrute' occurs in Milton's *A Maske* in the Elder Brother's discourse on divine philosophy. There, 'by leud and lavish act of sin' (465) 'The soul grows clotted by contagion, / Imbodies, and imbrutes, till she quite loose / The divine property of her first being' (467–69). Likewise, Satan reduces his own formerly archangelic spirit by debasing and commingling it with brutish matter. Satan's repugnance marks a key difference between the imbruted fiend and the incarnate Son. Whereas the Son will 'Freely put off' (3.240) divine glory, Satan is sickened by his reptilian possession, a 'foul descent' by which he is 'now constraind / Into a Beast, and mixt with bestial slime' (9.163–65).[7] Satan's extreme measures reveal more about his own baseness in his determination to imbrute himself in a creature less than human. Satan's juxtaposition of Incarnation and imbrutation evinces the qualitative difference in these two kinds of human and serpentine tenure that the Son and Satan choose. The juxtaposition also elicits two very distinct teleologies. The Son freely humiliates himself on the scale of being by assuming flesh to save humankind, whereas Satan resents impairing his being by imbruting serpentine slime to ruin the human race. Satan attempts to revenge himself upon Godhead by afflicting the Father through His innocent children, 'To wreck on innocent frail Man his loss' (4.11) and hurt creatures 'who wrong me not' (4.387). The Son heals humanity's wound and thwarts Satan by taking the hurt and wrong upon himself.

After priding himself on his mission to spite God by imbrutation, Satan offers a second motivation in his soliloquy. He plans to discomfit:

> him who next
> Provokes my envie, this new Favorite
> Of Heav'n, this Man of Clay, Son of despite.
> Whom us the more to spite his Maker rais'd
> From dust; spite then with spite is best repaid.
> (9.174–78)

Satan's periphrasis for Adam as 'Favorite of Heav'n' as readily accommodates God's only begotten Son. Raphael's narrative of the Son's anointing recounts how Satan was 'fraught / With envie against the Son of God' (5.661–62), a detail that makes

---

[7] Mary Christopher Pecheux has explored Satan's incarnational parody: ' "O Foul Descent!": Satan and the Serpent Form', *Studies in Philology*, 62 (1965), 188–96.

Satan's words here seem to do double duty for Adam and for God's original 'Favorite', the Son. The double reference persists in Satan's venomous titles for Adam as 'this Man of Clay, Son of despite'. 'Clay' here identifies 'the human body (living or dead) as distinguished from the soul; the earthly or material part of man' (*OED* def. 4a), so that 'Man of Clay' is an embellishment for Adam, formed from the dust (10.208). 'Man of Clay' derides Adam's earthy origins as well as anticipating the Son's future Incarnation. Specifically, Satan's words summon up the Pauline contrast between the first Adamic man who is terrestrial, and the second semi-divine man who is celestial: 'The first man was from the earth, made of dust, the second man is from heaven' (1 Cor. 15:47). What Satan cannot realize is that God's preexistent and only-begotten Son, a heavenly man, will become a mortal 'Man of Clay' sent to reform the chaos Satan wreaks. The second possible rendering of 'Man of Clay' has a further piquancy when one remembers that having 'feet of clay' can symbolize 'a fundamental weakness in someone supposedly of great merit' (*OED* def. 4c). The prophet Daniel interprets King Nebuchadnezzar's dream of a statue with feet of iron and 'miry clay' (Dan. 2:41) as a symbol of a kingdom divided against itself whose weak foundations will make it topple (Dan. 2:31–47). On one level Satan disdains the vulnerability of Adam, whose estate is moulded out of dust, but on another level God's Son may also be inferred. The preincarnate Son will become a 'Man of Clay,' a creature of earthly flesh and blood and apparent weakness, but Adam's 'Redeemer' will triumph on the cross 'by things deemd weak / Subverting worldly strong' (12.573, 567–68) and from death will be 'rais'd / From dust' to new life.

As a cracked archangel, Satan has acquired a perverted understanding of the Incarnation, resurrection, and ascension, and of Christ-like heroism, when he assures himself that one 'who aspires must down as low / As high he soar'd' (9.169–70). Leslie Brisman's analysis of the constructive use of irony clarifies Satan's mistaken slip into wisdom: 'An important weapon, irony remains an opening mode . . . One text overgoes the sublime of another not by mocking or dismissing it but by sinking more low to mount more high.'[8] Brisman's turn of phrase, *by sinking more low to mount more high*, glosses Satan's unintentional use of irony. Soaring low to mount more high duplicates, in part, the Miltonic pattern of a Christian hero, exalted after the experience of humiliation. By Christ's humiliation, an act of charity for humanity, the Son is raised up to a place of glory next to God. As with the opposing acts of imbrutation and Incarnation, the difference between Satan and the Son's methods is not only in the ends, but also in the means. Satan has already failed to aspire or soar in open war against God and he now chooses an alternative method to descend by deceit and then attempt to soar higher still from that descent. The motive forces driving the fiend are 'Ambition and Revenge' (9.168). Satan is a hopeless aspirant to what Geoffrey Hill styles 'haughty degradations' and is destined never to learn, as Shakespeare's Prospero finally does, that

---

[8] Leslie Brisman, *The Voice of Jacob: On the Composition of Genesis* (Bloomington, 1990), 113.

'The rarer action is / In virtue than in vengeance' (*Temp.* V.i.27–28).[9] Dejected upon Hell's bottom, Satan and his minions plan a similar travesty of the resurrection, a re-insurrection against God whereby:

> From this descent
> Celestial Vertues rising, will appear
> More glorious and more dread then from no fall,
> And trust themselves to fear no second fate.
>
> (2.14–17)

The Satanic pattern aspires to unlimited exaltation: glory progressing to still greater glory and to a position of power to be dreaded. For Satan, who cannot comprehend humility, the only way is up. Humility constitutes regression and failure to the Satanic mind. The diabolic cannot conceive of humiliation leading to exaltation, but hungers after exaltation leading to higher exaltation. 'Virtues' are equivocal in diabolic rhetoric, teetering between alternative meanings – the Aristotelian sense of 'goodness', therefore signifying 'good angels'; the Latin meaning of Roman imperial *virtus* as 'might', therefore 'celestial powers'; and Machiavellian, Italianate *virtù*, therefore 'celestial guile'. Adam and Eve's fallen speech similarly quibbles about the Forbidden Fruit's 'vertue' (9.973, 1033), either as a thing of intrinsic moral worth or, antithetically, as an instrument making them as powerful as Gods. Satan cannot understand how God can bestow Eden's various delights upon Adam, a humble man of clay, 'Exalted from so base original' (9.150). Satan is blind to God's redemptive plan and Jesus's resurrection as a promotion, exalted to God's side from 'so base original', that is predicated upon service and humility.

Satan's reasoning is forever stunted and foreclosed because the ingrate cannot find any justification for selfless love. Despite his obduracy Satan does know that all destructive inclination 'Bitter long back on it self recoiles' (9.172), yet he perseveres in his nihilistic code that 'Save what is in destroying, other joy / To mee is lost' (9.478–79). There is little to edify the reader in Satan's *modus vivendi*. '[T]he demonic has its own form of incarnation – bestial, not humane', Roland Mushat Frye writes, 'and with the object of securing man's subjection rather than his liberation, his death rather than his life'.[10] Satan desires a retributive economy of spite against Christ's agapic economy of grace. Satan would ruin an innocent 'to spite his Maker' (9.177), corrupt a child to injure its parent. There is little merit in the Satanic dictum, 'spite then with spite is best repaid' (9.178). Satanic spite with spite, the crudest form of *lex talionis* or retaliatory justice, can only be overmatched by the Son's altruistic offer, 'life for life', to become one with that human, 'base original', so that 'mee for him, life for life / I offer... Account mee man' (3.236–38).

[9] Geoffrey Hill, *Canaan* (London, 1996), 30; from '*De Jure Belli ac Pacis,*' I.11; Shakespeare, *Riverside*, 1682.
[10] Roland Mushat Frye, *God, Man, and Satan: Patterns of Christian Thought and Life in Paradise Lost, Pilgrim's Progress, and the Great Theologians* (London, 1960), 39.

III

Satan's goal, I suggest, is to mar Adam and Eve's pristine capacity to love God, self, and neighbour. Sinless Eve acknowledges that Adam is her 'Author and Disposer' and that 'so God ordains, / God is thy Law, thou mine' (4.635–37). This rather feudalized shape of things dictates that Adam is accountable to God and Eve, as Adam's subordinate, is accountable to Adam; but we saw above that all humans, fallen or unfallen, should abide by the natural law of the double love and are accountable to God, themselves, and one another. Sinful Eve's celebrated reconciliation speech is also mistaken when she confesses, 'both have sinnd, but thou / Against God onely, I against God and thee' (10.930–31), because both Adam and Eve have transgressed by sinning against the two loves. In this respect Milton's depiction of the Fall is a far cry from Augustine's: 'Now if Adams sinne be compared with the womans: in some things it will be found equall, In some things superiour, in some inferiour to it . . . As Augustine well noteth, *de Genes.* 11.42. the man sinned onely against God and himselfe, the woman, against God, her selfe, and her neighbour.'[11] Milton's couple violate the double love: 'Love was not in thir looks, either to God / Or to each other' (10.111–12). A. Bartlett Giamatti has called *Paradise Lost* 'a massive structure of ironies' and, indeed, in Milton's dramatization of the Fall, Adam and Eve's ironized versions, perversions, and deviations from the love of God and neighbour serve, at Satan's instigation, to bring about the Fall.[12] These variations also function proleptically to remind the reader that the Son will fulfil the double love and reconcile God to humanity.

   De Doctrina Christiana characterizes the love humans should show towards one another as the 'GENERAL VIRTUE' of 'CHARITY [*CHARITAS*]', founded 'IN CHRIST' and 'INFUSED INTO THE FAITHFUL' (*CE* 17.196). Michael esteems this love as preeminent among the virtues, 'Charitie, the soul / Of all the rest' (12.584–85). Adam and Eve are guilty of the two perversions of this love of one's neighbour, namely 'THE UNIVERSAL DUTY OF LOVE BOTH TOWARDS ONESELF AND TOWARDS ONE'S NEIGHBOUR' (*CE* 17.196). By extension, their perversions of love of self and neighbour tarnish their love for God. The first perversion, to which Eve is susceptible, is 'φιλαυτία [*philautia*] or a preposterous love of oneself [*amor sui praeposterus*], whereby one either loves oneself above God or despises one's neighbour instead of oneself' (*CE* 17.200). Opposed to this excessive self-regard is 'a human being's charity towards the self, where one loves oneself in accordance with God's precepts [for the attainment of eternal life] and seeks both eternal and temporal good for oneself' (*CE* 17.200). Seeking temporal and eternal good entails 'the pursuing of external goods, but the repelling or enduring of external evils' (*CE* 17.202). The proof texts supplied to exemplify true charity are gospel texts in which Christ predicts his death and teaches that 'the one who finds his life will lose it, and the one having lost his life for my sake will find it' (Matt. 10:39; see Mark 8:35; John 12:25). Satan's temptation of Eve distorts this altruistic principle. She falls through a 'preposterous

---

[11] Andrew Willet, *Hexapla in Genesin* (Cambridge, 1605), 47.
[12] A. Bartlett Giamatti, *The Earthly Paradise and the Renaissance Epic* (Princeton, 1966), 295.

love' of self, preferring self-deification before consideration of God or Adam. In Genesis the serpent tempts Eve with the possibility that 'God doth know that in the day ye eat thereof, then your eyes shall be opened; and ye shall be as gods, knowing good and evil' (*AV* Gen. 3:5). Milton emphasizes this aspect of Eve's sin, her effecting of a disproportion in Creation by thirsting after Godhead. At the Heavenly Council God forecasts that the first human couple 'sinns / Against the high Supremacie of Heav'n, / Affecting God-head, and so loosing all' (3.204–06), and Book Three's prose 'Argument' summarizes that '*Man hath offended the majesty of God by aspiring to Godhead*'. Milton's poem carefully portrays the hubris of self-apotheosis demonstrated by the first man and woman (5.77–81; 9.546–48, 705–17, 873–78, 932–37). In Eve's dream Satan's tempting angel works upon Eve's fancy by cultivating the self-regard she showed immediately after her creation when entranced by her own reflection at the lakeside (4.449–91). The dream-Satan encourages Eve to leave the bower to be beheld by the moon and stars, Heaven's 'eyes', which are 'with ravishment / Attracted by thy beauty still to gaze' (5.44–47). He praises the Forbidden Fruit for being 'able to make Gods of Men' (5.70) and flatters Eve that she will 'be henceforth among the Gods / Thy self a Goddess, not to Earth confin'd' (5.77–78), coaxing her to 'Ascend to Heav'n, by merit thine, and see / What life the Gods live there, and such live thou' (5.80–81). Eve's dream functions as a mock-rehearsal for the temptation proper in which Satan again tempts her to overreach and crave divinity.

Book Nine's 'Argument' notes that Satan tempts by '*extolling Eve above all other Creatures*'. Ingratiatingly '[f]awning' and 'lick[ing] the ground whereon she trod' (9.526), Satan in the serpent feeds upon Eve's self-love and builds upon Adam's embroidered sublimation of Eve, which the reader has already witnessed in Adam's rhapsody to Raphael (8.546–59; see 5.18–19). Satan apotheosizes Eve with a galaxy of glorified titles and comparisons: 'sovran Mistress' (9.532), 'sole Wonder' (9.533), 'Heav'n of mildness' (9.534), 'Celestial Beautie' (9.540), 'Goddess among Gods' (9.547–48), 'Empress of this fair World' (9.568), 'Sovran of Creatures, universal Dame' (9.612), 'Empress' (9.626), 'Queen of this Universe' (9.684), and 'Goddess humane' (9.732). Satan's honorific 'Fairest resemblance of thy Maker faire' (9.538) is a muted blasphemy that implicitly undermines God and Adam by designating Deity by the simple, and Eve by the superlative, adjectival forms. Satan's sycophantic barrage aims to instigate Eve's presumption to Godhead. The root of Satan's fraud borrows directly from Genesis, that 'yee shall be as Gods' (9.708), instilling in Eve the desire to be 'ador'd and serv'd / By Angels numberless, thy daily Train' (9.547–48). Even while Eve plucks and eats, Milton's reader learns that 'nor was God-head from her thought' (9.790). There is little evidence to substantiate Diane McColley's reading that Eve 'does not merely reject the flattery but considers it a symptom of unsound reason'.[13] Eve repeats to Adam her fond wish that the Forbidden Fruit is 'of Divine effect / To op'n eyes and make them Gods who taste' (9.865–66) and she claims that the Fruit imparts the

---

[13] McColley, 197. McColley's interpretation is supported by Eve's initial response, which indicates some reservation: 'Serpent, thy overpraising leaves in doubt / The vertue of that Fruit' (9.615–16).

experience of 'growing up to Godhead' (9.877). The Fruit's effect upon them both is delusory, so that they 'fansie that they feel / Divinitie within them breeding wings' (9.1009–10).

Aged twenty-five, Milton describes the Fall in 'At a solemn Musick' (1633) as 'disproportion'd sin [that] / Jarr'd against natures chime' and 'Broke the fair musick that all creatures made' (19–21). As *De Doctrina Christiana*'s formulation of 'preposterous love' suggests, Satan works an imbalance within Creation out of Eve's privileging of her back-to-front self-love over her love of God or Adam. Satan's methods to make 'intricate seem strait' (9.632) give Eve a distorted perception of God and an inflated sense of herself. Because of God's single prohibition not to eat the Forbidden Fruit, Satan invites Eve to imagine Deity as 'the Threatner' (9.687) and, after eating the Fruit, Eve slanders God as a totalitarian dictator with an angelic police state, 'Our great Forbidder, safe with all his Spies / About him' (9.815–16). In fallen Adam's eyes, too, God degenerates into a 'Fickle' monarch (9.948–49), capriciously frolicking with His current favourites. Satan makes the cornerstone of his temptation the specious benefits that he promises would result from Eve's choice. Satan argues that Eve's supposed transgression would accomplish her rapid promotion within Creation, transforming her into a human goddess:

> That yee should be as Gods, since I as Man,
> Internal Man, is but proportion meet.
> I of brute human, yee of human Gods.
> So ye shall die perhaps, by putting off
> Human, to put on Gods, death to be wisht.
> Though threat'nd, which no worse then this can bring.
> And what are Gods that Man may not become
> As they, participating God-like food?
>
> (9.710–17)

Raphael and God envision an appropriate future time when humans would be promoted by merit and spiritual maturity to an ethereal and even God-like state (5.493–505; 7.155–61). Satan claims that, by eating the Fruit, an upwardly mobile creature can precipitate a spiritual evolution (or revolution), much as Satan, once Lucifer, sought to apotheosize himself by usurping God. By eating and transgressing, Eve disrupts Creation's hierarchy. Satan's temptation speech of hybridized 'brute humans' and 'human Gods' spoils the best of all possible worlds; yet once more irony prevails, since Satan's words pave the way towards restoration. Satan's confused oxymoronic phrases, 'brute human', 'human Gods', and 'Goddess humane' (9.732) register the violence and indignity of Satan's inducement of Eve to foment disorder. Eve is neglectful when she first notices in the speaking snake an irregular mixture of orders of knowledge and nature. Faced with this aberration, she merely wonders aloud, 'What may this mean? Language of Man pronounc't / By Tongue of Brute, and human sense exprest?' (9.553–54). With his rhetoric of brute humans and human gods Satan confuses the integrities and limitations of Creation's order through his rhetorical use (or misuse) of *catachresis* or *abusio*, the improper application of a word out of context in order to generate a contradictory or paradoxical logic. The degree to which Satan addles, muddles, and turns Creation's hierarchy topsy-turvy reflects the extent to which he conspires to abuse the divinely sanctioned order and wrench the cosmos out of joint. The reader may gauge more from Satan's confused speech, since his anarchic words gesture to the reinstatement of harmony through the Incarnation. The Son takes upon himself this disproportion to restore the crookedness of sinful human nature by reducing his divinity, putting on humanity, and becoming 'human God'. Satan's expression 'human Gods' comes close to the Origenic phrase *theanthropos* or 'God-man', the term *De Doctrina Christiana* deploys to describe the mediatorial Son as one who 'both is called and is God and human' (*CE* 15.272). This hybrid word echoes the 'human God' or 'Goddess humane' Eve aspires to become by rudely elbowing her way up the hierarchy, whereas the Son must become God-man by descending it. Satan's lure of 'putting off / Human, to put on Gods' (9.713–14) alludes to the Pauline teaching on the sinner's renovation in Christ who, 'having put off the old humankind with his machinations, has put on the new humankind, renewed', so that 'Christ is all and [is] in all' (Col. 3:9–10). All humanity shall indeed be invited to participate in 'God-like food' (9.717), partaking of, not the Forbidden Fruit Satan proffers, but the Eucharist, to memorialize the God-man's rectifying of the Creational disproportion initiated at the Fall.

If Satan's imbruting of himself in the serpent is a warped Incarnation, Eve's eating from the Forbidden Tree is a sour Eucharist. Just as a sacrament is the seal and symbol of grace imparted to the communicant, so the poem describes the Fruit as communicating its good. In Eve's dream the false angel teaches that the Forbidden 'Fruit Divine . . . since good, the more / Communicated, more abundant growes' (5.67, 71–72), and Eve later recollects these words when she dismisses God's prohibition as an act of divine jealousy that 'inferrs the good / By thee [the Tree] communicated' (9.754–55). Eve's disregard for the potentially fatal repercussions of her actions, 'Of God or Death, of Law or Penaltie' (9.775), enumerates the elements that their redeemer must respectively satisfy, defeat, fulfil, and pay. Eve's two ruinous gestures, 'she pluckd, she eat' (9.781), replicate the dream-Satan's phantom gesture, 'He pluckd, he tasted' (5.65). These paired actions foretell Jesus's sacramental institution of his atonement at the Last Supper and his invitation 'λάβετε φάγετε' or 'take, eat, this is my body' (Matt. 26:26). When Eve eats she is said to 'partake / Full happiness' (9.818–19; 5.75), evoking the participation of Christian communicants. The Fruit's power to 'Impart' (9.728) its virtue evokes the transference to communicants of the significance of the bread and wine, Christ's body and blood. Eve's intoxicating experience of the Forbidden Fruit is very different from the angelic celebration of 'Fruit of delicious Vines' (5.635), of which, repeating the gospel's sacramental refrain, the angels 'eate, they drink, and in communion sweet / Quaff immortalitie and joy' (5.637–38). The Fruit makes Eve giddy, 'highth'nd as with Wine, jocond and boon' (9.793), and with Adam 'As with new Wine intoxicated both' (10.1008). The Forbidden Fruit, a heady and deadly aberration of sacramental wine, is toxic and corrupting. Trusting in the empirical evidence of the talking serpent, Eve depends upon the auditory proof of the serpent's self-promotion and speaks of the 'credit' (9.649) of the Fruit's power. Eve's words direct the reader to the human debt of sin credited or entrusted to Christ and cancelled by his blood. Eve imagined that she would enjoy Godhead; yet, in one of the most biting turnabouts, no sooner has she eaten the Fruit than she becomes enthralled to idolatry in her adoration of the Tree. In Eve's arborilatrous address the ignominious tree of the cross is evoked. The Fruit's transient, stimulating effects have not yet dispersed to leave behind the overpowering sense of sin's burden. Delirious Eve believes that those who eat the Fruit shall 'the fertil burden ease' (9.801), yet eating from the Tree has really imparted a burden that the Son will shoulder upon the stark tree of the cross. Where the Forbidden Tree's branches are tantalizingly and licentiously 'offerd free to all' (9.802), the Saviour's blood imparts undifferentiated grace, available for all, whether Jew or Greek, slave or free, man or woman (Gal. 3:28; Col. 3:11). Whereas good works are traditionally the seal of grace for those who faithfully partake of a sacrament, Adam and Eve's lust in action after tasting the Fruit are 'of thir mutual guilt the Seale' (9.1043) and climax in a Shakespearean expense of spirit in a waste of shame.

As the narrative focus transfers from the Fall of Eve to the Fall of Adam, the first perversion of love of oneself in *De Doctrina Christiana*, preposterous and disproportionate self-love, now shifts into the treatise's other perversion of human charity, where the sinner 'despises one's neighbour instead of oneself [*proximum prae se contemnit*]' (*CE* 17.200). Eve's sin of egoism and pride, 'Her circuit ... straitened to the narrow compass of greedy self, and self itself to infant appetite', next generates envy of Adam.[14] Godhead was not absent from Eve's false reasoning, nor has Adam entered her thoughts or words since she separated from him and began conversing with the serpent. Her former desire to usurp God now results in a decision-making process whether to permit Adam to share in this anti-Eucharist and 'partake / Full happiness with [her], or rather not' (9.818–19). This anti-sacrament is apparently not graciously free to all, if Eve so decides to debar her spouse. Book Nine's 'Argument' summarizes that Eve '*deliberates a while whether to impart thereof to Adam or not*'. Knowledge is now power and the Fruit has become a commodity, a means to make the possessor, in Eve's solecism, 'more equal, and perhaps, / A thing not undesireable, somtime / Superior' (9.823–25). The troubling thought of a Lilith, of an '*Adam* wedded to another *Eve*' (9.828), resolves Eve's quandary. Like Satan binding one third of the angels to share in his perdition, Eve's hubris motivates her to coerce Adam to 'share with me in bliss or woe' (9.831). The quality of mercy is acutely strained in Eve's invidious formulation 'that with him all deaths / I could endure, without him live no life' (9.832–33). Eve's speculation, 'what if God have seen, / And *Death ensue?*' (9.826–27; emphasis added), commits her to a course of action that will rivet Adam's doom to hers. Persuading Adam to eat, Eve later protests:

> Were it I thought *Death menac't would ensue*
> This my attempt, I would sustain alone
> The worst, and not perswade thee, rather die

---

[14] McColley, 205.

>   Deserted, then oblige thee with a fact
>   Pernicious to thy Peace.
>   (9.977–81; emphasis added)

The echo of Eve's former words gives the lie to her Christ-like pretensions to sustain alone the worst of ensuing Death. Eve's complaint that, if Adam does not taste, she will 'then too late renounce / Deitie for thee, when Fate will not permit' (9.884–85), attempts to do what rebel angels and fallen humans do best: exculpate their mistakes with the language of 'Fixt Fate' (2.560) or 'necessitie, / The Tyrants plea' (4.393–94). Eve's 'too late' reveals her firm resolution never to abandon the divinity she imagines she has gained (in fact, Milton's reader knows that all seems lost), but her unspoken reluctance to 'renounce Deitie' evokes Christ, who surrenders to Death 'All that of me can die' (3.246). Eve's Fall retraces the shape of Satan's own. Her pride mutates into envy, a self-love that abnegates love of God, which, in turn, compounds with a self-love that despises her only neighbour, her sole partner. In Eve's transgression of love of neighbour, Eve is potentially the original human perpetrator of homicide, just as Satan was the original perpetrator of genocide in his spoliation of Creation.

IV

If Eve is the first human perpetrator of homicide, then Adam, by falling into his own trap of sinful disproportion, becomes the primal human perpetrator of suicide. Heedless of what Raphael has taught him of God's loving concern for Creation, Adam too risks self-deification and willingly binds his fate, in bliss or woe, with Eve's. *De Doctrina Christiana*, along with the excessive self-love to which Eve is prey, warns against another degradation of love of oneself, 'a perverse hatred of oneself [*odium sui perversum*]', which category includes suicides or, literally, 'those who inflict death upon themselves [*sunt qui mortem sibi consciscunt*]' (*CE* 17.200). The antidote the treatise offers to such perverted charity and self-hatred is Ephesians 5:29, which, appropriate to Adam's situation, concerns moderate self-love and the love a husband fosters for his wife, loving her as he loves himself. A husband's sacrificial love for his wife is compared with Christ's love in giving himself up for his Church. The cure of self-hatred is 'the righteousness of humanity towards itself . . . right reason in ruling and moderating oneself' (*CE* 17.202). When Adam is confronted with the choice whether to disobey for Eve's sake or obey for God's sake, he falls short on both counts, and neither exemplifies sacrificial love on behalf of his spouse nor uses right reason to devise a saving solution for Eve.

   Like Eve, Adam gulls himself into believing that, through some metaphysical loophole, the serpent has gained 'to live as Man / Higher degree of Life' (9.933–34). Adam entertains a notion of 'Proportional ascent, which cannot be / But to be Gods, or Angels Demi-gods' (9.936–37). At this stage Adam, though misguided, still acknowledges God as his 'Creator wise' (9.938) and he mollifies Satan and Eve's virulent blasphemies of God as a Stalinist Threatener and Forbidder with a more cautious, concessive 'Though threatening' (9.939). Nevertheless, God condemns Adam's credulity for being 'seduc't / And flatterd out of all, believing lies / Against his Maker' (10.41–43). Adam's desire to overreach obscures his reasoning. Adam's attraction to a dis-'Proportional ascent' to Deity is no less forceful than in Eve's case, although Adam betrays and then clumsily rescinds his hopes for the two of them 'to be Gods, or Angels Demi-Gods' (9.937). By Adam's embarrassed words he is known, since, like Eve and the serpent, he rhetorically confounds the ranks of the cosmic hierarchy.

Paradise Lost elides the Pauline view at 1 Timothy 2:14 that 'Adam was not deceived, but the woman was deceived and came to be in the transgression'. When the Son descends to judge the unhappy couple, he reprimands Adam for his irresponsibility: 'Was shee thy God, that her thou didst obey / Before [God's] voice' (10.145–46)? *De Doctrina Christiana* teaches that Adam fell 'for behaving uxoriously, she for not heeding her husband [*uxorius hic, mariti illa inobservantior*]' (*CE* 15.182); and Book Nine's 'Argument' describes Adam's lack of initiative, succumbing to Eve '*through vehemence of love*', a love that, etymologically speaking, 'drives him out of his wits' (Latin *vehere* + *mens*). The narrator stresses that Adam was 'not deceav'd, / But fondly overcome with Femal charm' (9.998–99), but Michael denies Adam the luxury of any bogus comfort that 'the tenor of Mans woe / Holds on the same, from Woman to begin' (11.632–33), reminding Adam of his preposterous love for Eve, 'From Mans effeminat slackness it begins' (11.634). Despite the narrator's disclaimer, then, Adam *is* guilty of a wilful and foolish self-deception. As Eve is deceived or 'dis-Eved' (a recurrent Miltonic pun), so Adam becomes vehemently uncoupled from his proper station in the hierarchy by distracting himself and pledging loyalty to Eve rather than to God. Hugo Grotius's Adam in *Adamus Exul* makes the same error of judgement by indiscriminately seeing 'two loves: on the one side God, on the other Eve: both are great' (1443–45).[15]

In Book Eight Adam's rapture at his unrestrained love for Eve and Raphael's reproof prepare the reader for Adam's Fall. In Book Nine's separation scene Adam reluctantly concedes that Eve might leave his side, addressing her as one exorbitantly 'to me beyond / Compare above all living Creatures deare' (9.227–28). Adam's praise, which verges more on idolatry than the uxoriousness critics often point to, refers beyond the historical moment to his immoderate love of Eve that inclines him to fall; it alludes to the Son's boundless love for humanity. Adam's adulation of Eve's person 'beyond compare' plays second fiddle to the inimitable Son, the first and best of all living creatures dear, in the parallel phrase, 'Beyond compare the Son of God was seen / Most glorious' (3.138–39). As God's perfect image, 'in him all his Father shon / Substantially exprest' (3.139–40). When Adam encounters a newly fallen Eve, in an internal monologue he continues his adoration of her at the point where the serpent, and he himself, left off:

[15] Hugo Grotius, *Adamus Exul*, in *The Celestial Cycle*, trans. and ed. Watson Kirkconnell (New York, 1967), 182.

> O fairest of Creation, last and best
> Of all Gods works, Creature in whom excelld
> Whatever can to sight or thought be formd,
> Holy, divine, good, amiable, or sweet!
>   (9.896–99)

Praise of Eve that exceeds the measure is a marked feature of prelapsarian Adam's speech. During Adam's vision of Eve's creation, she appears to him 'so lovly faire' that all of 'fair' nature 'seemd now / Mean, or in her summd up, in her contained' (8.471–73); and later Adam wakes Eve from her infected dream with the blandishment 'Heav'ns last best gift' (5.19). Yet again irony redirects Adam's inordinate worship of Eve to denote the Son, the firstborn and best of God's Creation. Adam, though, overlooks the divine altogether and sublimates Eve into an inordinately exalted creature, 'Holy, divine, good, amiable, or sweet!' I am hard pressed to be able to agree wholeheartedly with A. J. A. Waldock that Adam here embodies 'one of the highest, and really one of the oldest, of all human values: selflessness in love'.[16] Waldock's verdict seems to me exactly half right. Adam's fidelity to the 'Link' (9.914) or 'Bond of Nature' with Eve (9.956) completes only one half of the double love in its exclusion of God. Adam neglects the fact that all of nature, himself and Eve included, finds its ultimate source in God. Furthermore, Adam's sacrifice is diminished because he interprets his Fall solely from the human side of the double love and precludes the divine side of love's equation. Millicent Bell correctly concludes that, by electing his wife above his Maker, 'in the scale of Raphael's vision, which represents Milton's own deepest convictions concerning the ultimate proportions of things, Adam's love is sinful'.[17]

The perennial temptation among Miltonists tends to be either to heroize Adam's decision, *pace* Waldock, or to offer various judicious alternatives to what Adam should have done. John Tanner applauds Adam's 'gallant decision to die for love, if he must, with erring Eve'.[18] Northrop Frye's uncommonly severe solution was that this 'is the point at which Adam should have "divorced" Eve'.[19] Joan Bennett proposes that Adam and Eve, instead of being hasty and rash, should have kept their dialogue open long enough for the prudent exercise of *recta ratio*.[20] Philip Gallagher recommends that Adam should have vented his spleen and repudiated his wife.[21] Yet, as with Eve's Fall, genuine altruism has no real place in Adam's motivation to disobey. Adam deforms, admittedly less brazenly than Eve, Christ's fulfilment of love of God and neighbour. Margaret Justice Dean characterizes this deformation, perceiving that 'Adam becomes a false martyr, suffering for his conscientious, but idolatrous,

---

[16] A. J. A. Waldock, '*Paradise Lost*: The Fall', in *Milton's Epic Poetry: Essays on 'Paradise Lost' and 'Paradise Regained'*, ed. by C. A. Patrides (Harmondsworth, 1967), 85.

[17] Millicent Bell, 'The Fallacy of the Fall in *Paradise Lost*,' *PMLA*, 68 (1953), 873.

[18] John S. Tanner, *Anxiety in Eden: A Kierkegaardian Reading of 'Paradise Lost'* (New York, 1992), 115.

[19] Northrop Frye, *Five Essays on Milton's Epics* (London, 1966), 69; see 83–84.

[20] Joan S. Bennett, *Reviving Liberty: Radical Christian Humanism in Milton's Great Poems* (Cambridge, Mass., 1989), 109–18.

[21] Gallagher, 104 and 127.

devotion to wrong causes (Eve, marriage, martyrdom itself)', and Anne Ferry finds
that Adam's 'choice is to die with Eve, not for her[, b]ecause his fear is for his own
loneliness without her, not for her plight'.[22] To my mind, Dennis Danielson's
interpretation of this critical moment gets to the root of Adam's error of judgement.
Danielson writes:

> In facing the predicament of the fallen Eve, therefore, Adam faced no real dilemma
> between loving Eve and obeying God. In an act of dazzling heroism such as only an
> unfallen person could perform, he could have done what the fallen Eve wished *she*
> could do and what the second Adam ultimately did do: to take the punishment of
> fallen humanity upon himself, to fulfill exactly 'The law of God,' as Michael puts it in
> Book 12, 'Both by obedience and by love'.   (12.402–03)[23]

Prelapsarian Adam has the opportunity to offer to do on Eve's behalf what Christ
accomplishes for all on the cross by his loving obedience to God and love of
neighbour: 'The Law of God exact [Christ] shall fulfill / Both by obedience and
by love' (12.402–03). Milton's telltale words are 'with' and 'without'. If theodical
embarrassment is to be avoided, the operative relation is not Eve's homicidal and
Adam's suicidal 'with' and 'without', but an altruistic 'for the sake of'. Eve selfishly
determines within herself that 'with him all deaths / I could endure, without him
live no life' (9.832–33), and she later professes to Adam, though her profession is
insincere, that 'I would sustain alone / The worst' (9.978–79). During the separation scene Adam vows that a husband to his wife 'with her the worst endures'
(9.269); and, later, questioning whether he should disobey God and eat, Adam asks
of Eve, 'How can I live without thee?' (9.908). He resolves that 'I with thee have
fixt my Lot' and 'to loose thee were to loose my self' (9.952, 959), only to regret
bitterly, after the fact, that he 'willingly chose rather Death with thee' (9.1167).
Alongside the preposition 'with', Adam and Eve's claims to make ventures 'for the
sake of' the other are inadequate or incomplete. Eve lies to Adam that she ate the
Fruit to grow up into Godhead, 'which for thee / Chiefly I sought, without thee can
despise' (9.877–78), when she in fact hoped to enjoy a lofty state that, if not divine,
would at any rate 'keep the odds of Knowledge' (9.820) in her power, making her
'more equal' (9.823) to Adam, if not his 'Superior' (9.825).

Adam's offer 'to undergoe like doom' (9.953), praised by Eve as 'Love so deare, /
To undergoe with mee one Guilt, one Crime' (9.970–71), is a mock redemption, a
decision so short-sighted that lovesick Adam, unmindful of the availability of God's
mercy for Eve, is blindly self-led into death 'with' rather than 'for' his spouse. On
making his fallen excuses to the judging Son, Adam later echoes his willingness to
'undergoe' the Fall's consequences with Eve. He further travesties the redemption
by imputing the blame to Eve for the whole transgression and expressing a selfish
reluctance 'to undergoe / My self the total Crime' (10.126–27). Before he falls,

---

[22] Margaret Justice Dean, 'Choosing Death: Adam's Temptation to Martyrdom in *Paradise Lost*',
Milton Studies, 46 (2007), 41; Ferry, 60.
[23] Dennis Danielson, 'Through the Telescope of Typology: What Adam Should Have Done',
Milton Quarterly, 23 (1989), 124.

Adam's criticism of God, though not as overtly irreverent as Eve's, is nevertheless skewed. At first Adam believes the Fall to be irreparable: 'But past who can recall, or don undoe?' (9.926). Shortly thereafter, Adam dimly recognizes that, should he eat the Fruit, God would probably restore humankind. Adam damagingly charges God with a pettish and overly proud disposition that would not countenance the inconvenience and shame of having to annihilate Creation:

> so God shall uncreate,
> Be frustrate, do, undo, and labour loose,
> Not well conceav'd of God, who though his Power
> Creation could repeate, yet would be loath
> Us to abolish, least the Adversary
> Triumph and say; Fickle their State whom God
> Most Favors; who can please him long? Mee first
> He ruind, Now Mankind; whom will he next?
> Matter of scorne, not to be giv'n the Foe.
>
>   (9.943–51)

Adam's conjecture shows that he has learned little about God's goodness from Raphael's narratives. He has forgotten God's disposition to create and retire Himself out of love so that His creatures, 'with strength entire, and free Will armd' (10.9; see 7.165–73), might enjoy life, liberty, and happiness. He attributes to God the correct providential purpose, an inclination to restore, but for all the wrong reasons. God will indeed 'be loath' to destroy what He has created and will, in *De Doctrina Christiana*'s words, as 'A PATEFACTION' or 'MANIFESTATION OF HIS POWER AND THE GLORY OF HIS GOODNESS' (*CE* 15.4), preserve the Old Creation by '*the renewing of all things*' through the Son ('Argument' to Book Ten). But Adam's disfiguring fancy that an omnipotent, omniscient Deity should *need* to preserve His reputation among His subjects is a deluded *non sequitur*.

Fallen Eve's responses to Adam's desperate gambit to risk all with her – 'O glorious trial of exceeding Love, / Illustrious evidence, example high!' (9.961–62), and again, 'This happie trial of thy Love' (9.975) – are flawed eulogies that lead backward and forward into the poem and compare Adam, to his detriment, with his exemplary redeemer. Backward, the angelic hymn praises the Son's selfless sacrifice as 'O unexampl'd love, / Love no where to be found less then Divine' (3.410–11). Forward, in Michael's revelation, Adam realizes the inferiority of all fallen acts of charity to Christ's 'suffering for Truths sake' (12.569), once 'Taught this by his example whom I now / Acknowledge my Redeemer ever blest' (12.572–73). These angelic and human affirmations recall the Pauline celebration of Christ as the *hypotyposis* or supreme example: 'Christ Jesus came into the cosmos to save sinners, of whom I am chief; but, because of this, I received mercy, in order that in me, the chief [of sinners], Jesus Christ might display all his longsuffering, as a supreme example to those who are going to have faith in him for eternal life' (1 Tim. 1:15–16). Milton's narrator casts further doubt upon Adam's suicidal choice, made without consideration of God's probable mercy, by deploring Adam's action in forensic soteriological discourse. As the narrator comments in a parenthetical aside,

Adam's decision to disobey and fall is a bad redemption, a flawed means to buy Eve back into God's good graces: '(for such compliance bad / Such recompence best merits)' (9.994–95).

Adam's mismanagement before and between both Falls – his lack of leadership in giving Satan the opportunity to compromise an isolated Eve; his inability to discern the mercy of his Maker or, as Dennis Danielson interprets the catastrophe, to negotiate a reconciliation between a fallen Eve and God; his misprision concerning God's nature; and his presumptuous intimation that he and Eve may achieve immortality and 'be Gods, or Angels Demi-gods' – Adam's choices implicate him with Eve in a transgression of the double love that can only be reversed by the suffering Son's fulfilment of the love of God and humanity. Eve begins the process of the Fall through an act of 'preposterous' self-love that leads to homicidal tendencies and Adam, through contempt for God and himself, completes the process by committing the original human suicide. Only the second Adam can justify the first Adam's fruitless resignation that 'Death is to mee as Life' (9.954). Christ's perfect love of God, self, and other makes right Adam's despair by bringing eternal life out of Adam's sin and death through the good communicated. This communicable good consists of both Jesus's victorious death upon the cross and his triumphant revival, a resurrection styled by Michael as 'A gentle wafting to immortal Life' (12.435).

6

Surprised by Sin, Assured by Grace:
Milton's Redeeming Irony

The works of Milton cannot be comprehended or enjoyed, unless the mind of
the reader co-operate with that of the writer. He does not paint a finished
picture, or play for a mere passive listener. He sketches and leaves others to fill
up the outline. He strikes the key-note, and expects his hearers to make out the
melody.

Thomas Babington Macaulay[1]

The very essence of Truth is plainesse, and brightnesse; the darknes and
crookednesse is our own.

Milton, *Of Reformation*

[W]hereas the paths of honesty and good life appear now rugged and difficult,
though they be indeed easy and pleasant, they would then appeare to all men
both easy and pleasant though they were rugged and difficult indeed.

Milton, *The Reason of Church-Government*

The end then of learning is to repair the ruins of our first parents by regaining
to know God aright, and out of that knowledge to love him, to imitate him, to
be like him, as we may the neerest by possessing our souls of true vertue, which
being united to the heavenly grace of faith makes up the highest perfection.

Milton, *Of Education*

MILTON'S REDEEMING IRONY

According to Milton's biographer John Aubrey, when John Dryden met Milton he
observed that the poet gave a hard pronunciation of *Littera canina*, the canine letter 'r',
'a certaine signe of a Satyricall Witt'.[2] Earlier I explored the possibilities of allegory for
Milton's epic, and I should now like to discuss Milton's 'canine letter', his deployment
of poetic irony.[3] Only in a secondary sense does irony denote a dry mock, speech that is

---

[1] Macaulay, *Literary and Historical Essays* (London, 1932), 10.
[2] Darbishire, ed., *Lives*, 6.
[3] For a previous study of Miltonic irony, see Victoria Silver, *Imperfect Sense: The Predicament of Milton's Irony* (Princeton, 2001), 64–76.

cynical and derisive. Irony is a species of allegory and these two rhetorical modes have much in common. Both modes, through obliquity, allusion, inference, and indirection, say one thing while intending another. The literal meaning of 'irony', from the Greek εἰρωνεία (*eironeia*), is a 'seeming', Classical and Medieval rhetorical taxonomies regularly placed irony alongside allegory. Quintilian understood irony as 'dissimulation [*dissimulationem*]', in which 'we should understand things contrary to what is spoken', and held that irony is 'a method of saying the contrary of what you want to be understood'.[4] Isidore of Seville compared allegory and irony and found that 'Allegory is "other-speaking", One thing is voiced, and quite another thing is understood'; 'Irony is expressing an opinion while having the contrary understood.'[5] Irony and allegory have 'a twin force' that 'figuratively indicates one thing beneath other things'.[6] Quintilian enlarged irony's parameters from tropic irony, which is limited to a single phrase or sentence, to figural irony, which is much more extensive than our modern conception of irony. In an ironic trope the gap is felt specifically and locally 'in two words', so that tropic irony is 'more concise' or 'limited' than figural irony.[7] In figural irony the accumulation of multiple ironic tropes may govern a whole discourse and direct a way of reading, rather as allegory functions as an extended metaphor, so that, 'as at some point a continued metaphor becomes allegory, so an entire [ironic] scheme may develop from the weaving together of [ironic] tropes'.[8] In figural irony the difference between 'the sense of the meaning and the speech [*sensus sermoni et voci*]' is sustained throughout an entire discourse.[9] Figural irony appertains to Milton's treatment of fallen poetic language.

Quintilian maintained that irony can indicate an ethical state, controlling 'both passages of text and sometimes the entire shape of a cause, since even an entire life may seem to represent irony, as was deemed of Socrates (for he was called εἴρων, who acted out the role of a fool and pretended to be an admirer of others and their supposed wisdom)'.[10] The power of Socratic irony, of Socrates's affected ignorance and intellectual deference before others, is legendary. Socrates is called an ironist twice within the Platonic corpus. In the *Republic* Thrasymachus chides Socrates for his 'well known irony [ἡ εἰωθυῖα εἰρωνεία]'.[11] In the *Symposium* Alcibiades calls Socrates an 'ironist [εἰρωνευόμενος]' and likens him to a superficially worthless statue of the pot-bellied, snub-nosed satyr Silenus that, once opened up, is found to be crammed with treasures and divine images.[12] In *Paradise Regain'd* the faint praise Jesus reserves for his damning of ancient wisdom alludes to the ironic shape to Socrates's life. Echoing Socrates's words from Plato's *Apology*, Jesus states that 'The first and wisest of them all professd / To know this onely, that he nothing

---

[4] Quintilian, *Institutio Oratoria*, vol. 3, 9.2.44.
[5] Isidore of Seville, *Etymologiarum Sive Originum Libri XX*, ed. W. M. Lindsay, vol. 1 (Oxford, 1985), 1.37.22–23.
[6] Ibid. 1.37.26.
    Quintilian, vol. 3, 9.2.46.
[8] Ibid. 9.2.47.
[9] Ibid.
[10] Ibid. 9.2.46.
[11] Plato, *The Republic*, vol. 1, trans. Paul Shorey (London, 1982), *Rep.* 1.337a.
[12] Plato, *Lysis; Symposium; Gorgias* (London, 1983), *Symp.* 216e.

knew' (4.293–94).[13] Milton's Jesus singles out this aspect of Socrates's life because it mirrors his own ironic destiny as humanity's Saviour. The gospel 'Lives' with which Socrates's life was often typologically compared present Jesus's life as dramatizing a succession of ironies: where God's Son is reared as a lowly carpenter's son in provincial Nazareth; where God's authentic Messiah is derided as King of the Jews; where God's viceregent is ridiculed in a mockery of state with a thorny wreath as a crown, a besmirched purple 'Robe of State', and a reed as a sceptre; and where the universal hero is suspected, condemned, and finally executed by the State as a Messianic pretender and political agitator. To quote Michael's ironic sentiment, humanity's Saviour is 'slaine for bringing Life' (12.414). The Pauline writings presuppose the gospels' ironic reading of Jesus's life and death. First Corinthians presents a salient tissue of ironies articulating the discrepancy between who Jesus was and how others perceived him. In Paul's discourse 'Christ crucified' signifies clandestine strength in apparent weakness and true wisdom in seeming foolishness, thus fulfilling Quintilian's designation of irony as antiphrasis or 'opposite speaking':[14]

> Christ [is] God's power and God's wisdom; because God's foolishness is wiser than humans and God's weakness is stronger than humans . . . But God has chosen the foolish things of the world that He might shame the wise; and God has chosen the weak things of the world that He might shame the strong; and God has chosen the base of the world and the things despised, things that are not, to nullify things that are, so that no flesh may boast before God.   (1 Cor. 1:22–25, 27–30)

This Pauline formulation is foundational to Adam's final revelation, who, schooled after the pattern of his suffering redeemer, looks past *superficies*:

>   with good
> Still overcoming evil, and by small
> Accomplishing great things, by things deemd weak
> Subverting worldly strong, and worldly wise
> By simply meek; that suffering for Truths sake
> Is fortitude to highest victorie,
> And to the faithful Death the Gate of Life;
> Taught this by his example whom I now
> Acknowledge my Redeemer ever blest.
>   (12.565–73)

Adam's education is preoccupied with securing a true perspective, an ironic perspective, on the spiritual reality that lies beyond appearances, and with discerning the potential for salvation and the hope for a Saviour in the least promising of places.

---

[13] 'This one among you, O humans, is wisest, who, like Socrates, knew that he was truly of no worth in regards to wisdom': Plato, *Euthyphro; Apology; Crito; Phaedo; Phaedrus*, ed. Jeffrey Henderson, trans. Harold North Fowler (London, 2001), *Apol.* 23b.

[14] Quintilian, vol. 3, 9.2.47.

A commitment to irony was a marked feature of the Protestant tradition Milton inherited. One cannot overstate irony's importance as a rhetorical and didactic strategy in the thought of Martin Luther, Milton, and, centuries later, Søren Kierkegaard.[15] Luther, perhaps the most influential exponent of Pauline irony within the Reformed tradition, developed in his 'Theology of the Cross' a complex ironic system proclaiming the crucified Jesus as a *Deus absconditus* or 'hidden God' and humanity's salvation upon the cross as a concealed revelation.[16] Luther passionately held, 'THE CROSS alone is our theology' and 'The Cross proves all!'[17] God both conceals and reveals Himself at Calvary. To the eye of reason the cross is foolish and scandalous, but to the eye of faith, as Adam discerns, the cross renovates and regenerates humanity and constitutes a show of strength overcoming apparent weakness and wisdom transcending apparent folly. According to Luther's doctrine of justification, a repentant sinner stood *simul iustus et peccator* as one who was simultaneously righteous and a sinner because, although fallen humans were intrinsically sinful, Christ's redemption made sinners righteous in God's eyes.[18] Christ's suffering represented God's *opus alienum*, something foreign to the divine nature, through which God worked out *opus proprium*, something proper to divinity.[19] Beyond God's unremitting *ira severitatis* or 'wrath of severity' during Christ's Passion, the repentant could discern God's *ira misericordiae* or 'wrath of mercy'.[20] Luther taught that God's mercy was even hidden within His shows of anger and that at the crucifixion God was both concealed and revealed; *Deus absconditus* implicit in and identical with *Deus revelatus*.[21] The repentant sinner remained a sinner *coram hominibus*, 'in the eyes of humans', but was a saint *coram Deo*, 'in God's sight.'[22] Luther maintained that these contrasts between things as they seem to be and things as they are would challenge the faithful to foster a divine perspective. Such a perspective would discern God as merciful behind His apparent wrath, Christ crucified as victorious and undefeated, and repentant sinners as justified, despite their abiding sinfulness, and not damned to perdition. Luther's formula for God's provision of salvation in the revelation of the cross, *abscondita sub contrariis* or 'things hidden beneath their contraries', resembles Quintilian's definition of irony as 'a method of saying the contrary of what you wish to be understood.'[23] Alister McGrath observes of the ironized Lutheran perspective, 'In the injustice, the shame, the weakness, the folly and the condemnation of the cross are revealed, and yet hidden, the righteousness, the glory, the wisdom, the strength and the salvation of God.'[24] To those without such belief, though, Christ's atonement is an 'alien work' showing only the severity of God's anger and God is a

---

[15] Consider Kierkegaard's 'Speech in Praise of Abraham', which is inspired by 1 Corinthians 1: 'greater than all was Abraham, great with that power whose strength is powerlessness, great in that wisdom whose secret is folly, great in that hope whose outward form is insanity, great in that love which is hatred of self'. See Søren Kierkegaard, *Fear and Trembling*, trans. Alastair Hannay (Harmondsworth, 1985), 50.

[16] I am indebted to Alister E. McGrath's *Luther's Theology of the Cross: Martin Luther's Theological Breakthrough* (Oxford, 1985), 95–175.

[17] Ibid. 152 and 159: '*CRUX sola est nostra theologia*' and '*Crux probat omnia*.'

[18] Ibid. 133–36.   [19] Ibid. 151–58.   [20] Ibid. 154.

[21] Ibid. 165.   [22] Ibid. 116.   [23] Ibid. 155.   [24] Ibid. 158.

'hidden God'. Luther recounted that his personal realization of this ironic way of theorizing the cross and the world was 'as though I had entered through opened doors into Paradise itself' and that 'Then an entirely other face of the whole of scripture was manifest to me.'[25] I propose that a fit reading of Milton's account of the Fall would adopt this Lutheran, ironic perspective – the same perspective Adam attains at the poem's climax.

Gordon Teskey recognizes, as did Quintilian, that irony is more than a trope, and that its ontology exceeds rhetoric and enters the domains of metaphysics and ethics. Irony can even behave like an ethical state. For Teskey, textual irony's effects 'approach chaos'.[26] Teskey's appropriation of Johannine rhetoric aids our understanding of his illogocentric analysis of irony's function: 'The text seems to contain under its surface not just a meaning but a reasoning power, a logos, which when carried to its limit is the logos that upholds the world.'[27] In Teskey's opinion such rehabilitations are cosmetic and illusory. Their superimposed logocentrism is a frail mask, the thinnest of veneers, disguising a severe disorder. Teskey's marshalling of metaphors from quantum physics, the indeterminacies of a black hole, a singularity, or an event, indicates his identification of a basic metaphysical irrationalism, the abyss 'on which the possibility of ordered relations inside the system is based' that falsifies 'the ground of the numinous'.[28] In consequence, 'words such as *numinousness, resonance, mystery, and vision*' disintegrate, decompose, and dematerialize.[29] Instead of the transcendent Lutheran Word that inheres in the immanent word and communicates the revealed and hidden God, 'what lies beneath visible signs is . . . mere noise', 'an underlying disorder' over which the self-deceiving interpreter conjures delusory meaning.[30] Hence Teskey disenchants. Yet the absolute attitude of negation that Teskey ascribes to the ironic does not apply so easily to irony's paideutic function according to the Lutheran, Miltonic, or Kierkegaardian worldview. Kierkegaard held that, through irony, 'One can deceive a person out of what is true, and – to recall old Socrates – one can deceive a person into what is true.' *De Doctrina Christiana* includes *ironiae* along with parables and didactic narratives among a family of discursive forms 'employed not to deceive but to educate with endeavour [*non fallendi sed erudiendi studio*]' (*CE* 17.300). Milton's ideal, amenable readers bring an identically earnest moral endeavour to their textual interpretations.[31]

Christian orthodoxy assumes brokenness, accepts fallenness, and comprehends Creation groaning in the throes of sin. One critical strain within Milton studies, influenced by the affective stylistics of Fishian analysis and Wolfgang Iser's reader-response theory, demonstrates how readers are surprised into a recognition of their own

---

[25] Ibid. 97: '*apertis portis in ipsam paradisum intrasse. Ibi continuo alia mihi facies totius scripturae apparuit.*'
[26] Gordon Teskey, *Allegory and Violence* (Ithaca, 1996), 57.
[27] Ibid. 65.   [28] Ibid. 63 and 66.
[29] Ibid. 65.   [30] Ibid. 66 and 65.
[31] Søren Kierkegaard, *The Point of View on My Work as an Author; The Point of View For My Work as an Author; Armed Neutrality*, ed. and trans. Howard V. Hong and Edna H. Hong (Princeton, 1998), 53–54.

fallenness and are made conscious of the ontological discrepancies between prelapsarian and postlapsarian conceptions of language and experience.[32] Yet in *Paradise Lost*'s postlapsarian scenes, where instances of irony are most concentrated, the ironic effect assures readers of the presence of grace. Teskey distinguishes how, where allegory 'may be thought of as leaning away at various oblique angles from soldierly directness, where what is said and what is meant coincide', irony perpetually negates because it is always 'opposing uprightness': irony 'spoils'.[33] Again, irony is a 'corrosively oppositional power'.[34] Surely, though, the positive or negative value of irony's power is contingent upon the point from which it executes its one-hundred-and-eighty-degree semantic turn. If applied to a fallen and broken world, such as Milton's postlapsarian, vitiated Eden, 'reforming' or 'redeeming' irony can be deployed logocentrically to affirm the presence of grace to the fit and few. Multiple ironic tropes, which amount to the activity of complex, schematic, figural irony, tell Milton's story of the Fall slant for his readers, correctly misleading them towards the idea of Christ crucified.

What I am proposing is a treatment of irony that is homeopathic in its results. Book Nine commences with the claim that the narrator 'now must change / Those Notes to Tragic' (9.5–6) and Milton's drama, with its extended dialogues, elaborate soliloquies, and static *mises en scène* beside the Forbidden Tree, at the place of judgement, and in gloomy, bosky shades adheres to the austere, spare structural principles of Attic tragedy. Milton, long choosing his great poem, early conceived of writing tragedy rather than epic and his theory of tragedy, propounded in the 'Preface' to *Samson Agonistes*, defends the homeopathic, tragic effect. Milton argues that tragedy should evoke 'a kind of delight', 'for so in Physic things of melancholic hue and quality are us'd against melancholy, sowr against sowr, salt to remove salt humours' (*SA* 'Preface'). Milton's redeeming irony, rather like the mythical Tele-phus's sword, heals Earth's fallen 'wound' (9.782) by this homeopathic principle, turning the reader conceptually about-face from the Fall's crisis to receive its redemptive solution. If redeeming irony operates upon benighted, faulty material, it can transfigure such negative stuff into something more auspicious. Redeeming irony educates and replenishes meaning by transforming fallen material into matter with restorative potential. 'Irony', Teskey avers, 'can disrupt anything', but when the object irony encounters in narrative is itself disrupted by Satan, Sin, and Death, then, to turn Teskey's thesis quite literally inside out, redeeming irony's action reconstructs the vestiges of a renewable world.[35] To borrow a Pauline idiom, readers may initially see 'in a mirror, in an enigma, but then face to face' (1 Cor. 13:12), because, read aright, the enigma contains sufficient material for its own solution. If Milton's readers are so inclined, their imperfect vision, polarized and perfected through redeeming irony, partakes of a fullness of knowledge that brings them 'face to face' with the epic's redemptive subject.

Milton's prose employs two images that aptly reproduce this concept. Milton explains how Jesus's teachings edify sinners by an 'art of powerfull reclaiming'

---

[32] See Stanley Fish, *Surprised by Sin: The Reader in 'Paradise Lost'* (London, 1967), especially 92–157.
[33] Teskey, *Violence*, 58–59.   [34] Teskey, 61.   [35] Ibid. 67.

(*CPW* 2.668) and he describes Jesus's educational technique with two analogies. First, he adopts the Aristotelian analogy of righting a twisted wand: 'as when wee bend a crooked wand the contrary way; not that it should stand so bent, but that the overbending might reduce it to a straitnesse by its own reluctance' (*CPW* 2.668).[36] Second, he introduces the analogy of a physician's therapeutic use of acid to purge corruptions: 'as the Physician cures him who hath tak'n down poyson, not by the middling temper of nourishment, but by the other extreme of *antidote*, so Christ administers heer a sharp and corrosive sentence against a foul and putrid licence; not to eate into the flesh, but into the sore' (*CPW* 2.668). Once this restorative epistemology is transferred to Milton's epic, it can cure infected language through redeeming irony. Redeeming irony can also mend, along with fallen utterance, a fallen world, reclaiming it from the abyss of the Fall and shepherding it towards salvation's light. The result is the regeneration of lapsed meaning. Milton's ironic method is inevitably most advantageous in fallen spaces, in Satan's Hell, postlapsarian Paradise, or Samson's eclipsed world. Here the reader might glimpse God's scheme of salvation glimmering faintly behind humanity's seemingly hopeless condition, tainted by Sin and terminated by Death: transcendence behind immanence, concord behind discord, order behind chaos, and wholeness behind waste. The suffering Christ, who hypostatizes irony when he enters the world as God made flesh and manifests strength through weakness, stands behind the web of redeeming ironies spun across Milton's fallen drama.

Richard Lanham remarks upon irony's convergence with allegory, 'the ironist depends on an allegorical habit of mind in his reader, a habit that will juxtapose surface and real meanings'.[37] To forge these juxtapositions requires that the reader is a willing participant in irony's discipline. As Glenn Holland states in his study of what he styles *divine irony*, 'A remark or situation might be potentially ironic, but it is not *actually* ironic until it is perceived as such.'[38] 'Since irony is a subversive reading of a text, it must always be to some extent hidden, and to the extent that it is hidden, there always remains the possibility that it will be overlooked.'[39] Thus, to appreciate irony, there must be a minimum of agreement within the community of writers and readers to keep one's eyes wide open.

One may count at least three ways in which Milton signals redeeming irony throughout the postlapsarian portion of his epic. First, Milton privileges his readers by permitting them a divine perspective that grants exclusive insights into the economy of grace established between the Father and the Son in the Empyrean, insights that, initially, Adam and Eve are denied on Earth. Examples of these divine

[36] Aristotle, *Nicomachean Ethics* 2.9. Francis Bacon's essay 'Of Nature in Men' adopts Aristotle's conceit: 'Neither is the Ancient Rule amisse, to bend *Nature* as a Wand, to a Contrary Extreme, whereby to set it right: Understanding it, where the Contrary Extreme is no Vice.' See Bacon, *The Essayes or Counsels, Civill and Morall*, ed. Michael Kiernan (Oxford, 1985), 119.
[37] Richard A. Lanham, *A Handlist of Rhetorical Terms* (2nd edn, London, 1991), 93.
[38] Glenn S. Holland, *Divine Irony* (London, 2000), 37. Holland draws upon the same exemplary texts as I do: specifically, the Platonic corpus, 1 Corinthians, *Oedipus Tyrannus*, and Job. A judicious generalist study of the literary–theological uses of irony is Anthony Esolen, *Ironies of Faith: The Laughter at the Heart of Christian Literature* (Wilmington, 2007).
[39] Holland, 48.

viewpoints are: in Book Three, the Heavenly Council during which the Son offers to atone; in Book Ten, the Son's justification of Adam and Eve externally and internally in God's sight so that, in Lutheran terms, they are simultaneously righteous and sinners; and, in Book Eleven, the Son's intercession in the Heaven of Heavens, appeasing the Father as High Priest and sacrificial victim.[40] The supernatural reality of the Son's mediation is withheld from Adam and Eve until Michael's narrative reveals it. This form of irony, Holland's divine irony, 'arises from a contrast between the way human beings perceive things and the way God or the gods are believed to perceive them'.[41] Milton's epic grants its readers 'a god-like perspective on the character and actions of the people who inhabit their narrative worlds' and this perceptible 'distance between the gods' perspective and the human perspective seems to produce an inevitable irony'.[42] The Book of Job, which inspired Milton's verse, also aided his architectonic design here. Without the frame to Job's narrative, in which Satan makes a wager with God about whether Job can endure his trials (Job 1:6–12, 2:1–7), the reader of Job's history would, like its patient hero, find God's ways inexplicable and approve the devastating advice of Job's wife to 'curse God, and die' (*AV* Job 2:9). Job's narrative frame, however, gives the reader a cause that Job is denied and makes the biblical hero's patience admirable. Holland reminds us, 'The ironist's use of irony is not only a manifestation of his or her adoption of the divine point of view, but an invitation to others to adopt the divine point of view as well.'[43] While Adam and Eve feud, lament, commiserate, and despair, readers have the advantage of knowing that the Son procures a hidden remedy. He descends as 'mild Judge and Intercessor both' (10.96), clothes and justifies their 'inward nakedness, much more / Opprobrious, with his Robe of righteousness' (10.221–22), and returns to God's inner sanctum, having 'appeas'd / All', and graciously 'mixing intercession sweet' (10.226–28). Even while Sin and Death wreak 'waste and havoc' (10.617), the Son is thwarting these Cerberean 'Dogs of Hell' (10.616). Readers are fully apprised of the salvific machinery backstage, which provides 'Prevenient Grace descending' (11.3). In Book Ten the justifying, interceding, and appeasing Son secures grace throughout Adam's experience of despair and Eve's proposal of suicide by preventing or 'coming before' the fallen couple to sustain them as they work out their salvation.

By a second use of redeeming irony, Adam, Eve, and Satan employ a redemptive discourse, the language of satisfaction and sacrifice and the mercantile argot of credit and debt, that further elucidates the ironies between their ignorance about salvation and the reader's insight into the atonement. One Miltonist has expressed relief that critics have 'lost interest in prescriptive criteria and have at least made

---

[40] Benjamin Myers's insightful comparison between Adam's speech to Eve (11.141–61) and the Son's ongoing petition to the Father (11.22–44) further illustrates Milton's redeeming irony. Milton's verbal and dramatic irony successfully bridges the distance between the reader's divine perspective of a loving Son mediating for humanity on high, and Adam and Eve's incomplete human perspective from below, ignorant of their mediator's charitable works. Michael's vision-narrative closes the hiatus between Adam's obliviousness to and the reader's cognizance of the Son's intercessory presence. See Myers, 157–58.

[41] Holland, 149.   [42] Ibid. 58 and 69.   [43] Ibid. 160.

some effort at clearing out an obstructive theology of essentialist meaning' from Milton's epic.[44] Another claims that ' "The Christian Tradition" [is] a dull set of immobile dogmas, recognized by all, interesting to none'; yet another considers that the redemptive theme in Milton amounts to 'the squeezing of the dense poetry of prelapsarian paradise into a thin line of doctrine'.[45] Nevertheless, one does not have to be one of Empson's culturally despised neo-Christian critics to appreciate that disregarding or, worse, jettisoning the atonement is tantamount to fracturing the poem's integrity. Book Ten's redemptive discourse animates the meaning of Milton's verse, repeatedly and indirectly directing the reader of Milton's narrative of the Fall's aftermath to human salvation.

In the third place, Milton's representation of the Fall assumes a tragic form that lends itself to dramatic irony, that is, to situational as well as verbal irony. This kind of irony draws upon the duplicities and ambiguities of language that may rise towards a semantics of restoration as much as they decline towards a semantics of the Fall. In Attic tragedy the Athenian audience would typically come to a fresh rendering of a beloved myth – *Oedipus Tyrannus* would be a classic example – to discover how the tragedian's arrangement of the plot would lead the protagonists into fulfilling their destinies. The reader similarly comes to Milton's adaptation of the Fall to discover how the action unfolds and how the epic gradually brings Adam and Eve to a stage where they can overcome their plight, acknowledge their redeemer, and realize the meaning of the cross encrypted within the *protevangelium* (10.179–92). In the three structural, verbal, and dramatic strategies of irony highlighted above, Milton invites his readers to discern the atonement when Adam and Eve are at their lowest existential and spiritual depths. What more pertinent moment could Milton have chosen to demonstrate the antiphrastic, allegorical, and oppositional potential of his redeeming irony? What better episode could the poet have selected to display irony's capacity, in Milton's words, to overbend the crooked timber of fallen humanity towards restoration, 'to a straightnesse by its own reluctance'?

TAUGHT TO RESOUND FAR OTHER SONG: REDEEMING IRONY AFTER THE FALL

Following Book Nine, redeeming irony is most energetic in lending grace notes to the discord of fallen language. *De Doctrina Christiana*'s soteriological scheme aids the reader in comprehending the pattern of lapsed Adam and Eve's spiritual progress. Humanity's restoration comprises two elements, redemption and renovation. Redemption is where 'CHRIST, . . . SENT IN THE FULLNESS OF TIMES, REDEEMS ALL THOSE BELIEVING, WHO ARE THOROUGHLY DISCHARGED AT THE PRICE OF HIS OWN VOLUNTARILY OFFERED BLOOD' (*CE* 15.252). Renovation, the fruit of redemption, is the action of grace assisting the individual will as it turns towards God,

---

[44] Gordon Teskey, *Delirious Milton: The Fate of the Poet in Modernity* (Cambridge, Mass., 2006), 50.
[45] Poole, 195; Rosenblatt, *Torah*, 216.

so that the believer 'IS LED AWAY FROM A STATE OF CURSE AND DIVINE ANGER TOWARDS A STATE OF GRACE' (*CE* 15.342).[46] The most contemptible figures in God's sight are the unrepentant, who exist in a cursed state and undergo penance for their sins. God's transformation of Satan and the devils into snakes, and His provocation of their appetite with succulent fruits that burst into dust and ashes in their mouths 'to aggravate / Thir penance' (10.549–50), afford a suitable poetic example of God's penance. Penitent sinners, who progress from a cursed state towards a state of grace, outshine those sinners who merely serve penance. The first 'alteration' towards grace within the sinner is temporary and comprises 'penitence and, corresponding to it, faith' (*CE* 15.356). The 'natural mind and will having been partially renovated, they are divinely moved towards a knowledge of God' (*CE* 15.352, 354). Penitence is a partial view of God, limited to His wrath and judgement: 'Penitence, also called μεταμέλεια, is where someone abstains from sinning through fear of punishment [*poenae metu*] and turns to God, when He calls, solely for their own salvation' (*CE* 15.358). Penitent sinners feel remorse, regret, and sorrow for their misdeeds, but lack a developed, rounded understanding of God's mercy. Penitence is superior to penance, since the sinner defers to God's justice. To the penitent, God is a hard taskmaster, so that penitence, like penance, is effectively penal. There is a difference, though. Penitence is a considered and contrite response to the experience of sin. Adam, for example, adopts a penitent disposition as his major soliloquy proceeds (10.720–862).

Penitence 'is common to the regenerate and to the unregenerate' (*CE* 15.358). A penitent sinner who is faithful can advance to regeneration and repentance and can receive grace. *De Doctrina Christiana*'s two dyads, penitence and faith, and repentance and saving faith, have a synergistic relationship because, 'as penitence bears itself in relation to repentance, so, in this way, does faith to saving faith' (*CE* 15.356). The repentant sinner who possesses saving faith has a refined perception of God's mercy, whereas the penitent sinner has only a cowed apprehension of divine anger. However, 'REPENTANCE [*RESIPISCENTIA*]' or 'μετάνοια', a term Milton derives from Lactantius, literally means a spiritual 'change of heart'. Repentance is:

> THE GIFT OF GOD WHEREBY SOMEONE WHO IS REGENERATED, FEELING AND SORROW-ING THAT HE HAS OFFENDED GOD BY HIS SINS, DENOUNCES AND FLEES THOSE SINS AND, FROM A SENSE OF DIVINE MERCY, TURNS TO GOD WITH THE GREATEST HUMILITY [*EX SENSU DIVINAE MISERICORDIAE AD DEUM HUMILLIME CONVERTIT*] AND FROM THE BOTTOM OF HIS HEART IS ZEALOUS TO FOLLOW WHAT IS RIGHT. (*CE* 15.378)

Milton's formulation of repentance reflects the ironic perspective of Luther's repentant believer. It mirrors Luther's realization of the 'other face of the whole of Scripture', the 'hidden God' of the cross, and God's wrath of mercy concealed within His wrath of severity. The sinner of the treatise is altered from a penitent 'STATE OF CURSE AND DIVINE ANGER' to a repentant 'SENSE OF DIVINE MERCY'. Such is Adam and Eve's improved condition by the close of Book Ten. *De Doctrina*

---

[46] 'IS AB STATU MALEDICTIONIS ATQUE IRAE DIVINAE AD STATUM GRATIAE DEDUCITUR'.

Christiana's fully regenerate, repentant sinner perceives God's mercy manifesting itself in 'The external cause of regeneration or sanctification', which 'is Christ's death and resurrection' (*CE* 15.376). 'THE GIFT OF GOD' proceeds 'from the Father, through the Son' (*CE* 15.378), and flows from Christ's resurrection and exaltation. The treatise gives Acts 5:31 to substantiate this transmission of grace. The other effect of regeneration, 'SAVING FAITH', is: 'A FULL PERSUASION INBORN IN US BY THE GIFT OF GOD WHEREBY, BECAUSE OF THE VERY AUTHORITY OF GOD'S PROMISE, WE BELIEVE THAT ALL THOSE THINGS WHICH HAVE BEEN PROMISED TO US IN CHRIST WILL BE OURS; ESPECIALLY THE GRACE OF ETERNAL LIFE BY THE GIFT OF GOD' (*CE* 15.392). Michael's vision-narrative, crowned by Adam's 'Redeemer ever blest' (12.573), confirms Adam and Eve's saving faith. Bearing in mind the treatise's process of spiritual conversion from penitence to repentance, let us now trace the operation of redeeming irony throughout Book Ten's postlapsarian drama.

Anne Ferry observes that Milton's ironic and duplicitous use of 'the verb "seem" is almost always a warning against oversimplification'.[47] The verb's function as a moralizing device is at least as old as Spenser's heroic poetry. Book Five's anointing scene models Milton's Satanic application of the verbs 'seem' and 'appear' when Satan silently seethes with envy among his fellow angels at the Son's exaltation. The narrator divulges inside information that 'All seemd well pleas'd, all seemd, but were not all' (5.617). The Satanic use of 'seem' has a high incidence in Book Nine. Satan's locomotion within the serpent, like his two-faced, double-tongued locu- tion, 'made intricate seem strait' (9.632). Satan meets Eve as a 'seeming Friend' (10.11) and his glozing words are reasonable 'to [Eve's] seeming' (9.738). As Eve eats the apple, 'such delight till then, as seemd, / In Fruit she never tasted' (9.787–88), an illusion the narrator soon dissolves, since really Eve 'knew not eating Death' (9.792). Later Adam regrets, too late, his over-zealous praise of Eve's fallen beauty, 'overmuch admiring / What seemd in [Eve] so perfet' (9.1178–79). After the Fall the formerly duplicitous connotations of 'seem' and 'appear' are reversed so that ostensibly hopeless and irresoluble situations ironically conceal grace and hint at restoration. The moment Adam eats the Fruit, he submits 'to what seemd remedi- less' (9.919) and, as the couple's squabbling intensifies, 'of thir vain contest appeerd no end' (9.1189). These phrases allude to God's economy of salvation, which is actively working behind the scenes of the fallen drama, and suggest a remedy for and cessation to apparently 'remediless' human strife with 'no end' appearing.

In the Fall's wake Adam and Eve demonstrate their estrangement from God and neighbour. Each seeks, with figleaves, 'to hide / The Parts of each from other' (9.1092–93), 'vain Covering if to hide / Thir guilt and dreaded shame' (9.1113–14), and to conceal their guilty persons from their Maker behind 'thickest Trees' (10.101). Their human nakedness is intrinsic as well as extrinsic, their 'native Righteousness' gone (9.1056): 'naked left / To guiltie Shame: [Adam] coverd, but his Robe / Uncoverd more' (9.1057–59). Adam's eyes are opened to his

[47] Ferry, 61.

impoverished knowledge of good and evil that comprises 'Good lost, and Evil got' (9.1072). Adam's new condition is proleptic of his future revelation that, in the cross, 'all this good of evil shall produce, / And evil turn to good' (12.470–71). However, until the Son descends to judge them, Adam and Eve cannot break the deadlock of 'mutual accusation' (9.1187). Milton deploys forensic redemptive language to convey their fault-finding, rather than their acceptance or sharing of guilt. Eve's complaint, 'Imput'st thou that to my default' (9.1145), parodies the Son's imputation of righteousness, not blame, to sinners. An 'incenst *Adam*' rebuts, 'Is this the Love, is this the recompence / Of mine to thee' (9.1162–64), burlesquing the Son's exchange of sin for grace by, instead, requiting sin for sin. The fallen couple, interminably wrangling, so it seems, with 'no end' (9.1189), have nothing to give in reparation and must rely, in one of Satan's characteristic half-truths, upon being 'quit / The debt immense' (4.51–52) by redemption.

The epic identifies the Son as Adam and Eve's divine judge. Milton expands upon God's 'walking in the garden in the cool of the day' (*AV* Gen. 3:8) in his description of the balm of the Son's soothing influence upon fallen Nature. A pathetic verity rather than a pathetic fallacy, the Son's pacifying charisma adds to the 'Eevning coole, when he from wrauth more coole' (10.95) descends. The Son discovers the discountenanced couple with signs of the vitiated love of God and neighbour upon them: 'Love was not in thir looks, either to God / Or to each other' (10.111–12). Adam's inculpation of Eve reveals how far he has declined from his earlier willingness 'to undergoe like doom' (9.953) and 'To undergoe with [Eve] one Guilt, one Crime, / If any be, of tasting this fair Fruit' (9.971–72). He now echoes these words to extenuate his betrayal of Eve and substitutes self-preservation for self-sacrifice by opting for the latter of two alternatives, 'either to undergoe / My self the total Crime, or to accuse / My other self, the partner of my life' (10.126–28). He implicates Eve because he is unprepared to 'undergoe' a punishment that would evoke Christ's altruistic bearing of sin's burden: 'Least on my head both sin and punishment, / However insupportable, be all / Devolv'd' (10.133–35). The terse confession with which Eve blames the serpent occupies a single, colourless line of verse, 'The Serpent me beguil'd and I did eate' (10.162). Neither Adam nor Eve accepts personal blame and a joint reluctance to own their faults exacerbates their culpability.

Despite the spiritual devastation of Milton's tragic Fall, the merciful divine framework contains and buttresses the unforgiving human framework, 'the cosmic theme . . . framing and interpreting the human theme'.[48] The Son's justification, delivery of the *protevangelium*, and intercession in Heaven counteract judgement with mercy. As *De Doctrina Christiana* states, God 'preceded the condemnation of humanity with His gratuitous redemption' (*CE* 15.252). When Adam attempts to exonerate himself by explaining that Eve's transgression 'seemd to justifie the deed' (10.142), Adam's self-justification and his transfer of blame onto Eve unwittingly evoke Jesus's redemptive assumption of blame to 'justifie' repentant sinners. Not one hundred lines after Adam's whining protest the Son commences that process of

---

[48] Helen Gardner, *A Reading of 'Paradise Lost'* (Oxford, 1965), 77.

justification. He protects Adam and Eve's exposed bodies with animal skins, imputes righteousness to them, and justifies their inner selves, 'coverd from his Fathers sight', 'with his Robe of righteousness' (10.223). The Son's act of justification, 'As when he washd his servants feet' (10.215), alludes to the Johannine pericope where Jesus teaches love of one's neighbour on the Passover night before his crucifixion: 'if I, your Lord and Teacher, washed your feet, you also ought to wash one another's feet' (John 13:14). Notably, Milton's Son labours 'to cloathe his Enemies' (10.219) and performs the utmost of neighbourly love, love of one's enemy, since Adam and Eve are the original ancestors of those who will persecute and torture the Son when he fulfils the divine–human love upon the cross. How else could the Son be said to be clothing his enemies? The Son next re-ascends to Heaven to perform 'intercession sweet' (10.228) before God's Mercy-seat and he continues to do so throughout Book Ten. The Son's renovation of the oblivious Adam and Eve from behind the scenes forms the divine backdrop to Book Ten's seemingly thankless human drama.

Although Adam's soliloquy is perhaps the poem's darkest episode, the possibility of the redemption irradiates Adam's despondent words. The operation of irony, and especially of syllepsis, is dynamic and the texture of redemptive images is subtle and deft. Citing Michael Riffaterre, Derek Wood has stressed the importance of syllepsis for interpreting Milton's poetry. Wood notes how 'syllepsis consists in the understanding of the same word in two different ways at once, as *contextual meaning* and as *intertextual meaning*.'[49] Fit interpreters of Adam's soliloquy must exceed the immediate context of his speech through irony and syllepsis and must look past the *de contemptu mundi* tradition to which Adam's lament is formally indebted. Readers need to appreciate in Adam's speech the complex skein of allusions to Pauline soteriology that affords a prospect of salvation.

Jason Rosenblatt grants that Adam's speech displays the 'thinness of a Pauline conception of Torah', but determines that, 'Bereft of grace or the language of grace, Adam's soliloquy represents a law that works wrath in a language unremittingly legalistic.'[50] There is, however, a counter-movement where redeeming irony retrieves a Pauline theology of grace amid Adam's despondency. Adam's self-involved speech reveals that, where knowledge of sin abounds, there does grace much more abound. As Hugh MacCallum comments, 'Adam's hesitant progress towards an understanding of atonement is the result of grace extended to him through the mediation of the Son, and there is thus a kind of benign irony about the limits of his vision.'[51] As Adam speaks, the sun is setting and, later, Adam refers to his experience of Sin and Death as 'this days Death' and 'A long days dying to augment our paine' (10.962–64). These lyrical phrases recall the Pauline utterance that 'I die

[49] Derek N. C. Wood, *'Exiled from Light': Divine Law, Morality, and Violence in Milton's 'Samson Agonistes'* (Toronto, 2001), 40. Wood cites Michael Riffaterre, 'Syllepsis', *Critical Inquiry*, 7 (1980), 637.
[50] Rosenblatt, *Torah*, 206.
[51] MacCallum, *Sons of God*, 170; see ch. 5. My reading of Adam's threnody is indebted to MacCallum's magisterial scholarship.

every day' (1 Cor. 15:31), but Adam's tragic fatalism is qualified by the Pauline assurance that, 'if indeed our outer man is decaying, yet our inner man is being renewed day by day' (2 Cor. 4:16). All things, death included, are put under Christ's feet so that, 'as in Adam all die, so also in Christ all will be made alive' (1 Cor. 15:22). George Herbert's 'Affliction (2)' pays homage to this Pauline text when the speaker, reassured by the redemption, beseeches God, 'Kill me not ev'ry day, / Thou Lord of life; since thy one death for me / Is more then all my deaths can be' (1–3).[52] Milton's reader needs a lexical and doctrinal anamorphoscope, so to speak, to rescue these obliquities and distortions from fallen language and revive the revelation of grace.

Adam and Eve are unique among the human race in their experience of an Edenic bliss that is rudely shattered by Sin and Death's cataclysmic usurpation. Milton's two protagonists are the first and sole human beings to feel keenly the hateful siege of contraries between possessing and losing Paradise. Once Sin and Death's pernicious influence first taints 'liveless things' (10.707), next systematically infects the plant kingdom, 'Herbs, and Fruits, and Flours', and the animal kingdom of 'Beast next, and Fish, and Fowle' (10.603–04; see 10.710–12), the contagion spreads ultimately to Adam. In the Genesis tradition Adam's lamentation conventionally either preceded God's judgement or came shortly after Adam and Eve's expulsion.[53] Milton saw the structural advantages of positioning the lament between divine judgement and expulsion, but before Michael's vision-narrative of humanity's redeemer, as a vehicle for illustrating redeeming irony and the hidden evidences of God's grace. There is far more to Adam's elaborate repining than 'misery's sluggish whirlpool – Why was I born? Why don't I die? – stirred for 125 lines'.[54] The *mise en scène* for Adam's intricate soliloquy is a fallen environment contaminated by Sin and Death in which creatures discount God, fear those stronger than themselves, and prey upon one another:

> Thus began
> Outrage from liveless things; but Discord first
> Daughter of Sin, among th' irrational,
> Death introduc'd through fierce antipathie:
> Beast now with Beast gan warr, and Fowle with Fowle,
> And Fish with Fish; to graze the Herb all leaving,
> Devourd each other; nor stood much in awe
> Of Man, but fled him, or with count'nance grim
> Glar'd on him passing: these were from without
> The growing miseries, which *Adam* saw
> Alreadie in part, though hid in gloomiest shade,
> To sorrow abandond, but worse felt within,
> And in a troubl'd Sea of passion tost,
> Thus to disburden sought with sad complaint.
> (10.706–19; see 11.184–89)

---

[52] Herbert, 62. The speaker of one of Donne's *Holy Sonnets* confesses, 'They kill'd once an inglorious man, but I / Crucifie him daily, being now glorified' (7–8): see Donne, *Divine Poems*, 9.
[53] John Martin Evans, *'Paradise Lost' and the Genesis Tradition* (Oxford, 1968), 290–91.
[54] Broadbent, 265.

Twice before, the poem gives glimpses of this viciousness within fallen Nature and its law of tooth and claw. First, the narrator digresses upon humanity's propensity for warmongering and 'Wasting the Earth, each other to destroy' (2.502). Second, the narrator artfully contrasts the sinless, 'frisking' animal kingdom, where Isaian lions dandle kids, and bears and tigers gambol together (4.340–52), with Satan's discordant metamorphoses into predatory beasts, a 'Lion' that 'stalkes with fierie glare' (4.402) and 'a Tiger' that would seize 'two gentle Fawnes at play', 'Grip't in each paw' (4.403–08). These incongruities anticipate the Fall and source Creation's vitiation in Satan who, like his biblical type Nimrod, is a hunter of men (12.24–37).

Internecine strife, a state of anomie between and within species, fascinated Renaissance thought. In *King Lear* Albany presages a condition of lawlessness where 'Humanity must perforce prey on itself, / Like monsters of the deep' (*Lr.* IV.ii.48–49).[55] In *Leviathan* Thomas Hobbes, the 'monster of Malmesbury', reasons that the human natural condition is 'this war of every man against every man'.[56] One century later Voltaire's *Zadig* concludes, 'men appeared in effect such as they are, insects devouring one another upon a tiny atom of mud'.[57] I previously examined how Milton exegetes a perfect human natural law consisting of sympathy and the love of God and neighbour. Its aberration manifests itself where 'Love was not in [human] looks, either to God / Or to each other' (10.111–12). *De Doctrina Christiana*'s remedy to the loss of the double love is atonement, where Christ 'fulfilled the Law by his most perfect love of God and his neighbour until, obedient to his Father in all things, he sought death for his brothers' (*CE* 15.316). A convincing source for Milton's anomic vision of 'fierce antipathie' (10.709) within Nature and species that 'Devour'd each other' (10.712) is Galatians, which citing Leviticus 19:18, emphasizes the importance of the love of others in order to undo this vicious, anarchic state:

> Because you, my brothers, were called for freedom. Only do not use freedom for the advantage of the flesh, but serve one another through love. For in one statement the entire Law has been summed up in the single utterance, 'You shall love your neighbour as yourself.' But if you bite and devour one another, beware lest you be destroyed by one another [εἰ δὲ ἀλλήλους δάκνετε καὶ κατεσθίετε, βλέπετε μὴ ὑπ' ἀλλήλων ἀναλωθῆτε]. (Gal. 5:13–15)

Love of God, self, and neighbour is apparently extinguished in Adam's soliloquy, which he delivers from a spiritual nadir. Milton converges this interspecific and intraspecific 'fierce antipathie' upon the psychic rift within Adam's fallen selfhood, separated and alienated from the spouse he has betrayed. The moment Sin and Death contaminate Adam's person, 'His thoughts, his looks, words, actions all infect' (10.608). Adam's outburst articulates his cursed state. Because of Adam's unprecedented experience of sin, critics have emphasized the tragic pathos of his

[55] Shakespeare, *Riverside*, 1331.
[56] Thomas Hobbes, *Leviathan*, ed. Edwin Curley (Indianapolis, 1994), 78.
[57] Voltaire, *Zadig and Other Stories*, ed. H. T. Mason (Oxford, 1971), 100.

desolate lament. Adam's prone situation, 'On the ground / Outstretcht he lay, on the cold ground' (10.850–51), expresses his debased position on the scale of being, since Adam, created as one 'not prone / And Brute as other Creatures, but endu'd / With Sanctitie of Reason, might erect / His Stature, . . . upright with Front serene' (7.506–09). Neil Forsyth observes how Adam's outstretched posture resembles the apostate Satan's devolved and dejected attitude, 'stretcht out huge in length' (1.209) upon Hell's bottom.[58] Emily Wilson detects Satanic traces in Adam's words and compares Satan's Niphates speech on the loss of his angelic state with Adam's loss of Edenic happiness.[59] Adam's 'Sea of passion tost' (10.718) recalls Satan's rancorous 'passion' (4.114). Adam's angst, 'from deep to deeper plung'd' (10.844), imitates Satan's depravity that eventually opens 'in the lowest deep a lower deep' (4.76) to devour him. However, in making these comparisons, critics should stress the disparities as well as the resemblances between Adam's and Satan's predicaments. The narrator differentiates how the devils 'oft they fell' (10.570), whereas fallen humanity 'once lapst' (10.572). At this stage Adam's apprehension of God is restricted to a penitent's consciousness, subjected to divine wrath. Nevertheless, unlike Satan and the rebel angels, the penitent Adam yearns for his transgressing and suffering to cease and craves deliverance from an 'Abyss of fears' (10.842).

Adam's speech enacts the dark night of his soul. Kester Svendsen has analysed how Adam's chaotic rhetoric reflects his spiritual turmoil: 'the abrupt changes in subject and tone'; 'the many contrasts, broken lines, and the high proportion of double caesuras'; 'the repetition of ideas, words, and even sounds'; the 'twin themes of immortality and death' evinced in 'synonyms and figures'; and 'the words *death* or *dies* and *curse*' criss-crossing Adam's soliloquy 'like dark threads'.[60] Despite the soliloquy's preponderance of negative images, Adam's obsessive antinomy of death and immortality is only perfectly synthesized in Christ's death and resurrection to immortal life. Adam's theodical 'reasonings' strike him as 'evasions vain' and drive him 'through Mazes' of convoluted thought (10.829–30). His dilemma may seem Satanic, like Hell's philosopher-devils who, in trying to discern providence, 'found no end, in wandring mazes lost' (2.561). Adam may also resemble Satan, who is so entangled in his own illogic that he deceptively 'made intricate seem strait' (9.632). Yet there is a Messianic solution to Adam's crisis. Adam's discursive reasoning becomes clarified through redeeming irony, just like the angels' dancing that 'Resembles nearest, mazes intricate, / Eccentric, intervolv'd, yet regular / Then most, when most irregular they seem' (5.622–24). Milton retains the momentous word 'seems' for Adam's supposed inability to reverse the Fall and understand God's ways. Adam bemoans that 'inexplicable / Thy Justice seems' (10.754–55). Adam's word 'seems' unravels the Latinate 'inexplicable', which etymologically

---

[58] Forsyth, 310.
[59] Kester Svendsen, 'Adam's Soliloquy in Book X of *Paradise Lost*', in *Milton: Modern Essays in Criticism*, ed. Arthur E. Barker (New York, 1965), 328–35; Emily R. Wilson, *Mocked with Death: Tragic Overliving from Sophocles to Milton* (Baltimore, 2004), 167–68; see ch. 8.
[60] Svendsen, 332.

means 'unable to be disentangled', like the massed wreaths of Satan's serpent's tail. God's justice only becomes explicable if Milton's redeeming irony unsnarls its knotty coils. As penitent, Adam can only see God's justice and wrath, but his words begin to discover God's grace and mercy. Adam may find his meditations labyrinthine, 'out of which / I find no way' (10.843–44), but his broken arguments are thick sown with seeds of grace planted by the Son, who is 'the way, the truth, and the life' (John 14:6). He only fully appreciates this fact on learning of his 'Redeemer ever blest' (12.573), but the tangles of his multi-faceted debate contain clues to resolving his spiritual crisis within the dense doctrinal subject matter and the Messianic subtext to his discourse.

Adam's opening apostrophes 'O miserable of happie' (10.720) and 'Accurst of blessed' (10.723) invert the providential principle of Milton's epic and *De Doctrina Christiana* that God draws good from evil, creating 'something good and just, as if He always creates and elicits light from darkness' (*CE* 15.74; 15.68, 72–80; see 12.470–71). The angelologist Henry Lawrence advocated an identical theodical maxim where 'it is Gods way, and it illustrates exceedingly his goodnes, and bounty, rather to bring greater goods out of evill'.[61] *In alia verba*, where sin abounds, God's grace eventually arises to supplant it. Adam's theory that his descendants, born into sin, will anathematize him so that 'all from mee / Shall with a fierce reflux on mee redound' (10.738–39) is a Satanic sentiment (1.209–20; 3.80–86, 128–30; 7.613–16; 9.171–73; *PR* 1.124–29). Unlike Adam, Satan is impenitent and unrepentant:

> If then his [God's] Providence
> Out of our evil seek to bring forth good,
> Our labour must be to pervert that end,
> And out of good still to find means of evil
> (1.162–65)

Conversely, God devises a plan for humans who wish to repent. The Son undergoes penal substitution so that 'Man therefore shall find Grace, / The other [the fallen angels] none' (3.131–32). Satan's commitment to malevolence diverges from Adam's detestation of sin and fear of penal reflux because the Son's mediation provides sufficient grace for Adam's race.

Adam is tormented by what *De Doctrina Christiana* calls 'THE STATE OF CURSE AND DIVINE ANGER' and dreads the contagion of his vitiated seed as a 'propagated curse' (10.729). Cursed humanity is 'Through Sin to Death expos'd by [Satan's] exploit' (10.407). The 'propagated curse' evokes traducianism, the doctrine holding that sin blights or traduces future generations that proceed from the corruption of Adam and Eve's original transgression. Satan plots the Fall on a traducian basis and seeks to induce the ruin of 'The onely two of Mankinde, but in them / The whole included Race, his purposd prey' (9.415–16). To fallen Adam, God's benediction to '*Encrease and multiplie*' (10.730; Gen. 1:28) now stands degraded as a curse perpetuating intergenerational sin. Adam's perception obscures the *protevangelium*

---

[61] Lawrence, *Angells*, 68.

where the redeemer, Adam and Eve's descendant and the seed of woman, shall bruise or defeat Satan, Sin, and Death. Michael describes the crucified Messiah as 'A shameful and accurst' (12.413), a humiliated state so abject it lacks a substantive. Michael's description alludes to a Deuteronomic text that was long interpreted as a Passion prediction: 'His body shall not remain all night upon the tree, but thou shalt in any wise bury him that day; (for he that is hanged is accursed of God)' (*AV* Deut. 21:23). Paul interprets the tree as foreshadowing the cross and argues that the crucified Christ became a curse: 'Christ redeemed us from the curse of the Law, becoming a curse for us, because it has been written, "Accursed is everyone hanging upon a tree"' (Gal. 3:13). Citing Galatians 3:13 in conjunction with Deuteronomy 21:23, *De Doctrina Christiana* narrates that during the crucifixion, 'The curse owed by us was transferred upon [Christ], Gal. 3:13 [*exsecratione nobis debita in se translata*]' (*CE* 15.304). Herbert's 'Prayer (2)' resumes this theme. Herbert's speaker wonders at that 'unmeasurable love' of which Christ was 'possest, who, when thou couldst not die, / Wert fain to take our flesh and curse' (13–15).[62] *De Doctrina Christiana* re-applies the Galatians text in four other soteriological contexts, in chapters concerning human restoration and redemption, the Son's mediation, the administration of redemption, and Christian liberty (*CE* 15.254, 292; 16.132, 140).

Elsewhere the treatise's chapter 'ON THE MANIFESTATION OF THE COVENANT OF GRACE' provides a cure for Adam's distress. The treatise holds that Paul resolved his 'agitation under the Law's malediction' when 'he gave thanks to God because of Christ' (*CE* 16.108). The treatise's Latin equivalent for the Greek *katara* or 'curse' is *execratio*. Adam uses this Latinate synonym in words recalling Paul's thanksgiving for grace rendered 'because of Christ'. (The Latin word *gratia* equally means 'thanks' or 'grace.') Adam pictures a resentful future descendant who 'will curse / My Head' and object, 'Ill fare our Ancestor impure, / For this we may thank *Adam*' (10.734–36). Adam wryly concludes, 'but his thanks / Shall be the execration' (10.736–37). Through the syllepsis of thanks (or grace) and execration Adam invokes the typology of a second Adam who, through the first Adam's lineage, will provide the means of grace or 'thanks' for his unworthy subjects by himself becoming a curse or 'execration'. Salvation permeates and undercuts Adam's self-pity: 'for what can I encrease / Or multiplie, but curses on my head?' (10.731–32). Christ, who is truly 'Accurst of blessed', undoes Adam's damage by assuming humanity's curse of sinning and dying to become 'A shameful and accurst' (12.413). When Adam groans that 'in mee all / Posteritie stands curst' (10.817–18) and fears lest his 'Son / Prove disobedient' (10.760–61), his hypocrisy undermines his self-pitying presentments, for Adam's disobedience towards God instigated the curse. Adam's words recall Pauline theology and the professed subject matter of the exordia to Milton's diffuse and brief epics (*PL* 1.1–5; *PR* 1.1–7), which illustrate how Christ, Adam's distant son, proves obedient by being accursed upon the cross: 'as through one man's disobedience many were constituted sinners, so by one man's obedience many will be constituted righteous' (Rom. 5:19).

---

[62] Herbert, 103.

The sense of insufficiency and futility Adam's execrable state provokes causes him to repeat his earlier wish, 'hide me from the face / Of God' (10.723–24; see 9.1088–90), and, later, to sympathize with his fallen offspring, 'how can they then acquitted stand / In sight of God?' (10.827–28). The dramatic, situational irony is such that, even while Adam utters these words, the Son has 'coverd' the unhappy pair 'from his Fathers sight' (10.223) and personally stands 'in sight / Before the Fathers Throne' (11.19–20; 10.224–28), reconciling God to humanity. Adam's question furnishes its own solution, for the word 'acquit' invites a raft of redemptive terms: atoning for another, cancelling a debt, clearing a debtor, releasing another from an obligation or burden, delivering, ransoming, liberating, exonerating, and exculpating (*OED* def. 1.1–5, 2.6–7, 3.8–13). The signal word 'quit' derives from *acquitare* and signifies liberation, deliverance, absolution, and redemption (*OED* def. 1.1). Humanity stands acquitted in God's sight because the incarnate Son has 'quitted all to save / A world from utter loss' (3.307–08).

Adam's inadequacy to repair matters and his inability 'to performe / [God's] terms too hard' (10.750–51) overwhelm him, but again he inadvertently fumbles 'TOWARDS A STATE OF GRACE' (*CE* 15.342), even in its seeming absence. He grieves that his paradisiacal pleasures were 'deare bought' (10.742) for his present sufferings and he begs God to 'reduce me to my dust' (10.748) and allow him to 'render back' (10.749) what he received. His words again evoke the Son's Incarnation and humiliation. The exalted Son is the *dux* or 'head' of Creation (3.319–20; 5.606, 842–43; *CE* 15.100) and the 'Second Omnipotence' (6.684) after the Father, yet he willingly reduces himself to humanity's size (*Christus redux*) to atone, rendering back humanity, 'Forfeit to Death' (10.304), by a redemption dearly bought. Christ's charisma insistently surmounts Adam's sullied thoughts of damnation and annihilation.

Another mainspring of Adam's complaint is his bewilderment at Death's 'tardie execution' (10.853). The apparent contradiction of God's vow that Adam will die on the day he eats the Fruit (see 4.425–27) increases Adam's confusion. Why, then, does he still live? In this way Adam might be said to 'overlive' (10.773), but he is also living on the extended credit guaranteed by his Saviour's blood, by which he may enjoy the prospect of a second, eternal life. The suffering Messiah, invested in mock-regal trappings, will be derided for being what, ironically, the canonical gospels portray him to be – King of the Jews. In the Passion narratives Christ, not Adam, is 'mockt with death' (10.774) and challenged, if he is God's Son, to save himself and descend from the cross. The resurrected God-man's conquest over Sin and Death shall be 'length'nd out / To deathless pain' (10.774–75). Even Adam's expression, 'how glad would lay me down / As in my Mothers lap' (10.777–78), only superficially refers to Mother Earth, from whose clay God moulded Adam. Adam's lying down in his 'Mothers lap' evokes the numerous *pietà* and deposition scenes in Renaissance poetry, painting, and sculpture, in which Christ's deposed corpse languishes against Mary's bosom.[63] Adam's phrase, 'lay

---

[63] Such Marian depictions are not the exclusive province of the Catholic tradition. Consider Mary's soliloquy in *Paradise Regain'd* (2.60–108) or Milton's *Fair Infant*, where, just as Mary mourned at the Deposition, 'the mother of so sweet a child' (71) laments her 'false imagin'd loss' (72).

down', reinforces this Passion allusion; for the Johannine Jesus repeats this idiom of 'laying down' his life for others each time he foretells his crucifixion (see John 10:15–19, 13:37–8, 15:13; 1 John 3:16).

Adam's confused oxymora reflect his inner strife. In a wider context they recall the grim amphibologies of Milton's Hell, of 'darkness visible' (1.63), the 'fiery Deluge' (1.68), and 'Black fire' (2.67), and Samson's hopeless self-definitions in his own fallen soliloquy as a 'living death' (*SA* 100) or a 'moving Grave' (*SA* 102). Yet Adam's contradictions proliferate along an unswerving thematic axis: 'deathless pain' (10.775), 'a living Death' (10.788), 'deathless Death' (10.798), and 'endless miserie' (10.810). Adam's oxymora rebuke a God who eternizes death, but he is unaware of God's plan to provide eternal life through the paradoxical death of the deathless Christ. His terrified interrogation of God, 'Can he make deathless Death?' (10.798), summarizes Christ's removal of death's sting. Adam's equivocation alludes to 1 Corinthians 15:53–54 and evokes the Pauline typology of the first and second Adam. Jesus's resurrection victory 'make[s] deathless Death' because redemption enables 'this perishable body to put on the imperishable [τὸ φθαρτὸν τοῦτο ἐνδύσασθαι ἀφθαρσίαν]' and enfranchises 'this one liable to death to put on deathlessness [τὸ θνητὸν τοῦτο ἐνδύσηται ἀθανασίαν]'.[64] Adam conceives this 'Strange contradiction' (10.799) of death-in-life as a negative spiritual state of moribund and Godless perpetuity. Marvellous contradictions are the stuff of Luther's hidden and redeeming God and of Jesus's Christological role as servant-king and *theanthropos*, forging eternal life amid death. Adam's philosophy upholds *De Doctrina Christiana*'s axiom that God is incapable of contradiction (*CE* 14.50), but Milton's epic celebrates the reconciliation between God and humankind through the paradox of the Incarnation. Hebrews 12:3 explores divinity's 'Strange contradiction' at the crucifixion when Jesus 'endured such a contradiction [ἀντιλογίαν] of sinners against himself'. Adam is more perceptive than he knows when he finds that God's making 'deathless Death' constitutes an 'Argument / Of weakness, not of Power' (10.800–01). His loaded phrase communicates the weak-ness-in-power that 'Christ crucified' represents for Paul (1 Cor. 1), whereby Jesus, apparently enervated upon the cross, *re vera* displays hidden strength. A Christia-nized Adam realizes that the Passion succeeds 'by things deemd weak / Subverting worldly strong' (12.567–68). In *Paradise Regain'd* Jesus nearly duplicates Adam's suggestion of the strength-in-weakness of Christ crucified. Jesus criticizes Rome's 'ostentation vain of fleshly arm' (*PR* 3.387) as an 'argument / Of human weakness rather then of strength' (*PR* 3.401–02). Jesus's formula differs from Adam's in the added epithet 'human', for therein lies the difference between the bloated vainglory of human empire and the God-man's powerful redemptive suffering. Redeeming irony reconciles Adam's puzzling contradictions and furnishes the answer of redemption for Adam's negating rhetorical question, 'Can [God] make deathless death?' (10.798). Unlike Adam, who is entangled in a continuing theological

---

[64] Satan's recommendation to Eve, by 'putting off / Human, to put on Gods' (9.713–14), also alludes to 1 Corinthians 15:53–54 in the moment prior to Eve's fall.

quandary, the reader benefits from hindsight and recourse to those many scriptural instances where Christ is praised for eliciting life from death.[65]

In one of the speech's myriad shifting perspectives, Adam professes a version of mortalism or thnetopsychism. Martin Luther, William Tyndale, and Isaac Newton espoused this doctrine, which taught that at death the soul perishes or 'sleeps' with the body.[66] *De Doctrina Christiana* teaches that the saints' souls slumber with their bodies until the *eschaton* and their resurrection to eternal life. In the chapter 'ON THE DEATH WHICH IS CALLED BODILY' (*CE* 15.214–51) the treatise asserts that until the resurrection of the dead, 'not whatsoever before *Christ's illustrious advent*' (*CE* 15.224), 'God denounced the death of the whole sinning man without the exception of any part' (*CE* 15.218).[67] Adam repeats the treatise's teaching that 'the whole man dies' (*CE* 15.226) and that 'the soul . . . is also able to die a natural as well as a violent death' (*CE* 15.228). Fallen Adam's own brand of mortalism is predictably bleak so that 'All of me then shall die' (10.792). Death for him is ignominious, terminal, and bereft of any consolation of a future resurrection to eternal life. Adam's logic that 'it was but breath / Of Life that sinnd; what dies but what had life / And sin' (10.789–91) discounts Christ's death and resurrection, which guarantee immortality, and of which Adam is unaware. The balm of Christ's redemption provides, for those 'whom [Christ] redeems, a death like sleep, / A gentle wafting to immortal Life' (12.434–35). At this juncture, however, Adam's terror of ravenous death dominates his consciousness. Paul's famous outcry, followed by his eureka, directly answers Adam's pessimism: 'I am a wretched man. Who will deliver me from the body of this death? But thanks be to God through Jesus Christ our Lord!' (Rom. 7:24).

In lines influenced by Genesis 2:7, Adam declares that he owes his existence to 'pure breath of Life, the Spirit of Man / Which God inspir'd' (10.784–85). *De Doctrina Christiana* accepts this Creational model of divine inspiration or 'in-breathing': 'From a kind of breath of life divinely inspired to man [*Ex inspirato . . . vitae halitu*], what was imparted from God to man was not a divine part of God's essence, but something human and proportionate to divine virtue' (*CE* 15.38). The treatise's traducian view dictates that after the Fall 'sin is inborn and passed along from the parents to the child [*peccatum ingeneratur atque traducitur a parentibus ad filium*]' (*CE* 15.46) and that 'no one will deny that all sin proceeds, in the first instance, from the soul' (*CE* 15.46). In Augustinian terms the contamination of original sin is transmitted across the generations from one begotten human soul to another. In *Paradise Lost* God's incarnate, only 'begott'n Son' (5.835) has a sinless, 'unspotted Soule' (3.248). *De Doctrina Christiana* concurs that, 'As for the soul of Christ, its generation was supernatural', and so Jesus 'is called the seed of woman,

---

[65] The texts are John 5:24; Rom. 5:10, 17–21; 6:3–4, 23; 8:1–2; 2 Cor. 2:16; 4:10–12; 1 John 3:14–15; 2 Tim. 1:8–10.

[66] For Milton's mortalism, see Gordon Campbell, 'The Mortalist Heresy in *Paradise Lost*', *Milton Quarterly*, 13 (1979), 33–36.

[67] The idea is repeated 'with God denouncing death on the entire sinning man' (*CE* 15.226). *De Doctrina Christiana*'s eschatology dispenses that 'The resurrection of the dead and the Last Judgement will follow Christ's Second Coming' (*CE* 16.348).

David's seed according to the flesh, that is, indubitably, according to his human nature' (*CE* 15.52). God housed the Son's immaculate, supernaturally generated soul within an incarnate body, the 'woman's seed' miraculously formed within Mary's womb. The unnamed name to Adam's query, 'what dies but what had life / And sin?' (10.790–91), is Adam's redeemer. Christ enjoyed incarnate life and, although his soul, which was produced supernaturally, was sinless, yet, in an extraordinary Pauline declaration, at the redemption his soul was *made sin*. Paul asserts that Christ, 'one not knowing sin, was made sin [ἁμαρτίαν ἐποίησεν] for us, that we might become God's righteousness in him' (2 Cor. 5:21). In keeping with the poem's mortalism, the treatise maintains that, 'if Christ really died, then both his body and soul [*anima . . . cum corpore*] died on the same day'; that 'God raised the Lord Jesus's total person [*totam . . . personam*] from the dead'; that 'Christ was killed as a sacrifice in his divine and human nature'; and that 'the whole of Christ [*totus . . . Christus*] was as a slain lamb' (*CE* 15.306, 308). Adam's lamentation that, through sin, 'All of me then shall die' (10.792) chimes in with the Son's sacrificial offer that, though sinless, upon the cross he will surrender up 'All that of me can die' (3.246). The Son foretells his revival to 'sit incarnate' as 'Both God and Man' (3.315–16) and his restoration of humanity. Jesus repairs Adam's 'loss' (10.752) or damnation (Latin *damnum* – 'loss'), since he alone can pay humanity's 'Sufficient penaltie' (10.753).

Adam's declared intention is to purge his grief through lamentation, 'to disburden . . . with sad complaint' (10.719), but he acknowledges his inability to find relief: 'Fond wish! couldst thou support / That burden heavier then the Earth to bear' (10.834–35)? Hugh MacCallum notes that Adam 'gropes toward the idea of atonement, yet despairingly, because he knows himself incapable of bearing the weight of God's wrath, that burden heavier than the earth. Thus Milton has managed to combine a moment of tragic intensity with the doctrine that man can be saved only by the righteousness of Christ.'[68] MacCallum's insight nevertheless leaves much unsaid. A brief digression will help to illuminate the rich theological heritage behind Adam's utterance. Although the metaphor of sin's burden is scriptural (Matt. 11:30, 20:12; 2 Cor. 12:16; Gal. 6:5; Rev. 2:24), the Medieval theologian Anselm of Canterbury accommodated the conceit to the argument of his soteriological treatise *Cur Deus Homo* [*Why God Became Man*] (1098 C.E.). In the section 'How Heavy the Burden of Sin is' Anselm famously exhorts the human need for redemption: 'You have not yet considered how heavy the burden of sin is [*Nondum considerasti, quanti ponderis sit peccatum*].'[69] The topic of humanity's insupportable burden of sin segues into Anselm's true subject, his theory of satisfaction. Anselm interprets Christ's Passion as the satisfactory punishment, recompense, and appeasement of divine justice. He explains why it befitted God to assume flesh to save humankind. He argues, 'Every person who sins is indebted to repay to God the honour they have taken from Him; and this is the satisfaction

---

[68] MacCallum, '"Most Perfect Hero"', 105.
[69] Anselm, '*Cur Deus Homo*,' *Florilegium Patristicum*, vol. 18, ed. Bernard Geyer and John Zellinger (Bonn, 1929), 33: 1.21.

which every sinner is indebted to make to God.'[70] Humanity is obliged to satisfy
for sin and yet is incapable of making recompense for sin's debt or, as Milton's
Adam styles it, is 'unable to performe / Thy terms too hard' (10.750–51).
Therefore, if 'nobody except God can make satisfaction and nobody is indebted
except humanity, it behooves the God-man to make that satisfaction'.[71] The only
one competent to make recompense would need to be 'perfect God and perfect
man'.[72] A God-man so committed would be able to redeem humanity in his divine
capacity, but would also be obliged to make reparation in his human capacity:

> For God will not do it, because He will not be indebted to do it; and a human will not
> do it, because he will not be able to do it. In order, therefore, for a God-man to do
> this, it is necessary that the same person should be perfect God and perfect man, since
> He cannot do this, unless He is a true God, and he is not indebted to do this, unless
> he is a true man.[73]

Anselm's atonement model was a landmark in Christian theology. Thomas Aquinas
amalgamated the theory into his *Summa Theologiae* (AD 1265), where he argued
that Jesus's love was great enough, his life of sufficient dignity, and his suffering
comprehensive enough to satisfy for humanity.[74] Anselm's satisfaction theory was
secure within Christian philosophy, where it found acceptance within Catholic
and, later, Protestant orthodoxy.

In my opening chapter I touched upon how *De Doctrina Christiana* and *Paradise
Lost* are fully committed to Anselm's satisfaction theory.[75] The treatise classifies
satisfaction as essential to understanding the administration of redemption: 'SATIS-
FACTION is where CHRIST THE GOD-MAN, BY FULFILLING THE LAW AND PAYING THE
JUST PRICE, FULLY SATISFIED DIVINE JUSTICE FOR ALL' (*CE* 15.314). Christ's
satisfaction is sufficient and efficacious for both the reprobate and the elect (*CE*
15.320, 324, 326). Summarily, 'the satisfaction is the effect and the end of
[Christ's] whole administration' (*CE* 15.330); 'the reconciliation of God the Father
with humankind is equivalent to the effect of satisfaction' (*CE* 15.332); and
'Christ's blood has fully satisfied for us, and rendered us thoroughly pure from
every stain' (*CE* 15.338). Milton's Son promises that he will 'mitigate [humanity's]
doom / On mee deriv'd' (10.76–77) by tempering divine justice with mercy and
appeasing God through an act that renders all creatures 'fully satisfi'd' (10.79).
Michael, too, styles the crucifixion 'this his [Christ's] satisfaction' (12.419). The
Son's staunching of the Fall's otherwise eternally mortal wound underscores
Adam's succession of rhetorical questions, which concerns Adam's penitence and
his anxiety about God's infinite wrath. Adam's conclusion that he will die absolutely, his soul expiring, imprisoned within his body, 'appease[s] / The doubt'
(10.792–93) that he has concerning his fate. Milton's choice word 'appease' recalls
the Anselmian *topos* of God's satisfaction and appeasement:

---

[70] Ibid. 18: 1.11.   [71] Ibid. 42: 2.6.   [72] Ibid. 43: 2.7.   [73] Ibid. 43: 2.7.

[74] Brian Davies, *The Thought of Thomas Aquinas* (Oxford, 1993), 327–32.

[75] William Rewak has explored Milton's esteem for Anselmian soteriology. See Rewak, 'Book III of
Paradise Lost: Milton's Satisfaction Theory of the Redemption', *Milton Quarterly*, 11 (1977), 97–102.

> For though the Lord of all be infinite,
> Is his wrauth also? be it, Man is not so,
> But mortal doomd. How can he exercise
> Wrauth without end on Man whom Death must end?
>
>   .   .   .   .   .
>
>   Will he draw out.
> For angers sake, finite to infinite
> In punisht Man, to satisfie his rigour
> Satisfi'd never
>
>   (10.794–97, 801–04)

The Son's gracious undertaking answers Adam's dilemma. Jason Rosenblatt notes how Adam's confusion as to how he might 'satisfie [God's] rigour' resonates with the Son's offer to 'pay / The rigid satisfaction, death for death' (3.211–12).[76] The Father further resolves Adam's conundrum by approving along Anselmian lines that, once the Son becomes God-man, 'Both God and Man, Son both of God and Man' (3.316), 'So Man, as is most just, / Shall satisfie for Man' (3.294–95). The seventeenth-century preacher Stephen Lobb composed a précis of the doctrine of satisfaction that mirrors the complex themes and images rippling through Adam's lamentation, including the incarnate Son's penal satisfaction and instantiation of himself both as sin and a curse to redeem others:

> That all who believe, might escape the Wrath to come, and have Everlasting Life, the Lord Jesus undertakes for us, by making *satisfaction* both to *punitive* and *remunerative* Justice; and that he might do so, he put himself into our *place, state* and *condition*; so that, whereas we were *Sin* and under a *Curse*, by this blessed *change*, Christ is made *Sin* and a *Curse*, and we delivered from *Sin* and the *Curse*, 2 *Cor.* 5:21, *Gal.* 3.13.[77]

Joseph Summers detected in the timbres of Milton's epic characters the speech-pattern of the self-giving 'voice of the redeemer'.[78] Adam's doleful words replicate that speech-pattern here. Summers noted certain nuances that were characteristic of the style in which the Son couches his redemptive offer: 'the continual recurrence of the long *e*'s' and 'repetitions of the sound . . . in the initial or final foot of a line or immediately before or after a caesura'.[79] Adam's complaint travesties this pattern and transforms the Son's altruistic tones into an unhealthy, self-pitying egocentrism. He bewails how:

>   upon me, all from mee
> Shall with a fierce reflux on mee redound,
> On mee as on thir natural center light
> Heavie, though in thir place
>
>   (10.738–41)

---

[76] Rosenblatt, *Torah*, 213.
[77] Stephen Lobb, *A Report of the Present State of the Differences in Doctrinals* (London, 1697), 5.
[78] Joseph H. Summers, *The Muse's Method* (London, 1962), 176–85.
[79] Ibid. 178.

The enjambement in Adam's words of a punishing burden that shall 'light / Heavie' alludes to Christ's saying that 'my yoke is easy, and my burden is light' (Matt. 11:30). The sinner's onerous burden, so important within Anselm's soteriology, is transplanted from the justified sinner's shoulders onto Christ, just as John Bunyan's Christian is relieved of his pack of sin when it drops from his back into Christ's tomb. Adam's repetition of the objective pronoun 'mee' and his conceit of a relieved burden in the word 'light' evoke the Son's prediction of his redemptive undertaking, that 'the worst on mee must light, / When time shall be' (10.73–74). Adam's borrowed accents from the patient Son's voice are crucial to interpreting Adam's plaintive, self-absorbed soliloquy. Milton reintroduces these ideas as Adam's soliloquy concludes – the pronominal redeemer's accents ('mee'), the exoneration of human sin that lightens sinners' burdens, and the satisfaction of God's wrath:

> first and last
> On mee, mee onely, as the sourse and spring
> Of all corruption, all the blame lights due;
> So might the wrauth. Fond wish!
>
> (10.831–34)

Adam recaptures once more the cadences of the Son's redeeming offer and recycles the ploche on the pronoun 'mee': 'Behold mee then, mee for him, life for life / I offer, on mee let thine anger fall; / Account mee Man' (3.236–38). Adam's expression 'first and last' re-sounds God's apocalyptic proclamation that, 'I am Alpha and Omega, the beginning and the end, the first and the last' (*AV* Rev. 22:13). Milton's reader should remember that God avows that providential mercy, not wrath and justice, will be His first and last words and that, *prior to* the Son's expressed wish to save humanity, God decrees that 'Mercy first and last shall brightest shine' (3.134).

Adam interprets his lapse as a spoiled inheritance and spiritual bankruptcy and regrets the 'Fair Patrimonie' (10.818) he will bequeath to his 'disinherited' posterity (10.821). Yet here too Adam's cynicism brightens by way of scriptural remembrance. In the Epistle to the Romans the Son, obedient even to the cross, inherits his Father's fair patrimony and enables the faithful to become 'heirs of God and joint-heirs with Christ' (Rom. 8:17) by imputed righteousness. *De Doctrina Christiana* makes God's adoption of fallen humanity a beneficial effect of their justification in Christ: 'GOD ADOPTS TO HIMSELF AS HIS CHILDREN THOSE WHO ARE JUSTIFIED THROUGH FAITH' (*CE* 16.50) and, 'from adoption we are even constituted heirs in Christ', enjoying a 'new generation', 'nature', and 'glory' (*CE* 16.54). The supporting texts attribute to Christ's saving work the adoption of sinners to the status of God's children (Gal. 3:29, 4:7; Heb. 2:11–12; Rom. 8:17). Mistakenly believing his progeny to be alienated, disinherited, and intestate, Adam will learn from Michael that the redemption, God's 'Fair Patrimonie', will restore God's faithful to His bosom.

As redeeming ironies amass throughout Adam's lament, a not inconsiderable body of evidence shows that Adam's soliloquy is not 'one of the loneliest scenes in literature'.[80] Adam's speech is more of a monologue than a soliloquy, because his ironic language proves that he is not isolated, but is being sustained by grace and supervised by an unseen divine audience. Unknown to Adam, he has been 'taught [to] resound farr other Song' (10.861–62) than a hopeless dirge. Adam's language is interlaced with subtle redemptive associations and his words confirm the grace issuing, without his knowledge, from the Son's intercession before God in the Empyrean. Throughout his remaining soliloquy Adam's benighted reasoning is still a long way from grasping the redemption and God's mercy, colleague with His wrath. Adam is in desperate need of absolution and yet, in a startling manoeuvre, he deigns to justify God's ways when he pardons his Maker, 'Him after all Disputes / Forc't I absolve' (10.828–29); Adam's impieties persist when he curses Creation and challenges 'Justice Divine' (10.858). Throughout he fails to recollect the *protevangelium*'s recondite promise of salvation. When Eve arrives and interrupts Adam's reverie, he demeans her to the status of a synecdochic 'Rib / Crooked by nature', a redundant and expendable 'part sinister' and 'supernumerarie' (10.884–88). Worse still, Adam rubbishes woman as if she were, in quasi-Aristotelian terms, an unfinished man and a 'fair defect / Of Nature' (10.891–92). James Grantham Turner justifiably deplores 'Adam's shower of misogynistic clichés – woman came from a crooked rib, woman is the sole cause of the fall, woman was made only for childbearing – [as] Milton's epic expansion of the first fallen excuse'.[81] Above all, Adam's rancorous gibes derogate Eden's matriarch, through whom the Messianic seed of woman shall all restore (12.623). Satan blames God for His ordering of Creation and, by extension, for causing the angelic fall, because God did not form him as a less ambitious, 'inferiour Angel' (4.59). Adam likewise evades accountability for his mistakes by reprehending God for having failed to populate the world with an alternative, 'woman-free' manner of procreation. He asks himself why God did not instead fashion a race of 'Angels without Feminine, / Or find some other way to generate / Mankind' (10.893–95). Yet, in Adam's flagrant condemnation of God's biological mandate and his spurning of God's gift of marriage as the means to procreate, he is oblivious to the potential for salvation glimmering within the *protevangelium*. Human salvation is predicated upon nuptial love, sexual delight, and the epiphany of a Messiah, a seed, not of man, but of woman, who will flourish from the Davidic line in Mary, the *Theotokos* or 'God-bearer'.

Miltonists of every sect have evaluated Eve's patient response to Adam's misogynistic tirade, her winning speech of reconciliation that begins, 'Forsake me not thus, *Adam*' (10.914–36).[82] Her unprecedented, charitable, and selfless gesture evokes a

---

[80] Svendsen, 329.

[81] James Grantham Turner, *One Flesh: Paradisal Marriage and Sexual Relations in the Age of Milton* (Oxford, 1987), 164.

[82] To give a baker's dozen: Arnold Stein, *Answerable Style: Essays on 'Paradise Lost'* (Minneapolis, 1953), 118; E. M. W. Tillyard, 'The Crisis of *Paradise Lost*', in *Milton: 'Paradise Lost': A Collection of Critical Essays*, ed. Louis L. Martz (Englewood Cliffs, 1966): 156–82; Summers, *Method*, 176–85; Frye, *Five Essays*, 66–69; Fish, *Surprised By Sin*, 273; J. Douglas Canfield, 'Blessed are the Merciful: The Understanding of the Promise in *Paradise Lost*', *Milton Quarterly*, 7 (1973), 43–47; Anthony C.

particular heroine from the chronicles of David. Eve's supplication pre-echoes the biblical Abigail's dutiful plea to David to spare her husband Nabal.[83] Elsewhere Eve's devotion in accompanying Adam into a hostile world east of Eden anticipates the pious Ruth's willingness to face an uncertain future beside her mother-in-law Naomi (12.614–19; Ruth 1:16–17).[84] Appropriately, Eve and Ruth are key figures within the Messianic line running from Adam and Abraham to Jesse and David to the house of Jesus's surrogate father Joseph. The incarnate Son is adopted and affiliated within this genealogy (see 5.385–87; 10.183; 11.158–61; Matt. 1:1–17).[85] Yet Abigail and Ruth's loving gestures, which are embodied in Eve's altruistic words and actions, are pale shadows of the Son, who is the overarching antitype for Eve's supplication of Adam in Book Ten.

Eve joins her voice to her redeemer's when she offers to be Adam's substitute and the 'onely just object of [God's] ire' (10.936). In Book Ten's emotional and dramatic context Eve's kenotic, self-emptying attitude is an abrupt and unforeseen event, especially coming after Adam's desperate monologue and misogynistic invective. No human activity preceding Eve's petition can prepare the reader for her surprising act of charity: not Eve's homicidal intent to have Adam fall with her, for better or worse; not Adam's willingness to die with, but not for, Eve; and certainly not Adam and Eve's propensity to blame others for their transgression. Eve's speech absorbs the negative energy of desolation and anguish generated since the Fall and, in its place, creates a peace within which the two sinners may work towards reunion. Eve begins to reconcile one half of the love between God and humanity, specifically, neighbourly love, and heals over the scar of interpersonal schism. How uplifting Eve's healing response is may be measured by comparing her with Hugo Grotius's Eve in *Adamus Exul*. Grotius's Eve emboldens her spouse by chiding him to be less 'timid [*timidum*]' (1748) and to 'rely upon masculine strength [*Virtute fretus mascula*]' (1750) or, if Adam is set upon committing suicide, to immolate her before he annihilates himself (1806–07).[86] Grotius's awestruck Adam reacts to Eve's stoicism, 'Whence does this great, emerging virtue shine forth amid such great evils?' (1754–55).[87] The sterner stuff Grotius's Eve recommends to her spouse – to do all that may become a man – is worlds apart from the humility and sacrificial love Milton's Eve manifests to mend human relations. Milton's Eve shapes herself after her redeemer, not only by accepting responsibility for her

Yu, 'Life in the Garden: Freedom and the Image of God in *Paradise Lost*', *Journal of Religion*, 60 (1980), 247–71; Christopher, 163–74; McColley, 209–11; Daniel W. Doerksen, '"Let There be Peace": Eve as Redemptive Peacemaker in *Paradise Lost*, Book X', *Milton Quarterly*, 31 (1997), 124–29; Richard Strier, 'Milton against Humility', in *Religion and Culture in Renaissance England*, ed. Claire McEachern and Debora Shuger (Cambridge, 1997), 272–73; Forsyth, 285–300.

[83] Compare Eve's demeanour at 10.909–13 and her words at 10.933–36 with 1 Sam. 25:23–31.
[84] See Barbara Lewalski, *'Paradise Lost' and the Rhetoric of Literary Forms* (Princeton, 1985), 277; and Cheryl H. Fresch, '"Whither thou goest": *Paradise Lost* XII, 610–23 and the Book of Ruth', *Milton Studies*, 32 (1995), 111–30.
[85] See Kristin Pruitt McColgan, '"God is also in Sleep": Dreams Satanic and Divine in *Paradise Lost*', *Milton Studies*, 30 (1993), 145–46.
[86] Grotius, *Adamus Exul*, 202 and 204.
[87] Ibid. 202.

offence against God and her spouse, but also, in an unforeseen act of altruism, by assuming the guilt of her husband who, only hours before, had informed on her to their divine judge and, moments before, had affronted her with a vile torrent of verbal abuse. With the exception of the Son's voice itself, Eve's adoption of her redeemer's voice sounds the epic's warmest note of selfless love. As David Gay observes, 'Eve initiates the redemptive countermovement to the Fall in the poem (a countermovement already realized in the Son's prophetic narrative in Book 3).'[88] The poem's other imitations of the redeemer's voice do not ring so true. Hubristic Satan travesties it when boasting of his self-elevation from dumb snake to brute human: 'look on mee, / Mee who have toucht and tasted' (9.687–88); and Adam, we saw, in deploring his misfortune, querulously and self-pityingly mimics his redeemer's voice. In Eve's speech the egoistic 'I' cedes to the self-giving 'mee', to that definition of love where 'Love is not a being-for-itself quality but a quality by which or in which you are for others.'[89]

Eve achieves her petition that 'Between us two let there be peace' (10.924). In so doing, she mimics the Son, whom the Father honours as 'in Heav'n and Earth the onely peace / Found out for mankind under wrauth' (3.274–75). Moreover, Eve's beseeching words and Adam's placatory response perform a cameo version of the reconciliation within the Godhead between the Son who satisfies and appeases all and the mollified Father who accepts the Son's sacrifice. Eve '*persists and at length appeases*' Adam ('Argument' to Book Ten), just as the Son seeks 'to appease [God's] wrauth' (3.406) and strives to have Adam and Eve 'fully satisfi'd, and [God] appease' (10.79). Eve's language and diction are inscribed with the figure of the suffering Messiah. Eve's opening words, 'Forsake me not thus, *Adam*' (10.914), which implore Adam's clemency, recall the crucified Jesus's Aramaic cry of derelic-tion as he satisfies for sin, '*Eloi, Eloi, lama sabachthani*' or 'O God, my God, why have you forsaken me?' (Mark 15:34; see Matt. 27:46). *De Doctrina Christiana* associates God's satisfaction with Christ's desolate cry from the cross, exclaimed during Christ's 'dreadful sensation of the divine anger being poured out upon him, from which proceeded that dying outcry' (*CE* 15.304, 306). Likewise Eve, imaging the placating Christ, wishes to be the 'onely just object of [God's] ire' (10.936). Adam submits to Eve's supplication and 'with peaceful words uprais'd her soon' (10.946), just as Christ, his satisfaction completed, is 'by [God] rais'd' (3.258) from the grave and victoriously re-enters Heaven. Just as in the satisfied Father's 'face . . . no cloud / Of anger shall remain' (3.262–63), Adam assumes the appeased Father's role as 'his anger all he lost' (10.945). The narrator describes the effect of Eve's humiliation as 'reconcilement' (10.943) with Adam and the Son similarly predicts 'peace assur'd, / And reconcilement' (3.263–64) between God and hu-manity. Eve's description of herself to Adam as one 'Restor'd by thee, vile as I am, to place / Of new acceptance' (10.971–72) makes her promotion to Adam's side coincident with the Son's restoration to a place of new acceptance at his Father's side (12.451–58). Eve's reconciliation with Adam, neighbour with neighbour, is a fragile, but vital, opening move towards reconciliation between God and humanity. Eve's confession of sin, 'vile as I am', distinguishes her from Christ, whose 'unspotted Soule' (3.248) qualifies him to intercede for humanity. By Book Ten's conclusion Adam and Eve *'seek Peace of the offended Deity, by repentance and supplication'* ('Argument' to Book Ten), and temporarily believe that their prayers are intrinsically unsupported and self-sufficient. The reader's broader perspective can comprehend, through the diminishing thundercloud about God's throne, that it is properly the Son who successfully pacifies the Father. Immediately after the Fall Milton depicts God sitting in 'his secret Cloud, Amidst in Thunder' (10.32–33). On the mild Son the mitigated Father 'Blaz'd forth unclouded Deitie' (10.65) and the Son's intercession mollifies the Father, now 'without Cloud, serene' (11.45), so that He is inclined to receive the fallen couple's prayers, which are no longer fuming and incensed. Although Eve possesses limited, fallen powers, she alone breaks this seemingly interminable cycle of hatred and introduces into the human tragedy a heroic, reviving, and welcome note of Christic love and reconciliation. Eve's humiliation motivates the fallen couple's spiritual metamorphosis from penitence in fearing God's justice, anger, and punishment to repentance in recognizing God's mercy, love, and grace.

As a result of Eve's breakthrough Adam is roused to a new spiritual maturity. Adam alludes to the teaching of Galatians 6:5 that 'each person will bear his own burden' when he recognizes that Eve is 'ill able to sustaine / [God's] full wrauth' and so should 'Beare thine own first' (10.950–51). Rather than 'blame / Each other, blam'd anough elsewhere' (10.958–59), Adam applies the lesson from Galatians 5:13–15 to love and not bite and devour one another and advises that they should 'strive / In offices of Love' (10.959–60). Adam's phrase evokes Christ's threefold 'office of mediator [*mediatoris officium*]', of prophet, priest, and king, 'by which HE GLADLY ANSWERED FOR, AND EVEN NOW ANSWERS FOR, ALL THOSE RESPONSIBILITIES THROUGH WHICH PEACE WITH GOD AND ETERNAL SALVATION ARE ACQUIRED FOR THE HUMAN RACE' (*CE* 15.284). Through these loving offices Adam advises that they should determine 'how we may light'n / Each others burden in our share of woe' (10.960–61), again advancing the Pauline counsel that humans should 'bear one another's burdens, and so you will fulfil Christ's law' (Gal. 6:2). Adam regrets the future pain 'to our Seed (O hapless Seed!) deriv'd' (10.965), unknowingly prophesying a time when the immaculate Jesus, the truly undeserving seed of woman, will vicariously 'derive' human suffering to himself. Above all, Adam's wording recalls the Son's willingness to 'mitigate [humanity's] doom / On mee deriv'd' (10.76–77).

Eve's unexpected proposal to fix on either sexual abstinence and 'wilful barrenness' (10.1042) or suicide and self-extinction does not undermine all that she has hitherto accomplished. Eve's initiative goads Adam to reason his way towards redemption by arguing against her proposal. Suicide will not 'exempt' (10.1025) or 'release' them (Latin *exemptus*) from the debt of sin they 'are by doom to pay' (10.1026). Rather, Adam is 'with such counsel nothing sway'd' (10.1010) and contemplates the Christic sublimity, literally, the 'up-raisedness' (Latin *sublimis*) of the exalted state into which he raised Eve from her humiliated posture. Eve's altruistic 'contempt of life and pleasure' (10.1013) communicates to Adam 'somthing more sublime / And excellent then what thy minde contemnes' (10.1014–15) and her humiliation has 'rais'd' 'To better hopes his more attentive minde' (10.1011–12). Her self-giving germinates within Adam a fresh awareness of mercy. Summers perceives here the restoration of the double love, love of neighbour evolving into love of God, so that 'the resulting reconciliation between man and woman is the inevitable prologue and type of the ensuing reconciliation between man and God'.[90] Readings have tended to regard Eve's supplication as an essential stage in the process of human–human and divine–human reconciliation and one unfortunate consequence of this focus is to draw attention away from Eve's suicide speech (10.966–1006). Eve's suicide speech is no less pivotal, for, in another of the poem's proliferating ironies, Eve's suicidal and genocidal overture prompts within Adam a rousing motion concerning God's gracious means. Adam's words immediately preceding Eve's suicide speech, which concern the suffering 'to our Seed (O hapless Seed!) deriv'd' (10.965), convey, in addition to Adam's apprehensions about Sin and Death contaminating the human race, Christ's future unmerited suffering prophesied in the *protevangelium*. Eve's plan to eradicate humanity would eclipse this Messianic oracle and would thus prevent any hope of reconciliation between God and humankind. The potential devastation resulting from Eve's proposition moves Adam to recollect both the *protevangelium* and the Son's piteous expression in delivering the oracle. There is little evidence, as Richard Strier proposes, that Miltonic heroism is 'against humility' and that it embodies Aristotelian *magnanimitas* and Roman *dignitas* nor that Eve manifests 'proper pride' by 'presumptuously trying to outsmart God ("to evade / The penalty")'.[91] The self-sacrificial quality to Eve's previous heroic speech defines true Miltonic magnanimity. Miltonic magnanimity is rich in humility and adamantly unAristotelian. As we will see, Jesus's innovation in *Paradise Regain'd* is to re-evaluate and reorient the virtue of magnanimity *away from* its Aristotelian definition towards charity and kenosis, where 'to lay down / [is] Far more magnanimous, then to assume' (*PR* 2.482–83).

Redeeming irony once more opposes and subverts negation. Eve's proposal 'ere Conception to prevent / The Race unblest' (10.987–88) is an abortive depravation of God's plan to redeem and preserve humanity by preventing or 'coming before' damnation with 'Prevenient Grace' (11.3). Contrary to Eve's statement, because the fallen couple has lapsed they cannot fully 'satisfie [Death's] Rav'nous Maw' (10.991), but Christ, from God and Adam's seed derived, *can* satisfy. Adam and Eve neither 'make short' (10.1000) through suicide nor decide 'both our selves and Seed at once to free' (10.999), but the Son as *Christus liberator* establishes Christian liberty and emancipates humanity from sin's bondage by lowering himself to participate in Adam and Eve's genealogy. Eve's doctrine of annihilation, 'Destruction with destruction to destroy' (10.1006), is a solecism R. A. Shoaf deems 'the infinite regress that characterizes unredeemed signification'.[92] A redeemed

---

[90] Summers, *Method*, 176.
[91] Strier, 'Humility', 260–61 and 273.
[92] R. A. Shoaf, *Milton: Poet of Duality* (Gainesville, 1993), 103.

signification overturns Eve's hopelessness. Describing Christ's intercession, Paul holds that sinners 'are to God a sweet smell of Christ among the ones being saved and among the ones perishing: to those perishing, a fragrance of death unto death [ἐκ θανάτου εἰς θάνατον], to those being saved, a fragrance of life unto life [ἐκ ζωῆς εἰς ζωήν]' (2 Cor. 2:15–16). Milton intercalates this passage when God characterizes Christ's sacrifice as a 'rigid satisfaction, death for death' (3.212), and the Son revitalizes the Father's grave formulation with the oath, 'Behold mee then, mee for him, life for life / I offer' (3.236–37). In Milton's pristine Eden Creation is each morning sufficient to convey, from the 'Earths great Altar', 'silent praise / To the Creator, and his Nostrils fill / With grateful Smell' (9.195–97). In a spoiled Eden the only worthy offering or fit praise for God must first be arrayed in Paul's 'sweet smell of Christ'. Eve's abnegation of God, self, and other in her phrase 'Destruction with destruction to destroy' anticipates the Son's sacerdotal mediation when, before God's throne, Adam and Eve's repentant prayers are 'clad / With incense . . . By thir Great Intercessor' (11.17–19). The Son refines these prayers into a 'smell of peace toward Mankinde' (11.38) or, in Paul's imagery, 'a sweet smell of Christ', and resumes his offer of 'life for life', since 'for these my Death shall pay' (11.36). The epic thus elaborates the concord of divine–human relations, brokered through Christ's sacrifice, and opposes Eve's 'Destruction with destruction to destroy' with Christ's voluntary sacrifice of his life for life to live.

Eve proposes '*violent wayes*' '*to evade the Curse likely to fall on thir Ofspring*', and her error allows Adam, '*conceiving better hope*', to put '*her in mind of the late Promise made them, that her Seed should be reveng'd on the Serpent*' ('Argument' to Book Ten). Georgia Christopher attributes the dramatic turning point, Adam's sudden perception of God's mercy, to his remembrance of the *protevangelium*. Christopher determines that 'deliverance comes from a divine voice, or more precisely from the memory of a divine oracle and its reinterpretation'.[93] While, admittedly, Adam deduces from the riddling oracle that Eve's 'Seed shall bruise / The Serpents head' (10.1031–32) and equates 'our grand Foe / *Satan*' (10.1033–34) with the serpent, the oracle remains obscure to him. Adam continues to interpret the redemptive bruise as a literal act of retaliatory vengeance rather than as a symbol of Christ's patient suffering. Michael later disabuses Adam of this fallacy of construing the bruise 'As of a Duel, or the local wounds / Of head or heel' (12.387–88). Strictly speaking, it is not the *protevangelium* itself, but Adam's recollection of the Son's demeanour as he imparts the *protevangelium* that constitutes the *anagnorisis* of the drama and moves Adam and Eve to repentance. Adam's consideration of Eve's suicide bid, 'so thinking to evade / The penaltie pronounc't' (10.1021–22), reminds him of the manner of the Son's pronouncement as much as the nature of the penalty. Adam accepts God's 'just yoke' (10.1045), but his spiritual perception penetrates further, beyond God's justice, to the mild yoke of God's mercy that the Son bears for all. Adam has already beheld the Son's loving aspect reflected in Eve's countenance as she delivered her sublime speech of supplication. Now Adam links in his mind the two gracious dispositions of his loving

---

[93] Christopher, 164.

judge and his loving wife. Adam's words support this reading. He remembers that his 'gracious Judge [was] without revile' (10.118) and enjoins Eve, 'Remember with what mild / And gracious temper he both heard and judg'd / Without wrauth or reviling' (10.1046–48). Even while the Son sentenced them, there was a 'look serene, / When angry most he seemd and most severe, / What else but favor, grace, and mercie shon?' (10.1094–96). Earlier Adam's flawed memory recoiled from the Son as a 'dreadful voice' that 'Would Thunder in my ears' (10.779–80). In Genesis 'the voice of the Lord God' (*AV* Gen. 3:8) judges Adam and Eve, and Adam's recollection of a thundering voice plays on the Hebrew word *kol* for 'voice' in Genesis, which is also the Hebrew word for 'thunder'. Milton radically re-imagines the 'voice of God' (10.97). The poet transforms his biblical antecedent, an outraged God's stentorian thundering, into the unambiguously compassionate and indulgent tones of the merciful Son, who descends as a 'mild Judge and Intercessor both' (10.96). Until Adam realizes that God intertwines mercy with justice and, to paraphrase Psalm 85, allows these divine attributes to kiss in the Son's 'mild / and gracious temper' (10.1046–47), he has been wilfully mishearing God's voice and mistaking serene clemency for indignant fulminations. Perplexed by how the *protevangelium* occults 'piteous amends' (10.1032), Adam nonetheless remains reassured by his memory of the Son's mien, 'pittying how they stood / Before him naked to the aire' (10.211–12). Adam is ignorant of the Son's justification of their souls, but he does remember the Son's pity and the care with which he shielded their exposed bodies, for he reminds Eve that 'his hands / Cloath'd us unworthie, pitying while he judg'd' (10.1058–59).

Milton's reader once again has the advantage of the divine perspective. The angels celebrate the Son's atonement by which he will 'end the strife / Of Mercy and Justice in [God's] face discernd' (3.406–07) and execute acts of mercy which epitomize God's first and last principle of Being. The appeased Father receives the 'accepted Son' (11.46) with a tranquil countenance, 'without Cloud, serene' (11.45). Adam, without access to these evidences of grace in the Empyrean, nevertheless makes the vital connection between Eve's loving humility and the Son's gracious aspect and, accordingly, postulates mercy as an essential attribute of a good God. Adam's fresh insight that God is disposed to 'pitying while he judg'd' (10.1059) and will 'his heart to pitie incline' (10.1061) reiterates the angelic hymn that the Son, 'to appease [God's] wrauth' (3.406), will dispose the Father to 'much more to pitie encline' (10.402) and to be 'much more to pitie enclin'd' (3.405). Adam's renewed outlook leads to the revelation that the 'place of [divine] judgement' (10.932) may simultaneously be a place of divine mercy, rather as Luther made the crucifixion the site for the outpouring of God's wrath and the demonstration of His love. At the cross each divine aspect is hidden and revealed. Corresponding to *De Doctrina Christiana*'s soteriological scheme, Adam and Eve's penitence yields to repentance and, concomitantly, divine justice to divine mercy. Adam's acknowledgement of divine pity moves 'our Father penitent' (10.1097) to advise their confession, contrition, and 'humiliation meek' (10.1104) at the same site where the Son judged them. On this spot Adam and Eve 'in lowliest plight repentant stood' (11.1). The human pride and envy that incurred the Fall give way to human sympathy and mutuality. Recognizing grace,

Adam and Eve 'both confessd' (10.1100). Where in prelapsarian Eden they sang their morning and evening psalms of thanksgiving to God as duets, they now beseech divine compassion from their Merciful Maker in unison.

Following the Fall Adam and Eve undergo interpretive labour pains that translate them from a state of curse to a state of grace, from penitence to repentance, and from an apprehension of divine wrath to a recognition of divine mercy. Throughout Book Ten's human drama they take up and discard soteriological doctrines, emend their words, amend their deeds, and adopt roles with varying degrees of selfishness and selflessness that bring them closer to and, at times, farther away from the redemptive solution to their sinful estate. As Book Eleven opens, Adam and Eve's knowledge of the Son's ways to lapsed humankind is incomplete. Adam and Eve may still entertain the illusion that they can reside in Eden 'though in fall'n state, content' (11.180), and that they can labour there 'now with sweat impos'd' (11.172), but their spiritual perception of God as 'placable and mild' (11.151) and of the Son as a 'Judge', 'infinite in pardon' (11.167), has developed considerably. They have worked out a path to salvation in fear and trembling: they are confirmed in God's goodness, grace, and mercy, and their hearts and minds, having attained an attitude of repentance, faithfulness, and responsiveness to God, are prepared for the unveiling of the mystery of the suffering God-man in Michael's narrative. Michael can now disclose to them the efficacy of a newfound faith, what *De Doctrina Christiana* styles a 'SAVING FAITH' (*CE* 15.392), in a God who saves through His Son, since prevenient grace descends from the Mercy-seat, allowing 'new flesh / Regenerat [to] grow instead' (11.4–5). The double love is restored and the covenant between God, Adam, and Eve somewhat mended through the Son's mediation. Moreover, their education has progressed, insofar as they have learned 'to be merciful to one another so that they can then comprehend God's mercy'.[94] They are well on the way to what Milton called the end of learning, 'regaining to know God aright, and out of that knowledge to love him, to imitate him, to be like him' (*CPW* 2.366–67) after their redeemer's pattern, the very image of Milton's invisible God (Col. 1:15). It remains for Michael to impart the *protevangelium*'s redemptive significance within human history but, for those who have ears to hear, the manifold and overlapping redeeming ironies have already spelled out the twofold reconciliation in Christ between human and human and between God and humanity.

In Book Ten Milton communicates the tacitly understood presence of God's mercy to the reader through multiple and accumulating redeeming ironies. The Puritan poet also reveals God's mercy to Adam and Eve through the Son's loving countenance that pities while it judges. Milton's subtle strategy of conveying divine mercy is anticipated early in the epic, once again in the motif of the Son's compassionate aspect. Following the Son's speech, in which he bestows himself 'as a sacrifice / Glad to be offerd' (3.269–70):

---

[94] Canfield, 46.

His words here ended, but his meek aspect,
Silent yet spake, and breath'd immortal love
To mortal men, above which onely shon
Filial obedience

(3.266–70)

The Son's 'meek aspect, / Silent yet spake', is as important to Adam and Eve's salvation as the Son's annunciation of the *protevangelium* or Eve's redeeming and reconciling voice. The Son's face is the mnemonic that guides the fallen couple towards a more developed awareness of God's mercy and discloses the hidden, loving aspect of Deity. The self-sacrificing Son's ironic facial expression, 'Silent yet spake', is an apt symbol for Milton's strategy of edifying irony, which is concealed within the epic for the fit reader. Through redeeming irony Milton's fit audience is 'taught' to 'resound farr other Song' (10.861–62) than a fallen lamentation. That 'other song' is a redemption song where grace trumps sin, hope prevents despair, and a restorative re-ascent annuls the Fall's degenerative effects. Amid human despondency the ostensibly tragic debacle of the epic's two fallen protagonists, who are surprised by sin, is subverted, supplemented, and revised by Milton's redeeming irony, which leaves Adam, Eve, and the fit reader assured by grace.

7

Paradise Found: Milton's Messiah
and the Argument of Weakness
in *Paradise Regain'd*

He plainely shewed that his own profession
Was virtue, patience, grace, love, piety:
And how by suffering he could conquer more
Than all the Kings that ever liv'd before.
Aemilia Lanyer, *Salve Deus Rex Judaeorum*[1]

Thou hast said much here of *Paradise lost*, but what hast thou to say of *Paradise found?*

> Words reportedly spoken by Thomas Ellwood
> to John Milton after reading *Paradise Lost*[2]

For who is ther almost that measures wisdom by simplicity, strength by suffering, dignity by lowlinesse, who is there that counts it first, to be last, somthing to be nothing, and reckons himself of great command in that he is a servant? yet God when he meant to subdue the world and hell at once, part of that to salvation, and this wholly to perdition, made chois of no other weapons, or auxiliaries than these whether to save, or to destroy. It had bin a small maistery for him, to have drawn out his Legions into array, and flankt them with his thunder; therefore he sent Foolishnes to confute Wisdom, Weaknes to bind Strength, Despisednes to vanquish Pride. And this is the great mistery of the Gospel made good in Christ himself, who as he testifies came not to be minister'd to, but to minister; and must be fulfil'd in all his ministers till his second comming.

> Milton, *The Reason of Church-Government*

In this final chapter I wish to undertake a close reading of *Paradise Regain'd*. I will demonstrate that, during the *agon* between Jesus and Satan, Milton in myriad subtle and indirect ways foregrounds the atonement through strategies of irony, parody, and biblical and classical allusion. The early commentator Henry Todd queried Milton's choice of the gospel temptation narratives for the poem's subject.

---

[1] Aemilia Lanyer, *The Poems of Aemilia Lanyer*, ed. Susanne Woods (Oxford, 1993), 92.
[2] Lewalski, *Life*, 444.

Todd writes, 'It may seem a little odd, that Milton should impute the recovery of Paradise to this short scene of our Saviour's life upon earth, and not rather extend it to his agony, crucifixion, etc.'[3] Todd's judgment has not abated. John Rogers recently proposed that *Paradise Regain'd* advances an exemplarist model of salvation. Rogers maintains that 'Milton's lifelong poetic neglect of the Crucifixion and its theological implications' is manifest in *Paradise Regain'd* and that 'Milton's neglect of the Crucifixion' is replaced by 'a provisional faith in man's ability to effect his own salvation, without the help of a sacrificial redeemer'.[4] Rogers claims, first, that Jesus's resistance to Satan's temptations lacks any redemptive overtones and, second, that Jesus's conduct fashions an imitable paradigm of moral exertion. As we will discover, neither of these hypotheses withstands scrutiny when measured against the poem's content. An enquiry into why Milton selected the temptation narratives over the crucifixion will never be wholly satisfied, but certainly his unfinished occasional piece *The Passion* reveals that he found a straightforward poetic account of the crucifixion too restrictive. The Passion ode's representation of divine suffering 'confine[s] my roving vers' (22) and leaves '*Phoebus*' his Muse 'To this Horizon . . . bound' (23). His subject, to sing 'Of labours huge and hard, too hard for human wight' (14), may have been beyond Milton's fledgling poetic powers. His appended prose admission of disappointment, astonishing in its candour, seems to indicate as much, in which he confesses that the work was left unfinished because he found the subject '*above the yeers he had, when he wrote it, and nothing satisfi'd with what was begun*'. Young Milton discovered that a direct rendering of the Passion would seriously limit his imaginative scope and hamper the technical amplitude and virtuosity required of his subject.[5] The four canonical gospel Passion narratives that meticulously record Jesus's walk to the cross, undergone in near total silence, afforded little room for poetic exposition and amplification through dialogue or drama. In contrast, Milton was less straitened by the temptation accounts. The form of a Socratic dialogue between Satan and Christ enabled Milton to debate and justify the virtues of Jesus's extraordinary life, a life endured even to the death.

The temporal framework of *Paradise Regain'd* is one structural aspect that reinforces its Passional theme. Christian typology conceived of Jesus as a second Moses who hungered, thirsted, and fasted in the wilderness for forty days and nights (Matt. 4:2; Luke 4:2).[6] Moses similarly fasted on Mount Sinai for forty days and nights when he interceded for Israel: 'I fell down before the Lord, as at the first, forty days and forty nights: I did neither eat bread, nor drink water, because of all your sins which ye sinned, in doing wickedly in the sight of the Lord, to provoke him to anger' (*AV* Deut. 9:18). Moses fasts to redeem God's

[3] Henry J. Todd, ed., *The Poetical Works of John Milton*, vol. 5 (London, 1809), 5; note to *PR* 1.3.

[4] John Rogers, 'Milton's Circumcision', in *Milton and the Grounds of Contention*, ed. Mark R. Kelley, Michael Lieb, and John T. Shawcross (Pittsburgh, 2003), 189 and 190.

[5] For an alternative reading of Milton's avoidance of a direct representation of the crucifixion, see Erin Henriksen, *Milton and the Reformation Aesthetics of the Passion* (Leiden, 2009).

[6] See Austin Farrer, *The Triple Victory: Christ's Temptations according to Saint Matthew* (London, 1965), 15–18.

people after they have murmured against Yahweh for want of bread (Exodus 16), tempted God at Massah for failing to procure water (Exodus 17), and apostatized by idolatrously worshipping the golden calf (Exodus 32). In Christian typology Jesus's wilderness ordeal for forty days and nights harbingers his Passional sufferings through which he intercedes for humanity. The mutual time scheme of forty days and nights, which encourages thematic parallels between the atonement of the Old Testament Moses and of the New Testament Messiah, furnishes an intercessory framework that informs the patient heroism of Milton's Jesus, who 'Full forty days he passd' (1.303). As I shall demonstrate, throughout what is arguably his last major poem Milton deploys analogous sophisticated literary strategies to assert the inseparability of Jesus's identity as Messiah from his atoning office.

I

Studies of Milton's brief epic have dwelt upon the significance of the poem's explication of Jesus's identity as the Son of God. Barbara Lewalski finds that 'A most important aspect of the poem's theme and the central issue in the dramatic encounter between Christ and Satan is the problem of determining, as Satan puts it, "In what degree or meaning thou art call'd / The Son of God" (4.516–17)', and Louis Martz holds that the narrative's goal is to define 'the nature of the Son of God' and to deduce 'what it means to be a Son of God.'[7] Peter Angelo and Ashraf Rushdy challenge this interpretation by pointing out that, even before the temptations proper begin, Milton is careful to establish that Jesus possesses foreknowledge that his way lies even to the death.[8] This detail makes the mode of Jesus's heroism as weighty as his nature. Angelo asserts, 'Jesus goes into the desert and experiences the subsequent confrontation with Satan with prior and full knowledge of his identity, as well as the redemptive end of his mission.'[9] Rushdy remarks that Jesus 'expresses the knowledge of death as the culmination of his second reading of the Law and as the defining feature of his identity', a discovery that 'bears immense possibilities for a richer understanding of Milton's christology'.[10] I would add that the poem's soteriology, the underlying issue Angelo and Rushdy address, is reinforced through another name, the name of Messiah. Jesus's Messianic identity clarifies our understanding of the kind of heroism he represents in *Paradise Regain'd*.

Although Milton's poem never adopts the Greek title 'Christ', Milton does include either its Hebrew equivalent 'Messiah' or the title's translated meaning 'Anointed'.[11] In the ancient Hebrew world the title 'Anointed' could denote a

---

[7] Barbara Lewalski, *Brief Epic*, 133–34; Louis L. Martz, *Milton: Poet of Exile* (2nd edn, New Haven, 1986), 254 and 256.
[8] Peter Gregory Angelo, *Fall to Glory: Theological Reflections on Milton's Epics* (New York, 1987), 103–04; Ashraf H. A. Rushdy, *The Empty Garden: The Subject of Late Milton* (Pittsburgh, 1992), 181–90.
[9] Angelo, 103.   [10] Rushdy, 181.
[11] For the title 'Messiah', see 1.245, 261; 2.4, 43; and 4.502; and for 'Anointed', see 2.50.

prophet, priest, or king. By the time of Jesus's birth Israel had been subjugated by a succession of empires, first by Babylon, next by Assyria, and later by Roman rule. The title of 'Messiah' reflected Israel's popular expectation of the advent of a powerful and righteous king who would liberate Israel from the imperial Roman yoke. According to the gospels, the *causa poenae* for Jesus's crucifixion entailed his public acceptance of the royal title of 'Messiah' during his trial before the Sanhedrin (see Matt. 26:63–67; Mark 14:61–65). To Israel's religious leaders such a claim was outrageous, if not blasphemous, and to the Roman authorities it threatened to incite sedition and foment popular unrest. The most fundamental creedal statements in the gospels promote this controversial claim, not only that 'Jesus is the one called the Messiah' (Matt. 27:17, 22), but also 'that the Messiah died for our sins in accordance with the scriptures' (1 Cor. 15:3). The early Christians comprised a Messianic sect, an offshoot of mainstream Judaism, which espoused a highly controversial messianology in which it was thought necessary for the Messiah to have been crucified for the welfare of humanity. Thus the Lukan gospel makes the radical claim, 'Was it not necessary that the Messiah must suffer these things and enter into his glory?' (Luke 24:26). Justin Martyr's apologetic dialogue has its Jewish interlocutor Trypho react to the idea of a Messiah whose mission was not to conquer Rome and restore Israel's political independence, but rather to suffer and die: 'But what we want you to prove to us is that [Jesus] was to be crucified and to be subjected to so disgraceful and shameful a death (which even in the Law is cursed). We find it impossible to think that this could be so.'[12] As the theologian Martin Hengel writes, '*a crucified Son of God* – i.e., a crucified God, Kyrios [Lord], Soter [Saviour] or Messiah – *was an offense without analogy*'.[13]

Milton's *The Passion* delineates the paradoxical idea of a Messiah who comes not to rule but to serve and whose service from the cross saves his people. In the ode the crucified Jesus acts as God's Anointed and 'stoop[s] his regall head / That dropt with odorous oil down his fair eyes' (15–16). Throughout *Paradise Regain'd* Milton stresses the discrepancy, frequently enunciated in the Pauline writings, between the expectation of an invincible Messianic conqueror and the paradoxical Messianic idea realized in the figure of Jesus. When Milton's Satan dwells upon Jesus's obscurity as 'unknown, unfriended, low of birth' (2.413), or regards Jesus as 'unexperienc't ... Timorous and loth, with novice modesty, ... Irresolute, unhardy, unadventrous' (3.240–43), he touches upon the supreme irony of Messianic victory. Jesus is a servant-king who, to worldly eyes, is without adequate regal attributes. D. H. Juel has illuminated the subtle relationship between appearance and reality that is played out throughout the Markan Passion narrative in a manner applicable to Milton's brief epic:

> Mark's story is predicated on the tension between what everyone thinks and expects of the Messiah and what is in fact the case. Mark's story is deeply ironic, and the irony

[12] Justin Martyr, 291; ch. 90.
[13] Martin Hengel, 'Christological Titles in Early Christianity', in *The Messiah: Developments in Earliest Judaism and Christianity*, ed. James H. Charlesworth (Minneapolis, 1992), 428.

is bound up with the royal imagery that dominates Mark's narrative of the passion. As readers we know that Jesus is the Christ (1:1, 14:62, *inter alia*). The great irony is that it is Jesus's enemies who 'invest' him as king and 'pay homage'. They offer testimony of what the reader knows to be the truth.[14]

Messianic irony pertains to all four canonical Passion narratives. The Roman soldiers clothe Jesus in mock-royal rudiments. The sarcastic inscription Pilate affixes to the cross reads 'The King of the Jews', while Jesus's mockers goad him from the foot of the cross with the titles of Christ or Messiah. And yet, for the four Evangelists these titles are properly his. By the prerogatives of the Empire and the State Jesus is executed for claiming dominion over an eternal kingdom that he is actually heir to. The ironies multiply as Joseph of Arimathea attempts to honour Jesus posthumously by enclosing his corpse within a tomb that cannot contain his resurrection body and by bestowing a funeral tribute upon Jesus's mortal flesh that will soon be clothed in immortality. Through manifold narrative ironies the Evangelists express the gap between human perversity and the spiritual reality that corrects such fleshly mistakenness. In *Paradise Regain'd* irony 'is the only suitable vehicle' for narration because, as Juel puts it, 'Truth is not identical with appearance but must in some way be in tension with it. Jesus is a hero who does not look like a hero – and thus conventional ways of narrating stories about heroes are not sufficient as vehicles for the evangelists.'[15]

During his first extended soliloquy Milton's Jesus reveals that, while he was revolving the Law and the Prophets, he sought 'what was writ / Concerning the Messiah' and 'soon found of whom they spake / I am' (1.261–63). Albert Schweitzer observes that Jesus's life entailed his redemptive death so that 'all that belongs to the history of Jesus, in the strict sense, are the events which lead up to His death[. T]he real "Life of Jesus" [consists of] the deliberate bringing down of death upon Himself'.[16] The New Testament texts to which Jesus's words allude underscore this anticipation of his death. His awareness that he is 'Born to that end, born to promote all truth, / All righteous things' (1.205–06) evokes his future reply to Pontius Pilate prior to his sentence and execution. The Johannine Jesus stands trial for claiming to be the Messiah and 'Pilate said to him, "So, are you a king?" Jesus answered, "You say that I am a king. *For this I was born and for this have I come into the world*, that I might witness to the truth"' (John 18:37; emphasis added). In equal measure Jesus's recollection that 'The Law of God I red, and found it sweet, / Made it my whole delight' (1.207–08) re-echoes Paul's realization of his incapacity to fulfil the Law's prescript and his consequent praise of Christ as his deliverer:

> For I delight in God's law according to the inner man, but I see a different law in my members warring against the law of my mind and taking me captive by the law of sin which is in my members. What a wretched man am I! Who will deliver me from the body of this death? Thanks be to God through Jesus Christ our Lord. (Rom. 7:22–25)

[14] D. H. Juel, 'The Origin of Mark's Christology', in *The Messiah*, 453.
[15] Ibid. 458.
[16] Albert Schweitzer, *The Quest of the Historical Jesus*, trans. W. Montgomery (Baltimore, 1998), 392.

Jesus explicitly connects his Messianic vocation with his future suffering on the cross:

> this chiefly, that my way must lie
> Through many a hard assay eev'n to the death,
> Ere I the promisd Kingdom can attain,
> Or work Redemption for mankind, whose sins
> Full weight must be transferrd upon my head.
>
> (1.263–67)

In Book Two, after Satan essays his first temptation and before the fiend launches the second barrage against Jesus that is sustained until the poem's close, God confirms Jesus's sense of his redemptive mission. Jesus descends into himself 'with holiest Meditations fed' and:

> at once
> All his great work to come before him set:
> How to begin, how to accomplish best
> His end of being on Earth, and mission high
>
> (2.110–14)

Satan admits that 'Of the Messiah I have heard foretold / By all the Prophets' (4.502–03), but Jesus is clear that 'what the means' of Messianic victory shall be eludes Satan's understanding. Jesus explains that, regarding a spiritual triumph by humiliation that will lead to the regaining of a 'Kingdom' of which 'there shall be no end', 'It is not for thee to know, nor mee to tell' (4.151–53). Milton clearly signposts Jesus's foreknowledge concerning Messianic victory through redemption and he indicates that, although such knowledge is denied Satan, it is available to Jesus before his wilderness temptations and prior to embarking upon his ministry.

Satan continually probes Jesus's mind for a definition of Messianism so that he can use this knowledge to undermine his opponent. Satan envisions Messianism as worldly kingship. Therefore, during the banquet temptation Satan ensures that 'A Table [is] richly spred, in regal mode' (2.340). Satan next proffers riches with which Jesus may regain '*Judahs* Throne; / (Thy throne)' (2.424–25) and urges Jesus to be zealous 'To sit upon thy Father *Davids* Throne' (3.153) and to enjoy his 'endless raign' (3.178). Satan presents Parthian prowess to entice Jesus, one already 'so apt, in regal Arts, / And regal Mysteries' (3.248–49), into vindicating himself through military might; with Parthia's aid Satan might 'reinstall thee / In *Davids* royal seat' (3.372–73). In offering Rome, Satan praises Jesus as one 'Indu'd with Regal Vertues' (4.989) and fit to usurp Tiberius's throne, 'in his place ascending' (4.101). Satan claims that the learning of Athens, too, will eventually 'mature thee to a Kingdoms waight' and 'render thee a King compleat' (4.282–83). Each time Satan renews his temptations, he re-invokes the Messianic theme in reductively materialist terms by suggesting the ways in which Jesus might establish his rightful kingdom.

The disparity between Satan's worldly idea of kingship and the spiritual reality of Jesus as servant-king exacerbates the arch-enemy's perplexity that Jesus 'seem'st otherwise inclin'd / Then to a worldly Crown' (4.212–13). Satan is puzzled that Jesus wishes for 'what Kingdom, / Real or Allegoric I discern not' (4.389–90), and his perplexity arises from his inability to perceive that Jesus's exaltation is contingent upon his humiliation and that his everlasting kingdom will outlast a temporal one. Jesus prophesies, 'I shall raign past thy preventing' (4.492), but Satan cannot reconcile the afflictions awaiting Jesus at the end of his earthly ministry with the kingdom with 'no end' (4.153) that Jesus looks to inherit from withstanding those trials. The blind Milton's favourite motto, which he or his amanuenses habitually inscribed alongside his autograph, was the text of 2 Corinthians 12:9. This verse reflects upon Jesus's teaching that 'My grace is sufficient for you, because my strength is made perfect in weakness' (*CE* 18.271). The verse restates the classic Pauline paradox of Christ crucified, which derives from 1 Corinthians 1:18–31, a message of wisdom in its apparent foolishness and power in its seeming weakness. Paul confesses, 'Because of this I revel in weaknesses, in insults, in hardships, in persecutions, and in troubles, all for Christ's sake. For when I am weak, then I am powerful' (2 Cor. 12:9–10). In *Paradise Regain'd* the Father explains to Gabriel that Jesus's heroism will conform to a sacrificial act by 'strong Sufferance' (1.160). In *Paradise Lost* Michael speaks of the Christian saints as 'in mind prepar'd, if so befall, / For death, like that which the redeemer dy'd' (*PL* 12.444–45), and describes them as being *'able to resist Satans assaults, . . .* Though to the death' (*PL* 12.491, 494; emphasis added). In the brief epic God recalls and trumps Michael's words concerning the saints' imitation of their Messiah when He praises Jesus as one *'far abler to resist / All* [Satan's] *sollicitations*, and at length / All his vast force' (1.151–53; emphasis added). Jesus will 'earn Salvation for the Sons of men' (1.167) in accordance with Milton's esteemed Pauline text and will defeat Sin and Death 'By Humiliation and strong Sufferance' (1.160). Furthermore, 'His weakness shall orecome Satanic strength' (1.161).

   In the original Pauline text Milton's motto of strength in weakness accompanies an enumeration of Christ-like woes that biblical theologians term a *peristasis* catalogue. On three occasions Milton's brief epic replicates similar *peristasis* catalogues in connection with Jesus's Passional regaining of a kingdom. Before Jesus can earn his kingdom, he discerns:

> I shall first
> Be try'd in humble state, and things adverse,
> By tribulations, injuries, insults,
> Contempts, and scorns, and snares, and violence,
> Suffering, abstaining, quietly expecting
> Without distrust or doubt, that he [the Father] may know
> What I can suffer, how obey? who best
> Can suffer, best can do; best reign, who first
> Well hath obeyd; just tryal ere I merit
> My exaltation without change or end.
>
> (3.188–97)

Jesus equates his sufferings with efficacious redemption and understands his trials as a temporary ordeal that is not without its rewards. His fortitude bests Satan and the devils, who barely abide their deathless aches and pains during the War in Heaven. Jesus's formulation of a true Messiah counters the defeated Satan's apothegm that 'to be weak is miserable / Doing or Suffering' (*PL* 1.157–58). *De Doctrina Christiana* teaches that Jesus endured, 'first in a state of humiliation, then in a state of exaltation' (*CE* 15.302). Jesus's understanding of his 'just tryal' as a prelude to meritorious 'exaltation' comprehends the cross as an ephemeral experience of humiliation before lasting triumph. Jesus forecasts his gaining of an endless Messianic kingdom in ways that escape Satanic faculties.

In another *peristasis* catalogue Satan claims to discern that Jesus's afflictions are written in the stars. The fiend claims that these portents:

> give me to spell,
> Sorrows, and labours, opposition, hate,
> Attends thee, scorns, reproaches, injuries,
> Violence and stripes, and lastly cruel death,
> A Kingdom they portend thee, but what Kingdom,
> Real or Allegoric I discern not,
> Nor when, eternal sure, as without end,
> Without beginning

> (4.385–92)

Satan's imagination cannot travel beyond the idea of an earthly kingdom and yet his biblical phrase, 'without end, / Without beginning', refers to the high priest Melchizedek, who was a type for Christ's exalted, sacerdotal role. The Epistle to the Hebrews holds that Jesus was one who, 'with neither beginning of days nor end of life, was made like the Son of God, and remains a priest for perpetuity' (Heb. 7:3). *De Doctrina Christiana* cites this text and affirms that 'Christ is the only priest [*sacerdos unicus*] of the New Testament, Heb. 7:23, 24' (*CE* 16.206). Hebrews distinguishes Jesus from all other priests, including Melchizedek, because, as the absolute atoning sacrifice, he gives himself up for human sin once and for all, and continues to intercede for humanity before God (Heb. 7:23–27). Milton's Satan is stone deaf to his own inadvertent Christological allusion. Not one hundred lines later he marvels that Jesus is destined to travail through 'many a hard assay / Of dangers, and adversities and pains, / Ere thou of *Israels* Scepter get fast hold' (4.478–80), as though Jesus were still intent upon regaining the earthly kingdom of Israel. Satan echoes Jesus's earlier words presaging a redemption to be accomplished 'Through many a hard assay eev'n to the death' (1.264), words alluding to the Philippians doxology that Christ must 'be obedient to the death, even to death upon the cross' (Phil. 2:8).

And so the poem gathers up multiple anticipations of the cross: Jesus's awareness of his Messianic destiny as an endurance even to death; God's prediction of His Son's victorious humiliation and weakness; and Satan's perplexity at a kingdom gained through the 'Violence and stripes' of the flagellation, the 'scorns, reproaches, injuries' of his tormentors, and 'lastly cruel death' on the cross. These anticipations of Christ's redemption are more than proleptic devices in Milton's theology. *De Doctrina Christiana* plainly states, 'CHRIST OFFERED HIMSELF ONCE [*SEMEL*] AS A VICTIM FOR THOSE SINNING, AND HAS ALWAYS [*SEMPER*] INTERCEDED FOR US, AND EVEN NOW [*ETIAMNUM*] INTERCEDES FOR US' (*CE* 15.290). Christ also 'OFFERED HIMSELF ONCE. Indeed, he did this virtually [*virtute*] and its efficacy [*efficacia*] was from the very beginning of the world [,] but in actual fact [*ipso facto*] he offered himself at the consummation of the ages; and that one time [*semel*]' (*CE* 15.294). The treatise champions what contemporary theologians term a 'realized' rather than an 'end-time' eschatology in its declaration that Christ both virtually and efficaciously administers the redemption and offers all creatures the gifts of life and eternal life once, even now, and for all time. As John Martin Evans has noted, Milton adopts this principle of omni-temporal redemptive efficacy as early as *The Nativity Ode*, which concludes by at once announcing an ending and a beginning. Although *The Nativity Ode* commences with the promise of dawn breaking at the Christ-child's birth, it concludes with the suggestion of nightfall. The Virgin 'Hath laid her Babe to rest' (238) while 'Each fetter'd Ghost slips to his severall grave' (234). These images connote the entombment of the adult Christ's body at the same instant that the Christ-child newly enters the world. Evans comments, 'What began as an *aubade* is ending as a lullaby . . . A poem on "the morning of Christ's nativity" has become a poem on the mourning of Christ's nativity.'[17] Milton re-incorporates within his brief epic *The Nativity Ode*'s complex, simultaneous sense of the present and past efficacy of the future redemptive event. Book One's exordium 'now' sings of 'Recoverd Paradise to all mankind' (1.2–3) and yet simultaneously reflects upon Satan's disgraceful past, 'defeated and repulst, / And Eden rais'd' (1.6–7). The Father describes the Son earning salvation 'now' and 'hereafter' (1.164). Once Satan falls from the pinnacle in Book Four, the angels hymn Jesus's consummate victory of having 'aveng'd / Supplanted *Adam*' and 'regaind lost Paradise' (4.607–08), while they urge the Son, 'on thy glorious work / Now enter, and begin to save mankind' (4.634–35). So Satan 'never more hence-forth will dare set foot / In Paradise to tempt' (4.610–11) and, likewise, a future 'time shall be / Of Tempter and Temptation without fear' (4.616–17). As Stephen Fallon argues, *Paradise Regain'd*, like *The Nativity Ode*, displays 'the ancient Christian theme of the intersection of the timeless with time' so that 'Christ's passion is both a unique event in history and a sacrifice played out at all times'.[18]

Milton's conception of a continually efficacious, instantaneous Passion is not an eccentricity. Lancelot Andrewes preached, 'It is well known that Christ and His cross were never parted, but that all His life long was a continual cross. At the very cratch [manger], His cross began.'[19] The dying John Donne adorned his final sermon *Death's Duel* (1630) with an identical conceit:

---

[17] J. Martin Evans, *The Miltonic Moment* (Lexington, 1998), 35.

[18] Stephen M. Fallon, *Milton's Peculiar Grace: Self-Representation and Authority* (Ithaca, 2007), 250; and see 53–60.

[19] Lancelot Andrewes, 'Sermons Preached Upon Good-Friday: Sermon 3 [26 March, 1605]', *Works, Sermons, Volume Two*, ed. Marianne Dorman (Project Canterbury, Library of Anglo-Catholic

Our *criticall* day is *not* the *very day* of our *death*: but the whole course of our life. [S]ince all [Christ's] *life* was a *continual passion*, all *our Lent* may well bee a *continuall good Fryday*. *Christs* painefull life tooke off none of the paines of his death, hee felt not the lesse then for having felt so much before.[20]

The degree to which *Paradise Regain'd* employs the traditional *simul totum* effect of the atonement, with its power always already and its efficacy simultaneously now and not yet, indicates that the redemption is a priority in Milton's temptation narrative.

There are at least two further instances where the poem expresses the simultaneous immediacy and futurity of a realized eschatology. First, before the temptations begin God professes His intention, 'ere' Jesus conquers Satan, Sin, and Death, to exercise Jesus in the wilderness where he 'shall first lay down the rudiments / Of his great warfare' (1.155–58). God's words refer to the Latin phrase *ponere rudimenta*, a technical idiom from ancient Roman military practice where the young Roman soldier won his spurs by laying down his rudiments or by passing his novitiate in arms, before he advanced to grander military triumphs.[21] Perhaps the most notable instance of this martial idiom in ancient epic occurs in Virgil's *Aeneid*, where the Arcadian King Evander laments the tragic death of his son Pallas. Virgil pictures Evander grieving over Pallas's fatal experience of 'the cruel rudiments of close warfare [*bellique propinqui / dura rudimenta*]' (*Aen.* 11.156–57). Milton's Virgilian intertext gestures towards the Son's consummation of his ministry at the crucifixion even as Milton's God speaks of Jesus's preliminary trial in the desert, where he shall first lay down the rudiments of his great warfare.[22] Milton's association of the divine Father's prophetic words with Virgil's human father and, more exactly, with the Latian King mourning the death in battle of his valiant son, conjures up the Father's sufferance of His Son's death on the cross. Second, the 'consummat vertue' (1.165) God ascribes to Jesus anticipates the role Hebrews allots to Christ who, 'having endured the cross', is, literally, the 'consummator of the faith' (Heb. 12:2; Vulgate *consummatorem*). Such 'consummat vertue' also encompasses Christ's cry of victory, uttered from the cross, that 'It is finished!' (John 19:30; Vulgate *consummatum est*). As Francis Moloney remarks regarding this triumphant cry, through Jesus's crucifixion the 'task given to him by the Father (cf. [John] 4:34; 5:36; 17:4) has now been consummately brought to a conclusion'.[23]

II

The prominence the poem gives to John the Baptist's baptizing of Jesus in the Jordan further highlights the continuing importance of the Passion. In the gospels

Theology; published online 2001–03) ⟨http://anglicanhistory.org/lact/andrewes/v2/passion1605.html⟩ accessed 21 Nov. 2009.

[20] Donne, *Sermons*, vol. 10, 241 and 243.

[21] Charlton T. Lewis and Charles Short, *Latin Dictionary* (Oxford, 1879), 267.

[22] Virgil, *Aeneid VII–XII; Appendix Vergiliana*, trans. H. Rushton Fairclough, ed. G. P. Goold (London, 2000), 246.

[23] Francis J. Moloney, *The Gospel of John*, ed. Daniel J. Harrington (Collegeville, 1998), 504.

the baptism marks the commencement of Jesus's three years of public ministry, embarked on in his thirtieth year. The baptism also forms the induction of Milton's Messianic hero. The poem stresses the significance of Jesus's immersion in and emersion from the river by telling and retelling the event from the various perspectives of its characters. The baptism is recounted no fewer than eight times across the narrative: twice by the narrator (1.18–39; 2.1–6), three times by Satan (1.70–85, 326–34; 4.510–23), once by Jesus (1.268–89), once by the apostles Andrew and Peter (2.49–52), and once by Jesus's mother Mary (2.82–85). Milton himself interprets the sacramental significance of the baptismal rite in largely orthodox terms. The ritualized actions of plunging into and rising from the water point symbolically to Jesus's death, burial, and resurrection; they also enact his humiliation and subsequent exaltation from the grave. Michael explains to Adam that baptism memorializes Christ's atonement by reminding the baptized of his sacrificial death and purging of sin:

> Baptizing in the profluent streame, the signe
> Of washing them from guilt of sin to Life
> Pure, and in mind prepar'd, if so befall,
> For death, like that which the redeemer dy'd.
>   (12.442–45)

As Rushdy observes, 'Milton asserted that the Baptism was, for Jesus, a metaphoric signification of death.'[24] For *De Doctrina Christiana* all sacraments, including baptism, externally seal the covenant of grace in Christ and constitute 'that by which God seals saving grace or Christ's satisfaction by a visible sign, divinely instituted, for us who believe' (*CE* 16.164). The treatise defines baptism as that whereby 'THE BODIES OF BELIEVERS WHO PLEDGE PURITY OF LIFE ARE IMMERSED IN PROFLUENT WATER TO SIGNIFY OUR REGENERATION THROUGH THE HOLY SPIRIT AND ALSO OUR COALITION WITH CHRIST THROUGH HIS DEATH, BURIAL, AND RESURREC-TION' (*CE* 16.168). The treatise derives from Colossians 2:11 a certain 'analogy [*analogiam*] between baptism and circumcision' (*CE* 16.176). However, whereas circumcision 'was a little sign in the flesh, and an extremely obscure one, of the grace to be promulgated at a later time, baptism is a little sign of that grace already revealed, the remission of sins, sanctification, a sign of our death and resurrection with Christ' (*CE* 16.178). Scripture provides numerous proofs for a soteriological interpretation of baptism.[25] The treatise concludes, 'baptism figuratively signifies Christ's painful life, death, and burial, in which he was, as it were, immersed for a time' (*CE* 16.184), and goes on to assert that Paul confirmed this view by teaching 'that

---

[24] Rushdy, 185.
[25] The proof texts read: '[H]aving arisen, be baptized and wash away your sins' (Acts 22:16); '[D]o you not know that as many as were baptized into Jesus Christ were baptized into his death? Therefore we were buried with him through baptism into death' (Rom. 6:3–4); and '[B]uried together with him through baptism, you were also raised together with him through faith in God's method, who raised him from the dead' (Col. 2:12). See also Mark 10:38–40; Luke 12:50; 1 Cor. 6:11; 12:13; Gal. 3:27; Eph. 5:25–27; and Titus 3:4–5.

baptism is not only an initiation, but also a certain representation of our death, burial, and resurrection with Christ' (*CE* 16.190).

Regarding this aspect of sacramental theology Milton takes an orthodox line that comes close to the position of the Church Father John Chrysostom. Chrysostom held that 'In Baptism are fulfilled the pledges of our covenant with God; burial and death, resurrection and life; and these take place all at once. For when we immerse our heads in the water, the old man is buried as in a tomb below, and wholly sunk forever; then, as we raise them again, the new man rises in its stead.'[26] Thus, 'not only is Baptism called a "cross," but the "cross" is called "Baptism".'[27] Lancelot Andrewes appropriately termed Jesus's 'Passion . . . a second baptism, a river of blood, and He even able to have been baptized in it, as He was in Jordan'.[28] As Albert Labriola has shown, Milton's description of the Jordan as 'the laving stream' (1.280) plays upon the Church Fathers' naming of the baptismal pool or font as a purifying 'laver of regeneration'.[29] Yet 'the laving stream' also conforms to the baptismal formula in *The Book of Common Prayer* as 'the mystical washing away of sin' so that 'as [Christ] died and rose again for us, so should we, who are baptized, die from sin and rise again unto righteousness', casting off the old, sinful self and assuming the new, regenerate self.[30]

Satan recognizes John the Baptist's action as a rite that, in some undisclosed fashion, prepares the way for the Messiah. He acknowledges that it is a tributary act of anointing by water that confers on Jesus royal 'honour as thir King' (1.75).[31] For Satan the event has a purgative meaning, although his inability to foresee the means of grace obtained through humiliation makes him ridicule the event as make-believe. Satan reasons that, because Jesus is immaculate and cannot be baptized 'to be more pure' (1.77), his baptism 'in the Consecrated stream / Pretends to wash off sin' (1.72–73). Because Jesus enjoys a sinless state of *non-posse peccare*, of 'not being able to sin', the paradox becomes apparent of the perfect, sinless servant-king stooping to be washed in 'the laving stream' (1.280) by the Baptist, who is, after all, a sinful human. The gospels refigure this paradoxical conceit where the immaculate Jesus gains absolution for sinners through his own sinless person when they describe the anointing of Jesus's feet by the woman with the alabaster jar (Luke 7:36–50), and, again, Jesus's washing of his disciples' feet (John 13:1–20). Milton explicitly connects Jesus's washing of the disciples' feet with the Son's justification of Adam and Eve in 'the forme of servant' (*PL* 10.211–23). As Thomas Aquinas reasons, 'Christ was not baptized so that he might be cleansed,

---

[26] John Chrysostom, *Homilies on the Gospel of Saint John and the Epistle to the Hebrews*, ed. Philip Schaff (Peabody, 2004), 89.

[27] Ibid.

[28] Andrewes, 'Sermon 3'.

[29] See Albert C. Labriola, '*Christus Patiens*: The Virtue Patience and *Paradise Lost*, I–II', in *The Triumph of Patience*, ed. Gerald J. Schiffhorst (Orlando, 1978), 138–46.

[30] *The Book of Common Prayer* (Cambridge, 1968), 280 and 288.

[31] See Luke 4:18 and Acts 4:27–28. The Book of Acts describes baptism as 'how God anointed [*echrisen*] Jesus of Nazareth with the Holy Spirit and power' (10:37–38).

but so that he might cleanse.'[32] An appreciation of this paradox also helps to explain John the Baptist's initial refusal 'on [Jesus] his Baptism to conferr, / As much his greater, and was hardly won' (1.278–79). George Herbert's poem 'Marie Magdalene' makes the same point. Herbert's persona asks why the fallen woman with the alabaster jar anoints Jesus's feet: 'She being stain'd her self, why did she strive / To make him clean, who could not be defil'd?' (7–8). Herbert's final stanza resolves the dilemma:[33]

> Deare soul, she knew who did vouchsafe and deigne
> To bear her filth; and that her sinnes did dash
> Ev'n God himself: wherefore she was not loth,
>   As she had brought wherewith to stain,
>   So to bring in wherewith to wash:
> And yet in washing one, she washed both.
>
>   (13–18)

As orthodox Christian soteriology teaches, and as Herbert and Milton understood, Jesus fulfilled this paradoxical action upon the cross, where one who was spotless vicariously atoned for the culpability of others.

Milton's choice, not only of opening the epic action with Jesus's baptism, but also of frequently recollecting baptism through the characters inhabiting the brief epic, parallels the structure of his long epic. The Son's heavenly coronation in Book Five of *Paradise Lost* (5.577–657) maps neatly onto Jesus's earthly coronation in Book One of *Paradise Regain'd* (1.18–39). The chronological schemes of both epics begin with the Father's anointing and proclamation of His Son. Both royal unctions upset Satan. In *Paradise Lost* God announces His 'begetting' of the Son (*PL* 5.600–15) and proclaims the Son's promotion 'At [God's] right hand' (5.606). *De Doctrina Christiana* interprets this act of begetting as signifying metaphorically 'the Son's exaltation and mediatorial office' (*CE* 14.180). In the matching baptismal scene in *Paradise Regain'd* God concordantly 'proclaimd' (1.275) Jesus as God's Son 'as [he] rose out of the laving stream' (1.280). If one construes the baptismal scene in figurative terms, Jesus's emergence from the Jordan anticipates his future exaltation from humiliation and death to everlasting kingship and restoration at God's right hand.[34] It is with Jesus's resurrection, ascension, and session in mind, an exalted state that results from his earthly trials, that the narrator portentously esteems Jesus, risen from the Jordan's waters and about to commence his Messianic mission, as 'th' exalted man' (1.36).

The interlude of nearly three hundred lines with which Book Two begins merits discussion here. This interval prepares the reader for the poem's considerable

---

[32] Thomas Aquinas, *Summa Theologiae: The Life of Christ (3a.38–45)*, ed. and trans. Samuel Parsons and Albert Pinheiro, vol. 53 (London, 1971), 24; 3a.39.1: '*Christus non fuit baptizatus ut ablueretur, sed ut ablueret.*'

[33] Herbert, 173.

[34] According to the treatise, the Son's begetting has 'a double sense'. The literal sense refers to his 'production [*producendo*]' and the metaphorical sense relates to his 'exaltation [*exaltando*]' (*CE* 14.180).

treatment of the mode of Messianic victory before the dogged Satan unleashes his slew of temptations. This 'digression' grants the reader a window onto the Messianic hopes that the apostles Andrew and Simon Peter entertain and provides access to the private fears that Mary nurses concerning the implications of her son's Messianic destiny. Andrew and Peter's expectations for their teacher and Mary's disquiet over her son measure the extent to which these two sets of characters comprehend the Messianic means of victory. Milton's selection of Andrew and Peter as the representative disciples who ponder the nature of the Messianic fulfilment is appropriate. In the gospels these two apostles are conspicuous for correctly identifying Jesus as the Messiah, although they both prescribe for Jesus a destiny restricted to the advancement of Israel's national liberation. The Johannine Andrew approaches Peter with the claim that 'we have found the Messiah [τὸν Μεσσίαν] (which is translated Christ [Χριστός])' (John 1:41) and, in the Synoptic gospels, Peter makes a similar confession to Jesus at Caesarea Philippi (see Matt. 16:20–23; Mark 8:27–33). In *Paradise Regain'd* Andrew and Peter correctly interpret the supernatural tribute beside the Jordan as revealing 'Jesus Messiah Son of God declar'd' (2.4), yet they cling to the expectation of a Messiah who will be a political and militant zealot. Milton's Jesus reflects that in his boyhood he carefully weighed and then dismissed the legitimacy of such a Messianic model:

> To rescue *Israel* from the *Roman* yoke,
> Then to subdue and quell ore all the earth
> Brute violence and proud Tyrannick pow'r,
> Till truth were freed, and equity restor'd
> (1.217–20)

Andrew and Peter hope that in Jesus a Messianic freedom fighter, now declared by God 'In publick' (2.52), will soon 'arise and vindicate / Thy Glory, free thy people from thir yoke' (2.47–48). The disciples' suspense, their 'joy ... turnd / Into perplexity and new amaze' (2.37–38), suggests a timeframe within the gospel narratives that is proleptic of another period of waiting during their Messiah's absence: that doubtful period lasting from Jesus's death and burial until his resurrection. Just as, after Christ's death, the apostles feel cheated of their triumphalist Messianic expectation, so, in Milton's narrative, they feel robbed by his temporary absence. They complain that he is 'So lately found, and so abruptly gone' (2.10), they ask 'whither is he gone, what accident / Hath rapt him from us' (2.39–40), and they are fearful lest God will 'withdraw' or 'recall' him, or 'Mock us with his blest sight, then snatch him hence' (2.55–56). The gospels relate that God acts likewise with His resurrected Son, for the welfare of humanity, at Jesus's ascension. Milton blurs the lines separating these two periods of apostolic expectation in Andrew and Peter's jubilation: 'Now, now, for sure, deliverance is at hand, / The Kingdom shall to *Israel* be restor'd' (2.35–36). The disciples' words betray their narrow understanding of Messianic deliverance, but they also look forward to a time when, even with the resurrected Jesus standing before them, they continue to enquire in liberationist, Messianic terms, 'Lord, will you at this time restore the kingdom to Israel [Κύριε, εἰ ἐν τῷ χρόνῳ τούτῳ ἀποκαθιστάνεις τὴν βασιλείαν τῷ Ἰσραήλ]?' (Acts 1:6).

If Andrew and Peter conceive of Messianic victory in worldly, nationalist terms and imagine an exalted Messiah who will materially and temporarily emancipate a subjugated Israel from the oppressive Roman yoke, then Mary's trust in God errs too much in the other direction. Mary foresees her son's Messianic destiny as a series of woes. She envisions a process of unmitigated suffering and humiliation, devoid of exaltation, that must be endured as its own reward. Admittedly, Mary's experience teaches lessons of patience and fortitude.[35] She draws her lament from a well of 'Motherly cares', 'fears', 'troubl'd thoughts', and 'sighs' (2.64–65), and reflects upon motherhood as a sequence of discomforts, perils, and narrow escapes (2.69–78): the inhospitality she encountered on the night of Jesus's birth; the inclement weather and 'bleak air'; the harsh reality of delivering a child in an unromantic, cheerless, filthy stable, 'scarce a Shed'; their flight into Egypt for refuge shortly thereafter; and the mass infanticide of 'the Murd'rous King' Herod. Nonetheless, Mary's intimate participation in her son's life gives her an unparalleled insight into the persecution that lies ahead for him.

Mary recollects the prophecy of 'Just *Simeon*' (1.255; see Luke 2:25–35) that Jesus will become 'a sign / Spok'n against' (2.89–90) and she has prepared herself for her own private 'passion' of maternal loss. She remembers Simeon's prediction 'that through my very Soul / A sword shall pierce' (2.90–91; Luke 2:34–35). Renaissance visual art frequently represents Mary in crucifixion scenes with a sword piercing her heart as she kneels before the cross. Milton had ample precedent in Passion poetry for connecting Simeon's prophecy of the heart-piercing sword with Mary's anguish over her crucified son. Both the early Christian tragedy *Christos Paschon*, which was attributed to Gregory of Nazianzus and which Milton cited in his 'Preface' to *Samson Agonistes*, and Hugo Grotius's imitation *Christus Patiens* are dramatic poems that picture the realization of Simeon's prophecy at Jesus's crucifixion and entombment. Nazianzus's Mary bewails that 'awful brand, / Which violently makes me quiver and shakes my heart, / Running through my heart's core like the shudder of a drum' (27–29).[36] Grotius's Mary confirms that 'These things the aged Simeon saw, / When he looked into my soul's depths and saw the wound.'[37] Milton had also read Marco Girolamo Vida of Cremona's *Christiad* (1535) and praises Vida's epyllion in *The Passion* where 'Loud o're the rest *Cremona's* Trump doth sound' (26). Vida's *Christiad* depicts the Madonna grieving on Golgotha:

> *Terrificans senior luctus sperare iubebat,*
> *Et cecinit fore, cum pectus mihi figeret ensis.*
> *Nunc alte mucro, nunc alte vulnus adactum.*

---

[35] Achinstein, *Dissent*, 135–37.

[36] Gregory of Nazianzus, *La Passion du Christ: Tragédie*, trans. and ed. André Tuilier (Paris, 1969), 130: 'δεινὴν φλόγα, / ἣ σφόδρα μαιμάσσει με καὶ δονεῖ κέαρ / καὶ καρδίαν δίεισιν ὡς ῥόπτρον μέγα' (27–29).

[37] Hugo Grotius, *Christus Patiens* (Leiden, 1608), 55: '*Vidit haec Simeon senex, / Imaque in anima vulnus aspexit meum.*'

(The terrifying old man instructed me to hope for lamentation, and he prophesied that there would be a time when a sword would pierce my breast. Now, deeply, the point has been driven, now, deeply, the wound.)   (5.878–80)[38]

Finally, in Giles Fletcher's *Christ's Victorie and Triumph* (1610) the narrator expresses Mary's profound sympathy for her son by equating her cleft heart with Christ's stigmata:

> Ah blessed Virgin, what high Angels art
> Can ever coumpt thy teares, or sing thy smart,
> When every naile, that pierst his hand, did pierce thy heart?
> ('Christ's Triumph over Death', 65.6–8)[39]

Dayton Haskin observes that Milton's Mary fulfils a role as 'bearer of the Word' and mediatrix to Jesus of information concerning his earthly mission. Haskin believes that she is 'more adept at dealing with delays and disappointments than Andrew and Simon, who have only recently had their hopes raised'.[40] But Mary's anticipation of the Passion is more extraordinary than even Haskin allows for. She is the sole human agent to grasp the divine method and the paradox that Messianic victory is incumbent upon suffering, but she cannot see that her son's fall will precede an elevation to immortality. The outcome that she awaits is unremittingly lugubrious. She considers herself 'highly favour'd' to have been 'advanc't' 'to sorrows' and initiated into 'fears as eminent' (2.68–70) and she regards her patience as 'My Exaltation to Afflictions high' (2.92). Mary is as yet excluded from the fullness of a Christian revelation that exaltation *succeeds* affliction. For the time being she possesses a rather muddled perspective of God's providence. From within this incomplete perspective Mary attempts to understand herself as 'Afflicted...and blest' (2.93), yet accepts her vocation 'to wait with patience' (2.102) for the time of her son's humiliation. At this stage in salvation history she cannot see that humiliation is the prelude to resurrection victory and that night will bring forth the day. The disciples spell Messianic deliverance in mundane and patriotic, though exalted and hopeful, terms, and yet they spare no thought for a spiritual redemption that entails suffering and potentially emancipates humanity from the bondage of sin. In turn, Mary is confined to an understanding of exaltation that is cast in the exclusively Passional terms of carnal suffering and ignominy – 'to Honour? no, / But trouble, as old *Simeon* plain fore-told' (2.86–87). Mary cannot, as yet, imagine a promised resurrection and exaltation that will transcend Jesus's earthly existence.

---

[38] Marco Girolamo Vida, *The Christiad*, ed. and trans. Gertrude C. Drake and Clarence A. Forbes (Edwardsville, 1978), 232.

[39] Giles and Phineas Fletcher, *Poetical Works*, vol. 1, ed. Frederick S. Boas (Cambridge, 1970), 74.

[40] Dayton Haskin, 'Milton's Portrait of Mary as a Bearer of the Word', in *Milton and the Idea of Woman*, ed. Julia M. Walker (Urbana, 1988), 176 and 178.

III

I have assessed above the redemptive value that the poem attaches to Jesus's
Messianic role. I should now like to consider how Milton treats this urgent
atonement theme throughout the *agon* between Satan and Jesus. Satan's first two
assaults upon Jesus consist of the temptation to turn stones into bread and the
banquet temptation. Both temptations develop Eucharistic themes and anticipate
Jesus's instauration of the Last Supper and the figuration of his sacrifice in the
broken bread and the wine. In the first temptation Satan, disguised as a desert
hermit, goads Jesus to transform stones into bread and so 'save thy self and us
relieve / With Food' (1.344–45). Satan's words duplicate the unrepentant thief's
insulting challenge to Jesus at the crucifixion, 'Are you not the Messiah? Save
yourself and us [σῶσον σεαυτὸν καὶ ἡμᾶς]' (Luke 23:39). Satan and the thief are
oblivious to the place of suffering in the atonement. Moreover, Satan's deviation
from the gospel source, his addition of the phrase 'With Food', indicates his
inability to see beyond the merely physical to the spiritual sustenance that Jesus
brings to support his fallen creatures. Robert Entzminger perceives the sacramental purport of the bread that Milton's Jesus declines to produce: 'the physical
bread [Jesus] rejects as necessary in itself he will later reclaim as a symbol for the
nourishment he offers, both in feeding the multitude and in initiating the
Eucharist'.[41]

Jesus's reply to Satan elaborates upon the Deuteronomic text, 'man doth not live
by bread only' (*AV* Deut. 8:3). He marshals three biblical instances where God
nourishes His faithful: the feeding of Israel's wilderness generation on manna and
quail, the fortifying of Moses upon Mount Sinai, and the sustaining of Elijah upon
Mount Horeb. The Deuteronomic text Jesus cites refers to Moses's rebuke against
Israel for obsessing over the scarcity of heaven-sent bread rather than resting
confidently in God's assurances. In New Testament symbolism Jesus embodies
both God's 'Word' (John 1:1) and 'the bread of life' (John 6:35). Jesus's answer
points to the Johannine 'I am' saying that Jesus is 'the true bread from heaven'
(John 6:32) or, effectively, the true manna. *De Doctrina Christiana* also attests,
'The type of the Lord's Supper under the law was the manna' (*CE* 16.196).[42] In
the Johannine gospel, once Jesus has miraculously fed the multitude with loaves
and fishes during the Passover, he compares himself three times with the manna
that fed his forefathers in the wilderness (John 6:31–33, 49–50, 58). Jesus
proclaims himself the perfection of the heavenly manna God sent to nourish the
Hebrews and the consummation of the Torah God commissioned to Moses to
sustain Israel. Where the manna supported the wilderness generation for forty
years, Jesus implies that, as redeemer, he embodies the bread that grants eternal,
and not temporary, life:

---

[41] Entzminger, 107.
[42] '*Typus coenae Dominicae sub lege erat manna.*'

I am the bread of life. Your fathers ate manna in the wilderness and died. Here is bread coming down from Heaven so that anyone may eat of it and not die. I am the living bread that has come down from Heaven. If anyone eats of this bread, he will live for eternity. Also, the bread that I will give you is my flesh, [given] for the life of the world.   (John 6:48–51)

Milton's treatise links this passage with the atonement:

Therefore that living bread which Christ says is his flesh and that true drink which he says is his blood, what else can it be than the doctrine concerning Christ made man, that he pours forth his blood for us? A doctrine which, whoever perceives it with genuine faith, no less certainly will he live for eternity, as those who eat and drink to sustain this mortal life; yet, indeed, the former way is far more certain.   (*CE* 16.194)

This exegesis might serve as a useful commentary upon Jesus's repudiation of Satan's first temptation in *Paradise Regain'd*. To reinforce the correspondence between Jesus's redemptive office and the spiritual feeding of his people with the promise of eternal life through the atonement, an action remembered and repeated in the Eucharist, Milton has Satan's response betray his role as the Antichrist. Satan's hypocrisy is not difficult to detect. At one moment Satan tells Jesus that he has 'not lost / To love, at least contemplat and admire' (1.379–80), creaturely excellence in beauty or virtue, and the next moment he reveals his actual contempt for God's creatures and expresses his envy that 'Man, / Man fall'n shall be restor'd, I never more' (1.404–05). Between these contradictory lines Satan discloses his true purpose for humankind and his relationship with them as their tormentor. Satan lords it over humanity in the hope of damning them. Conversely, Jesus desires to serve humanity and, ultimately, to save them.

Satan unconsciously parodies the sacramental discourse of Jesus's altruistic mission as commemorated at the Last Supper. The fiend describes humans as 'Companions of my misery and wo' (1.398). Satan's words pun upon the etymology of 'Companions', the Late Latin word *com* + *panis*, which literally means 'those who break bread together'. For, under Satan's dominion, sinful humanity breaks the bread of misery and abjection in the company of fallen angels. The Satanic worldview, which determines that 'fellowship in pain divides not smart, / Nor light'ns aught each mans peculiar load' (1.401–02), fails to conceive the Messianic principle of success, already spelled out in Jesus's soliloquy, that the Messiah willingly receives 'sins / Full weight ... transferrd upon my head' (1.266–67). Satan lies and tempts for the personal satisfaction of witnessing others partake in his 'fellowship in pain', first 'leagu'd with millions' (1.359) of his lapsed angels, next with 'Man adjoind' (1.403) as 'Copartner' (1.392) in his separation from God. Despite his enjoyment of these sadistic pleasures, Satan can see that such bad company neither divides nor lightens his load of sin and despair. Jesus fulfils his Messianic purpose for humanity contrariwise, by reducing himself to undergo a sympathetic 'fellowship in pain' with humanity. The redemption does not divide, but lightens and relieves humanity from its peculiar load of sin so that believers can partake in the fellowship of grace symbolically rehearsed and sealed at Holy Communion. Satan's talk of bad company, a fellowship of perdition with creatures he has seduced into falling, develops the Eucharistic theme that pervades this temptation. Yet the devil's words also contain the hidden promise of Jesus's *good* company, a fellowship in which humanity may participate in salvation by confessing Jesus as the living bread. Satan, who is forever damned, is denied such restorative Communion, a fact that Jesus plays upon when he speaks of Satan's 'Lost bliss, to thee no more communicable' (1.419).

After Satan convokes his second diabolic council, Milton's narrator returns to Jesus, who is discovered exercising patience in the wilderness. Jesus is 'Now hungring first' (2.244) and reasons that suffering without God's support is proof of virtue, since otherwise 'what praise is it to endure?' (2.251). Satan's second temptation, his invitation to a banquet, a sensual symphony of pleasing sounds, sights, and smells, resumes the Eucharistic theme as an anti-sacrament or Satanic parody of the principles behind participation in Communion. Barbara Lewalski notes that, in Satan's travesty of Communion, the grove's vaulted roofs, majestic 'walks', and 'alleys brown' (2.293–94) that open out into a woody scene and a banqueting table evoke the procession along the nave to the high altar of 'an idolatrous Catholic cathedral'.[43] Thus the sumptuous spread 'alludes to superstitious and idolatrous worship, especially the Roman Catholic mass, which throughout history will seek to mislead the church of which Christ is head'.[44] George McLoone has argued that the debauched revels of Satan's banquet recommend 'the unholy alliance between courtly decadence and a wrongheaded eucharistic discipline'.[45] Lewalski and McLoone posit the principal discrepancy between the ostentatious entertainment Satan tenders and the reception Jesus deems fit for himself as Messiah. The banquet's lavish furnishings, decked 'in regal mode' (2.340), are at odds with the definition of kingship with which Jesus closes the banquet scene, when Jesus informs Satan that 'on [a true king's] shoulders each mans burden lies' (2.462). Satan's sumptuous and sybaritic outlay is too exorbitant for Jesus's altruistic idea of a servant-king for whom 'to lay down [is] / Far more magnanimous, then to assume' (2.482–83).

Jesus rejects Satan's banquet with the declaration, 'I can at will, doubt not, as soon as thou, / Command a Table in this Wilderness' (2.383–84). His allusion to Psalm 78, which Louis Martz calls 'a brief suggestion of the communion table', refers to Israel's weary Exodus generation, who murmured for manna and provoked and 'tempted God in their heart, by asking meat for their lust' (*AV* Ps. 78:17 18).[46] Jesus's allusion operates, not to identify himself with the hungry Israelites who challenge their Maker, but to associate himself, as the Messiah and sustainer of God's people, with Israel's God, who is the divine source and provider of grace. With its unrestrained luxury, pomp, and circumstance, Satan's banquet contradicts Jesus's self-understanding as a king who should relieve human destitution and sorrow by freely participating in his subjects' suffering. Because Jesus's idea

---

[43] Lewalski, *Brief Epic*, 217.   [44] Ibid.
[45] George H. McLoone, *Milton's Poetry of Independence: Five Studies* (London, 1999), 97.
[46] Martz, 257.

of kingship is predicated upon selflessly serving others, and not upon selfishly assuming advantages, he refuses Satan's jarring and superfluous offer.

Milton conveys the travesty of true kingship that Jesus's sitting and eating at Satan's banquet would entail through allusion to George Herbert's 'Love (3)'. Herbert's lyric presents a scene of hospitality in which a dialogue occurs between a host, Herbert's allegorical figure of 'Love', and Love's guest.[47] The poem's 'guest–host framework' and 'courtesy-contest' possess sacramental connotations.[48] In Herbert's *A Priest to the Temple* (1652) 'The Parson in Sacraments' directs the communicant to kneel and not to sit before the Eucharist, like the guest of 'Love (3)': 'The Feast indeed requires sitting, because it is a Feast; but man's unpreparednesse asks kneeling. Hee that comes to the Sacrament, hath the confidence of a Guest, and hee that kneels, confesseth himself an unworthy one, and therefore differs from other Feasters.'[49] The guest's perceived unworthiness, 'Guiltie of dust and sinne' (2), and contrite sense of self as an 'ungratefull' (9) or, perhaps, graceless prodigal, rehearses the posture of the humble communicant.

Interpreted as an allegorization of God's Son, Herbert's Love participates in human suffering through his Incarnation, and so receives his guest as one not 'unkinde' (9), that is, one not ungenerous or, Christologically, not dissimilar in nature to his divine humanity. Herbert's loving host bids the guest enjoy his meal, knowing that his reputation has earned a saving grace, because the host 'bore the blame' (15). Love's expression thinly veils the Son's redemptive burden. When the guest corrects the seeming breach of etiquette and challenges the perceived disgrace of a superior serving his inferior, Herbert's host concisely replies, 'You must sit down, sayes Love, and taste my meat' (17). Herbert's pun hinges upon the 'meat' as either choice cuts of meat or Love/Christ's self-sacrifice. One might construe the 'meat' as the host's body and blood figured in the Eucharistic bread and wine. The poem may allude to the gospel parable of the Messianic banquet where, when the parabolic Lord of the house returns home to discover his servants guarding his goods, like Herbert's host 'he shall gird himself, and make them to sit down to meat, and will come forth and serve them' (*AV* Luke 12:37). The guest's concluding explanation, delivered in six terse monosyllables, 'So I did sit and eat', concedes to the paradox of being esteemed as a dignitary by his superior. This paradox resembles Jesus who, despite Peter's protestations, washes his apostles' feet before the Last Supper (John 13:1–20). Herbert reproduces this trimeter elsewhere in *The Temple* in a Eucharistic context. In 'The 23d Psalme' Herbert's psalmist gives thanks to God, since 'thou dost make me sit and dine' (17).[50] Richard Strier judiciously summarizes the guest's acquiescence to the host's service: 'In the courtesy framework, the graciousness of grace is one with its irresistibility.'[51]

The circumstances of Herbert's 'Love (3)' parallel Milton's banquet scene. Both dramatizations involve a guest and a host and in each case the host wishes to

---

[47] Herbert, 188–89.
[48] I am applying Richard Strier's terminology here. See Strier, *Love Known: Theology and Experience in George Herbert's Poetry* (Chicago, 1983), 74 and 82.
[49] Herbert, 259.   [50] Herbert, 172–73.   [51] Strier, *Love Known*, 83.

entertain a reluctant guest. Milton's adaptation, however, devilishly burlesques its Herbertian original. Milton's fiendish host displays a false graciousness that would undermine rather than sustain his guest. Milton's guest, far from being unworthy and guilty of sin, like Herbert's guest, is the sinless Saviour and Arch-host through whom righteousness may be imputed to bankrupt sinners. The gaudy feast Satan tantalizes Jesus with is subordinated to that simpler meal of bread and wine that Herbert's poem elicits, humble fare that points beyond its literal signification to the salvation its host guarantees to those who gratefully sit, eat, and commemorate.

'So I did sit and eat' (18), the iambic trimeter that rounds off 'Love (3)', provides a stronger internal connection with Milton's poem. Milton's Satan repeatedly and unconsciously parodies the phrase. Three times Satan rallies to lure the Son to partake of the banquet and three times, in epistrophe, Satan presses him to enjoy the feast with the imperative Herbert's Love uses to invite his communicant to 'sit and eat' (2.336, 368, 377). Herbert's reconciled 'I did sit and eat' resonates throughout Satan's three exhortations, although the phrase's purpose has been drastically altered from its source. Satan's tone builds in hostility each time he adapts Herbert's phrase. He begins with a courteous invitation, 'onely deign to sit and eat' (2.336), that is decorous for Satan's 'fair speech' and courtly demeanour, apparelled 'As one in City, or Court, or Palace bred' (2.300–01). Snubbed, Satan's polite request tenses into a slightly piqued 'What doubts the Son of God to sit and eat?' (2.368). Finally, Satan's more urgent entreaty degenerates into a severe, peremptory imperative: 'What doubt'st thou Son of God? sit down and eat' (2.377). Satan claims that the feast's opulence, fit for an indulgent king, would please Jesus with an extravagant 'sweet restorative delight' (2.373). At Satan's banquet of excess, creatures should have to serve and slave under the Son with no promise of restoration or Christian liberty. Yet, as Satan's three echoes of Herbert's grateful guest's willingness to sit and eat intimate, such decadence is worlds apart from the sweet restoration Milton's Jesus purposes for humanity as its suffering servant-king. Milton's Son and Herbert's Love both intend to provide a spiritual rather than a physical restoration, of which the guest enjoys the benefits. Herbert's love feast and Milton's devilish banquet gesture to Holy Communion, where the guest/communicant faithfully sits, eats, and partakes, and the Eucharistic elements signify the host/Christ's atoning sacrifice.

In addition Jesus protests that he can, at any time, 'call swift flights of Angels ministrant / Arrayd in Glory on my cup to attend' (2.385–86). Charles Huttar has argued that Milton pre-echoes Jesus's supplication of his Father at his Agony that 'My Father, if it is not possible for this [cup] to pass away, unless I drink from it, let your will be done' (Matt. 26:42).[52] Depictions of the Agony from the early fifteenth century onwards customarily include an angel offering a cup or chalice to Jesus. Thomas Goodwin defined the chalice as 'that cup delivered to [Christ] at his crucifying . . . the bitter cup of Gods anger', and tradition identified it as the cup of wrath, suffering, or desolation mentioned by the Prophets (Isa. 51:17; Jer. 25:15,

---

[52] Charles A. Huttar, 'The Passion of Christ in *Paradise Regained*', *English Language Notes*, 19 (1982), 254.

49:12; Lam. 4:21; Ezek. 23:32–33).[53] The gospel Jesus prophesies that he must drain the cup to the dregs at his Passion to satisfy divine justice (Matt. 20:22–23, 26:27, 26:39, 42; John 18:11). Milton conflates, not one, but two motifs recollected from the Agony in Jesus's statement. The poem evokes, first, his petition to be relieved of the bitter cup and, second, his claim to be able to summon flights of angels to his aid. Milton's Jesus avouches that he could summon 'swift flights of Angels' to relieve him. When, in Matthew's gospel, elders and chief priests armed with swords and clubs come to arrest Jesus, one of Jesus's apostles slices off the ear of a servant of the high priest with his sword. Jesus checks his belligerent disciple and counsels that patience rather than violence is the divine method: 'Do you think that I am not able to ask my Father, and He will now provide for me more than twelve legions of angels? How then may the scriptures be fulfilled that say it must be thus?' (Matt. 26:53–54). Just as the Matthean Jesus prefers endurance on the cross to open hostility and would drain the bitter cup of divine wrath and forego angelic aid, so Milton's Jesus rejects the banquet and resists Satanic luxury to persevere in a mission that entails suffering.

Satan and Jesus's final exchange in Book Two elaborates upon the central virtue of patience for the Messiah's earthly ministry. Jesus's aim is neither to preserve his life nor to 'destroy[] life's enemy, / Hunger' (2.372–73), but to defeat Satan (whose Hebrew speaking name means 'enemy') and conquer Sin and Death by his redemption and resurrection. Death is life's true enemy and, as Paul states, 'The last enemy to be destroyed is death' (1 Cor. 15:26). Unable to tempt Jesus 'By hunger, that each other Creature tames' (2.406), Satan discards appetite, not realizing that Jesus's patient endurance of hunger contains the answer to his next dilemma. Satan asks, concerning Jesus's 'high designs, / High actions; but wherewith to be atchiev'd? / Great acts require great means of enterprise' (2.410–12). Milton's narrator describes Jesus's reply with the signal adverb 'patiently' (2.432) and this qualifier suggests the Messianic means of success. Throughout, the narrator chooses adverbial modifiers that qualify Jesus's responses to the various temptations. Resisting the banquet's delicacies, the Son answers 'temperatly' (2.378); to Satan's irritating provocations that Jesus's achievements are slight for his over-ripe years, Jesus answers 'calmly' (3.43); and, repelling a golden age of classical learning, Jesus responds 'sagely' (4.285), with true wisdom. Jesus's patient response, which dismisses riches as 'the toil of Fools' (2.453), moves on to a nobler subject by setting forth a blueprint for Messianic heroism where one 'so poor / . . . could do mighty things' (2.447–48):

> What if with like aversion I reject
> Riches and Realms; yet not for that a Crown,
> Gold'n in shew, is but a wreath of thorns,
> Brings dangers, troubles, cares, and sleepless nights
> To him who wears the Regal Diadem,
> When on his shoulders each mans burden lies:

[53] Thomas Goodwin, *A Childe of Light Walking in Darknes* (London, 1638), 149.

> For therein stands the office of a King,
> His Honour, Vertue, Merit and chief Praise,
> That for the Publick all this weight he bears.
>
> (2.457–65)

The Son's definition of kingship, falling upon Satan's deaf ears, audaciously subverts fallen values. A true Messiah is a giver, not a receiver. A true king accepts grave accountability so that 'To gain a Scepter, oftest better misst' (2.486). Jesus speaks of a 'wreath' rather than a thorny crown, evoking the mock-regal 'acanthine wreath [ἀκάνθινος στέφανος]', which the Roman soldiers, scoffing at Jesus's Messianic claim, planted on his head (Mark 15:17; see Matt. 27:29; John 19:2, 5). The 'weight' a true king bears 'for the Publick' recalls Jesus's earlier acceptance that, in 'work[ing] Redemption for mankind, [their] sins / Full weight must be transferrd upon my head' (1.266–67). Jesus's rejection of a 'Regal Diadem', assumption of a thorny wreath, and willingness to assume the immeasurable burden of human sin sabotage and diminish Satan's flashy and vainglorious portrayal of kingship. Satan's idea of kingship, which is valued for its wealth, pales before the authentic Messiah, who is valued for his self-sacrifice.

Jesus concludes Book Two with the maxim, 'to give a Kingdom hath been thought / Greater and nobler done, and to lay down / Far more magnanimous, then to assume' (2.481–83). Robert Entzminger interprets 'laying down' as 'giving up' and links this activity to the Incarnation, where the Son inhabits 'a darksom House of mortal Clay' (*The Nativity Ode* 14). There is, however, another kind of giving up in Jesus's kenosis or self-emptying upon the cross.[54] The gospel phrase 'to lay down one's life' (θεῖναι τὴν ψυχήν; Vulgate *ponere animam*) and the antithetical expressions 'lay down' and 'assume' (λαβεῖν; Vulgate *assumere*) are Johannine idioms. Laying down and assuming are Johannine symbolic actions analogous to Jesus's altruistic atonement. Thus Jesus presages:

> I am the good shepherd . . . I lay down my life for the sheep . . . Therefore, the Father loves me because I lay down my life in order to assume it again. No one takes it from me, but I freely lay it down. I have the authority to lay it down and I have the authority to assume it again. This command I received from my Father.   (John 10:14–18)

The Johannine Jesus elsewhere instructs, 'No one has greater love than this, that he should lay down his life for his loved ones' (John 15:13; see John 13:37–38). First John repeats the lesson that 'In this we have known love, because [Christ] laid down his life for us; and we should lay down our lives for our brothers' (1 John 3:16). For Milton's Jesus, to lay down a kingdom for others, a self-bestowing action supremely exemplified in the redemption, excels the assumption of personal privileges. The cadences of Johannine diction inform Jesus's lesson on true kingship here. The genuine Messiah discards a worldly crown 'Gold'n in shew' for 'a wreath of thorns'. The Messiah secures a deathless crown, not for himself, but for others, so that, by vicariously laying down his life, he establishes an eternal kingdom.

---

[54] Entzminger, 109.

IV

Throughout Book Three Jesus maintains his stance on the virtue of patience. Satan's disquisition on military glory is crafted to make Jesus feel like an under-achiever. To excite Jesus with thoughts of 'fame and glory' (3.25) Satan reels off a dazzling list of conquerors and potentates, and he especially extols those two 'Worthies' (3.74) Alexander the Great and Julius Caesar.[55] Jesus's riposte presents an anti-populist picture, shot through with Messianic irony, in which glory amounts to a short-lived 'blaze of fame' (3.47). Jesus reasons that glory, if measured by worldly categories, is specious and transient. The fickleness of vulgar opinion means that 'to be disprais'd were no small praise' (3.56). The one possessing true glory need not keep up appearances. Jesus substitutes the philosophy of 'The just man' (3.62), the one 'who dares be singularly good' (3.57), for Satan's idea of 'false glory' (3.69). Jesus recapitulates Michael's roll call of just men throughout human history, extending from Enoch and Noah to Abraham and Moses, and culminating in Christ and his saints. The ancient Worthies, together with the heroes and warriors of military history, epic, and old song, 'rob and spoil, burn, slaughter, and enslave / Peaceable Nations' (3.75–76), 'all the flourishing works of peace destroy' (3.80), and achieve glory by 'ambition, warr, or violence' (3.90). The just attain glory 'by means far different' (3.89), 'By deeds of peace, by wisdom eminent, / By patience, temperance' (3.91–92).

Jesus's re-evaluation of worldly values by divine standards ironizes the mundane perspective so that the shamed martyrs and marginalized saints are really glorious and the valiant and soldierly are instead weak. Jesus defines true glory as rarely discernible by worldly standards, but clear and commendable in heavenly eyes:

> This is true glory and renown, when God
> Looking on th' Earth, with approbation marks
> The just man, and divulges him through Heaven
> To all his Angels, who with true applause
> Recount his praises
>
>   (3.60–64)

Jesus's teaching again concerns virtuous patience and he provides two supporting examples of long-suffering, just men of biblical and classical provenance. The first is 'patient *Job*' (3.95), who bore Satan's 'wrongs with Saintly patience' (3.93), while the second is 'Poor *Socrates*', who earned his posterity 'By what he taught and sufferd for so doing, / For truths sake suffering death unjust' (3.96–98). Jesus surpasses these ancient types by his redemptive suffering. Jesus's vision of a God who approves the just man and divulges his merit to a host of applauding angels recalls God's speech about His Son's worth and the responsive angelic hymn from earlier in the brief epic. His vignette also evokes God and the angels' praise of the

---

[55] The Nine Worthies are, in Jewish history, Joshua, David, and Judas Maccabeus; in Greco-Roman history, Hector, Alexander, and Julius Caesar; and, in the Christian Era, Arthur, Charlemagne, and Godfrey of Bouillon.

Son from *Paradise Lost*'s Heavenly Council, responses arising from the Son's offer to redeem.

Barbara Lewalski has documented 'a tradition of commentary pointing to Socrates' death for truth's sake at the hands of the Athenian masses as foreshadowing Christ's death, and to his teaching as prefiguring Christ's doctrine.'[56] The Church historian Jaroslav Pelikan records that Justin Martyr regarded Socrates, like Moses, as 'a type and forerunner of Christ' and ' "a Christian before Christ" ', one who ' "was accused of the very same crimes as [Christians] are" and as Jesus was.'[57] Pelikan continues, 'Both Socrates and Jesus were outstanding teachers; both of them urged and practiced great simplicity of life; both were regarded as traitors to the religion of their community; neither of them wrote anything; both of them were executed.'[58] Should readers miss the resemblance between the patience of the singularly good and Jesus's redeeming death, Milton ensures that the phrase Jesus uses to describe Socrates's heroic martyrdom merges with Jesus's future role as redeemer. Just as Socrates was persecuted 'For truths sake suffering death unjust' (3.98), Milton's Adam duplicates Jesus's phrasing when he accepts, patterned after his Saviour's supreme example, 'that suffering for Truths sake / Is fortitude to highest victorie' (*PL* 12.569–70). Jesus's definition of 'true glory' recognizes his humiliation and glorification portended in one who dares to be singularly good. Milton valued John's gospel for its teachings on Christ's person and office, and it is a Johannine axiom that Jesus's 'lifting up' upon the cross was also inclusive of his exaltation (John 3:13–15; 8:28; 12:31–34), and that the glory God purposed for His Son incorporated the Messiah's death as well as his resurrection (see John 11:4, 40; 12:23–24, 31–34; 13:31–32; 17:1–5).[59]

Satan counters Jesus's argument with a variation upon his previous temptation to acquire glory. If worldly glory is undesirable, Satan questions, then what kind of God 'exacts' (3.120) tribute from His subjects as a usurer extracts credit from a debtor? Jesus reminds Satan that he has discounted God's economy of grace. Thanks or grace, deriving from the Latin *gratia*, is 'The slightest, easiest, readiest recompence' (3.128) remunerated to God by those who, now fallen into sin, have nothing of their own to give. In the Christian dispensation grace issues from God's gift of Christ's saving work. Phillip Donnelly's insight that 'what Satan seems most unable to anticipate is the experience of gift' underscores Satan's unwitting allusion to Paul on the bounty of grace imparted through the Son.[60] Satan criticizes a God who 'requires / Glory from men, from all men good or bad, / Wise or unwise, no difference, no exemption' (3.113–15), and who 'glory he receives / Promiscuous from all Nations, Jew, or Greek, / Or Barbarous, nor exception hath declar'd'

[56] Lewalski, *Brief Epic*, 240; see 240–49.

[57] Jaroslav Pelikan, *Jesus Through the Centuries: His Place in the History of Culture* (New Haven, 1999), 44.

[58] Ibid. 188.

[59] *De Doctrina Christiana* judges the Johannine gospel distinctive in its purpose 'to assert explicitly the Son's deity [*ut deitatem filii . . . palam assereret*]' (*CE* 15.302).

[60] Phillip J. Donnelly, '*Paradise Regained* as Rule of Charity: Religious Toleration and the End of Typology', *Milton Studies*, 43 (2004), 188.

(3.117–19). Galatians and Colossians implement an identical idiom to praise, not to condemn, God's impartial and unconditional bestowal of grace through Christ to all peoples without distinction of status, race, or gender. Galatians teaches, 'There is neither Jew nor Greek, there is neither slave nor freeman, there is neither male nor female; for you are all one in Christ Jesus' (Gal. 3:28); and Colossians maintains that 'there is neither Greek nor Jew, circumcision and uncircumcision, barbarian [βάρβαρος], Scythian, slave, freeman, but all things and in all things is Christ' (Col. 3:11; see 1 Cor. 1:22–24). Satan's caricature of a punitive and unrelenting God traduces the Pauline vision of an all-loving Deity who erases all differences, cancels all exceptions, and admits all persons who receive divine grace through His Son.

Jesus's response reverses Satan's indictment by asserting universal grace couched in sacramental terms. God is willing to 'impart / His good communicable to every soul / Freely' (3.124–26) so that every creature is at once indebted and discharged. Jesus also hints at the means of Messianic victory. The claim that those 'who advance [God's] glory, not thir own, / Them he himself to glory will advance' (3.143–44), evokes the Christ-like principle behind the Philippians doxology (Phil. 2:5–11). Gerard Manley Hopkins encapsulated this principle in his translation of the doxology when he observed that Christ thought equality with God to be οὐχ ἁρπαγμὸν, 'no snatching-matter'.[61] Because the Son does not regard equality with God as a snatching-matter (indeed, he refuses all earthly kingdoms), and because he undergoes Incarnation, humiliation, and obedience even to death, 'Therefore God exalted him and gave him the name that is above every name' so that 'at the name of Jesus every knee should bend . . . and every tongue should confess that Jesus Christ is Lord to the glory of God the Father' (Phil. 2:6–11).[62] The doxology teaches that Jesus's self-giving at his Passion promulgates his Father's glory. Moreover, his heroic act supplies universal grace to all without exception and thereby advances his Messianic glory. Milton's narrator poignantly follows Jesus's allusion to the Messianic humility that leads to a reunion with God and the exaltation of God's people with a brief contrastive sketch of Satan's brazen ambition. Satan has committed the sin of 'regard[ing] equality with God a thing to be grasped at' (Phil. 2.6) and 'himself / Insatiable of glory had lost all' (3.147–48).

Tangling himself in knots with 'his weak arguing' (3.4), Satan's next temptation reverts to 'Zeal and Duty' (3.172) and impresses upon Jesus the need to take up arms. Satan gives the example of Judas Maccabeus, the ancient Worthy and Israel's defender and emancipator. Satan attempts to incense Jesus by reminding him of the

---

[61] Gerard Manley Hopkins, *Poetry and Prose*, ed. Walford Davies (London, 1998), 153.

[62] Richard Crashaw's 'Christ Crucified' conveys God's gracious plenty through His Son. The image of Christ's hands transfixed to the cross forms the basis for his metaphysical conceit:

> Thy hands to give Thou canst not lift,
> Yet will Thy hand still giving be;
> It gives, but O, itself's the gift!
> It gives tho' bound, tho' bound 'tis free! (5–8)

See Arthur Quiller-Couch, ed., *The Oxford Book of English Verse: 1250–1900* (Oxford, 1900), 369.

Temple's repeated violation throughout Israel's history, its successive sacking by Pompey, Crassus, and Pilate, and the second Temple's desecration by Antiochus IV Epiphanes. The 'Zeal of thy Fathers house' (3.175) Satan incites Jesus to display amounts, to Satan, to a show of open and hostile outrage at the sacrilege against God's House. His words refer to Psalm 69: 'For the zeal of thine house hath eaten me up; and the reproaches of them that reproached thee are fallen upon me' (*AV* Ps. 69:9). John's gospel appropriates this Psalm to describe Jesus's indignation that his Father's house has been made into 'a house of merchandizing' (John 2:16) and his subsequent expulsion of the vendors and the money-changers from the Temple. Zeal demonstrated in a godly cause is a positive good in Milton's writings. In Sonnet Nine Milton likens the saintly Lady to one of the wise virgins of the parable (Matt. 25:1–13) who 'zealously attends / To fill thy odorous Lamp with deeds of light' (9–10) and who gains an audience with her bridegroom Christ. Milton's 'fervent Angel' Abdiel proudly shows his 'zeale' (5.849) when he defends God before Satan (5.849). *De Doctrina Christiana's* chapter 'ON ZEAL [*DE ZELO*]' validates the zeal Jesus demonstrates in his clearing of the Temple as 'an ardour and eagerness for sanctifying the divine name or an indignation against those things which pertain to the violation of or contempt for religion' (*CE* 17.152).[63] The Johannine text converts the past tense of the Hebrew verb 'to eat up' at Psalm 69:9 into the future tense and so transforms the Psalm into a riddling Messianic oracle of Jesus's death. The prophecy foretells a time when Jesus's zeal for his Father 'will' consume him and he will suffer reproach upon the cross (John 2:17). The Johannine Jesus promises a future 'sign' of zeal for his Father, 'Destroy this Temple, and in three days I will raise it up' (John 2:19). Jesus's conceit figures the three-day progress of his dead, buried, and resurrected body as the toppled and then miraculously restored Jerusalemic Temple. As the fourth gospel explicates, Jesus 'was speaking about the Temple of his body. Therefore, after he was raised from the dead, his disciples remembered that he had said this' (John 2.21–22). In *Paradise Regain'd* Jesus's zealous reply retrieves the Johannine adaptation of this Psalm as a prediction of Jesus's redemption. Milton's Jesus explains that, since suffering is doing, the Messiah must 'Be try'd in humble state' (3.189) before he can properly reign and 'merit / My exaltation' (3.196–97).

Satan's next shift is to toy with the possibility of benefiting from a diabolic reprieve through Jesus's intercession. Satan confesses that 'all hope is lost / Of my reception into grace' (3.204–05):

> [My crimes] will alike be punisht; whether thou
> Raign or raign not; though to that gentle brow
> Willingly I could flye, and hope thy raign,
> From that placid aspect and meek regard,
> Rather then aggravate my evil state,

---

[63] The concept is a Puritan commonplace. Henry Bullinger writes, 'There is an holy kind of anger, which the scripture disalloweth not . . . For a good man hath a zeal of God, and in that godly zeal he is angry at the iniquity and naughtiness of mankind': Elizabeth Heale, *The Faerie Queene: A Reader's Guide* (2nd edn, Cambridge, 1999), 72.

> Would stand between me and thy Fathers ire,
> (Whose ire I dread more then the fire of Hell)
> A shelter and a kind of shading cool
> Interposition, as a summers cloud.
>
> (3.214–22)

The passage is remarkable for Satan's hypocritical admission, coming soon after his chastisement of God as a hard taskmaster, that he can discern the attribute of mercy in the 'gentle brow' of Jesus's countenance. Lewalski marvels at 'the audacity of his suggestion that Christ become priest and mediator for him instead of his designated conqueror'.[64] Sanford Budick remarks, 'Willingly or not, [Satan] foretells the fulfillment of Christ's propitiatory role'; and Mary Ann Radzinowicz finds that Satan recognizes 'priestly implications in the Son's words' and 'acknowledges momentarily the Son's right to be intercessor'.[65] Satan sues for a respite as evanescent as a summer's cloud, an intermission that would briefly assuage the scorching heat of the sun's rays. Satan does not speak for all fallen creatures, not even for his fellow devils, but courts his own safety. He conveys his self-interested proposal for reconciliation with God in language proleptic of the Son's intercession with God for humanity. Even Jesus's 'placid aspect', which works to cool his Father's ire, evokes Jesus's placation of divine wrath.

Paradise Lost affords a complementary vignette of the Son's intercession for fallen humanity (11.1–71). Milton visualizes Satan's desired reconcilement, with Jesus 'stand[ing] between me and thy Fathers ire', as early as 1626 in his *Fair Infant* elegy. Milton's vision of the departed child encompasses the Christ-child's reconciliation of God and humanity, 'To stand 'twixt us and our deserved smart' (69). *De Doctrina Christiana* echoes Satan's conceit of his truce with God as 'a kind of shading cool / Interposition'. The treatise describes Jesus's satisfaction as mitigation 'interposed':

> But no one could have been thought worthy of a calling by grace, had not Christ's satisfaction been interposed [*nisi interposita Christi satisfactione*]. It was a satisfaction not only sufficient in itself but also efficacious for all people, insofar as it was permitted according to God's will, if indeed He calls in earnest. The calling and gifting is God's, the accepting is a matter of faith. If this [faith] in the efficacious satisfaction is lacking, this is not because the satisfaction has not been efficaciously given [by God in Christ], but that the gift has not been accepted. (*CE* 15.324)[66]

Satan's feeble, parodic version of Christ's satisfaction and reconciliation evinces yet another poetic strategy Milton exercises to communicate his redemptive model of Messianic heroism. Satan imagines only a temporary alleviation of his damnation, orchestrated through the Messiah's interposition, and a passing satisfaction of

---

[64] Lewalski, *Brief Epic*, 258.

[65] Radzinowicz, 45; Sanford Budick, *The Dividing Muse: Images of Sacred Disjunction in Milton's Poetry* (New Haven, 1985), 56.

[66] The rude obverse to Christ's saving interposition is the nightmarish causeway obtruding from Hell's mouth that 'With long reach interpos'd' (*PL* 10.321–23) between the 'Empyrean Heav'n' and 'this World'.

God's wrath. Those 'regal Mysteries' (3.249) or redemptive 'mysteries of the kingdom of heaven' (Matt. 13:11) upon which Satan's speech unwittingly touches are beyond him.

Satan commences his presentation of the kingdoms of the world with a panorama of the might and craft of Parthia. Once more he obsesses about the 'means' (3.355) and the 'means us'd' (3.356) by Jesus to secure Messianic victory, and once more he imagines Jesus's regaining of a kingdom in a geographical, localized context. He harps on the recovery of Israel as Jesus's main aim, the Israelites 'to deliver' and 'from servitude [to] restore / To thir inheritance' (3.380–82). The mode of victory Satan recommends exposes his limited methodology. Satan prefers strategies of force and fraud.[67] Thus Satan suggests that Jesus should enfranchise Israel forcefully or fraudulently, 'by conquest or by league' (3.370). Jesus explodes both possibilities as mere froth and vanity. Force is no more than:

> Much ostentation vain of fleshly arm,
> And fragile arms, much instrument of warr
> Long in preparing, soon to nothing brought
> (3.387–89)

Satan, despite his massive catalogue of Parthian might, has bombastically and windily enthused about fraud. He has:

> Vented much policy, and projects deep
> Of enemies, of aids, battles and leagues,
> Plausible to the World, to mee worth naught.
> (3.391–93)

Jesus engages in wordplay when he deflates these two strategies as 'Plausible'. The epithet, stemming from the Latin *plaudere*, denotes something 'worthy of applause', but it equally denotes an object only speciously or superficially reasonable or valuable (*OED*).

Jesus continues to refute fraud and force. He rebuffs the winding fraud of Satan's 'politic maxims' and the futile bulk of Parthia's 'cumbersome / Luggage of warr', yet he also tantalizes Satan with talk of the 'time' within which and the 'means' by which he will become victorious. The involved and intricate syntax that reflects Jesus's reasoning closes with an ambiguous phrase that he leaves suspended in an enigmatic relationship with the preceding clauses:

> Means I must use thou say'st, prediction else
> Will unpredict and fail me of the Throne:
> My time I told thee, (and that time for thee
> Were better fardest off) is not yet come;

---

[67] For a survey of the Satanic collocation of fraud and force, see my '"By Force or Fraud Weening to prosper": Milton's Satanic and Messianic Modes of Heroism', *Milton Quarterly*, 43 (2009), 17–38; James A. Freeman, *Milton and the Martial Muse: 'Paradise Lost' and European Traditions of War* (Princeton, 1980), 156–77.

When that comes think not thou to find me slack
On my part aught endeavouring, or to need
Thy politic maxims, or that cumbersome
Luggage of warr there shewn me, argument
Of human weakness rather then of strength.

(3.394–402)

With what substantive does Jesus's nominal phrase, 'argument / Of human weakness rather then of strength', agree? If the phrase lies in apposition with Satan's 'politic maxims' and 'Luggage of warr', then Jesus is appropriately excoriating Satanic force and fraud as a hopeless means to victory. Yet, if readers resist the temptation to select the readiest, easiest possible antecedents, they may associate the dependent clause concerning the argument of weakness with the time and means for Jesus's victory over Satan on the cross. The main idea of the sentence concerning the method of Messianic victory is then enfolded within and modified by the adverbial clause. Jesus's ambivalence makes both readings defensible. Jesus's suggestive syntax implies that his victory will paradoxically involve a heroic argument of human weakness upon the cross, 'By Humiliation and strong Sufferance' (1.160), rather than of strength in open warfare. Interpreted thus, Jesus engages in an intertextual dialogue with the Pauline proclamation of 'Christ crucified' (1 Cor. 1:23), where 'Christ [is] God's power', 'God's weakness is stronger than human strength', and, through atonement, 'God chose the weak things of the world in order to shame the strong things' (1 Cor. 1:24–27). Milton's personal motto suggests that the poet learned from the experience of his blindness that one's strength could be made perfect in weakness. Milton's Jesus similarly instructs readers to attend to his syntactical doubleness, reform their quality of vision, and assess the apparent worth of earthly things against their authentic heavenly value, *sub specie aeternitatis*. In Jesus's estimation an indomitable Parthian army amounts to an argument of weakness. Conversely, the crucified Messiah comprises God's argument of spiritual strength. *Paradise Regain'd* once again directs the reader's attention to the cross. Book Three, like Book Two, closes with the image of a king burdened by the cares of office. The poem insistently approves of a servant-king who, through his Passion, accedes to his rightful Messianic status as '*Israels* true King' (3.441).

V

Book Four opens with three similes that convey Satan's mounting perplexity 'at his bad success' (4.1). As I have showed elsewhere, of these three comparisons the second simile of the flies buzzing about a winepress has been neglected.[68] The oversight is unfortunate because the Christian imaginary had elaborated the

---

[68] See my 'The Wreath, the Rock, and the Winepress: Passion Iconography in Milton's *Paradise Regain'd*', *Literature and Theology*, 22 (2008), 387–405.

winepress image into a complex Passion symbol. Within the epic tradition the closest species of simile to Milton's winepress occurs in Homer's *Iliad*, where the swarming Greeks besieging Troy and the Greeks and Trojans quarrelling over the slain Sarpedon's spoils are as flies buzzing about a milk-pail (*Il.* 2.469–73; 16.641–43).[69] Young Milton appropriated this Homeric comparison for his neo-Latin epyllion on the Gunpowder Plot *In Quintum Novembris*, where the crowds congregating within the goddess Rumour's tower and stirring up gossip are 'like masses of flies which hum and buzz around milk-pails' (178–79).[70] In *Paradise Regain'd* Milton fuses the classical and biblical traditions in his winepress simile. He modifies the Homeric simile to meet his redemptive concerns by replacing the milk-pails with the winepress. Milton's principal inspiration is Isaiah 63:1–4, where one 'cometh from Edom, with dyed garments from Bozrah':

> Wherefore art thou red in thine apparel, and thy garments like him that treadeth in the winefat? I have trodden the winepress alone; and of the people there was none with me; for I will tread them in mine anger, and trample them in my fury; and their blood shall be sprinkled upon my garments, and I will stain all my raiment. For the day of vengeance is in mine heart, and the year of my redeemed is come. (*AV*)

For Justin Martyr, Isaiah's wine-stained man treading the winepress alone proclaimed the bloodstained and crucified Christ solitarily treading out the vintage for his redeemed.[71] Augustine endorses this hermeneutic for the winepress in his *Expositions of the Psalms*. Expounding Psalm 83, Augustine modifies the meaning of the image and figures Jesus as the bruised and crushed grape-cluster rather than as the grape-treader. Augustine praises Jesus, likening him to grapes prepared for the winepress, his skin flayed and his body wrung out upon the cross. Likewise, Augustine admonishes, Christians who prosper in their faith like rich grapes or olives should expect to follow Christ's example and be 'pressed' by their persecutors:

> This Psalm is inscribed, '*For the winepresses*'. [T]here are people ... who are conformed to the image of the only-begotten Son who, principally in his Passion, was wrung out as a mighty grape-cluster is pressed. Accordingly, people, before they accede to God's service, likewise enjoy a kind of delicious freedom in this world, as if they were hanging grapes or olives. But ... each person who accedes to God's service must be aware that they have come to the winepresses. They will be crushed, bruised, pounded, not so that they perish in this world, but so that they may flow down into God's wine-cellars ... This entire idea is about nothing except the pressing; for this reason, God's Churches in this age are named winepresses.[72]

In his discussion of Psalm 8 Augustine unites the Passional winepress with Numbers 13, where Moses's scouts reconnoitre the Promised Land and bring back a grape-cluster hanging upon a staff. Once again, the process of 'pressing' the grapes represents the persecution of Christ and his Church:

---

[69] John Milton, *Complete Poems and Major Prose*, ed. Merritt Y. Hughes (New York, 1957), 515.
[70] '*Qualiter instrepitant circum mulctralia bombis / Agmina muscarum*'.
[71] Justin Martyr, 186–87.
[72] Augustine, *Enarrationes in Psalmos, Corpus Christianorum*, vol. 39, ed. D. Eligius Dekkers and Johannes Fraipont (Turnhout, 1956), 1146; commenting upon Psalm 83, section 1.

There is another understanding concerning the winepresses, while simultaneously not abandoning their signification as Churches. For the divine Word can be understood as a grape. For even the Lord is called a cluster of grapes, which those who were sent forth by the people of Israel carried back from the Land of Promise, suspended from a tree as though it were crucified... The winepresses are also customarily accepted as martyrdoms, as though martyrs were trodden down by the affliction of persecutions for confessing Christ's name; their mortal remains abide back here on Earth like grape-skins, but their souls flow forth to a resting-place in a heavenly habitation.[73]

Representations of the Passional winepress prevailed in Medieval and Renaissance visual art. Gertrud Schiller's compendium of Passion iconography charts the evolution of the winepress conceit.[74] In the twelfth and thirteenth centuries artists depicted Jesus as a serene and beardless youth trampling the grapes without the fury of the Isaian treader. By the fifteenth century 'the ideas behind the typological image of the wine-treader changed and it was transformed into a eucharistic image of the Passion in the sense of a Man of Sorrows sacrificing his blood and suffering under the sins of mankind'.[75] While Jesus treads out the vintage, sacramental blood-wine spatters his raiment. Artists discovered new ways of amplifying the winepress scene. In some versions Christ shoulders the rood-shaped winepress beam; in others the Father, accompanied by a dovelike Holy Spirit, presses upon the beam. Angels and a wimpled Mary, her heart pierced by a sword, might stoop to collect the blood-wine running from the trough into a Eucharistic chalice. In Jorg Breu's naturalistic *Christ in the Winepress suffers for the sins of mankind* (*c.* 1520) a brutish mob encircles the trough and derides a bloodstained Christ, while a distressed angel, catching Jesus's expiatory blood in a chalice, covers its eyes in dismay.[76] Schiller chronicles how, during the Reformation and afterwards, the winepress conceit retained its respectability: 'Since the faith of this period stemmed not from speculative mysticism but from a direct relationship with the person of Christ and his suffering – *pro nobis* – the need for contemplation remained' so that winepress iconography 'received new stimulus in the seventeenth century.'[77]

The winepress conceit animates Lancelot Andrewes and John Donne's homilies. Andrewes preaches on the crucified Christ's sufferings, 'This was the pain of "the press", so the Prophet [Isaiah] calleth it, *torcular* ["winepress"], wherewith as if He had been in the wine-press, all His garments were stained and gored with blood.'[78]

---

[73] Ibid., vol. 38, 49–50; Psalm 8, sections 2.1–3.4.

[74] For representations of the winepress conceit, see Gertrud Schiller, *Iconography of Christian Art*, trans. J. Seligman, vol. 2 (London, 1972), 128–29 and 228–29; figures 432–33, 808, and 810–12; and Gabriele Finaldi, *The Image of Christ* (London, 2000), 186–89; figures 73 and 74. My thumbnail conspectus of the winepress image is indebted to Schiller and Finaldi's research.

[75] Schiller, 228.

[76] Ibid. figure 811.

[77] Ibid. 229.

[78] Andrewes, 'Sermon 3'. In a Paschal Sermon of 1623 Andrewes expatiates, 'Twice [Christ] was a *winepress*. On Good Friday when He was, like the grapes, trodden on and pressed, the other as on Easter day when He was the *winepress* and trampled upon sin, and drank the fruits of the winepressing for us': Andrewes, *Sermons*, vol. 2, 184.

In an Easter sermon on Isaiah 63 Andrewes discerns three winepresses manifested throughout Christian history.[79] The first was during Christ's Agony in Gethsemane, whose Hebrew name *gath shemanim* translates as 'the garden with the oil press' after the machine that stood amid Gethsemane's olive groves. Christ's 'unnatural' bloody sweat (Luke 22:44) was 'as if He had been wrung and crushed in a *winepress*' and at Calvary the forces of darkness trampled upon Christ as pounded grapes.[80] Second, Christ stamped out Sin and Death:

> Of *Calcatus* ["the Downtrodden", Christ] became *Calcator* ["the Treader"]. He who was thrown Himself, threw them now another while into the press, trod them down, trampled upon them as upon grapes in a fat, till He made the blood spring out of them, and all to sprinkle His garments, as if He had come forth of a winepress indeed. And we before, mercifully rather than mightily by His Passion, now mightily [are] also saved by His glorious resurrection.[81]

Third, interpreting Revelation 19:15, where God's Word 'treads the winepress of the furious wrath of God the Almighty', Andrewes predicts that at the Second Coming the Son will again tread the winepress and achieve an everlasting victory.[82] In his *Devotions Upon Emergent Occasions* John Donne maintains, 'It was for thy blessed, thy powerfull *Sonne* alone, *to tread the wine-presse alone, and none of the people with him.*'[83] Finally, in a Lenten sermon of 1620, Donne, expounding the knowledge of angels, imagines a dialogue between Christ and his angels during which Christ teases the celestial company with Isaian intimations of redemption:

> There [the angels] say with amazement, *Quis iste? Who is this that cometh from Edom, with dyed garments from Bozrah?* And Christ answers there, *Ego, it is I, I that speak in righteousness, I that am mighty to save.* The Angels reply, *Wherefore are thy garments red, like him that treadeth the wine-press?* and Christ gives them satisfaction, *calcavi;* You mistake not the matter, *I have trodden the wine-press*; and *calcavi solus, I have trodden the winepress alone, and of the people there was none with me.* The Angels then knew not this, not all this, not all the particulars of this; The mystery of Christs Incarnation for the Redemption of Man, the Angels knew in generall.[84]

Additionally, the Passional winepress features in English Protestant poetics. In Herbert's 'The Agonie' sin's burden excruciates Christ. From the lance-wound in Christ's side his precious redeeming blood flows forth, which the communicant enjoys as 'liquor' or wine:

> Who would know Sinne, let him repair
> Unto Mount Olivet; there shall he see
> A man so wrung with pains, that all his hair,
>   His skinne, his garments bloudie be.
> Sinne is that presse and vice, which forceth pain
> To hunt his cruell food through ev'ry vein.

[79] Andrewes, *Sermons*, vol. 2, 179–90.   [80] Ibid. 185–87.
[81] Ibid. 186.   [82] Ibid. 189.
[83] Donne, *Devotions Upon Emergent Occasions*, ed. Anthony Raspa (London, 1975), 27.
[84] Donne, *Sermons*, vol. 3, 217.

Who knows not Love, let him assay
And taste that juice, which on the crosse a pike
Did set again abroach; then let him say
    If ever he did taste the like.
Love is that liquor sweet and most divine,
Which my God feels as bloud; but I, as wine. (7–18)[85]

In Herbert's 'The Bunch of Grapes' the grape-cluster represents the Law's curse that Christ lifts, 'Who of the Laws sowre juice sweet wine did make, / Ev'n God himself being pressed for my sake' (27–28).[86] While Milton was probably not aware of all these versions of the redemptive winepress, yet their prevalence in early modern visual art, homiletics, and Protestant poetics testifies to the conceit's influence throughout seventeenth-century Northern European culture.

This brief retrospective of the development of the winepress motif reinforces how, in the hinterland of *Paradise Regain'd*'s simile, Milton's winepress is loaded with redemptive meaning. Satan's plaguing of Jesus is:

    as a swarm of flies in vintage time,
About the wine-press where sweet moust is powrd,
[which,] Beat off, returns as oft with humming sound
                    (4.15–17)

Although the immediate context concerns Satan's intensifying rancour before Jesus's patience, the simile broadens its frame of reference to encompass Satan's downfall at the Passion. Milton adds the innovation of a plaguing swarm of flies, which corresponds to the harassing figure of Satan. *De Doctrina Christiana* approves the name *Beel-zebub* as one of Satan's titles and argues, 'The devils also have their prince. Matthew 12:24: "Beelzebub the prince of the devils"' (*CE* 15.110). The Hebrew title *Beel-zebub*, which translates 'Lord of the Flies', matches the vehicle of Milton's comparison with its tenor and adds another Satanic resonance to the noisome swarm surging around the winepress. Milton refrains from specifying Jesus's relation to the winepress, but we can reasonably infer that he fulfils his conventional role of trampling the grapes of wrath or being crushed like a pressed grape. Just as the wine's 'sweet moust' allures the flies, so Jesus's goodness fascinates Satan. Satan is continually 'Beat off' and denied access to the must, the blood-wine and saving grace issuing from Jesus's sacrifice. Satan's redoubled efforts to over-throw Jesus, joined with Jesus's reiterated repulsion of Satan's assaults, only allow the redeemer's grace to abound all the more, since, as steadily as 'the sweet moust is powrd,' Satan 'returns as oft with humming sound'. The pestilent, greedy flies that untiringly molest the press expose Satan's insatiable ambition, driven by base cravings. The flies' doggedness also reinforces the sadistic pleasure Satan derives from incessantly tempting Jesus and exacerbating his trials, even while the blood-wine constantly outpouring from the winepress suggests the spiritual fruits of Jesus's longsuffering.

---

[85] Herbert, 37.   [86] Ibid., 128.

VI

Satan's offer of Rome's imperial seat develops logically out of his offer of Parthia. Parthia and Rome were two regnant principalities in Jesus's time. Yet the fiend is also building upon his previous temptation to zeal by tantalizing Jesus with the prospect of hegemony over Rome, since, as the preeminent global power, the Roman *imperium* had reduced Israel to a colonial province. Jesus responds by debunking Satan's lure of cosmopolitan Rome, the 'Queen of the Earth' (4.45), as 'this grandeur and majestic show / Of luxury, though calld magnificence' (4.110–11). He deflates Roman civilization's putative patrician values of Horatian simplicity and frugality and invokes an alternative vision of gluttonous, decadent Romans who 'quaff in Gold, / Crystal and Myrrhine cups' (4.118–19). Jesus next banishes this riotous picture of excess as quickly as he creates it and substitutes for the saturnalia a sketch of those suffering saintly endurance 'who thirst / And hunger still' (4.120–21). The patrician gourmands supping from 'Myrrhine cups' faintly allude to the Markan Passion when the crucified Jesus refuses the Roman soldiers' cup of 'wine mixed with myrrh [ἐσμυρνισμένον οἶνον]' (Mark 15:23). In the other gospels a Roman soldier provides wine mixed with vinegar or gall (Matt. 27:34; Luke 23:36–37; John 19:29–30). The Christian tradition taught that the offered mixture of wine and gall fulfilled the 'Messianic prophecy' of Psalm 69:21, where the righteous sufferer laments, 'They gave me also gall for my meat; and in my thirst they gave me vinegar to drink' (*AV*). Despite these minor gospel variations, myrrh, gall, and vinegar were commonly used in antiquity as narcotics, sedatives, and analgesics. In Mark's gospel, in order to complete his Passion Jesus refuses the release from bodily suffering that the 'Myrrhine' cup of wine would bring. As Donne explains, the 'blessed and glorious *Sonne*, being offered in the way to his *Execution*, a Cup of *Stupefaction*, to take away the sense of his paine, (a charity afforded to condemned persons ordinarily in those places, and times) refused that *ease*, and embraced the whole *torment*'.[87] Jesus's image of satisfied Romans contentedly quaffing wine from myrrhine cups should jar with the excruciated Jesus refusing the cup of wine mixed with the painkilling drug myrrh.

The second prong to Satan's Rome temptation concerns the appeal of expelling the 'lascivious' Emperor Tiberius (4.91) and his 'wicked Favourite' Sejanus (4.95). The Roman historians Tacitus and Suetonius graphically detailed Tiberius's 'horrid lusts in privat' (4.94) upon Capri.[88] Satan's attempt to kindle Jesus's righteous indignation into desiring to 'expell this monster from his Throne' (4.100) misfires because Jesus professes to conquer upon a cosmic rather than a local canvas. Jesus walks to the cross, not to 'expell / A brutish monster' like Tiberius, because eventually the depraved Emperor's 'tormentor Conscience [will] find him out', but to defeat 'a Devil who first made him such' (4.127–30). Satan unwittingly suggests the Passional 'Means' whereby Jesus achieves this expulsion, means that, Jesus states, 'Is not for thee to know, nor mee to tell' (4.152–53). Satan's

[87] Donne, *Devotions*, 108.
[88] See Suetonius, *Suetonius*, vol. 1, trans. J. C. Rolfe (London, 1989), 352–57; 3.43–45.

description of Jesus's potential usurpation of Tiberius, 'and in his place ascending /
A victor people free from servil yoke' (4.101–02), accidentally describes Jesus's
ascension following his resurrection by which he will oust, not a temporal potentate
like Tiberius, but the cosmic tyrant Satan. In Satan's place ascending, Jesus will
liberate neither nation nor Empire, but the human race. In Michael's words, 'to the
Heav'n of Heav'ns he shall ascend / With victory, triumphing through the aire' (*PL*
12.451–52).

Satan deems Jesus worthy of wearing the imperial laurel because he is naturally
'Indu'd with Regal Vertues' (4.98). 'To endue' is a specialized verb; its etymology
derives from the Greek verb ἐνδύω, 'to put on, clothe oneself in'. Paul uses the verb
to exhort early Christians that, since they are reborn in Christ, they should discard
their old, sinful selves and be clothed with new, regenerate selves in Christ. Christ's
followers should 'clothe themselves with Christ [Χριστὸν ἐνδύσασθε]' (Gal. 3:27),
'put on the new self [ἐνδυσάμενοι τὸν νέον]' (Col. 3:10), and 'put on . . . the bowels
of compassion ['Ενδύσασθε . . . σπλάγχνα οἰκτιρμοῦ]' (Col. 3:12). Jesus's atonement has swallowed up death in victory so that regenerate humanity may 'put on
[ἐνδύσασθαι]' incorruption, the perishable clothed with the imperishable and the
mortal nature arrayed in immortality (1 Cor. 15:53–54). 'To endue' is in Pauline
discourse a symbolic action concerned with the joint themes of Jesus's administration of redemption and humanity's renovation. Satan's temptation to install Jesus,
one whose bearing is endued with regal virtues, as Israel's political liberator from
Roman rule, opens into a vision of Jesus as *Christus Liberator*, freeing humanity
from sin. Jesus bases his rejection of transient Roman rule and ascension to the
Roman throne upon the limited beneficial effects that such usurpation would have.
Accepting Satan's offer of Rome would require Jesus not only to labour to
emancipate a people chronically 'degenerat, by themselves enslav'd', but also to
'of inward slaves make outward free' (4.144–45). Both obligations would be
fruitless. In contrast, the everlasting throne Jesus ascends to claim after his resurrection enables humanity to be inwardly free and equipped, if they so choose, to
discard the old self and become endued with the new. At the poem's climax Milton
reactivates this Pauline imagery. When Satan is dethroned at the pinnacle and the
exalted Jesus does ascend, uplifted by angels, the angels paean that Jesus is 'with
Godlike force indu'd' (4.602).

Exasperated by Jesus's rejection of Parthia and Rome, Satan offers him all the
kingdoms of the world on the single condition that Jesus falls prostrate and wor-
ships him as a 'superior Lord' (4.167) and 'God' (4.192). Jesus's willingness to
'endure the time, till which expir'd' (4.174), of Satan's illegitimate and finite power
restates patient Messianic heroism. However, the Son's rebuke, 'Get thee behind
me' (4.193), stresses the Passional subtext. Editors tend to cite as Milton's source
Jesus's repudiation of earthly kingdoms at Matthew 4:10 – 'Go away, Satan!' Yet
there are two other instances of this rebuke in Matthew and Mark's gospels that
occur, not in the temptation narratives, but during Peter's confession at Caesarea
Philippi (Mark 8:27–37; Matt. 16:20–26). Milton signals the importance of Peter's
confession by having Jesus utter the exact words with which he rebukes Simon
Peter, 'Get thee behind me, Satan ['Υπαγε ὀπίσω μου, Σατανᾶ]' (Matt. 16:23;

Mark 8:33), rather than the more succinct formula from the Matthean temptation of the kingdoms, 'Go away, Satan ['Υπαγε, Σατανâ].' At Caesarea Philippi Jesus reproves Peter, through whom Satan is working ill, for tempting him to understand Messianism in a worldly sense:

> From that time Jesus began to explain to his disciples that he must go to Jerusalem and suffer many things at the hands of the elders and chief priests and scribes, and be killed, and be raised on the third day. And Peter took him aside and began to rebuke him, saying, 'May God take pity upon you, Lord. This will never happen to you!' But Jesus turned about and said to Peter, 'Get you behind me, Satan! You are a stumbling-block to me, because you are not thinking of the things of God, but the things of humanity.' Then Jesus told the disciples, 'If someone wishes to follow me, let him deny himself and take up his cross and follow me. For whoever desires to save his soul will lose it. But whoever loses his soul for my sake will find it. For what will it benefit a man if he gains the whole world, but forfeits his soul? Or what will a man give in exchange for his soul?'   (Matt. 16:21–26)

Although Peter correctly confesses Jesus as Messiah, he abhors Jesus's prediction of Passional Messianism and his definition of a Messiah whose mission will involve trial, persecution, and torturous death. Jesus meets Peter's challenge with a rebuttal *De Doctrina Christiana* terms a kind of 'pious hatred [*odium . . . pium*]': 'Thus did Christ speak to Peter, who was otherwise most loved by him' (*CE* 17.258, 260). *Paradise Regain'd* dovetails Satan's Messianic concerns with Peter's offence. In both texts Jesus delivers the same rebuke to his two tempters, the one an apostle and the other the Devil, who are both guilty of narrowly defining kingship according to fallen, and not divine, categories. Satan's bafflement at Jesus's rejection of worldly kingship and his blindness to spiritual kingship rightly makes him wonder, 'thou thy self seem'st otherwise inclin'd / Then to a worldly Crown' (4.212–13).

Satan's next ruse is a survey of Athens contrived to lure Jesus 'To contemplation and profound dispute' (4.214) and to awaken in him a desire to 'Be famous then / By wisdom' (4.221–22). Satan again tries to appeal to Jesus's idea of Messianism and promises to 'render thee a King compleat' (4.283). Jesus's denunciation of Satan's synopsis of classical erudition troubles those who see Milton as an exponent of Christian humanism.[89] Jameela Lares notices how 'Milton typically invokes classical learning only to rank it as inferior to Christian revelation', while Ken Simpson cautions, 'it is not classical wisdom in itself that is rejected in this temptation, but classical wisdom offered by Satan as a source of fame and as a spiritual kingdom superior to Christ's'.[90] If Jesus's insistence upon the sufficiency of scripture alone seems to smack of radicalism, that is because it *is* a radical, though not an uncommon, assertion in Christian thought. Tertullian famously refuted Greek learning, 'What, therefore, has Athens to do with Jerusalem? What has the Academy to do with the Church? . . . After Jesus Christ, there is no need for curiosity. After the gospel, there is no need for inquisition. Since we believe, we

---

[89] For a critical reception history of the Athens temptation, see Lares, 173–82.

[90] Lares, 178; Ken Simpson, *Spiritual Architecture and 'Paradise Regained': Milton's Literary Ecclesiology* (Pittsburgh, 2007), 176; see 93–94.

desire nothing beyond believing.'[91] Jerome, too, singled out Second Corinthians 6:14–15, 'What fellowship has light with darkness? What concord has Christ with Belial or a believer with an unbeliever?' Jerome likewise challenged the canonicity of Rome's Golden Age: 'What has Horace to do with the Psalter? [Publius Virgilius] Maro with the gospels? Cicero with the apostle [Paul]? . . . We should not simultaneously drink from Christ's chalice and from the chalice of devils.'[92]

One crucial Pauline text from First Corinthians informs Satan's Athens temptation and Jesus's rejoinder that is companionate with Jesus's renunciation of Parthian might and his advocacy of the 'strength-through-weakness' of the cross. The Pauline teaching concerning the 'wisdom-through-folly' of 'Christ crucified' identifies the cross as 'foolishness to the gentiles', where 'the foolishness of God is wiser than man's wisdom', where Christ embodies 'the wisdom of God', and where, through redemption, 'God chose the foolish things of the world to shame the wise' (1 Cor. 1:23–25, 27). Satan contends that Jesus's acquaintance with classical learning will enable him to evangelize effectively, because 'The Gentiles also know . . . And with the Gentiles much thou must converse . . . Without thir learning how wilt thou with them, / Or they with thee hold conversation meet?' (4.227–32). Satan pointedly uses the designation 'Gentiles' instead of 'Greeks' or 'Romans', and so he replicates the Greek of Paul's text, which employs the phrase 'foolishness to the gentiles [ἔθνεσιν]'. Satan's injunction to Jesus to 'revolve' pagan learning to 'mature thee to a Kingdoms waight' (4.281–82) recalls another instance where the verb 'revolve' has a meditative sense. As a youth, Jesus 'revolv'd / The Law and Prophets, searching what was writ / Concerning the Messiah' (1.259–61). Superior biblical study enlightened Jesus that the Messiah must endure 'eev'n to the death' (1.264) to 'work Redemption for mankind' (1.266). Jesus's sentiments mirror those of the Puritan Richard Greenham. Greenham deplored preachers who felt the Athenian itch for Atticisms and 'plausible novelties' and who stressed rhetorical preciosity, ostentation, and wit instead of teaching the central Christian verities: 'They whose knowledge is in swelling words, and painted eloquence of humane wisdome, being but a doctrine of the letter, in their death they are as if they knew nothing of Christ crucified.'[93]

Point for point Jesus's palinode undermines Satan's truncated curriculum of ancient philosophy and exposes pagan folly after pagan folly, yet Jesus speaks 'sagely' (4.285) as he epitomizes Christian wisdom. Jesus distinguishes true wisdom from the foolishness of classical learning and he cautions Satan to 'Think not but that I know these things, or think / I know them not; not therefore am I short / Of knowing what I ought' (4.286–88). Jesus is cool in his opinion of Socrates, whom Satan extols as the 'Wisest of men' (4.276), and he judges him to be a primary exponent of *docta ignorantia*: 'The first and wisest of them all [for professing] / To know this onely, that he nothing knew' (4.293–94). Plato is no more than a fabler

[91] Tertullian, *De Praescriptione Haereticorum Ad Martyras: Ad Scapulam*, ed. T. Herbert Bindley (Oxford, 1893), 40–41; ch. 7.
[92] Jerome, *Select Letters of St. Jerome*, trans. F. A. Wright (London, 1975), 124; Letter 22.29.
[93] Richard Greenham, *Workes* (London, 1605), 20.

(4.295), and the Sceptics 'doubted all things, though plain sense' (4.296). Aristotelian and Peripatetic eudaimonism defines the happy life as a lifetime of virtue in action, sustained by external goods, and so, according to Milton's Jesus, misguidedly emphasizes 'vertue' as earthly 'felicity' and 'riches and long life' (4.297–98). Jesus somewhat oversimplifies, but is no less scathing about, the Epicurean worldview as embracing 'corporal pleasure' and 'careless ease' (4.299). The Stoic's 'Philosophic pride, / By him calld vertue' (4.300–01), causes him to deem himself 'Wise, perfet in himself, and all possessing / Equal to God' (4.302–03). This verbal touch, 'possessing / Equal to God', transliterates the Greek of the Philippians doxology and erects an implicit antithesis between the Stoic and the Messianic states. Where the hubristic Stoic thinks himself a petty God, the Messiah, who 'did not regard being equal with God a thing to be grasped at [ἁρπαγμὸν ἡγήσατο τὸ εἶναι ἴσα θεῷ]' (Phil. 2:6), is exalted because of his kenosis on the cross.

Jesus completes his methodical refutation by concluding that ancient philosophical systems lack any valid conceptual framework for comprehending who made the world and how humanity lapsed. Consequently, for all its erudition, classical philosophy is deficient:

> Alas what can they teach, and not mislead;
> Ignorant of themselves, of God much more,
> And how the World began, and how man fell
> Degraded by himself, on Grace depending?
> (4.309–12)

The dangling participial clause depending from this enumeration of fundamental Christian doctrines of God, Creation, and the Fall – 'on Grace depending' – is the essence and the attribute of Jesus's question. The workings of divine grace actively salvage fallen human history and rescue humanity from its sinful predicament. Jesus's question is rhetorical only insofar as Satan is incapable of answering it. Jesus argues that the wisdom of antiquity, whether Platonism or Scepticism, Stoicism or Epicureanism, cannot provide an adequate exposition of either grace or its soteriological foundation. As in the concessive clause of *Paradise Lost*'s first invocation, where the fallen human predicament appears hopeless 'till one greater Man / Restore us' (*PL* 1.4–5), the fact of divine grace colours and revises our reading of Jesus's sentence. Next to the foolish wisdom of the Messiah crucified in Pauline teaching, classical antiquity cannot offer 'True wisdom', but instead holds out 'delusion', wisdom's 'false resemblance', which is at best 'An empty cloud' (4.319–21). The syntax of Milton's verse and the span of fallen human history that the syntax encompasses are reformed by the means of grace promised through Jesus's atonement. Paul's words are particularly apt here as a gloss upon the rejection of worldly wisdom by Milton's Jesus and the priority of the knowledge of God's grace. Paul discourses upon Christ as one 'in whom are hidden all the treasures of wisdom and knowledge' (Col. 2:3). He cautions, 'Beware lest anyone take you captive through philosophy and empty deceit according to the tradition of men, according to the elementary principles of the world, and not according to Christ' (Col. 2:8). Jesus's disparagement of classical philosophy, poetry, and oratory, when compared with scripture, as being barely 'worth a spunge' (4.329) evinces its expendability as knowledge that is easily absorbed and just as easily dissipated. Yet, as with Jesus's verbal icons of the 'wreath of thorns' or the 'Myrrhine cups', the worthless sponge hints at another Passion instrument in the Greek '*spongos* [σπόγγος]' or sponge that was doused in vinegar, set upon a branch of hyssop, and then pressed to Jesus's dying lips (John 19:29; Mark 15:36; Matt. 27:48).[94] As with the thorny wreath or the bitter cup, the gospels narrate that the acidic, distasteful sponge was considered worthy of the crucified Christ, who nevertheless stood strong in his apparent weakness and wise in his putative folly.

VII

Satan's supernaturally generated storm and Jesus's excruciating ordeal at the pinnacle put into practice the philosophical theory Milton has mapped out throughout Jesus and Satan's exchange, namely the heroic idea of a physically suffering and glorified Messiah. Satan's masterminding of these two trials puts Jesus's disquisition on Passional kingship to the test. As Satan states, Jesus shows that his heart has 'the perfet shape' (3.11) and 'What best to say canst say, to do canst do; / Thy actions to thy words accord' (3.8–9), when, self-balanced upon the pinnacle, Jesus perfectly weds word to deed and concertedly 'said and stood' (4.561). Before Satan deploys physical force against the Son, he enlists scare tactics. He attempts to make Jesus despair by retracting his offer to 'have set thee in short time with ease / On *Davids* Throne' (4.378–79). Moreover, he reminds Jesus that, since his ripe years stand 'Now at full age' and 'fulness of time' (4.380), his prospects are nearly eclipsed. Satan uses astrology to foresee a 'contrary' fate (4.382) for Jesus and reviews a catalogue of woes awaiting him. The catalogue resembles the Pauline *peristasis* catalogue we examined above. As David Gay has shown, Jesus's destiny 'brings "scorns, reproaches, injuries, / Violence and stripes, and lastly cruel death" and a promised kingdom (4.387–8). Satan sees only the material spectacle of Jesus' suffering and death.'[95] Satan's expression 'fulness of time', which he takes to signify the *kairos* or 'opportune time' for Jesus's entry into earthly prosperity, is, like the verb 'endue', a New Testament idiom fraught with soteriological meaning. So Paul writes:

> But when the fullness of time [τὸ πλήρωμα τοῦ χρόνου] came, God sent forth His Son, born of woman, born under the law, to redeem those under the law, so that we might receive adoption as [God's] children. (Gal. 4:4–5)

---

[94] David Gay tells me that the word 'sponge' appears in scripture in the three accounts of the crucifixion alone, which suggests that this reading of the 'spunge' as a prolepsis of the cross may withstand scrutiny.

[95] David Gay, 'Astrology and Iconoclasm in Milton's *Paradise Regained*', *Studies in English Literature, 1500–1900*, 41 (2001), 186.

> In [Christ] we have redemption through his blood, the forgiveness of trespasses, according to the riches of his grace, which he lavished on us...which [God] purposed in [Christ] for the economy of the fullness of times [τοῦ πληρώματος τῶν καιρῶν]. (Eph. 1:7, 9–10)

De Doctrina Christiana uses the phrase in an identical sense when it asserts that 'REDEMPTION IS THAT WHEREBY...CHRIST, SENT IN THE FULLNESS OF TIMES [*IN PLENITUDINE TEMPORUM*], REDEEMS ALL THOSE BELIEVING, WHO ARE THOROUGHLY DISCHARGED AT THE PRICE OF HIS OWN VOLUNTARILY OFFERED BLOOD' (*CE* 15.252).[96] Satan's prescience stops short of Jesus's accession to an endless kingdom and can only foresee Jesus's death. Yet Satan is sure enough of his prediction to engender a tempest designed to give Jesus a foretaste of, and distaste for, his future sufferings.

Satan's storm is an elaborate *pièce de théâtre* charged with a foreboding of the Passion. Satan assaults Jesus's constitution externally and internally. Just as Satan once squatted like a toad at the slumbering Eve's ear and blew infections into her dreams (*PL* 4.799–803), so now the enemy, though 'Feigning to disappear' (4.397), watches at Jesus's head and 'with ugly dreams / Disturbd his sleep' (4.408–09). Satan compounds this psychic attack with a physical storm consisting of a chaotic confusion of elements, of rain, wind, lightning, thunder, and fire. He is aided by 'terrors dire' (4.431), the supernatural agency of 'Infernal Ghosts, and Hellish Furies' (4.422), that howl and shriek at Jesus to wear down his resolve. Despite this fiendish attrition and despite the fact that Jesus is sleepless and, 'After his aerie jaunt, though hurried sore, / Hungry and cold', his equanimity prevails 'with untroubl'd mind' (4.401–03). Jesus's passive obedience summons up Shakespeare's description of an unruffled, constant love, unaltered and unalterable, as 'an ever-fixèd mark / That looks on tempests and is never shaken' ('Sonnet 116' 5–6).[97] Jesus's attitude is supremely Passional. The narrator apostrophizes him, 'ill wast thou shrouded then, / O patient Son of God, yet onely stoodst / Unshak'n' (4.419–21), and his paramount epithet 'patient' is redolent of the cross.

The narrator further admires how 'thou / Sat'st unappalld in calm and sinless peace' (4.424–25). The negative epithets 'ill...shrouded' and 'unappalld' derive, respectively, from the burial shroud or linens and the pall or heavy cloth that covers a coffin. Jesus's endurance is conveyed in terms that evoke the preparation of his body for burial and entombment. An additional paradox corroborates Jesus's Passional stance. No sooner has Jesus 'betook him to his rest' (4.403) than Satan beleaguers him. We are informed that Jesus 'onely stoodst / Unshak'n' and then,

---

[96] Expounding Gal. 4:4–5, John Donne's 1625 Christmas sermon exegetes 'fullness of time' to incorporate Christ's entire life lived out in the shadow of his Passion:

> Onely to Christ Jesus, *the fulnesse of time* was at his birth; not because he also had not a painfull life to passe through, but because the work of our redemption was an intire work, and all that Christ said, or did, or suffered, concurred to our salvation, as well his mothers swathing him in little clouts, as *Iosephs* shrowding him in a funerall sheete; as well his cold lying in the Manger, as his cold dying upon the Crosse; as well the *puer natus*, as the *consummatum est*; as well his birth, as his death is said to have been *the fulnesse of time*. (Donne, *Sermons*, vol. 6, 333)

[97] Shakespeare, *Riverside*, 1864.

five lines later, that he 'Sat'st unappalld in calm and sinless peace'. How is this apparent contradiction to be resolved? The best solution may be that the quintessentially Miltonic heroic state of spiritually 'standing' beckons to Jesus's station upon the cross. Just as the seated Jesus 'onely stoodst / Unshak'n', adopting an inward Passional attitude, so in *Paradise Lost* the unfallen angels 'stand unshak'n, from within / Or from without' (*PL* 4.64–65). During the Heavenly War God's angels demonstrate saintly patience when they are bowled over by the rebel angels' cannonry such that 'none on thir feet might stand, / *Though standing else as Rocks*, but down they fell / By thousands, Angel on Arch-Angel rowld' (*PL* 6.592–94; emphasis added). Lancelot Andrewes similarly imagines Jesus's Agony experience as 'an internal cross, the passion of Gethsemane'.[98] In Milton's evocation of the patient Son braving the storm and being able to stand even while he sits, the Puritan poet foreshadows Christ's station upon the cross.

Satan's goal in executing these unearthly pyrotechnics is not merely to discourage Jesus from executing his redemptive mission with a staged rehearsal of the Passion. He also aims to impute the blame for Jesus's suffering to God. Although Satan concocts an alibi that during the storm he 'Was distant' (4.454), Jesus blasts this diabolic excuse out of the water, charging that these 'false portents [were] not sent from God, but thee' (4.491), and that Satan 'storm'st refus'd, thinking to terrifie / Mee to thy will' (4.496–97). Satan's description of the storm as a 'rack' (4.452) aligns the tempest with the crucifixion and anticipates the poem's showdown at the pinnacle. The primary sense of the word 'rack' conveys a storm, a mass of cloud driving before the wind (*OED*), but the word also connotes the idea of stretching, a meaning that even extends to the act of torturing. 'Rack' originates from the Old English *reccan* and the German *recken*, which mean 'to stretch' or 'strain'. In a domestic context the verbal noun conveys the action of drawing off wine or other liquor from the lees; in agriculture it denotes a trough used for animal fodder. Yet from 1447 John Holland, the fourth Duke of Exeter and the constable of the Tower of London, introduced the Recke or Rackbank, an instrument of torture that, in slang, was named 'the Duke of Exeter's daughter' or, more commonly, 'the rack'. A crucifix, a transverse frame of wood across which the condemned is stretched, resembles a rack. Early modern preachers clearly thought so. John Flavel drew this connection and in a sermon 'Of the Nature and Quality of Christ's Death' he preached, 'The cross was a rack as well as a gibbet.'[99] Lancelot Andrewes, too, diagnosed the pains the crucified Christ experienced: 'those are properly "straining pains, pains of torture." The rack is devised as a most exquisite pain, even for terror. And the cross is a rack, whereon He was stretched, till, saith the Psalm, all His bones were out of joint.'[100] Herbert's 'Christmas' exceeds the Christ-child's rude accommodation in a lowly manger and stable and envisions Jesus's heavenly glorification after his ignominious death. Herbert's persona wishes for

---

[98] Andrewes, 'Sermon 3'.

[99] John Flavel, *The Fountain of Life*, in *The Works of John Flavel*, vol. 1 (London, 1968), 322; see Sermon 26.

[100] Andrewes, 'Sermon 3'.

Jesus 'A better lodging then a rack or grave' (14).[101] So, too, in 'The Temper (1)'
Herbert's speaker identifies with his crucified Saviour's afflictions when he begs, 'O
rack me not to such a vast extent' (9). The speaker asks, 'Wilt thou meet arms with
man, that thou dost stretch / A crumme of dust from heav'n to hell?' (13–14).[102]
Just as Satan's *son et lumière* tempest adumbrates Jesus's forthcoming 'dangers, and
adversities and pains' (4.479), so the devil's talk of the storm as a 'rack' could be
pointing to that engine of State torture on Golgotha where Jesus's patience is tested
to its mortal limits.

VIII

Elsewhere I have suggested that the pinnacle episode functions as a kind of trap that
God primes for Satan with the bait of the Son's mysterious person.[103] Yet Milton
also loads the pinnacle scene with symbolic meaning. Milton fastidiously relates
Satan's transportation of Jesus from the wilderness to the topmost pinnacle of the
Hekal, that is, the Herodian Temple Mount. The poem's grammar conveys this
centralizing movement as it shifts from simple to comparative to superlative
epithets. Their flight telescopes from the 'Wilderness' and the 'Plain' to Jerusalem's
'high ... Towers,' to the 'pile' of the 'higher ... glorious Temple', to the 'highest
Pinnacle' atop the central shrine or Holy of Holies, 'appearing like a Mount / Of
Alablaster' (4.543–48). The Holy of Holies, which, in the case of the first and
second Jerusalemic Temples, housed the Mosaic Tablets of the Law within the Ark
of the Covenant, was a later, static form of the mobile Tabernacle that the Hebrews
brought with them to the Promised Land. According to ancient Hebrew lore, the
Ark stood at the world's navel. The Ark was flanked by the images of two sentinel
Cherubim and was crowned with a headpiece – *kapporeth* in Hebrew, *hilasterion* in
Greek, *gnadenstuhl* according to Luther, and the Mercy-seat according to William
Tyndale. Milton's deliberate alteration of the gospels, where Jesus teeters precari-
ously upon the Temple pinnacle instead of perching upon the *pterugion*, the
Temple's 'wing-tip' or cornice, makes of the poem's climactic scene a powerful
textual icon saturated with redemptive overtones. Readers have noted the ways in
which Milton shapes the pinnacle scene to resemble the crucifixion.[104] Northrop
Frye recognized that Jesus's station, poised above the Sanctuary, means that 'the

[101] Herbert, 81.   [102] Ibid. 55.
[103] See my '"O What a Mask Was There, What a Disguise!": The Mechanism of Satanic Defeat in
Paradise Regained', *Milton Studies*, 49 (2009), 167–91.
[104] For the most representative studies, see: Edward Cleveland, 'On the Identity Motive in *Paradise
Regained*', *Modern Language Quarterly*, 16 (1955), 232–36; Lewalski, *Brief Epic*, 312–21; Frye, *Five
Essays*, 149; William B. Hunter, Jr, 'The Obedience of Christ in *Paradise Regained*', in *Calm of Mind:
Tercentenary Essays on 'Paradise Regained' and 'Samson Agonistes'*, ed. Joseph A. Wittreich, Jr
(Cleveland, 1971), 235–57; Nelson, 80–100; Ira Clark, 'Christ on the Tower in *Paradise Regained*',
Milton Quarterly, 8 (1974), 104–07; Mary Wilson Carpenter, 'Milton's Secret Garden: Structural
Correspondences Between Michael's Prophecy and *Paradise Regained*', *Milton Studies*, 14 (1980),
153–82; Huttar, 236–60; MacCallum, *Sons of God*, 262–67; and James H. Sims, 'Jesus and Satan as
Readers of Scripture in *Paradise Regained*', *Milton Studies*, 32 (1995), 187–215.

centre of religion passes from the temple Christ is standing on into the Christian temple, the body of Christ above it'.[105] The reader can easily miss what Frye detects: the allegorical meaning of the Holy of Holies for seventeenth-century Puritan thought and Milton's condensation of spatial symbolism and the semantics of the atonement in Jesus's ultimate moment of endurance.

The Pauline writings interpret Jesus's person as a Tabernacle and construe his relation to God and the fallen world, covering, propitiating, and interceding for human sin, as the realization of the symbolic relationship between the Mercy-seat and the Ark. As the Mercy-seat covers the Ark, so God's mercy, embodied in Christ, covers divine justice and satisfies divine wrath (compare Exod. 25:17–22 with Heb. 9). The symbolic association between Christ and the Ark–Mercy-seat device intrigued Puritan thinkers.[106] Milton's early prose asserted that 'The whole ceremoniall law, and types can be in no law else, comprehends nothing but the propitiatory office of Christs Priesthood' (*CPW* 1.770–71). Even after the Temple's destruction the 'pattern and modell of the Temple', with its rites and ordinances, shadowed forth in Ezekiel's vision (Ezek. 40–48) the expectation of 'a new and more perfect reformation under Christ', albeit expressed in a 'typicall and shadowie' manner (*CPW* 1.756–57). Standard scriptural proof texts maintained that 'God set forth [Jesus] as a propitiation [ἱλαστήριον] through faith in his blood' (Rom. 3:25) and that Jesus 'is the propitiation [ἱλασμός] for our sins, and not only for our sins but also for the whole cosmos' (1 John 2:2). Milton may well have been contemplating the new covenant's re-evaluation of the old covenant's cultic symbolism of the Ark and Mercy-seat in his artistic programme to *The Reason of Church-Government*: 'to celebrate in glorious and lofty Hymns the throne and equipage of Gods Almightinesse, and what he works, and what he suffers to be wrought with high providence in his Church' (*CPW* 1.817).

Among Milton's contemporaries, Puritan luminaries expanded upon Christ's expiatory role as the fulfilment of the Mercy-seat device. John Norris, Peter Sterry, John Lightfoot, Thomas Godwyn, Thomas Taylor, John Smith, Henry More, Pilgram Marbeck, William Guild, Andrew Willet, and Samuel Mather represent only a handful of those Protestant theologians who invested in the conceit.[107]

---

[105] Frye, *Five Essays*, 151.

[106] For Milton's adoption of Temple symbolism, see Michael Lieb, *Poetics of the Holy: A Reading of 'Paradise Lost'* (Chapel Hill, 1981), especially chs 6 and 10. In *Samson Agonistes* Milton adapts the symbolic tearing of the Temple veil to elicit parallels between Samson and Christ. See my 'Grotius's *Christus Patiens* and Milton's *Samson Agonistes*', *The Explicator*, 65 (2006), 9–13.

[107] See, seriatim, John Norris, *Christian Blessedness* (London, 1690), 132–33; Peter Sterry, *Discourse*, 233–34; Sterry, *The Rise, Race, and Royalty of the Kingdom of God in the Soul of Man* (London, 1683), 381; John Lightfoot, *Horae Hebraicae Et Talmudicae*, vol. 3, ed. Robert Gandell (Oxford, 1859), 443–44; Lightfoot, *An Handfull of Gleanings out of the Book of Exodus* (London, 1643), 44–46; Thomas Godwyn, *Moses and Aaron* (London, 1634), 72–73; Thomas Taylor, *Christs Combate and Conquest* (Cambridge, 1618), 160–63; John Smith, *Select Discourses* (London, 1690), 324; Henry More, *An Explanation of the Grand Mystery of Godliness* (London, 1660), 292; More, *Divine Dialogues*, vol. 2 (London, 1668), 108–13; Pilgram Marbeck, 'Concerning the Lowliness of Christ' (1547), in *The Writings of Pilgram Marbeck*, trans. and ed. William Klassen and Walter Klaassen (Scottdale, 1978), 431 and 435–36; William Guild, *Moses Unvailed* (London, 1626), 100–03; Andrew Willet, *Hexapla: that is, a Six-Fold Commentarie vpon the Most Diuine Epistle of the*

Mather, for example, gives a comprehensive explanation of the symbolic relationship between the Ark and the Mercy-seat:

> The Hebrew word for [Mercy-seat] is *Capporeth*, from *Caphar*, to cover with Pitch, and in another Conjugation, to expiate, atone, appease. It implieth a merciful covering of our Sins. The Septuagint call it sometimes *hilasterion* [ἱλαστήριον]. a propitiatory Covering, and sometimes *epithema* [ἐπίθεμα], a Lid or Covering laid on. The Apostle applies it to the Blood of Christ, and the Satisfaction made thereby to the Justice of God for our Sins, *Rom.* 3.25. *1 John* 2.2 ... Here is the Law kept in this blessed Ark of the Covenant ... Therefore here is a Mercy-seat upon the Ark, a propitiatory Covering, in the passive Obedience of Jesus Christ, whereby he hath not only kept the Law, but satisfied for our breaking of it. Draw near to God in the Faith and Mediation of this Mystery.[108]

Peter Sterry, who served the Commonwealth at Whitehall alongside Milton, is characteristically more sublime:

> In the Holy of Holies was placed a Mercy-Seat all of Beaten Gold, the Throne of Grace, the Throne of Love. Out of this Throne of one piece with it, rose up two Cherubims of Beaten Gold. They stretched forth their Wings, they set their faces one to the other. They together looked down to the Mercy-Seat. This is the Heavenly Figure of your Christ, and you, O ye Children of Love, in your Love-Union, and Spiritual Communion. God in *Christ*, Christ in the Glory of the Father is the Golden Mercy-Seat, the Throne of Love.[109]

The Cambridge Platonist John Smith imagines the celestial significance of the device in the context of a heavenly theatre: 'Christ our true High priest is ascended up into the Holy of holies, and there in stead of the bloud of Bulls and Goats hath sprinkled the Ark and Mercy-seat above with his own bloud.'[110]

The textual culture of Reformation and post-Reformation England admitted magnificent illustrations of the Temple structure. In depicting the Tabernacle and the Temple, Protestants felt validated by scripture. God had sanctioned Moses to design the original Holy of Holies, the *mishkan* or portable Tabernacle in the desert, and had commissioned Israel's architect Bezaleel and his assistant Aholiab to construct it (Exod. 31:1–11). Thus William Tyndale interleaved eleven second-hand woodcuts, previously printed in a Flemish Bible, within his contraband translation of the *Pentateuch* of 1530. The woodcuts picture the Tabernacle furniture precisely as they are described in Exodus, and they would have helped to inculcate these divinely warranted forms upon the hearts and minds of England's pre-Reformation readers. The Geneva Bible of 1560 contains cartoons of the Tabernacle objects placed between the lines of the sacred text.[111] John Field, the

---

holy Apostle S. Paul to the Romanes (Cambridge, 1611), 169–70; Samuel Mather, *The Figures or Types of the Old Testament* (London, 1705), 406–12.

[108] Mather, *Figures*, 411–12.
[109] Sterry, *Rise*, 381.
[110] Smith, *Discourses*, 324.
[111] The 1560 Geneva Bible is pictorially spare and includes one other major woodcut, 'The Forme of the Temple and citie restored', interleaved within the Book of Ezekiel.

printer to Cambridge University's Press, decorated his popular 'Field' Bible with luxurious 'chorographical sculps' of the Herodian Temple designed by John Ogilby. One plate portrays the Temple Mount rising prominently above the Temple Complex, the vestibule and outer sanctum cocooning the inner Sanctuary. Another plate lays out the interior of the Holy of Holies, together with the Temple furniture, the candelabra, the table for shewbread, the altar of incense, and the Ark.[112] John Baptist Villalpandus and Jerome de Prado jointly composed a monumental three-volume commentary on Ezekiel's vision entitled *Explanations on Ezekiel and the Apparatus of the City and the Jerusalemic Temple* (1596–1604). The third volume contains illustrated reconstructions of the Temple Courts and the Holy of Holies with its sacred furniture. The royalist cleric Brian Walton incorporated Villalpandus and Prado's commentary and illustrations within the introductory first volume of his *Biblia Sacra Polyglotta* (1655–1657). Milton, acting in his capacity as censor and supported by the esteemed Christian Hebraist John Selden and the Archbishop of Armagh James Ussher, directly petitioned Parliament to assist Walton in his preparation of his polyglot Bible edition; he also sought permission for the importation of tax-free paper to aid Walton in the Bible's composition.[113] A wealth of textual material gave Milton ample opportunity to visualize the Herodian Temple Mount and accommodate it to the spectacular climax of his brief epic.

Sanford Budick has demonstrated how Jesus's supervenient position above the Holy of Holies bodies forth his mediatorial role, physically interposed between Heaven and Earth.[114] Before Satan transports Jesus to the Sanctuary he calls Jesus 'a Center' (4.534). Satan's naming of Jesus as 'a Center' and his placing of Jesus over the Holy of Holies, the cynosure of the Hebrew universe, are two actions that suggest that the Temple's significance as the *omphalos* or world's navel is transferred from the symbolic apparatus of the Ark and the Mercy-seat to Christ's actual incarnate person. Milton's reading of Josephus's *The Jewish War* and the *Mishnah* would have apprised him that the Ark and the Mercy-seat were absent from the Herodian Temple Sanctuary.[115] Josephus states explicitly, 'And absolutely nothing stood in [the inner sanctum], but it was inaccessible and inviolable and invisible to all; it was called the Holy of Holies.'[116] In Villalpandus and Prado's commentary Villalpandus disputes Josephus's observation concerning the Ark's absence:

> And accordingly, since Herod possessed neither the Ark of glory, nor the glory of God's presence, nor any remaining marvels, which were glorious portents from God: respecting which, if Christ had not come, nothing Herod made by the addition of gold or silver could have been comparable to this glory; not even if Herod had heaped

---

[112] *The Holy Bible*, vol. 1 (Cambridge, 1660). Ogilby's sculps appear between pages 102–03, 442–43, and 102–03.
[113] Lewalski, *Life*, 288 and 634 fn. 52.
[114] See Budick, 52–55, 68–69, and 142–48.
[115] See especially the section entitled *Middoth* or 'Measurements' in *The Mishnah*, trans. and ed. Herbert Danby (Oxford, 1992), 589–98; Josephus, *The Jewish War: Books IV–VII*, trans. H. St. J. Thackeray (Cambridge, Mass., 1968), 254–75; Book 5.184–237.
[116] Josephus, *Jewish War*, 266; Book 5.219.

up superior riches or more wealth than Solomon; because it would have been absolutely impossible.[117]

Suspended above the vacant Holy of Holies, Milton's Jesus is not only the propitiatory supplement for the present absence of the Ark–Mercy-seat array in the Herodian Sanctuary. He actually overcompensates for the absence of the sacred device by reifying or enacting, both now and not yet, the function of these symbols in his office as redeemer, expiator, and reconciler.

Noam Reisner has remarked how, as Milton's narrative progresses, the poem zones in upon the images of the Temple furniture and focuses them upon the figure of Jesus.[118] During the first temptation Jesus refers to his silencing of all oracles and his purpose as God's 'living Oracle', sent 'Into the World' (1.460–61). *The Oxford English Dictionary* indicates that from 1440 the word 'oracle' designates 'That part of the Jewish Temple where the divine presence was manifested; the holy of holies; also, the mercy-seat within it' (*OED* def. 3a). The opening lines of *Paradise Lost* thus indicate the Temple Sanctuary, since Siloa's brook flows 'Fast by the Oracle of God' (*PL* 1.12). Menahem Haran notes that the Tabernacle and Temple designs were constructed so that the layers of ingress towards the core of the holy structure, the Holy of Holies, were graded materially and ranked sociologically in 'concentric circles'.[119] Haran notes how 'In the focal point we find the *kapporet* with its cherubim, the holiness and the value of an object progressively diminishing with its distance therefrom.'[120] The arrangement is hierarchical and describes a sacred spatial order that increasingly excludes social strata as the devotee progresses further inwards. This sacral arrangement is most clearly demarcated in the architecture of the Temple complex where there are, *seriatim*, a Court of Women, a Court of Israelites, a Court of Priests, and a series of thirty-eight cells for the Priests. At the Temple's heart stands the Sanctuary, which is divided into the outer and inner sancta. Only the High Priest can pass through the inner sanctum, and even then he is only permitted to do so on the Day of Atonement when he enters the Holy of Holies to anoint the Mercy-seat with sacrificial blood.

Throughout *Paradise Regain'd* Satan's argument progresses through the Temple's graded order as Satan attempts to understand Jesus's significance. Satan first perversely compares himself with 'the Hypocrit or Atheous Priest' (1.487), a phrase that perhaps recollects the biblical priest Eli or one of his impious sons. Satan further compares Jesus with the altar standing in the Court of Priests

---

[117] Villalpandus and de Prado, *In Ezechielem Explanationes et Apparatus Urbis, ac Templi Hierosolymitani*, vol. 2 (Rome, 1604), 586 and 588: '*Josephus negat Arcam in templo Herodiano fuisse*'; '*Atque adeo cum Herodes neque Arcam gloriae habuerit, neque gloriam praesentiae Dei, aut reliqua miracula, quae Deo erant gloriosa: si in illud Christus non venisset, nihil ad huius gloriae collationem faceret Herodes addito auro, vel argento; etiamsi divitias superiores, aut plures coacervasset, quam Salomon; quod omnino impossibile fuit.*'

[118] Reisner interprets Jesus's attitude atop the pinnacle as 'a miraculous and paradoxically "non-skillful" *speech* act that already encodes the destruction of the structure on which he stands and its eventual re-edification in Christ's resurrected body' (178). See Reisner, 'Spiritual Architectonics: Destroying and Rebuilding the Temple in *Paradise Regained*', *Milton Quarterly*, 43 (2009), 166–82.

[119] Menahem Haran, *Temples and Temple-Service in Ancient Israel* (Oxford, 1978), 164–65.

[120] Ibid. 165.

and imagines himself in relation to the Son as 'tread[ing God's] Sacred Courts, and minister[ing] / About his Altar, handling holy things' (1.488–89). Later, Satan proceeds deeper within the Temple's spatial hierarchy. He portrays himself as the Aaronic High Priest wearing the coruscating *ephod* when he consults Jesus, whose wisdom is 'as the Oracle / *Urim* and *Thummim*, those oraculous gems / On *Aarons* brest' (3.13–15). Satan now figures himself as approaching the Ark and the Mercy-seat, since Aaron wore the breastplate before entering the Holy of Holies. However, Satan, whose violence against Jesus brings God's Son into an emblematic relation with the Temple Mount at the poem's close, never fully realizes Jesus's propitiatory mission and his embodiment of the Mercy-seat's function. The angels' final hymn celebrates this aspect of Jesus's saving work when they sing of their incarnate hero, 'remote from Heaven, enshrin'd / In fleshly Tabernacle, and human form, / Wandring the Wilderness' (4.598–600). The angels' words recall the exordium to John's gospel, where the incarnate Logos is 'the Word became flesh and tabernacled among us' (John 1:14). The Greek ἐσκήνωσεν or 'tabernacled' derives from σκηνή or 'tent'. Jesus becomes the portable Tabernacle, since he diffuses God's mercy through his mediatorial person and office. Henry More likewise reasoned, 'Christ was also ναὸς θεοῦ [God's sanctuary] in the most eminent manner imaginable: For in him dwelt the Godhead bodily.'[121]

Angels upraise Jesus from the pinnacle 'As on a floating couch' (4.585) in what Budick terms a reconstitution of 'the fixed Old Testament mercy seat . . . as a propitiatory "couch" without specified location'.[122] 'The redeemed image . . . is no longer localized and restricted in a particular place, but is made infinitely accessible in the mercy of Christ's intervention.'[123] Jesus's relief following his last stand upon the pinnacle parallels his exaltation following his last stand upon the cross. His 'uneasie station' (4.584) upon the pinnacle's point illustrates that his standing is, above all, a trial of withstanding. The other instance of the word 'uneasie' in Milton's major poetry expresses Satan's painful discomfiture as he picks his 'uneasie steps / Over the burning Marle' of Hell's floor (*PL* 1.295–96). Across *Paradise Lost* the word 'ease' and its cognates are Satanic terms that connote sloth, luxury, irresponsibility, negligence, apathy, and moral slackness. Thus the fallen angels slumber at their 'ease' (1.320); Belial counsels 'ignoble ease' (2.227) and 'the easie yoke / Of servil Pomp' (2.256–57); Beelzebub, acting as Satan's stooge, proposes the 'easier enterprize' (2.345) of unseating Earth's 'punie habitants' (2.367); Satan entices Sin and Death to prey upon Creation, there to 'dwell at ease' (2.841) and 'live at ease' (2.868); and Satan 'with ease / Wafts' his way to taint Eden (2.1041; see 3.563; 4.187). Satan sums up his nihilistic creed, 'For onely in destroying I finde ease' (9.129). 'Spirits perverse' pass between Hell and Earth on destructive errands 'With easie intercourse' (2.1030–31). Satan 'easily destroyd, and still destroyes' (3.301), humanity and, in *Paradise Regain'd*, preferring Earth's milder climate to Hell's, he winds his way to tempt Jesus with 'easie steps' (1.120). In Milton's moral universe acts of sinful disobedience and apostasy are always committed with ease, yet

---

[121] More, *Explanation*, 292.   [122] Budick, 52.   [123] Ibid. 69.

the Fall's effects are diseased and the remedy for sin is a trial of unease. To resist the Forbidden Fruit in Eden is 'this easie charge' (4.421) and 'One easie prohibition' (4.433), but, once Adam and Eve have transgressed, a world of woe is unleashed that only the Messiah can restore. Likewise, Sin misuses her key to Hell's gates and unfastens them 'with ease' (2.878) to free Satan. Hell's gates, though, once opened, 'to shut / Excelld [Sin's] power' (2.883–84). The Son alone can immure Satan, Sin, and Death and 'obstruct the mouth of Hell / For ever' (10.636–37).

The primary dictionary definitions of 'ease' are to relieve from pain and to disburden, lighten, or set free a person from a burden, pain, anxiety, or trouble (*OED* def. 1–5). For those creatures sustained or redeemed by grace, ease is a solace or relief. It is a quality of existence disburdened of sin. Satan imagines, but cannot fathom, a state of grace where one can honestly admit 'what burden then?' (*PL* 4.57). Fallen Adam conceives (or tries to) of God's wrath, 'That burden heavier then the Earth to bear' (*PL* 10.835). The redeeming Son is the solution to Satan's frustration and Adam's angst. Milton's Christ disentangles this semantic skein of ease, unease, and burdensomeness by assuming sin's load and satisfying God's anger so that a believer's yoke is easy and their burden light (Matt. 11:30).

Evidence abounds in British Renaissance verse for these relieving, restorative connotations of ease and unease. Ben Jonson's verse epistle 'To Heaven' laments sin's burden and implores grace when its speaker beseeches, 'Is it interpreted in me disease, / That, laden with my sins, I seek for ease?' (3–4).[124] Herbert's 'The Holy Communion' praises Christ, 'Thou hast restor'd us to this ease / By this thy heav'nly bloud' (37–38).[125] The fulcrum of Herbert's 'Iesu' is a pun that turns upon the interchangeability of the letters 'I' and 'j' in Renaissance typography, so that 'Iesu' accomplishes for the sinner an '*I ease you*' (9). In Herbert's 'The Crosse' the repentant devotee petitions his Creator to 'ease my smart' (31) with 'a crosse felt by thy Sonne' (35).[126] In Henry Vaughan's 'The Sap' the communicant imbibes Christ's 'balm' (44), his 'Cordial' (27) or heart-blood, and enjoys 'Such perfect Ease, and such a lively sense / Of grace against all sins' (47–48).[127] Milton's adaptation of the ease granted by redemption is fundamentally unchanged from his early occasional poem *Upon the Circumcision*, in which the Christ-child's first experience of pain prefigures Golgotha. The child, like the man, 'bleeds to give us ease' (11) and 'the full wrath beside / Of vengeful Justice bore for our excess' (23–24). Jesus's 'uneasie station' upon the pinnacle's tip is a stirring reminder that Messianic victory entails humiliation and that propitiation requires sacrifice. Milton therefore retraces and fulfils the semantics of the Ark–Mercy-seat apparatus renovated in Christ. The potent icon of Milton's Jesus, poised uneasily above the Sanctuary, anticipates and engages with the mystery of redemption, where Christ

---

[124] Ben Jonson, *The Complete Poems*, ed. George Parfitt (New Haven, 1975), 119.
[125] Herbert, 53.
[126] Ibid. 112 and 164.
[127] Henry Vaughan, *The Complete Poetry of Henry Vaughan*, ed. French Fogle (New York, 1965), 244.

covers Satan's destruction, Adam's sin, and God's justice, and proves that 'love covers a multitude of sins' (1 Pet. 4:8).

At the poem's close a 'meek', 'unobserv'd', and 'privat' Jesus returns to Mary's house after his ordeal. And yet he is simultaneously 'our Saviour' and 'Sung Victor' (4.636–39), since the Messianic victory at the Passion, rehearsed in Jesus's uneasy station at the pinnacle, stands for all time. Jesus re-enters a world of Satan, Sin, and Death to provide grace with the Passion already and not yet before him. Jesus's willing return to a sinful world resonates with Adam and Eve's reluctant departure from Eden in *Paradise Lost*'s final lines. Adam and Eve are disquieted by the prospect of entering a world plagued by Satan, Sin, and Death, but they are assuaged by prevenient grace and comforted that the promise of redemption lies already and not yet before them. In Milton's scrupulous Passion poem his theological poetics came full circle.

Regina Schwartz cautions readers to be more attentive to the issue of salvation in *Paradise Regain'd* and remarks how 'The vital connection between the person of Christ and work of Christ has not always been apparent to the Miltonists who have engaged in debates about the person of Jesus to the neglect of salvation.'[128] My concluding chapter has attempted to elucidate this 'vital connection' for Milton's brief epic. I have endeavoured to establish that *Paradise Regain'd* examines the nature of Messianic heroism and the Messianic mode of salvation. The qualities of altruistic endurance and patience communicate the substance of Milton's understanding of kingly values and are at the core of Milton's poetics. Scrutiny of the intricate shifts in debate and action throughout Jesus and Satan's spiritual duel indicates that the Passion is the poem's overwhelming concern. The poem's central interests are expressed by the patient heroism and obedience of Milton's Messiah, that 'one greater Man' (*PL* 1.4) who 'learned obedience from the things he suffered' (Heb. 5:8).[129]

---

[128] Regina M. Schwartz, 'Redemption and *Paradise Regained*', *Milton Studies*, 42 (2003), 29–30.

[129] The narrator of *Paradise Regain'd* honours Jesus as 'Saviour' or 'our Saviour' at least twenty times: *PR* 1.187, 406, 465, and 493; 2.283 and 338; 3.43, 121, 181, 266, 346, and 386; 4.25, 170, 285, 367, 401, 442, 615, and 636.

Conclusion: 'High Actions, and High Passions Best Describing'

I am moved by fancies that are curled
Around these images, and cling:
The notion of some infinitely gentle
Infinitely suffering thing.

T. S. Eliot, 'Preludes'

A true Critick ought to dwell rather upon Excellencies than Imperfections, to discover the concealed Beauties of a Writer, and communicate to the World such Things as are worth their Observation.

Joseph Addison[1]

Plunged into Hell's murk, the best that Satan's newly fallen angels can do in praise of the leader who has brought them to a state of sin and damnation is to parody the reverence that humans share for their redeemer. The epic voice describes the last vestiges of angelic goodness reflected in their misconceived applause:

> Nor faild they to express how much they prais'd,
> That for the general safety he [Satan] despis'd
> His own; for neither do the Spirits damnd
> Loose all thir vertue
>
> (PL 2.480–83)

Satan's show of altruism for 'the general safety' is characteristically a specious and invidious distortion of Christ's vicarious atonement. In early modern English the word 'Safety', which is nowadays a rather bloodless noun, signified, from its Latin root *salvus*, the 'Salvation (of the soul)' (*OED* def. 1b). Though the fallen angels extol Satan as their deliverer and saviour, he has already been the agent of their damnation. The fiend's supposedly magnanimous voyage, a mission of so-called liberation, is an offensive that is hell-bent on the destruction, rather than the salvation, of the Earth and its inhabitants. Satan's conquest of Paradise secures for himself and his subjects only a brief respite and a temporary dominion, and works for Hell's inhabitants a further damnation of devil with devil damned.

---

[1] Steele and Addison, 423.

The main purpose of this study has been to demonstrate that an appreciation of the myriad ways in which Milton expresses his esteem for the atonement and 'the general safety' for humankind that the atonement brings constitutes the right handle with which to take hold of the bundle of his manifold poetry. To paraphrase the words of Joseph Addison above, this study has attempted to show that Milton's treatment of the redemption is the true excellence of his poetry and the flower of his theology. A reading that depreciates the importance of redemptive theology for Milton's thought will remain partial and incomplete. Readers inclined to discount or diminish the importance of the cross in Milton's poetic or who mistake the form that Milton's imaginative treatment of the redemption takes may find themselves, like Milton's fallen angels, philosophically disoriented or imprisoned in epistemological obscurity, in wandering mazes lost. This kind of reading inevitably comes up against a hermeneutic impasse. Long before Milton pictured Jesus explaining to Satan that fallen and insufficient man is 'Degraded by himself, on Grace depending' (*PR* 4.312), the twenty-six-year-old poet had encapsulated, in the closing lines of *A Maske Presented At Ludlow-Castle*, the great moral argument existing at the heart of his evolving corpus of verse. Between the lines of the Attendant Spirit's counsel Milton's reader can construe the familiar Protestant assurance that human 'Vertue', though 'feeble' or incapable of its own salvation, relies entirely upon the supernatural assistance of its redeemer, ever blessed. Only a hero who stoops to succour a fallen Earth and endures his humiliation and afflictions high could finally merit the exaltation he secures for those faithful perseverers who would believe in him:

> Mortals that would follow me,
> Love vertue, she alone is free,
> She can teach ye how to clime
> Higher then the Spheary chime;
> Or if Vertue feeble were,
> Heav'n it self would stoop to her.
>   (1018–23)

Bibliography

MILTON EDITIONS

Bentley, Richard, ed., *Milton's 'Paradise Lost'* (New York, 1974).

Darbishire, Helen, ed., *The Poetical Works of John Milton* (London, 1958).

Fowler, Alastair, ed., *Paradise Lost* (2nd edn, Harlow, 1998).

French, J. Milton, *Life Records of John Milton*, 5 vols (New Brunswick, 1949–58).

Hughes, Merritt Y., ed., *John Milton: Complete Poems and Major Prose* (New York, 1957).

Hume, Patrick, ed., *The Poetical Works of Mr. John Milton* (London, 1695).

Newton, Thomas, ed., *Paradise Lost: A Poem, in Twelve Books*, 2 vols (London, 1749).

Patterson, Frank A., *et al.*, eds, *The Works of John Milton*, 18 vols (New York, 1931–38).

Richardson, Jonathan, Jr and Sr, eds, *Explanatory Notes and Remarks on Milton's 'Paradise Lost'* (London, 1734).

Todd, Henry J., ed., *The Poetical Works of John Milton*, 7 vols (2nd edn, London, 1809).

Tonson, Jacob, ed., *Paradise Lost: A Poem, in Twelve Books* (London, 1688).

Williams, Charles, ed., *The English Poems of John Milton* (Oxford, 1940).

Wolfe, Don M., *et al.*, eds, *Complete Prose Works of John Milton*, 8 vols (New Haven, 1953–82).

PRIMARY SOURCES

Andrewes, Lancelot, *The Sermons of Lancelot Andrewes*, ed. Marianne Dorman, 2 vols (Edinburgh, 1992–93).

—— *Works, Sermons, Volume Two*, ed. Marianne Dorman (Project Canterbury, Library of Anglo-Catholic Theology; published online 2001–03) ⟨http.//anglicanhistory.org/lact/andrewes/v2/passion1605.html⟩ accessed 21 Nov. 2009.

Anselm, '*Cur Deus Homo*', in *Florilegium Patristicum*, ed. Bernard Geyer and John Zellinger, vol. 18 (Bonn, 1929), 1–65.

Aquinas, Thomas, *Summa Theologiae*, gen. ed. Thomas Gilby and S. F. Parmisano, 61 vols (London, 1964–81).

Ariosto, Ludovico, *Orlando Furioso*, trans. Guido Waldman (Oxford, 1974).

Aristotle, *The Physics*, trans. Philip H. Wicksteed and Francis M. Cornford, 2 vols (London, 1929).

Augustine, *Confessions*, trans. William Watts, 2 vols (London, 1918).

—— *Enarrationes in Psalmos*, ed. D. Eligius Dekkers and Johannes Fraipont, *Corpus Christianorum*, vol. 38–40 (Turnhout, 1956).

—— *Opera Omnia*, 11 vols (2nd edn, Paris, 1836–38).

—— *Sermons*, trans. Edmund Hill, ed. John E. Rotelle, 11 vols (Hyde Park, 1990–97).

—— *The Writings against the Manichaeans, and against the Donatists*, NPNF, vol. 4 (Peabody, 2004).

Bacon, Francis, *The Essayes or Counsels, Civill and Morall*, ed. Michael Kiernan (Oxford, 1985).

Biblia Sacra iuxta Vulgatam Versionem, ed. Robert Weber, 2 vols (Stuttgart, 1969).

Biddle, John, *A Twofold Catechism* (London, 1654).

Blake, William, *The Poems of William Blake*, ed. W. H. Stevenson and David V. Erdman (London, 1971).

The Book of Common Prayer (Cambridge, 1968).

Browne, Thomas, *Religio Medici*, ed. W. Murison (Cambridge, 1922).

Calvin, John, *Calvin's Commentaries: The Gospel according to St. John*, trans. T. H. L. Parker, ed. David W. Torrance and Thomas F. Torrance (Edinburgh, 1959).

——*Institutes of the Christian Religion*, ed. John T. McNeill and Ford Lewis Battles, 2 vols (Philadelphia, 1960), 282.

Cheynell, Francis, *The Christian Belief* (London, 1696).

Chrysostom, John, *Homilies on the Gospel of Saint John and the Epistle to the Hebrews*, ed. Philip Schaff (Peabody, 2004).

Coleridge, Samuel Taylor, *Aids to Reflection*, ed. John Beer (London, 1993).

Corpus Christianorum, Series Latina, 176 vols (Turnhout, 1954–65).

The Coverdale Bible (1535), ed. S. L. Greenslade (Folkestone, 1975).

[Culpeper, Nicholas] *Treatise of Aurum Potabile, Being A Description of The Three-fold World Viz. Elimentary, Celestiall, Intellectual* (London, 1656).

Donne, John, *The Complete Poetry and Selected Prose of John Donne*, ed. Charles M. Coffin (New York, 2001).

——*Devotions Upon Emergent Occasions*, ed. Anthony Raspa (London, 1975).

——*The Divine Poems*, ed. Helen Gardner (Oxford, 1969).

——*The Sermons of John Donne*, ed. George R. Potter and Evelyn M. Simpson, 10 vols (Berkeley, 1953–62).

Douglas, J. D., ed., *The New Greek–English Interlinear New Testament*, trans. Robert K. Brown and Philip W. Comfort (Wheaton, 1990).

The Early Lives of Milton, ed. Helen Darbishire (London, 1932).

Eliot, T. S., *Collected Poems, 1909–1962* (London, 1963).

Flavel, John, *The Works of John Flavel*, 6 vols (London, 1968).

Fletcher, Giles and Phineas, *Poetical Works*, ed. Frederick S. Boas, 2 vols (Cambridge, 1970).

Gillespie, Patrick, *The Ark of the Couenant Opened* (London, 1677).

Godwyn, Thomas, *Moses and Aaron* (London, 1634).

Goodwin, Thomas, *A Childe of Light Walking in Darknes* (London, 1638).

Greenham, Richard, *Workes* (London, 1605).

Gregory of Nazianzus, *La Passion du Christ: Tragédie*, trans. and ed. André Tuilier (Paris, 1969).

Gregory the Great, *Morals on the Book of Job*, 3 vols (Oxford, 1844–47).

Grotius, Hugo, *Adamus Exul*, in *The Celestial Cycle*, trans. and ed. Watson Kirkconnell (New York, 1967), 96–220.

——*Christus Patiens* (Leiden, 1608).

Guild, William, *Moses Unuailed* (London, 1626).

Herbert, George, *The Works of George Herbert*, ed. F. E. Hutchinson (Oxford, 1941).

Herrick, Robert, *Poems*, ed. L. C. Martin (London, 1971).

Hill, Geoffrey, *Canaan* (London, 1996).

Hobbes, Thomas, *Behemoth* (London, 1679).

——*Leviathan*, ed. Edwin Curley (Indianapolis, 1994).

The Holy Bible, 2 vols (Cambridge, 1660).

Homer, *Opera*, ed. David B. Monro and Thomas W. Allen, 5 vols (Oxford, 1966–69).

Hopkins, Gerard Manley, *Poetry and Prose*, ed. Walford Davies (London, 1998).

Hutchinson, Lucy, *Order and Disorder*, ed. David Norbrook (Oxford, 2001).

Isidore of Seville, *Etymologiarum Sive Originum Libri XX*, ed. W. M. Lindsay, 2 vols (Oxford, 1985).

Jackson, Thomas, *A Treatise of the Divine Essence and Attributes* (London, 1628).

Jerome, *Select Letters of St. Jerome*, trans. F. A. Wright (London, 1975).

Johnson, Samuel, *Lives of the English Poets*, ed. George Birkbeck Hill, 3 vols (Oxford, 1905).

Jonson, Ben, *The Complete Poems*, ed. George Parfitt (New Haven, 1975).

Josephus, *Works*, trans. H. St. J. Thackeray, Ralph Marcus, Allen Wickgren, and Louis H. Feldman, 9 vols (Cambridge, Mass., 1926–65).

Justin Martyr, *Writings of Saint Justin Martyr*, trans. Thomas B. Falls (Washington, DC, 1948).

Kierkegaard, Søren, *Fear and Trembling*, trans. Alastair Hannay (Harmondsworth, 1985).

—— *The Point of View on My Work as an Author; The Point of View for My Work as an Author; Armed Neutrality*, ed. and trans. Howard V. Hong and Edna H. Hong (Princeton, 1998).

—— *Works of Love*, trans. Howard V. Hong and Edna H. Hong (Princeton, 1995).

The King James Version of 1611: Standard Text Edition (Cambridge, 1992).

Lanyer, Aemilia, *The Poems of Aemilia Lanyer*, ed. Susanne Woods (Oxford, 1993).

Lawrence, Henry, *An History of Angells* (London, 1649).

Lewis, Charlton T., and Charles Short, *Latin Dictionary* (Oxford, 1879).

Lightfoot, John, *Erubhin or Miscellanies Christian and Judaicall, and Others* (London, 1629).

—— *An Handfull of Gleanings out of the Book of Exodus* (London, 1643).

—— *Horae Hebraicae Et Talmudicae*, ed. Robert Gandell, 4 vols (Oxford, 1859).

Lobb, Stephen, *A Report of the Present State of the Differences in Doctrinals* (London, 1697).

Luther, Martin, *Lectures on Genesis: Chapters 26–30*, ed. Jaroslav Pelikan (Saint Louis, 1968).

Marbeck, Pilgram, *The Writings of Pilgram Marbeck*, trans. and ed. William Klassen and Walter Klaassen (Scottdale, 1978).

Mather, Samuel, *The Figures or Types of the Old Testament* (2nd edn, London, 1705).

Mirandola, Giovanni Pico della, *Oration on the Dignity of Man*, trans. A. Robert Caponigri, (Washington, DC, 1956).

The Mishnah, trans. Herbert Danby (Oxford, 1992).

More, Henry, *Divine Dialogues*, 2 vols (London, 1668).

—— *An Explanation of the Grand Mystery of Godliness* (London, 1660).

Norris, John, *Christian Blessedness* (London, 1690).

Norton, John, *A Discussion of that Great Point in Divinity, the Suffering of Christ* (London, 1653).

Owen, John, *Vindiciae Evangelicae* (Oxford, 1655).

The Oxford Book of English Verse: 1250–1900, ed. Arthur Quiller-Couch (Oxford, 1900).

The Oxford English Dictionary, ed. J. A. Simpson and E. S. C. Weiner, 20 vols (2nd edn, Oxford, 1989).

Patrologiae Cursus Completus, Serie Graeca, ed. J. P. Migne, 161 vols (Paris, 1857–66).

Plato, *Euthyphro; Apology; Crito; Phaedo; Phaedrus*, ed. Jeffrey Henderson, trans. Harold North Fowler (London, 2001).

—— *Lysis; Symposium; Gorgias*, trans. W. R. M. Lamb (London, 1983).

—— *The Republic*, trans. Paul Shorey, 2 vols (London, 1963).

Prado, Jerome de, and John Baptista Villalpandus, *In Ezechielem Explanationes et Apparatus Urbis, ac Templi Hierosolymitani*, 3 vols (Rome, 1596–1604).

Quintilian, *Institutio Oratoria*, trans. H. E. Butler, 4 vols (London, 1953).

The Racovian Catechisme (Amsterdam, 1652).

Reuchlin, John, *De Rudimentis Hebraicis* (Pforzheim, 1506).

Shakespeare, William, *The Riverside Shakespeare*, ed. G. Blakemore Evans and J. J. M. Tobin (2nd edn, Boston, 1997).

Sidney, Sir Philip, 'The Defence of Poesy', in *Sir Philip Sidney*, ed. Katherine Duncan-Jones (Oxford, 1989), 212–50.

Smith, Henry, *Satans Compassing the Earth* (London, 1592).

Smith, John, *Select Discourses* (London, 1690).

Spenser, Edmund, *The Faerie Queene*, ed. A. C. Hamilton (2nd edn, Harlow, 2007).

Sterry, Peter, *A Discourse of the Freedom of the Will* (London, 1675).

—— *The Rise, Race, and Royalty of the Kingdom of God in the Soul of Man* (London, 1683).

Suetonius, *Suetonius*, trans. J. C. Rolfe, 2 vols (London, 1989).

Tasso, Torquato, *Discorsi Dell' Arte Poetica e Del Poema Eroico*, ed. Luigi Poma (Bari, 1964).

——*Jerusalem Delivered; Gerusalemme Liberata*, ed. and trans. Anthony M. Esolen (Baltimore, 2000).

Taylor, Thomas, *Christs Combate and Conquest* (Cambridge, 1618).

——*Christ Revealed: or The Old Testament Explained* (London, 1635).

Tertullian, *Adversus Praxean Liber*, ed. and trans. Ernest Evans (London, 1948).

——*De Praescriptione Haereticorum Ad Martyras: Ad Scapulam*, ed. T. Herbert Bindley (Oxford, 1893).

——*De Resurrectione Carnis Liber*, ed. and trans. Ernest Evans (London, 1960).

Toland, John, *Christianity not Mysterious* (London, 1702).

Vaughan, Henry, *The Complete Poetry of Henry Vaughan*, ed. French Fogle (New York, 1965).

Vida, Marco Girolamo, *The Christiad*, ed. and trans. Gertrude C. Drake and Clarence A. Forbes (Edwardsville, 1978).

Virgil, *Eclogues; Georgics; Aeneid I–VI*, trans. H. Rushton Fairclough, ed. G. P. Goold (London, 1999).

——*Aeneid VII–XII*, trans. H. Rushton Fairclough, ed. G. P. Goold (London, 2000).

Voltaire, *Zadig and Other Stories*, ed. H. T. Mason (Oxford, 1971).

Willet, Andrew, *Hexapla in Genesin* (Cambridge, 1605).

——*Hexapla: that is, a Six-Fold Commentarie vpon the Most Diuine Epistle of the holy Apostle S. Paul to the Romanes* (Cambridge, 1611).

Williams, Griffith, *Seven Goulden Candlesticks* (London, 1624).

SECONDARY SOURCES

Achinstein, Sharon, *Literature and Dissent in Milton's England* (Cambridge, 2003).

——'Toleration in Milton's Epics: A Chimera?', in *Milton and Toleration*, ed. Sharon Achinstein and Elizabeth Sauer (Oxford, 2007), 224–42.

Allen, Don Cameron, 'Two Notes on *Paradise Lost*', *Modern Language Notes*, 68 (1953), 360–61.

Altizer, Thomas J. J., *The Contemporary Jesus* (Albany, 1997).

Angelo, Peter Gregory, *Fall to Glory: Theological Reflections on Milton's Epics* (New York, 1987).

Anon., 'Milton on *Christian Doctrine*', *The Eclectic Review*, 25 (1826), 1–18.

Bauman, Michael, *Milton's Arianism* (Frankfurt, 1987).

Bell, Millicent, 'The Fallacy of the Fall in *Paradise Lost*', *PMLA*, 68 (1953), 863–83.

Bennett, Joan S., *Reviving Liberty: Radical Christian Humanism in Milton's Great Poems* (Cambridge, Mass., 1989).

Borris, Kenneth, *Allegory and Epic in English Renaissance Literature: Heroic Form in Sidney, Spenser, and Milton* (Cambridge, 2000).

——'Allegory in *Paradise Lost*: Satan's Cosmic Journey', *Milton Studies*, 26 (1990), 101–33.

——'Milton's Heterodoxy of the Incarnation and Subjectivity in *De Doctrina Christiana* and *Paradise Lost*', in *Living Texts: Interpreting Milton*, ed. Kristin A. Pruitt and Charles W. Durham (London, 2000), 264–82.

——'Union of Mind or in Both One Soul: Allegories of Adam and Eve in *Paradise Lost*', *Milton Studies*, 31 (1995), 45–72.

Brisman, Leslie, *The Voice of Jacob: On the Composition of Genesis* (Bloomington, 1990).

Broadbent, J.B., *'Some Graver Subject': An Essay on 'Paradise Lost'* (London, 1960).

Bryson, Michael, *The Tyranny of Heaven: Milton's Rejection of God as King* (Newark, 2004).

Budick, Sanford, *The Dividing Muse: Images of Sacred Disjunction in Milton's Poetry* (New Haven, 1985).

Campbell, Gordon, 'The Mortalist Heresy in *Paradise Lost*', *Milton Quarterly*, 13 (1979), 33–36.

——'The Son of God in *De Doctrina Christiana* and *Paradise Lost*', *Modern Language Review*, 75 (1980), 507–14.

——and Corns, Thomas N., John K. Hale, David I. Holmes, and Fiona J. Tweedie, 'The Provenance of *De Doctrina Christiana*', *Milton Quarterly*, 31 (1997), 67–117.

——and Corns, Thomas N., John K. Hale, and Fiona J. Tweedie, *Milton and the Manuscript of 'De Doctrina Christiana'* (Oxford, 2007).

Canfield, J. Douglas, 'Blessed are the Merciful: The Understanding of the Promise in *Paradise Lost*', *Milton Quarterly*, 7 (1973), 43–47.

Carey, John, *Milton* (London, 1976).

Carpenter, Mary Wilson, 'Milton's Secret Garden: Structural Correspondences between Michael's Prophecy and *Paradise Regained*', *Milton Studies*, 14 (1980), 153–82.

Chadwick, Owen, *The Penguin History of the Church: Volume Three: The Reformation* (London, 1990).

Chaplin, Gregory, 'Beyond Sacrifice: Milton and the Atonement', *PMLA*, 125 (2010), 354–69.

Christopher, Georgia B., *Milton and the Science of the Saints* (Princeton, 1982).

Clark, Ira, 'Christ on the Tower in *Paradise Regained*', *Milton Quarterly*, 8 (1974), 104–07.

Cleveland, Edward, 'On the Identity Motive in *Paradise Regained*', *Modern Language Quarterly*, 16 (1955), 232–36.

Cope, Jackson I., *The Metaphoric Structure of 'Paradise Lost'* (Baltimore, 1962).

Council, Norman, '"Answering His Great Idea": The Fiction of *Paradise Lost*', *Milton Studies*, 32 (1996), 45–62.

Coward, Barry, *Oliver Cromwell* (London, 1991).

Crump, Gilbraith Miller, *The Mystical Design of 'Paradise Lost'* (Lewisburg, 1975).

Danielson, Dennis, 'Milton, Bunyan, and the Clothing of Truth and Righteousness', in *Heirs of Fame: Milton and Writers of the English Renaissance*, ed. Margo Swiss and David A. Kent (Lewisburg, 1995), 247–69.

——*Milton's Good God: A Study in Literary Theodicy* (Cambridge, 1982).

——'Through the Telescope of Typology: What Adam Should Have Done', *Milton Quarterly*, 23 (1989), 121–27.

Davies, Brian, *The Thought of Thomas Aquinas* (Oxford, 1993).

Davies, Stevie, *Images of Kingship in 'Paradise Lost': Milton's Politics and Christian Liberty* (Columbia, 1983).

——and William B. Hunter, Jr, 'Milton's Urania: "The Meaning, Not the Name I Call"', *Studies in English Literature, 1500–1900*, 28 (1988), 95–111.

Dean, Margaret Justice, 'Choosing Death: Adam's Temptation to Martyrdom in *Paradise Lost*', *Milton Studies*, 46 (2007), 30–56.

Diekhoff, John S., *Milton's 'Paradise Lost': A Commentary on the Argument* (London, 1958).

Doerksen, Daniel W., '"Let There Be Peace": Eve as Redemptive Peacemaker in *Paradise Lost*, Book X', *Milton Quarterly*, 31 (1997), 124–29.

Donahue, John R., and Daniel J. Harrington, eds, *The Gospel of Mark* (Collegeville, 2002).

Donnelly, Phillip J., '*Paradise Regained* as Rule of Charity: Religious Toleration and the End of Typology', *Milton Studies*, 43 (2004), 171–97.

Duncan, Joseph E., *Milton's Earthly Paradise: A Historical Study of Eden* (Minneapolis, 1972).

Dzelzainis, Martin, 'Milton and Antitrinitarianism', *Milton and Toleration*, 171–85.

Empson, William, *Milton's God* (Cambridge, 1981).

Entzminger, Robert L., *Divine Word: Milton and the Redemption of Language* (Pittsburgh, 1985).

Esolen, Anthony, *Ironies of Faith: The Laughter at the Heart of Christian Literature* (Wilmington, 2007).

Evans, John Martin, *The Miltonic Moment* (Lexington, 1998).

—— *'Paradise Lost' and the Genesis Tradition* (Oxford, 1968).

Fallon, Stephen M., *Milton among the Philosophers: Poetry and Materialism in Seventeenth-Century England* (Ithaca, 1991).

—— *Milton's Peculiar Grace: Self-Representation and Authority* (Ithaca, 2007).

—— 'Milton's Sin and Death: The Ontology of Allegory in *Paradise Lost*', *English Literary Renaissance*, 17 (1987), 329–50.

Farrer, Austin, *The Triple Victory: Christ's Temptations according to Saint Matthew* (London, 1965).

Ferry, Anne, *Milton's Epic Voice: The Narrator in 'Paradise Lost'* (Chicago, 1983).

Finaldi, Gabriele, *The Image of Christ: The Catalogue of the Exhibition Seeing Salvation* (London, 2000).

Fish, Stanley E., *How Milton Works* (Cambridge, Mass., 2001).

—— *Surprised by Sin: The Reader in 'Paradise Lost'* (London, 1967).

—— 'Why Milton Matters; Or, Against Historicism', *Milton Studies*, 44 (2005), 1–12.

Flannagan, Roy, 'Reflections on Milton and Ariosto', *Early Modern Literary Studies*, 2.3 (1996), 4.1–16 (published online 16 Dec. 1996) <http://purl.oclc.org/emls/02–3/flan-milt.html> accessed 21 Nov. 2009.

Fleming, James Dougal, *Milton's Secrecy and Philosophical Hermeneutics* (Aldershot, 2008).

Fletcher, Angus, *The Transcendental Masque: An Essay on Milton's Comus* (London, 1971).

Forsyth, Neil, *The Satanic Epic* (Princeton, 2003).

Freeman, James A., *Milton and the Martial Muse: 'Paradise Lost' and European Traditions of War* (Princeton, 1980).

Fresch, Cheryl H., '"Whither thou goest": Paradise Lost XII, 610–23 and the Book of Ruth', *Milton Studies*, 32 (1995), 111–30.

Frye, Northrop, *Five Essays on Milton's Epics* (London, 1966).

Frye, Roland Mushat, *God, Man, and Satan: Patterns of Christian Thought and Life in 'Paradise Lost', 'Pilgrim's Progress', and the Great Theologians* (London, 1960).

Gallagher, Philip J., *Milton, the Bible, and Misogyny*, ed. Eugene R. Cunnar and Gail L. Mortimer (Columbia, 1990).

Gardner, Helen, *A Reading of 'Paradise Lost'* (Oxford, 1965).

Gay, David, *The Endless Kingdom: Milton's Scriptural Society* (Newark, 2002).

Giamatti, A. Bartlett, *The Earthly Paradise and the Renaissance Epic* (Princeton, 1966).

Goldberg, Jonathan, '*Virga Iesse*: Analogy, Typology, and Anagogy in Milton's Simile', *Milton Studies*, 5 (1973), 177–90.

Greenlaw, Edwin, 'A Better Teacher than Aquinas', *Studies in Philology*, 15 (1917), 196–217.

Gregg, Robert C., and Dennis E. Groh, *Early Arianism – A View of Salvation* (London, 1981).

Grossman, Marshall, '*Authors to Themselves*': *Milton and the Revelation of History* (Cambridge, 1987).

——'"In Pensive trance, and anguish, and ecstatic fit": Milton on the Passion', in *A Fine Tuning: Studies of the Religious Poetry of Herbert and Milton*, ed. Mary A. Maleski (Binghamton, 1989), 205–20.

Haller, William, *The Rise of Puritanism* (New York, 1938).

Hamlet, Desmond M., *One Greater Man: Justice and Damnation in 'Paradise Lost'* (Lewisburg, 1976).

——'Recalcitrance, Damnation, and the Justice of God in *Paradise Lost*', *Milton Studies*, 8 (1976), 266–91.

Hanford, James Holly, 'The Temptation Motive in Milton', *Studies in Philology*, 15 (1918), 176–94.

Haran, Menahem, *Temples and Temple-Service in Ancient Israel* (Oxford, 1978).

Harnack, Adolf, *The Apostles' Creed*, trans. Rev. Stewart Means, ed. Thomas Bailey Saunders (London, 1901).

Haskin, Dayton, 'Milton's Portrait of Mary as a Bearer of the Word', in *Milton and the Idea of Woman*, ed. Julia M. Walker (Urbana, 1988), 169–84.

Heale, Elizabeth, *The Faerie Queene: A Reader's Guide* (2nd edn, Cambridge, 1999).

Hengel, Martin, 'Christological Titles in Early Christianity', in *The Messiah: Developments in Earliest Judaism and Christianity*, ed. James H. Charlesworth (Minneapolis, 1992), 425–48.

Henriksen, Erin, *Milton and the Reformation Aesthetics of the Passion* (Leiden, 2009).

Hillier, Russell M., '"Betwixt Astrea and the Scorpion Signe": The Conjunction of Astrology and Apocalyptic in Milton's Psychostasis', *The Cambridge Quarterly*, 37 (2008), 305–23.

——'Spatial Allegory and Creation Old and New in Milton's Hexaemeral Narrative', *Studies in English Literature, 1500–1900*, 49 (2009), 121–43.

——'"By Force or Fraud Weening to prosper": Milton's Satanic and Messianic Modes of Heroism', *Milton Quarterly*, 43 (2009), 17–38.

——'The Good Communicated: Milton's Drama of the Fall and the Law of Charity', *Modern Language Review*, 103 (2008), 1–21.

——'Grotius's *Christus Patiens* and Milton's *Samson Agonistes*', *The Explicator*, 65 (2006), 9–13.

——'Milton's Dantean Miniatures: Inflections of Dante's *Inferno* and *Purgatorio* within the Cosmos of *Paradise Lost*', *Notes and Queries*, 56 (2009), 215–19.

——'Milton's "Genial Angel": The Identity and Salvific Office of the Son in Adam's Narrative of Creation and Recreation', *Studies in Philology*, 107 (2010), 366–400.

——'Milton's *Paradise Regain'd* and Herbert's "Love (3)"', *The Explicator*, 66 (2007), 4–9.

——'"O What a Mask Was There, What a Disguise!": The Mechanism of Satanic Defeat in *Paradise Regained*', *Milton Studies*, 49 (2009), 167–91.

——'The Patience to Prevent that Murmur: The Theodicy of John Milton's Nineteenth Sonnet', *Renascence*, 59 (2007), 247–73.

——'To Say it With Flowers: Milton's "Immortal Amarant" Reconsidered (*Paradise Lost* III.349–61)', *Notes and Queries*, 54 (2007), 404–08.

——'Two Patristic Sources for John Milton's Description of the Sun (*Paradise Lost* III.591–95)', *Notes and Queries*, 53 (2006), 185–87.

—— 'The Wreath, the Rock, and the Winepress: Passion Iconography in Milton's *Paradise Regain'd*', *Literature and Theology*, 22 (2008), 387–405.

Holland, Glenn S., *Divine Irony* (London, 2000).

Hughes, Merritt Y., 'Milton's Limbo of Vanity', in *Th' Upright Heart and Pure: Essays on John Milton Commemorating the Tercentenary of the Publication of 'Paradise Lost'*, ed. Amadeus P. Fiore (Pittsburgh, 1967), 7–24.

—— ' "Myself Am Hell" ', *Modern Philology*, 54 (1956), 80–94.

Hunter, Jr, William B., 'The Heresies of Satan', in *Th' Upright Heart and Pure*, 25–34.

—— 'The Obedience of Christ in *Paradise Regained*', in *Calm of Mind: Tercentenary Essays on 'Paradise Regained' and 'Samson Agonistes'*, ed. Joseph A. Wittreich, Jr (Cleveland, 1971), 235–57.

—— *Visitation Unimplor'd: Milton and the Authorship of 'De Doctrina Christiana'* (Pittsburgh, 1998).

—— and J. H. Adamson, and C. A. Patrides, eds, *Bright Essence: Studies in Milton's Theology* (Salt Lake City, 1971).

Huttar, Charles A., 'The Passion of Christ in *Paradise Regained*', *English Language Notes*, 19 (1982), 236–60.

Ide, Richard S., 'On the Begetting of the Son in *Paradise Lost*', *Studies in English Literature, 1500–1900*, 24 (1984), 141–55.

Isitt, Larry R., *All the Names in Heaven: A Reference Guide to Milton's Supernatural Names and Epic Similes* (London, 2002).

Juel, D. H., 'The Origin of Mark's Christology', in *The Messiah*, 449–60.

Kaske, Carol V., 'The Dragon's Spark and Sting and the Structure of Red Cross's Dragon-Fight: *The Faerie Queene*, I.xi–xii', in *Essential Articles for the Study of Edmund Spenser*, ed. A. C. Hamilton (Hamden, 1972), 425–46.

Kelley, Maurice, *This Great Argument: A Study of Milton's 'De Doctrina Christiana' as a Gloss upon 'Paradise Lost'* (Princeton, 1941).

Kerrigan, William, *The Sacred Complex: On the Psychogenesis of 'Paradise Lost'* (Cambridge, Mass., 1983).

Knoespel, Kenneth J., 'The Limits of Allegory: Textual Expansion of Narcissus in *Paradise Lost*', *Milton Studies*, 22 (1986), 79–99.

Kranidas, Thomas, *Milton and the Rhetoric of Zeal* (Pittsburgh, 2005).

Labriola, Albert C., '*Christus Patiens*: The Virtue Patience and *Paradise Lost*, I–II', in *The Triumph of Patience*, ed. Gerald J. Schiffhorst (Orlando, 1978), 138–46.

—— 'The Medieval View of Christian History in *Paradise Lost*', in *Milton and the Middle Ages*, ed. John Mulryan (Lewisburg, 1982), 115–32.

—— ' "Thy Humiliation Shall Exalt": The Christology of *Paradise Lost*', *Milton Studies*, 15 (1981), 29–42.

Lanham, Richard A., *A Handlist of Rhetorical Terms* (2nd edn, London, 1991).

Lares, Jameela, *Milton and the Preaching Arts* (Cambridge, 2001).

Lauter, Paul, 'Milton's "Siloa's Brook"', *Notes and Queries*, 5 (1958), 204–05.

Leonard, John, *Naming in Paradise: Milton and the Language of Adam and Eve* (Oxford, 1990).

Lewalski, Barbara K., *The Life of John Milton* (Oxford, 2003).

—— 'Milton and *De Doctrina Christiana*: Evidences of Authorship', *Milton Studies*, 36 (1998), 203–28.

—— *Milton's Brief Epic: The Genre, Meaning, and Art of 'Paradise Regained'* (Providence, 1966).

—— *'Paradise Lost' and the Rhetoric of Literary Forms* (Princeton, 1985).

Lewalski, Barbara K., 'Why Milton Matters', *Milton Studies*, 44 (2005), 13–21.

——, John T. Shawcross, and William B. Hunter, Jr, 'Forum: Milton's *Christian Doctrine*', *Studies in English Literature, 1500–1900*, 32 (1992), 143–66.

Lewis, C. S., *A Preface to 'Paradise Lost'* (Oxford, 1971).

——*Spenser's Images of Life*, ed. Alastair Fowler (Cambridge, 1967).

Lieb, Michael, *Poetics of the Holy: A Reading of 'Paradise Lost'* (Chapel Hill, 1981).

—— *The Sinews of Ulysses: Form and Convention in Milton's Works* (Pittsburgh, 1989).

—— *Theological Milton: Deity, Discourse and Heresy in the Miltonic Canon* (Pittsburgh, 2006).

Linden, Stanton J., *Darke Hierogliphicks: Alchemy in English Literature from Chaucer to the Restoration* (Lexington, 1996).

Loewenstein, David, *Representing Revolution in Milton and His Contemporaries: Religion, Politics, and Polemics in Radical Puritanism* (Cambridge, 2001).

Low, Anthony, 'Angels and Food in *Paradise Lost*', *Milton Studies*, 1 (1969), 135–45.

——'Siloa's Brook: *Paradise Lost*, I, 11', *Milton Quarterly*, 6 (1972), 3–5.

Lull, Janis, *The Poem in Time: Reading George Herbert's Revisions of The Church* (London, 1990).

Macaulay, Thomas Babington, *Literary and Historical Essays* (London, 1932).

MacCallum, Hugh, *Milton and the Sons of God: The Divine Image in Milton's Epic Poetry* (Toronto, 1986).

—— ' "Most Perfect Hero": The Role of the Son in Milton's Theodicy', in *'Paradise Lost': A Tercentenary Tribute*, ed. Balachandra Rajan (Toronto, 1969), 79–105.

Madsen, William, *From Shadowy Types to Truth: Studies in Milton's Symbolism* (New Haven, 1968).

Martin, Catherine Gimelli, *The Ruins of Allegory: 'Paradise Lost' and the Metamorphoses of Epic Convention* (Durham, 1998).

Martindale, Charles, *John Milton and the Transformation of Ancient Epic* (London, 1986).

Martz, Louis L., *Milton: Poet of Exile* (2nd edn, New Haven, 1986).

McClung, William A., 'The Pinnacle of the Temple', *Milton Quarterly*, 15 (1981), 13–15.

McColgan, Kristin Pruitt, ' "God is also in Sleep": Dreams Satanic and Divine in *Paradise Lost*', *Milton Studies*, 30 (1993), 135–48.

McColley, Diane Kelsey, *Milton's Eve* (Urbana, 1983).

McGrath, Alister E., *Luther's Theology of the Cross: Martin Luther's Theological Breakthrough* (Oxford, 1985).

McLoone, George H., *Milton's Poetry of Independence: Five Studies* (London, 1999).

McManus, Hugh F., 'The Pre-existent Humanity of Christ in *Paradise Lost*', *Studies in Philology*, 77 (1980), 271–82.

Miller, Clarence H., 'Christ as the Philosopher's Stone in George Herbert's "The Elixir"', *Notes and Queries*, 45 (1998), 39–41.

Miller, Leo, ' "Siloa's Brook" in *Paradise Lost*: Another View', *Milton Quarterly*, 6 (1972), 5–7.

Mohamed, Feisal G., *In the Anteroom of Divinity: The Reformation of the Angels from Colet to Milton* (Toronto, 2008).

Moloney, Francis J., *The Gospel of John*, ed. Daniel J. Harrington (Collegeville, 1998).

Musacchio, George, *Milton's Adam and Eve: Fallible Perfection* (New York, 1991).

Myers, Benjamin, *Milton's Theology of Freedom* (Berlin, 2006).

Nelson, Cary, *The Incarnate Word: Literature as Verbal Space* (Urbana, 1973).

Nuttall, Anthony D., *The Alternative Trinity: Gnostic Heresy in Marlowe, Milton, and Blake* (Oxford, 1998).

Painter, John, *The Quest for the Messiah: The History, Literature, and Theology of the Johannine Community* (Edinburgh, 1991).

Patrides, C. A., *Milton and the Christian Tradition* (Oxford, 1966).

——'Renaissance Interpretations of Jacob's Ladder', *Theologische Zeitschrift*, 18 (1962), 411–18.

Pecheux, Mary Christopher, '"O Foul Descent!": Satan and the Serpent Form', *Studies in Philology*, 62 (1965), 188–96.

Pelikan, Jaroslav, *Jesus Through the Centuries: His Place in the History of Culture* (New Haven, 1999).

Poole, William, *Milton and the Idea of the Fall* (Cambridge, 2005).

Radzinowicz, Mary Ann, *Milton's Epics and the Book of Psalms* (Princeton, 1989).

Rajan, Balachandra, 'Milton Encompassed', *Milton Quarterly*, 32 (1988), 86–89.

Reisner, Noam, 'Spiritual Architectonics: Destroying and Rebuilding the Temple in *Paradise Regained*', *Milton Quarterly*, 43 (2009), 166–82.

Revard, Stella Purce, *War in Heaven: 'Paradise Lost' and the Tradition of Satan's Rebellion* (Ithaca, 1980).

Rewak, William J., 'Book III of *Paradise Lost*: Milton's Satisfaction Theory of the Redemption', *Milton Quarterly*, 11 (1977), 97–102.

Ricks, Christopher, *Milton's Grand Style* (Oxford, 1963).

Riffaterre, Michael, 'Syllepsis', *Critical Inquiry*, 7 (1980), 625–38.

Robins, Harry F., 'Satan's Journey: Direction in *Paradise Lost*', *Journal of English and Germanic Philology*, 60 (1961), 699–711.

Rogers, John, 'Delivering Redemption in *Samson Agonistes*', in *Altering Eyes: New Perspectives on 'Samson Agonistes'*, ed. Mark R. Kelley and Joseph Wittreich (Newark, 2002), 72–97.

—— *The Matter of Revolution: Science, Poetry, and Politics in the Age of Milton* (Ithaca, 1996).

——'Milton's Circumcision', in *Milton and the Grounds of Contention*, ed. Mark R. Kelley, Michael Lieb, and John T. Shawcross (Pittsburgh, 2003), 188–213.

Rosenblatt, Jason P., *Renaissance England's Chief Rabbi: John Selden* (Oxford, 2006).

—— *Torah and Law in 'Paradise Lost'* (Princeton, 1994).

Rumrich, John P., 'Milton's Arianism: Why It Matters', in *Milton and Heresy*, ed. Stephen B. Dobranski and John P. Rumrich (Cambridge, 1998), 75–92.

——'Milton's *Theanthropos*: The Body of Christ in *Paradise Regained*', *Milton Studies*, 42 (2002), 50–67.

Rushdy, Ashraf H. A., *The Empty Garden: The Subject of Late Milton* (Pittsburgh, 1992).

Ryken, Leland, *The Apocalyptic Vision in 'Paradise Lost'* (Ithaca, 1970).

Samuel, Irene, *Dante and Milton: The 'Commedia' and 'Paradise Lost'* (Ithaca, 1966).

Schiller, Gertrud, *Iconography of Christian Art*, trans. Janet Seligman, 2 vols (London, 1972).

Schwartz, Regina M., 'Redemption and *Paradise Regained*', *Milton Studies*, 42 (2003), 26–49.

Schweitzer, Albert, *The Quest of the Historical Jesus*, trans. W. Montgomery (Baltimore, 1998).

Sensabaugh, George F., *Milton in Early America* (Princeton, 1964).

Shawcross, John T., *Rethinking Milton Studies: Time Present and Time Past* (Newark, 2005).

Shoaf, R. A., *Milton, Poet of Duality* (Gainesville, 1993).

Silver, Victoria, *Imperfect Sense: The Predicament of Milton's Irony* (Princeton, 2001).

Simpson, Ken, *Spiritual Architecture and 'Paradise Regained': Milton's Literary Ecclesiology* (Pittsburgh, 2007).

Sims, James H., 'Jesus and Satan as Readers of Scripture in *Paradise Regained*', *Milton Studies*, 32 (1995), 187–215.

Sims, James H., 'The Miltonic Narrator and Scriptural Tradition: An Afterword', in *Milton and Scriptural Tradition: The Bible into Poetry*, ed. James H. Sims and Leland Ryken (Columbia, 1984), 192–205.

——'*Paradise Lost*: "Arian Document" or Christian Poem?' *Études Anglaises*, 20 (1967), 337–47.

Snare, Gerald, 'Milton's "Siloa's Brook" Again', *Milton Quarterly*, 4 (1970), 55–57.

Steadman, John M., 'The Tree of Life as Messianic Symbol', in *Milton's Epic Characters: Image and Idol* (Chapel Hill, 1968), 82–89.

Steele, Richard, and Joseph Addison, *Selections From 'The Tatler' and 'The Spectator'*, ed. Angus Ross (London, 1988).

Stein, Arnold, *Answerable Style: Essays on 'Paradise Lost'* (Minneapolis, 1953).

Steiner, George, *Real Presences* (Chicago, 1989).

Strier, Richard, *Love Known: Theology and Experience in George Herbert's Poetry* (Chicago, 1983).

——'Milton against Humility', in *Religion and Culture in Renaissance England*, ed. Claire McEachern and Debora Shuger (Cambridge, 1997), 258–86.

——'Milton's Fetters, or Why Eden is Better Than Heaven', *Milton Studies*, 38 (2000), 169–97.

Summers, Joseph H., *George Herbert: His Religion and Art* (Binghamton, 1981).

—— *The Muse's Method: An Introduction to 'Paradise Lost'* (London, 1962).

Svendsen, Kester, 'Adam's Soliloquy in Book X of *Paradise Lost*', in *Milton: Modern Essays in Criticism*, ed. Arthur E. Barker (New York, 1965), 328–35.

Swete, H. B., *The Apostles' Creed: Its Relation to Primitive Christianity* (Cambridge, 1908).

Talmage, Frank Ephraim, 'Apples of Gold: The Inner Meaning of Sacred Texts in Medieval Judaism', in *Apples of Gold in Settings of Silver: Studies in Medieval Jewish Exegesis and Polemics*, ed. Barry Dov Walfish (Toronto, 1999), 108–50.

Tanner, John S., *Anxiety in Eden: A Kierkegaardian Reading of 'Paradise Lost'* (New York, 1992).

Teskey, Gordon, *Allegory and Violence* (Ithaca, 1996).

Tillyard, E. M. W., 'The Crisis of *Paradise Lost*', in *Milton: 'Paradise Lost': A Collection of Critical Essays*, ed. Louis L. Martz (Englewood Cliffs, 1966), 156–82.

——*Milton: Revised Edition* (New York, 1967).

Tobin, J. J. M., 'A Note on Luther, Arius and *Paradise Lost*, X, 504ff', *Milton Quarterly*, 11 (1977), 38–43.

Treip, Mindele Anne, *Allegorical Poetics and the Epic: The Renaissance Tradition to 'Paradise Lost'* (Lexington, 1994).

Turner, James Grantham, *One Flesh: Paradisal Marriage and Sexual Relations in the Age of Milton* (Oxford, 1987).

Ulreich, Jr, John C., 'Making the Word Flesh: Incarnation as Accommodation', in *Reassembling Truth: Twenty-First-Century Milton*, ed. Charles W. Durham and Kristin A. Pruitt (Selinsgrove, 2003), 129–44.

——'Milton on the Eucharist: Some Second Thoughts about Sacramentalism', in *Milton and the Middle Ages*, ed. John Mulryan (Lewisburg, 1982), 32–56.

Waldock, A. J. A., '*Paradise Lost*: The Fall', in *Milton's Epic Poetry: Essays on 'Paradise Lost' and 'Paradise Regained'*, ed. C. A. Patrides (Harmondsworth, 1967), 74–91.

Watson, J. R., 'Divine Providence and the Structure of *Paradise Lost*', *Essays in Criticism*, 14 (1964), 148–55.

West, Robert Hunter, *Milton and the Angels* (Atlanta, 1955).

Whiting, George Wesley, *Milton and This Pendant World* (Austin, 1958).

Wiles, Maurice, *Archetypal Heresy: Arianism Through the Centuries* (Oxford, 1996).

Wilkes, G. A., *The Thesis of 'Paradise Lost'* (London, 1961).

Williams, Rowan, *Arius: Heresy and Tradition* (London, 2001).

Wilson, Emily R., *Mocked with Death: Tragic Overliving from Sophocles to Milton* (Baltimore, 2004).

Wittreich, Joseph, 'Why Milton Matters', *Milton Studies*, 44 (2005), 22–39.

Wood, Derek N. C. *'Exiled from Light': Divine Law, Morality, and Violence in Milton's 'Samson Agonistes'* (Toronto, 2001).

Yu, Anthony C., 'Life in the Garden: Freedom and the Image of God in *Paradise Lost*', *Journal of Religion*, 60 (1980), 247–71.

Index